STAGING THE WORLD

ASIA-PACIFIC:

Culture, Politics, and Society

Editors: Rey Chow, H. D. Harootunian,

and Masao Miyoshi

REBECCA E. KARL

STAGING THE WORLD

Chinese Nationalism at the Turn of the Twentieth Century

DUKE UNIVERSITY PRESS

Durham and London 2002

Designed by Amy Ruth Buchanan
Typeset in Quadraat by Tseng
Information Systems, Inc. Library
of Congress Cataloging-in-
Publication Data appear on the
last printed page of this book.

For my parents, Dolores M. and Frederick R. Karl

CONTENTS

PREFACE AND ACKNOWLEDGMENTS

In 1986, while I was teaching in Hunan Province, I met a group of Filipino communists, who had fled the Philippines in the late 1960s after their plot to assassinate then-president Ferdinand Marcos had been discovered. They had looked upon their giant neighbor, the People's Republic of China, as a natural ally and historical model. Arriving in China at the height of the Cultural Revolution, they were met in Beijing by Mao Zedong, welcomed as fraternal revolutionary allies, and provided political refuge, housing, and employment in Changsha. There, for two decades they raised their families while struggling to retain a sense of solidarity and revolutionary optimism. By the time I met them, many of those sentiments—in relation to China at least—had dissipated and been replaced by frequent despair. Despite what he saw as China's hopeless situation, Fernando, as I knew him, remained absolutely committed to his hopes for a better future for the Philippines, and when Corazon Aquino's "people's power" movement toppled Marcos, Fernando decided it was a propitious time to return to his homeland to put his hopes into action. One cold night in February 1987, Fernando left Changsha, with a send-off party attended by his friends, albeit pointedly avoided by representatives of the province and city who, in a different era, had been his enthusiastic hosts. Less sanguine about Aquino's new regime, most of the other exiles remained in China. Several months later, at a different gathering, I learned that Fernando had been executed by Aquino's army, and that his wife and children were in hiding in the south.

In some retrospective way, the initial motivation for this study emerged from my encounters with Fernando and his fellow Filipino revolutionaries, for this study traces the historical conditions that made a revolutionary dialogue on and in the world possible and significant in China. However, the book concerns itself with the initial moment of this possibility, at the turn of the twentieth century. The world around which this dialogue was formed at that time was the uneven world of modernity, as seen from the perspective of Chinese intellectuals'/activists' emerging understandings of the colonized world, which was just then coming into Chinese view, as one place after the next erupted in anticolonial and nationalist revolution. In the following chapters, I argue that this global historical moment of the turn of the century came to be conceptually linked to China's post-1895 intellectual and social crisis, and became crucial to the original formulations of Chinese nationalism, as a discursive formation and an elite orientation. In some ways, the book implicitly laments the overwriting of this expansive moment of modern Chinese history in the academic and global rush to write and forge narrower histories that contribute to a different kind of normative History altogether, even as it also acknowledges that that global moment has passed and that a new moment of global and national activism is now required.

I began this project a long time ago as a dissertation, with a vaguely sentimental idea of the topic. My graduate training at Duke University, under Arif Dirlik's rigorous and decidedly unsentimental—albeit very sympathetic—guidance, helped me refine my theoretical approaches, as well as the historiographical and historical problematics through which the theory could be posed and elaborated. I am deeply grateful for Arif's commitment to me and to this project. In addition, other members of my dissertation committee—Fredric Jameson, Andrew Gordon, and Kären Wigen—were also consistently supportive through the initial years of research, conceptualization, and writing. A constant stream of funding at Duke, for which I thank the History Department, the Asia/Pacific Studies Institute, and the Graduate School, was indispensable. Subsequently, a summer grant from the Office of Sponsored Research at the University of Florida allowed me to finish research for the book in Tokyo and Beijing, while a semester of teaching relief in spring 1998 at New York University gave me time to begin rewriting the text.

Over the years, in the PRC, librarians at the Beijing University library, pre-1911 journals division; the Beijing Library; the Modern History Institute Library at the Chinese Academy of Social Sciences; the Nanjing University library; the Jiangsu Provincial Library, journals division; and the Shanghai Library, all graciously fulfilled my copious requests. In Taiwan, the Modern History Institute archives at the Academia Sinica assisted at an early stage; while in Japan, the Toyo-Bunko Library; Tokyo University Library; and the Tokyo Municipal Library all were cooperative and efficient. Among the many people who assisted me in my research abroad, I particularly thank Xu Xiuli, Yu Keping, Wang Lie (Beijing); Hamashita Takeshi, Kondo Kuniye, Kanada Shinji, Wada Haruki (Tokyo); Lu Zhe, Yang Jianya (Nanjing); Chang P'eng-yuan, Ursula Richter (Taipei); Guo Xuyin, Bu Guilin (Shanghai); and Danny Kwan (Hong Kong).

This project, originally conceived and written in Durham, N.C., was reconceived and rewritten over a span of several years in Gainesville, Florida, New York City, and Hurley, N.Y. I thank Bruce Cumings, then of Northwestern and now of University of Chicago; the NYU History Department and East Asian Studies Program; and Huri Islamaglu, Visiting Professor at NYU's Kevorkian Center for inviting me to present portions of this work while I was rethinking it. Among friends and colleagues, I am grateful to, in Durham, Michael Hardt, Cesare Casarino, Neferti Tadiar, Jon Beller, Sara Danius, Stefan Jonsson, Joanne Filley, Wan Shuping, Hwang Dongyoun, Tang Xiaobing, and Zhang Xudong; in Gainesville, Louise Newman, Mark Thurner, Kathryn Burns, Maria Todorova, Holly Hanson, Kiran Asher, Susan Hegeman, Phil Wegner, and Sheryl Kroen; in no particular location, Peter Zarrow, Caroline Reeves, and Giovanna Merli.

Since arriving at NYU, I have been overwhelmed by the generosity of my colleagues. I especially thank Harry Harootunian, Marilyn Young, and Moss Roberts, who have read and discussed with me every part of this book, among many other things. For intellectual and personal support, I am also grateful to Joanna Waley-Cohen, Louise Young, Meg McLagan, Hyon-Ok Park, Christina von Koehler, and Zia Jaffrey. I thank Yva and John for their house, and Ken Kawashima and Katsuhiko ("Mariano") Endo, who showed iron will in keeping me in good humor in summer 1998 and beyond. I especially thank Kristin Bayer for the bibliography and her general assistance. For reading and laboriously commenting on the entire first draft, I am grateful to Marilyn Young, Xudong Zhang, Louise Newman, and Ann Farnsworth-Alvear.

The readers chosen by my editor, Ken Wissoker, took their jobs seriously; their probing comments and suggestions were most helpful in guiding my revisions. The copyeditor's heroic struggle with my prose can only be commended. Naturally, I alone am responsible for what remains.

Finally, I acknowledge with love and gratitude how Christopher, Sophia,

Nora, Tepi, and Channa, as well as their parents, Deborah and Bob, Judith and John have indulged and delighted me over the years; and am grateful for the generosity of my Aunt Dotte and late Aunt Jo. To my parents, Dolores and Frederick Karl, there is nothing I can say that could properly express my appreciation for all the years of love, encouragement, and support; thus, simply, I dedicate this book to them.

PART I

1 INTRODUCTION: SHIFTING PERSPECTIVES ON MODERN CHINESE NATIONALISM

Politics is primarily conflict over the existence of a common stage and over the existence and status of those present on it. It must first be established that the stage exists for the use of an interlocutor who can't see it and who can't see it for good reason *because* it doesn't exist.[1]

This book traces the process through which certain central concepts that came to constitute a discourse of nationalism were produced in China. It concentrates on the late Qing period (1895–1911), when these concepts and indeed the formation of nationalist discourses and understandings were first systematically and systemically explicated and debated. In broadest terms, the study figures the period as a progressively narrowing process of conceptual incorporations, through which a set of unstable historicized formulations that came to define nationalism as an intellectual orientation in the Chinese context was temporarily stabilized. This process is traced from an initially expansive global or internationalist moment of identification (1895–1905) through a gradual reduction to a conceptualization of racial-ethnic revolution in pursuit of state power (1905–1911). The results of this conceptual narrowing helped inform the basic ideological premises for the overthrow of the dynastic system in general—the Qing dynasty in particular—and the establishment of the Chinese Republic in 1911.

Specifically, the book's inquiry focuses on how—during this crucial period of intellectual, social, economic, and political crisis in China and the world—China's situation at the turn of the twentieth century was conceptually linked to the world around it, and particularly to emergent nationalist and anticolonial movements in the non-Euro-American world of the time. While noting that the specific linkages were ultimately ephemeral, the main premise of the book is that it was a growing Chinese sense of identification with the non-Euro-American world at the turn of the century that initially made the modern world visible as a structured totality.[2] I argue that it was by reference to the conceptual production of this totality, seen as dominantly marked by the ongoing creation of global unevenness in economy, politics, culture, representation, and power, that the basic ideological components of nationalist discourse were incipiently worked out in China. The study analyzes, in an overlapping (rather than linear narrative) structure, the three arenas of concept-formation most evident and most debated in the publicly available journalistic, editorial, and historical literature at the time: newly articulated relationships between global and national space, between revolutionary process and imperialist/nationalist ideology, and between ethnicity, citizenship, and nationality.

The inquiry, rather than concentrating on the turn-of-the-century world "stage" from an accustomed focus on Euro-American-Japanese philosophical and institutional influences on China, shifts perspectives to focus on another, albeit intimately linked, world "stage": that stage unstably comprised by the first post–Latin American wave of anticolonial and nationalist revolutions of the late nineteenth and early twentieth centuries. To be sure, the unity of this latter stage—or its very presence—was no more and no less imaginary (that is, no more or less "real" or "unreal") than the tendentially totalizing one of the Euro-American imagination. Indeed, the inherent impossibility of both stages—the "Western" just as the "non-Western"—is well encapsulated in the citation taken from Jacques Rancière noted at the top of this chapter: "Politics is primarily conflict over the existence of a common stage and over the existence and status of those present on it. It must first be established that the stage exists for the use of an interlocutor who can't see it and who can't see it for good reason *because* it doesn't exist." Taking the "stage" as a global historical and political conceit, then, this study highlights the formation of Chinese discourses of nationalism in relation to the non-Euro-American world. Such a defamiliarizing approach and historical problematization not only complicates the more usual West(Japan)/China confrontation that forms the implicit or explicit paradigm around which inquiries on modern Chinese history are usually organized, but it also allows us to see modernity—of which nationalism is a central (albeit far from exhaustive) expression—as a global material and representational structure, whose tendential unities are underpinned by the expansion of capitalism in its imperialist forms.

No doubt, this view of modernity, as tendential unity held together by a capitalism purportedly emanating from a central point, *could* confirm a familiar normative picture of the modern world in a staged diachronic temporal hierarchy of difference and spatial distance from the putative center of Euro-America (that centered unity usually called "the West"). In other words, it could yield that very diachronic "staging" of modernity that forms a core content of Euro-American-centered ideologies of modernization, which normatively represent History as universal, teleological, and as hegemonically foreclosed by Euro-American trajectories. However, my focus on the historical formation of a non-Euro-American consciousness of globality from the Chinese perspective is intended to bring into view a recognition of modernity that leads to a different staging of the world—that is, a staging that makes visible a world of synchronic temporality emphasizing historical identification and spatial proximity. In China's case, this latter staging of the world was expressed as an immanence of global transformation: an immanence recognized and performed in and through the non-Euro-American world.[3] Uncovering the modalities through which this immanent synchronicity—with both its possibilities and constraints—was produced and incorporated into Chinese intellectual practice at the turn of the twentieth century is the primary topic and intellectual strategy of this study.

On this view, the formation of Chinese nationalism—understood here primarily as a historically specific process of concept-formation and intellectual reorientation—can only appear as part of a global historical problematic, where "historical problematic" is understood as a theoretical entity, which, in Fredric Jameson's words, "must be grasped in a different way from the traditional representational or philosophical one."[4] In conceptualizing the problem in this manner, this book represents an attempt to think through early-twentieth-century nationalism generally and Chinese nationalism particularly by linking them—as historical problematics and as material historicities—to a properly productive global moment. As such, if we take seriously, as historian Zheng Zengqun has noted, that "when the world entered China, China entered the world,"[5] then one crucial step toward understanding the full contours of the historical crisis precipitated by the irruption and incorporation of the world into Chinese consciousness by the late Qing period, is to recognize the truly global nature of the world that "entered," by centrally including within it—as did Chinese intellectuals at the time—non-Euro-American-Japanese histories and concerns. Such a recognition not only allows a theoretical break from the narrow confines of historiographical emphasis on the West–Japan/China dyad that dominates narratives of China's "struggle with modernity," but it allows us to figure the late Qing Chinese "struggle" as one not *with* (or *against*) but completely *of* modernity.

The analysis hence engages two intimately linked realms of inquiry: a historical and a theoretical one. Historically, it foregrounds repressed aspects of the early-twentieth-century development of Chinese nationalism by reading texts written from 1895 to 1911 within the context of global modernity, as the latter was produced, illumined, and recognized through the most visible spaces of unevenness in the modern world: its imperialized and colonialized places. Theoretically, the book proposes that this historical focus becomes available only when modern Chinese experiences and recognitions of modernity and nationalism are neither assimilated into dominating Euro-American perspectives[6] nor rooted in reified local-place identifications and/or in notions of continuous traditional, dynastic, or statist-defined bounded national space.[7] Such a focus is thus also available only when statism and nationalism, as historical topoi and processes, are separated.

As such, the book also takes up several well-entrenched historiographical paradigms in the China field as well as in current theorizations of nationalism. These include recent critiques of nation that conflate nationalism with nation-statism (state-building) by establishing an axiomatic functional narrative relationship between the two; state-centered approaches to Chinese nationalism, which lead to a fundamental neglect of the broader sources and inspirations for Chinese nationalist imaginings and conceptual formation; and the concept of a global structure whose encompassing totality is assumed to be exhausted by a "West" (plus Japan)/China dyad that purports to define "the world." The remainder of this introduction establishes the theoretical points and historical background through which the particular topics taken up in detail in the ensuing chapters have been rethought.

Recognizing a Historical Problematic: The World and China

Ernst Gellner long ago observed that "it is nationalism which engenders nations, and not the other way around."[8] While the simple causality suggested in this observation cannot be taken at face value, Gellner's point is nevertheless a useful reminder that any analysis of the coming into being of the "nation" (understood by Gellner as the nation-state)[9] must be rooted in the emergence of nationalism as a historical problematic. In exploring the posing of the historical problematic of nationalism in China at the turn of the twentieth century, this study posits that the particular nationalism of China must be seen as part of the general global problematic in which it was embedded, lest the inquiry become trapped in a rhetoric of exclusivity and pure authenticity or become merely a catalog of the reactive replication in China of globally existing institutional forms and ideologies. This is precisely how Chinese intellectuals viewed the problem, beginning from the traumatic Chinese defeat in the Sino-Japanese War of 1895 up through the Republican revolution of 1911. For it was during this crucial extended historical moment that nationalism as a historical topos, systematic discursive formation, and systemic intellectual practice emerged as a way to reconceptualize internal and global relationships; it was also during this period that the emerging concepts that were to comprise nationalism in the Chinese context were in most urgent and debated flux.

By the same token, Benedict Anderson's *Imagined Communities* suggests that the establishment of a sense of temporal simultaneity was integral to the formation of an imagined community of the nation.[10] The seemingly accidental nature of this temporal apprehension leads Anderson to posit that nationalism became a function of this temporal order; nationalism, or what really amounts to nation-statism in Anderson's narrative, then congealed this temporality into state form, a form that, once invented, became available for adoption by disparate peoples around the globe in modern times. Partha Chatterjee, in his exploration into the cultural dimensions of nationalism in nineteenth- and twentieth-century India, has contested this modular model of political-territorial nationalism by reinjecting a "native" imaginary into the historical process.[11] As Chatterjee states, "The most powerful and the most creative results of the nationalist imaginations in Asia and Africa are posited not on an identity but rather on a *difference* with the 'modular' forms of the national society propagated by the modern West."[12]

Chatterjee's rejection of nationalism as purely state form is helpful. However, his binary of identity and difference establishes a false historical dichotomy between what is "external" and what is "internal," because of his designation of "native" imaginings as emanating from some culturally defined notion of authentic experience (pure internality). To avoid both traps—that is, the reduction of nationalism to temporal statism (or state-form) and the positing of a historical culturalist internality—I wish to repose both Anderson's accidental temporal proposition and Chatterjee's culturalist challenge to ask: what happens when the purportedly coincidental temporal nature of "events" comes to be spatially understood? That is, what happens when historical-spatial logic comes to *explain* the seemingly arbitrary temporal unity and coincidence of disparate events? And, what happens when those events, that temporality, and that spatiality are understood not merely as statist or culturalist but as global historical issues? Once these questions are asked the space of "national" imagining can no longer be confined to an a priori state-defined space, and the emergence of a national imaginary can no longer be understood as a process necessarily bounded by the overlap among a unique language, culture, state, or territory, or yet by a purely internalist logic. Indeed, the imaginary process must be opened up in a number of different and perhaps even contradictory directions.

This study is most concerned with the simultaneous growth of nationalism and a global historical logic in China, through which the seemingly arbitrary co-temporality of events around the world and in China came to be seen as held together by their shared contemporary historical relationship in and to global modernity. Yet, in much of the secondary literature, the problem of Chinese nationalism is discussed either in terms of a confrontation with and selective absorption of Western (and Japanese) philosophical knowledges and political *forms* into programs for transforming China—that is, as a functional mobilization of set doctrines; or in terms of a confrontation and grappling with China's past traditions and legacies—that is, as a continuation or rejection of past forms and knowledges. Both conceptualizations are partial at best.

On the relationship of past to present, there can be no doubt that China's past, or rather the reinterpretations of that past in light of China's new crises, was of fundamental significance to the ways in which the contemporary moment was viewed. By the same token, it seems unreasonable to assume that Chinese were any more imprisoned by their past than any other people might be. In this light, the historiographical argument over continuity and discontinuity is a red herring. On the relationship of Euro-America-Japan to China, undeniably, there was an urgency produced by the demonstrably great power of Euro-America-Japan in China, an urgency, as many scholars have noted, that grew after the 1895 Sino-Japanese War into a persistent tendency among many Chinese to unfavorably compare

China's contemporary situation with the national unifications and historical trajectories of the world's powers. These latter intellectual and political urgencies are without a doubt the most obviously visible part of the historical record, a visibility that, in large part, derives from the immediate presence in China of Euro-Americans and Japanese, and from their direct roles through the nineteenth and into the twentieth century as violent invaders, instructors, advisers, administrators, builders of modern factories, hospitals, schools, and so on. The visibility of Euro-America-Japan is both symptom and consequence of the ongoing restructuring of the late-nineteenth-century world by capitalism, colonialism, and imperialism,[13] wherein the realities of global power and what appears as a "natural" historical diachrony all lend an unquestioned truth-value to the historiographical centrality accorded to them in the modern history of China. In short, as tangible bearers of modernization in and perpetrators of violence against China, the insistent *presence* of Euro-America-Japan is hard, and indeed unnecessary, to contest.

To put this issue more philosophically: "the West" is generally the geopolitical category "through which the historical predicate of modernity is translated into a geographical one," as Naoki Sakai and Peter Osborne have separately argued.[14] The "translator" in this process is understood to be "the West" itself (along with, in East Asia's case particularly after 1905, Japan). From at least the nineteenth century onward, this translation process strove to present itself as normative and to order its ambitions for temporal totalization into a global diachronic time-space that located the Western world at its most developed end, and the rest of the world in various stages of behind-ness. One result of this global diachronic narrative and practice is what Johannes Fabian has called the West's denial of coevalness to the non-West,[15] or, differently phrased by Xiaobing Tang for China, it forms a "lasting dilemma" of modernity.[16]

As persuasive and widespread as this figuration is—it does, after all, conform to and confirm the world as it was and remains most readily visible—such accounts nevertheless present a major disjuncture from the way the intertwined problems of nation, history, and global modernity were figured in many Chinese texts at the turn of the twentieth century. This disjuncture, at its most basic, appears as an occlusion of the mediating structure of the rest of the world in the formation of late Qing Chinese nationalist concepts and global consciousness.[17] In other words, colonized or imperialized world spaces prolifically appear in the primary texts of the time as major constitutive and productive aspects of the very *process* of the formation of a consciousness of the world and the Chinese nation at the time. It is these very spaces that disappear from historiographical accounts.

In this light, we can tentatively restate the problem of the "translation" of modernity in the late Qing Chinese context. The conceptualizations of globality (geopolitics + geography) and its relationship to China in the late Qing period cannot be encoded merely as acts of recognition, acquiescence, or even of resistance to the space of geopolitics translated as geography ("the West"). That is, if we concede that "the West" was neither recognizable as such for most of the nineteenth century—it was an imaginary "stage" that was being produced but did not exist as such—and that "China" was not an already constituted national concept at the time (without denying that the Qing dynasty was obviously a polity and recognized as one), then inquiring into the formation of such overarching categories of historical conceptualization as "the West" and "China"—among others—must form a central part of the historian's task. This task requires inquiring into the process through which the historicized concepts of nationalism and globality came to be specified simultaneously in concrete time and space.

Through such a reorientation, we can see that the contemporaneous global space through which the historical predicate of modernity and nationalism could be translated in China did not appear primarily *as* an existing nor *in* an alternative *form* to that proposed by "the West" (and Japan), but as a material historicity through which world, nation, and social transformation—as concepts—were understood as linked parts of the interconnected historical formation of global modernity. As such, late Qing globality and nationalism are most plausibly seen not as blinding recognitions of an already constituted "West" that defined and translated "the world" encroaching upon "China," but rather as layered processes that required the appropriation of uneven global spaces into a redefinition of China and the world as unfinished historical projects.[18] This process was "translated" through the colonized and imperialized spaces of the world because it was precisely there, as many Chinese intellectuals recognized, that the relationships among global unevenness and modernity, nationalism and revolution, politics and social transformation were being posed most urgently and visibly at the time.

On this view, the aforementioned lasting "dilemma of modernity" can be exposed as both a historical and historiographical dilemma. Historically, as Xiaobing Tang has written, the dilemma was raised in and by Chinese experiences and narrativizations of modernity as contradictorily both global and particular. Historiographically—that is, as paradigm[19]—the dilemma is produced and reproduced by the representation of non-Western histories in a hegemonic perspective that subordinates historical realities outside the West in treatments that consistently conceal a vital dimension of global modernity: the constitutiveness of the "international overhearings"[20] forged within those very same globally uneven spaces that seem to lend unquestioned historical priority and centrality to "the West." V. Y. Mudimbe, writing of African history, has called this practice "epistemological ethnocentrism," or, the view that "there is nothing to be learned from 'them' unless it is already 'ours' or comes from 'us.'"[21] This very same epistemology also implicitly maintains that there was nothing "they" could have learned from one another in "their" historical passages through the contradictions of modernity, since "they" could only learn (either well or poorly) from "us."

Having stated as much, I would reemphasize that it is undeniably true that Euro-America–Japan had multiple practical links to China that set them in direct relationships of domination and power vis-à-vis China, both in terms of actual impingements on China's territory, political integrity, and economic sovereignty as well as in terms of philosophical and discursive claims to universality in time and space. However, the central fact of this power—the politics of *presence*—has unreasonably led to a historiographical and theoretical blindness to the fact that the turn-of-the-century world was a complicated one, and that what Chinese intellectuals saw when they looked out across that world from a Chinese situation in increasing turmoil and flux was not a world neatly bifurcated into a "West/Japan" and "China" (nor, even, a slightly more complex triangulated "West," "Japan," and "China"), but a disjunct world striving to reconfigure itself. It was with this disjunctness that Chinese intellectuals often identified. It is possible to pursue these identifications as a legitimate problem in modern Chinese history only if we discard the epistemological and historiographical conventions that have led historians to disregard those parts of the world deemed less important in the march of History toward modernity (or, really, modernization). Pursuing such a history, therefore, requires paying attention to "the rupture in what resembles a repetition of a theme," in Rey Chow's words, a rupture that allows for different types of questions to be asked and different types of histories to be written.[22]

Renarrating Modern Chinese History through Globality

Consciousness of a new globality began to take shape in China in the mid-nineteenth century, following the violent incursions of Euro-America in the First Opium War (1839–1842) and the consequent forced entry of China into a new phase of the formation of a capitalist world system.[23] In the wake of that war, the scholar-official Wei Yüan wrote of the changing relational position of the Qing empire to the world. Through his observations on the British-mediated opium trade, Wei became aware that India was being drawn closer to the Qing in the context of an inchoately recognized connection between foreign assault on and commercial practices linking the Qing with its neighboring states. As Wei commented in summary to his observations: "India is nearby and must not be considered [a] barren land on the periphery [of the world]."[24] Wei's view of India as proximate to the Qing helped him articulate a new awareness of the world, in which the Qing empire would need to pursue a global approach to accumulating local threats.[25] By the same token, Wei's recognition of a changing world did not as yet impinge upon his, or his contemporaries' certainty about the Qing dynastic sociopolitical order.

By 1895, a half-century of massive internal rebellions and continued assaults by European imperialist powers on China was capped by the defeat of the Qing armies in Korea by the rising power of Meiji Japan. The defeat helped crystallize the prior fifty years of dynastic difficulty, social and economic upheaval, and increasing Euro-American—and, after 1895, Japanese—demands on China's territory, resources, and polity into an urgent sense of sociopolitical and global crisis. The urgency helped propel a small but disproportionately influential group of Chinese educated elites to look anew at China's problems. As this process got under way, the acquisition of knowledge about other places and the incorporation of this new knowledge into new structures of knowledge and social practice became a major pursuit of many educated elites. These very pursuits, in their increasing disconnection from direct service to the dynastic state, came to mark these elites as a new social group of intellectuals. The emergence of journalism and the explosion of print media after 1895 was also crucial to this development. Indeed, as Liang Qichao, the first professional Chinese journalist and one of the most influential of this new group of intellectuals, realized early on, newspapers and print media could both produce and be produced by changes in what constituted proper knowledge and by new types of sociopolitical power that could derive from the mobilization of such new knowledge.

Out of this rearticulation of knowledge and power quickly emerged a secularized realm of politics, increasingly dissociated from both the dynastic state and ritual knowledge.[26] Yet it was not knowledge qua knowledge that was most important in this process; rather, it was the ways in which the texts produced in the process of knowledge accumulation helped produce a new sense of China's situation. In other words, the texts were situated against and with the multiple contemporary contexts, which were not external to, but rather were produced by and in the texts themselves. As such, these texts were not merely functionally produced in the service of different types of (power-centered) ideologies or institutions; instead, powerful social ideologies and discourses were being produced in and through the texts.[27] Thus, as integral as they were to the new articulation of politics as an internal proposition, journalism and the new print media also simultaneously opened a global space of politics that fed and was fed by both internal and external upheavals. For the concern with politics was not limited to bounded notions of "China," "West," or "Japan"; rather, the concern with politics helped produce a new global consciousness through which all of these could be rethought as mutually productive discourses.

By 1897, in what is perhaps the first Chinese statement of the nature of the relationship between the commercial and territorial expansionism of Euro-America and cultural/textual production, Liang Qichao wrote of the tight nexus between Western ideology and conquest: "I read Western newspapers and they report on . . . the disorder in the Chinese polity . . . This has been going on for the past few decades. Since September or October of last year [1896], they have even more openly and brazenly publicized how wild and uncivilized the Chinese are, how ignorant and dishonest, how empty Chinese Confucianism is. The meaning is clear: they will eliminate China at once."[28] Identifying China as one among many targets of Western ambitions—with Turkey and India noted elsewhere as similar targets—Liang demonstrated an awareness not only of the leveling power of Western violence for all who were its objects; he also evinced an incipient understanding of how imperialism worked to ideologically create its object. In other words, as Liang insightfully saw, "China" appears differently when read through imperialist ideology masquerading as mere "texts." As with Wei Yüan earlier, however, Liang still wanted to assert China's superiority to a

Turkey or an India. "Westerners, you are wrong! China cannot be compared to India or Turkey!" he wrote; he thus wanted to assert the ability of what he called "true" Confucianism to combat imperialism's homogenizing tendency.

Soon enough—in fact, by the end of the summer of 1898—Liang *was* comparing China to Turkey and India, among many other countries, and finding in their modern experiences clues for linked solutions to what he now apprehended not as only *Chinese* problems solvable in uniquely *Chinese* ways, but rather as problems of the modern world itself. This incipient global logic took on particular significance after the summer of 1898, for in that summer a reform movement arose (the *wuxu* or hundred-day reforms), which was directed by a small number of nonbureaucratic elites led by Liang and his teacher Kang Youwei, in concert with a handful of reform-minded officials within the dynastic state. The movement's political aim was to guide the dynasty to efficiency through top-down institutional reform. It briefly captured the support of the Emperor Guangxu, but after 103 days, the threat posed to vested interests prompted the Empress Dowager Cixi to stage a coup d'état to suppress the movement's perceived radicalism. The emperor was placed under house arrest (where he died a decade later), and Beijing was cleansed of "radicals." Pushed into exile—to Japan and the *nanyang* (Southern Seas) primarily—or underground in other parts of the Qing empire, many educated elites, such as Liang, Kang, and many others, went back to the drawing board to rethink, for a second time in three years, strategies and goals of change. At this juncture, many intellectuals began to lose faith in the ability of the dynasty to reform itself, and some soon turned to yet more radical solutions to China's problems. From the September 1898 coup onward, therefore, debates within Chinese intellectual circles abroad and in China—separately and in concert—became increasingly contentious, even as the rethinkings continued to overlap considerably in substance and terminology.

These rethinkings were in part abetted and informed by the newfound currency of conceptual formations derived from translated Euro-American political and philosophical texts, with the foremost social philosophy at the time being Spencerian Darwinism, which introduced "race" and "struggle" as fundamental categories of internal and global relations.[29] Indirectly linked to these new categories, the very concept of revolution (*geming*) was also fundamentally transformed by 1903: from its traditional meaning of "overthrowing the mandate of heaven"—or, replacing one dynasty with another—*geming* now came to encompass a fundamental restructuring of the premises of political organization, which centrally included the rearticulation of the relationship between the state and the people into a new concept of nation. This rearticulation became pervasive in part because it was also at this juncture that much of the intellectual ferment over the modalities, directions, and goals of change began to be phrased alternately in the political terms of nation-statism (*guojia zhuyi*) and/or the racial terms of "ethno-nationalism" (*minzu zhuyi*). Never a unitary set of ideas or practices, these concepts and the sociopolitical-economic practices they might require to be fulfilled—of intellectuals, the people, the state, and so on—became the subjects of the contentious specification of China's historical project from the early 1900s onward.

New types of histories were also written at the time, prominent among them a new genre called *wangguo shi* (lost country histories). These flourished in the first years of the twentieth century after the allied occupation of Beijing in the wake of the Boxer Rebellion (1900–1901),[30] and they were part of an overall dramatic increase at the time in writings on the world and translations from Euro-America and Japan.[31] The numerous *wangguo shi*—covering such distant examples as Babylonia, ancient Greece, and Rome and such modern ones as India, Poland, Egypt, and Vietnam, among others—narrativized the historical "failure" of peoples and states to properly recognize the twin problems of foreign assault and internal decline into an inexorable "perishing" or "loss" (*wang*) of the state. Through these histories and the new view of the world they enabled and produced, *wangguo* too was rearticulated away from its traditional Chinese meaning of a change of dynasty to a modern meaning of colonization. In this latter form, *wangguo* was linked to imperialism into a new view of modern world dynamics, relationships, and representations—or, into a view of modernity. This new view of what was often called in the late Qing either "national imperialism" (*guojia diguo zhuyi*), just "expansionism" (*pengzhang zhuyi*), or *wangguo* also lent historical relevance to revolution and nationalism, for in a most basic sense, if *wangguo*—as colonization—was to be avoided or contested, then struggle, against both ineffective internal rule and foreign occupiers, needed to be launched.[32]

It was precisely in these intellectually exciting and extremely messy years after 1898 that dramatic turn-of-the-century global events also became particularly important to Chinese intellectuals. For, in the post-1898 period, just as many Chinese intellectuals began to abandon the dynastic structure of state as the inevitable form and guarantor of "China" and to look around for solutions to China's accumulating crises, they, for the first time, also began to see the modern world as an ongoing historical process. This immanent reconfiguration of global structure was made visible through a cluster of events in the colonized and imperialized world that drew Chinese attention from 1898 to 1911. These included the Philippine, Hawaiian, and Cuban struggles against Spain and the United States; the incipient Indian nationalist movement; the Boer struggle in South Africa against Britain; Poland's, Egypt's, and Ottoman Turkey's reformisms, struggles against territorial partition, and attempts to reconstitute themselves as national polities; Vietnam's struggle against the French; Japanese expansionism into Korea, Taiwan, and Manchuria; and a host of others.

The contemporaneity of these events as well as the specific and general concerns that motivated them seemed to Chinese observers to overlap exactly with China's situation; they thus helped point to a fundamental problem and a new opportunity for China. The problem: how a diachronically Darwinian staged world could be constituted as an active site of global reimaginings within the context of overwhelming Euro-American-Japanese power. The opportunity: how this world could be transformed into an immanent stage upon which the Chinese, and others along with them, could act against the very global unevenness that was constitutive of their shared moment. This was the complex terrain of the world "staging" of identification and proximity that Chinese intellectuals consciously entered and constructed at the turn of the twentieth century; and it was on this stage that the combining of ideas of race, struggle, revolution, and *wangguo* concerns into a synchronic modern global temporality and uneven global spatiality allowed for the decentering of both Chinese and global spatialities, and permitted Asia, the Pacific, Africa, and other places to emerge into view, not as inert geographical designations, nor as fatally "lost" (*wang*) places, but as material sites for the production and performance of new global, national, and local meanings, practices, and histories.

To be sure, the historical possibility opened by these latter places was inextricably bound up with the limitations inherent in the uneven global space of modernity, limitations that imposed upon Chinese nationalist and global discourses a certain derivativeness from Euro-American-Japanese philosophical premises and formal structures of nation-state sovereignty, territorial boundedness, and Enlightenment ideologies.[33] That is, each successive instance of struggle taken up in the world, recognized as a "nationalist" or "anticolonial" struggle, and thus incorporated into Chinese conceptualizations of their own situation, served to normalize and confirm "nation" as a fixed and necessary signified for China and the world. Nevertheless, the possibilities opened by interpreting the events that transpired in these places also pointed to a dynamic global space produced and enabled precisely by that unevenness: a dynamic space animated by the very transformative internal and global struggles upon whose path Chinese intellectuals aspired to launch China.

It was this world stage that became the literal and metaphorical place and space from which global unevenness and China came to be discursively repositioned, not merely as negative spaces of "lack" and "incompletion," but as positive spaces for an ongoing project of dynamic sociopolitical and cultural transformation. And it is in *this* context that this study situates the formation of specific components of a discursive nationalism, primarily the relationship between territoriality and globality; revolution and history; race/ethnicity and nationality—as each came under intensive review and redefinition in the 1895–1911 period.

Reconfiguring a Historical Problematic: Statism and Nationalism

Finally, then, the history pursued in this study is possible only if the historical process of nationalism—as concept-formation—and that of statism—as either the retrospective renarration of the nation in light of the achievement of nation-statism or as the purely functional pursuit and institutional elaboration of state power—are disentangled. While the historical production of nationalist discourse—in China as in many histories and theoretical treatments—is usually tightly linked historiographically to the institutional formation of the state, or the nation-state, these two processes cannot be seen as historically isomorphic with one another, as Gellner and other theorists suggest,[34] unless one overlooks the global dimension to nationalism as a historical problematic.

Recently, deconstructing the nation—as cultural artifact, as narrative practice, as hegemonic (male) subjectivity, as liberatory promise, as repressive or redemptive discourse and practice, or as postcolonial or postmodern fantasy—has become a dominant mode of inquiry (particularly in the wake of the new life and direction given to studies of nationalism by Anderson's *Imagined Communities*). Yet paradoxically, after all these years of subjecting nationalism to cultural and political critique, we seem to have ended up with a reinscription of the state as an ever more hegemonic and ever more dictatorial narrator of nation than we ever could have imagined before nation was proclaimed to be an essentially imagined community. Indeed, in its new fashionable form as cultural text, nationalism has become *more* isomorphic with statism, and nation more functional to the state than ever before.

The conflation of statism and nationalism has taken two dominant forms in recent critical writing. They are analytically conflated, on the one hand, in an effort to confirm (even while perhaps lamenting) the nation-state as the historically inevitable form of modern human social organization. This inevitability has an often unarticulated but nevertheless assumed axiomatic relationship to (capitalist) modernization, which is understood as modernity's essential content (as with Gellner). Studies that reveal this type of constructed statist triumphalism—even those that deplore its hegemonic hold and recognize its historicity—thus usually substitute modernization (as institutional and industrial form) for a more theoretically informed elaboration of modernity. Moreover, such studies have become theoretically unproductive, even within their own limits. For, on the one hand, the types of insights possible to generate out of them are generally limited to functional accounts of how completed states conceal their constructedness through cultural, political, economic, historical, or other suppressions. And, while local varieties of such inventions are endless, endlessly complex, and sometimes endlessly fascinating, the theoretical point of state-led national narrative construction has been made and the central insight has been established: multisided and ragged historical processes are almost inevitably overwritten by a teleology of statist outcomes once the nation-state has been established. On the other hand, such studies also usually end up in a vague comparative mode that often points to historical "failure," specifically, non-Western failure to replicate Western forms or outcomes.

The historiographical solution proposed for statist narrative suppressions—and this is the other dominant form that the conflation of statism and nationalism takes—is to historically "delink" messy local processes from the nation-state, and to offer these local "alternatives" as individual episodes that resist recuperation into nation-state narratives. These delinkings end up reinforcing the sense that nationalism is merely, and indeed can only be, an imposed state-led narrative tyranny. Meanwhile, the historiographical solution proposed for narratives of "failure," particularly in the China field, has been to write "insider" histories that altogether ignore or "delink" Chinese history from the global.

In recent writings on early-twentieth-century China this delinking strategy has received several related treatments. One type responds to and fuels a growing current concern with provincialism or other localisms, and is exemplified by a veritable explosion—in China as in the United States—in microeconomic studies and local social histories that aim to disaggregate "the nation" into smaller parts, conceived either sociologically (as gendered, racialized, or ethnicized) or as geographically, politically, or culturally circumscribed spatialities. Such explorations of "the local" are, in one sense, a welcome departure from many older studies of China that, rather than take the national unit as a historical question needing to be explained, take it as the self-evident premise from which to begin. Nevertheless, in deconstructing the a priori nation (whether culturally or politically understood), local studies tend to see nationalism as essentially irrelevant to local practices, thus tending to reinforce the synonymity of nationalism and the central state (or the pursuit of one).[35] In the end, nationalism is reduced to statism even when both become absent presences marked by either the presence or absence of the state.

One recent study in the China field, which has been extremely well received among scholars, ingeniously combines most of these tendencies. This is Prasenjit Duara's *Rescuing History from the Nation*, which, because of its deceptive clarity, merits fuller discussion. Duara goes one step further than other critics by condemning "nation" as historical category altogether. He begins by defining "nation" as a teleological universalist Hegelian *narrative* of statist triumph, imposed upon China (and India) by the West in the late nineteenth century. In thus immediately conflating nationalism and statism at the level of Historical universality underpinned by narrative teleology, Duara then goes on to propose dislodging the offensive "nation" category by recuperating local histories and by separating these histories out from the putative universal History of nation (which is really just the state narrative or the narrative of state). Thus displacing the universal onto Statist Idealism (via Hegel), Duara is able to reject universalism, and focus on the "real" messiness of local history, thereby apparently to "rescue" (Chinese) history from History (universal narrative) and thus from the repressive historical category of the nation altogether.[36]

To be sure, Duara successfully demonstrates that not all local episodes can be gathered into a nation-state narrative, while his effort to contest the a priori disciplinary boundaries presupposed by nations as historical objects of study is salutary. He nevertheless so thoroughly conflates universal History as *narrative* with global historical problematics and processes as to dissolve legitimate issues of historical interpretation and disciplinary practice into problems of narrative practice *tout court*. This he achieves by not making any distinction between "universal" and "global." That is, he conflates the narrative uses of Hegelian Idealist History—which focus on the State—with the modern global historical problematic of nationalism, which is more productively seen as a material reflection of and conceptual challenge to political, social, cultural, and economic relationships in an era of global modernity fueled by the expansion of capitalism as a representationally tendential unity. In so doing, Duara effectively conceals the (materiality of the) global under a misrecognized (idealist version of the) universal, thus allowing himself to brush away "nation" as just so much ideological (narrative) dross.

Yet surely the *narrative* problem—at whatever level—is consequent upon the global material problem, not the reverse; and just as surely, it is precisely *because* of the hegemony of the Historical narrative—that practice that presents European history as universal Historical teleology—that there is a necessity to reintroduce, rather than to elide, a material global dimension to local history. In other words, countering the hegemony of Euro-American-centrism in History, just as does countering a falsely conceived authentically "local" that is detached from anything larger, requires an effort to return a global historical condition to the picture, not as objective teleology (Idealist universal narrative), nor as homogenizing force, but as historically specific representational structure or tendential totality. Repudiating universalist hegemony—as worthy a cause as this may be—cannot be done by brushing away the materiality of global problematics: that just reconceals History under an idealist sign or reifies histories under an isolationist sign; rather, repudiating universalist hegemony must be done through an effort to recuperate interconnectedness *in global historical context*. It cannot be done, then, by rejecting the ideological *narrative* practice of Idealist universality and thereby declaring the global, national, or nonlocal contexts irrelevant and always universalizing, but by refiguring how those are mutually productive and constitutive at various levels of material historicities.

That said, the recent emphasis exemplified by Duara (and many others) on the Chinese nation as a construct raises good questions about a previously assumed entity called "China" that moves directly and diachronically through homogeneous time to the present (although Duara's claim that "nationalism" is not new to China because of the continuous and enduring sense of polity from the inception of the imperial period onward contradictorily runs against these claims, and smuggles a statist teleology as well as an enduring "China" back in). Nevertheless, the "local" emphasis has done little to explicate the problem of "locality" in an unreified way. For, by posing "nation" primarily in terms of the problem of state narrative (or, in assimilating nation historically either to a putatively Hegelian narrative of the ideal State or to a continuous Chinese polity), nationalism is still reduced to statism in an axiomatically functional relationship, where the local can only appear as an a priori resistance to an already constituted entity. More important for the present inquiry, however, is that in these perspectives the materiality of globality is completely erased.[37]

Historically, the tendency to conflate state and nation in modern China studies has proceeded as a dominant historiographical conceit in the past century; such a tendency was consolidated in Chinese Republican statist narratives soon after the fall of the Qing dynasty in 1911. Prior to the Republican revolution of that year, no contender for the postimperial state was able to hegemonically foreclose its claim to the "nation" or to the "state," although many tried. Indeed, in its final long decade of rule (1895–1911), the Qing state, for all its weaknesses vis-à-vis imperialist and growing provincial or local powers, was to some extent still able to exert control over the activities of oppositional elites and other social groups trying to claim the state away from the dynasty. As part of its attempt to reconsolidate its claims to the state and hence to a dynastically defined nation-statism, the Qing initiated many reforms (*xinzheng* reforms) after 1901 that were intended to reassert its grip on imperial state power and over the disintegrating socioeconomic structure, even while these reforms implicitly and explicitly acknowledged the inroads of the new historical situation (e.g., by abolishing in 1905 the millennium-old civil service exams). Despite these attempts, however, the Qing's social efficacy as a ruling power continued its rapid decline; and its ability to renarrativize itself as the future state of the new Chinese nation continued to be fatally compromised by a conjunction of developments. These included defeat in the Sino-Japanese War (1895), which exposed the dynasty's extreme weakness and the insufficiency of the previous decades' self-strengthening measures, which were primarily aimed at enhancing the technological and industrial capacity of China; the 1898 coup d'état by the Empress Dowager Cixi, which exposed the dynasty's resistance to change and its essential corruption; and the Boxer Rebellion debacle of 1901, during which the allied imperialist powers sacked Beijing and imposed crushing indemnities upon the country, while also helping prop up the prostrated dynastic state as the only guarantor of international treaties and the only plausible defense against complete social disintegration.

The compromised situation of the dynasty was quickly recognized by newly emergent elites, many of whom were increasingly detaching themselves from bureaucratic service and now explicitly positioning themselves as critics of dynastic politics and culture (either to reform or overthrow it). These educated elites—often backed by local entrepreneurial interests—began to publish journals in astonishing numbers to promote their views. The situation was also recognized by local elites, whose local governance and economic projects, ostensibly carried out with state sanction, ultimately helped weaken the dynasty's centralizing rule.

Given the realities of the weakness of late Qing dynastic state power, a "frustrated state" narrative of modern China emerged as historiographical conceit after the deposing of the dynasty in 1911. This statist narrative of modern Chinese history reconceptualized the period from the First Opium War (1840) through the Republican revolution (1911) primarily as an era of weakening state power and of staged diachronic "backwardness" vis-à-vis Euro-America and Japan, a weak-state narrative which then placed the historical burden of building national strength squarely in the realm of the state. This statist narrative quickly imposed an effective closure upon the types of questions posed about modern Chinese history. Indeed, the very instability of the Republican governments that succeeded the dynastic state, along with the snowballing Japanese and Euro-American incursions on China's territory, polity, culture, and economy from the 1910s through 1949, only served to focus historiographical attention more firmly on state weakness as one of the most central problems of modern Chinese history. As a consequence, there has been strong historiographical focus on the historical centrality of urgent efforts at making up for the legacy of "weakness" through state-building.

This focus has produced a contradictory situation. For, even though the postdynastic state was unstable and could hardly unambiguously lay claim to the "nation," the coming into being of the Chinese Republic itself—that is, the overthrow of the dynastic system—was nevertheless quickly consolidated into a narrative that presented dynastic overthrow and the Republic as the historically inevitable outcome of China's early modernization and thus as the historically inevitable basis for China's modernity.[38] This teleological political narrative of modernization/modernity, however, necessarily had to be emplotted as a tragic story of incompletion because of the utter fragmentation of the Republican state.[39] Thus, even while historians have moved away from centering the burden of state "failure" on either the personal history of Sun Zhongshan (Sun Yatsen, the Republic's ostensible "father"), and/or on the institutional history of Sun's Revolutionary Alliance (*Tongmeng hui*) as the (flawed) vehicle for China's political modernization, the narrative of state incompletion—where completion could only be strong state formation—has effectively contained the last century of modern Chinese historiography under the statist sign (even when the ostensible topic is not the state per se).

This contradiction, in turn, has led to an easy scholarly acceptance of a historical paradigm of bifurcation, first purveyed by philosopher Li Zehou, between political efforts to "save the nation [state]" (*jiuguo*) and cultural-intellectual trends toward "enlightenment" (*qimeng*).[40] In this formulation, the saving (embodied by political revolution and the pursuit of strong state-building) is said to have consistently suppressed the enlightenment (bourgeois democracy and intellectual freedom), a suppression that supposedly began in the late Qing and that purportedly continues to this day. Indeed, this putative suppression is currently often blamed for the incomplete social, intellectual, cultural, and political modernity and modernization of China today.[41]

Taking the implied incompletion of modernity as historical reality, then, recent Chinese historiographical efforts at recuperating the repressed other (enlightenment) of the purely political (the *guo*, or state) have dovetailed with postcolonial trends in the United States, such as Duara's, that concern themselves with marginalized or marginal forms. The problem with this approach has already been suggested above. That is, when the *guo* (nation) is taken to be synonymous with the *guo* (state) and is thus posed as the opposite of cultural-intellectual enlightenment, then the failure of the *guo* (state) to secure its own inevitability as national embodiment invariably leads its purportedly repressed historical other—enlightenment—to come back to haunt it. This "other" can take any form: cultural, economic, political, intellectual, and so on. Yet, whatever form it does take, it is in the *paradigmatic* acceptance of *guo* (state) as exhausting the historical possibilities of "nation" and the *historiographical* acceptance of statism as nationalism's inevitable and exhaustive content that intellectual and cultural trends oppositional to the state can be seen as pertaining to "alternative" spheres that appear as historical specters ("alternative modernities" in current parlance). It is also in this twin historical and historiographical acceptance that any relationship between globality and nationalism can be brushed aside as mere universalist or idealist ideology.

In sum, then, no matter whether the historiographical effort is to confirm the nation-state—in the unnamed name of modernization hitched to state triumphalism—or to deny the nation-state—in the name of seemingly autonomous resistant localisms and practices—"nationalism" as a historical problematic and "state" as its always-destined ventriloquist have become ever more historiographically fused in narrative complicity. No wonder, as Jacques Rancière has remarked in a very different context, the death of the king that "signifies that kings are dead as centers and forces of history," instead of leading somewhere completely different, has led to a relocation of historical centers and of historical forces to the "blindness" of life.[42] The paradox, as Rancière also notes, is that this "blindness" actually works to reinforce the old historical center itself.

Nationalism and the state are without a doubt related to one another, since, evidently, one goal of nationalism as a purely political project was and is the establishment of a state. However, the relationship is historical, not inevitable, and it needs to be specified contingently, not teleologically. To this end, as already noted, in this book I rejoin modern Chinese history to the global context, by taking Chinese nationalism as part of a modern historical problematic that was posed in the late nineteenth century, not only by and to the Chinese but simultaneously by and to others. I take nationalism to be a congeries of diverse intellectual praxes and concept-formations, which are not reducible to the pursuit of a political state, and which are endowed with translocal significance precisely because of the emergence of nationalism globally.[43] As a consequence of rerooting nationalism in globality and yet delinking it from an inevitable conjoining with statism, it becomes possible, on the one hand, to widen our view of nationalism away from the accustomed arena of inquiry (the emulation of Western-Japanese state forms and/or the remapping of traditional forms unto a new situation), and, on the other hand, to avoid a reified focus on an internality that putatively resides outside the broader histories in which it is perforce embedded.

A Note on the Book's Organization

As this book proceeds in a nonlinear fashion, I provide an overview of the chapters here. Chapter 2 introduces the major terms elaborated through the rest of the study. It almost literally sets the stage for the readings that follow by closely analyzing the textual and historical conditions of possibility for a 1904 production of a Beijing opera in Shanghai that concerns the partition of Poland and its modern resurgence as an ethno-nation. It starts the book's inquiry in chronological mid-stream, in order to indicate the historicity of the relationships established among some of the key terms in the text: *race*, *colonization* or *wangguo*, *globality*, *history*, *the people*, and so on.

Chapters 3 through 5, which comprise part 2 of the book, go back from the time of the opera to cover the same chronological period (1898–1904) through three different lenses. Each chapter takes up one or a cluster of related conceptual aspects of nationalism as each came to be elaborated through observations on or participation in particular events in the world, where each event helped bring one set of concepts and relationships to the fore of political and social analysis. They are: global space, territoriality, and deterritorialized political praxis, as seen through the "discovery" of Hawaii as a center of the Pacific and the constitution of overseas Chinese as potential "national people" (chapter 3); the relationship among revolution, representation, and history, as read through the Philippine revolution against the United States (chapter 4); and the connections between ethnicity and nationality, as seen through the lens of the Boer War in South Africa (chapter 5). I should emphasize that all of the events and concept-formations elaborated in these three chapters occurred simultaneously in real time; as a writing and intellectual strategy, I separate them out and go over the chronological period three times.

Following the decade during which this disarticulation of the components of nationalism proceeded, part 3 traces how these components were gradually reconstructed into a new whole. The first step was the reduction of the scope of imagination from the global to the regionally Asian (chapter 6), through which Chinese nationalist discourses were intimately tied to radical nationalist projects in Asia. The second step was the further reduction of this imaginary to a national revolutionary strategy that called for a specifically Han Chinese revolution against the Manchu Qing (chapter 7). In this last moment—which was partially derived from interpretations of Egypt and the Turkish revolution of 1908–1910—internationalism as such was rejected in favor of a much more limited statist notion of China. The book ends with a brief conclusion.

STAGING THE WORLD 2

Through four thousand years of history, we have witnessed both success and failure. Like actors in a drama, we perform on a stage. Borrowing the annals of light and darkness, we must urgently take over the right of education. The world is a theater, yet I suspect the stage might be too small.—Wang Xiaonong, 1904

On 5 August 1904, the Chunxian Teahouse on Wuma Road in central Shanghai[1] was crowded with people attending the debut of the well-known actor Wang Xiaonong's[2] new-style Beijing opera, *Guazhong lanyin*. Performed as the Russo-Japanese War was under way on the nearby Korean Peninsula, *Guazhong lanyin* concerns an ostensible war at an unspecified time between Poland and Turkey, which leads to Poland's defeat and partition. The first opera written to suit Wang's newly launched opera reform movement, *Guazhong lanyin* explicitly aimed to fulfill the reformist goals of incorporating themes from current events and foreign histories into new dramatic works.[3] As reform supporters put it, such dramas would "force people to think and feel for their country [*guo*] and [would] be a model for awakening our four hundred millions, allowing them to imbibe a sense of the ways of the world [*shidao*]."[4] Shanghai, it was thought, was a particularly promising site for such popular educational experiments, for, in contrast to the capital, where Beijing-style opera was attended mostly by officials and gentry, in Shanghai, common people constituted the majority of the audience.[5]

A full month prior to its debut, *Guazhong lanyin* was heralded as a major coming attraction in the Shanghai papers, as it promised an unprecedented combining of performers dressed in Western-style costumes with traditional musical and dramatic forms.[6] But, before its first performance, Wang Xiaonong was filled with anxiety about his opera's fate. He wrote of his doubts in one of the leading journals of the day: "[When] I stage this drama, if people flock to the doors, then [it means that] their hearts are ready to be seduced [*yiyou*]; if the contrary occurs and no one comes knocking at the door, then [it means that] our country is truly lost [*guo jen wang*]."[7] As it turned out, Wang need not have worried. The performance on August 5 of the first part of the opera produced an extraordinary hubbub, earning the Chunxian Teahouse a warning by Shanghai police to keep the crowds under control and the noise level down.[8] The second part of the opera was performed ten days later at the same venue to equally teeming crowds. Responding to audience demand, a playbill was printed for the second half of the opera; the text of its first half was published serially in the Shanghai-based daily *The Tocsin* (*Jingzhong ribao*), and other journals;[9] and, by late October 1904, a single-volume reprint of the script was put on sale.[10] By all available measures, then, the opera was a success with the public.

It was also a hit with reviewers, particularly those who were committed to the stated aspirations of opera reform to extend the relationship between local drama as mass entertainment and popular sociopolitical education.[11] Chen Qubing—an important figure on the Shanghai intellectual scene, the editor-in-chief of *The Tocsin*, and a co-founder with Wang Xiaonong of the opera reform movement's short-lived journal *The Twentieth-Century Stage* (*Ershi shiji dawutai*)[12]—was among the crowds at the Chunxian Teahouse on both August evenings. In an enthusiastic commentary for *The Tocsin*, Chen noted that the opera's "far-reaching import, felicitous structure, and tragic musical tonalities" along with its "unprecedentedly heroic" dramatizations would undoubtedly "enlighten" "lower-class society [*xiadeng shehui*]."[13] Other reviewers, circulating among the audiences during the performances, noted that "people were full of praise and said that the program stimulated their excitement and aroused their energies."[14]

That a curious public and politically sympathetic reviewers flocked to a major opera event may not be surprising in the bustling and turbulent context of Shanghai at the turn of the twentieth century. However, that an opera about the partition of Poland was written and performed in Shanghai at that time does require further commentary, as does the particular rendition of the world that the opera engages. In its broadest sense, *Guazhong lanyin* offers an account of the modern world from the perspective of the disjuncture and incoherence with which it seemed suffused, while, at the same time, in its staging of the world—its literal containment of the world on the stage as well as in its metaphorical reference to the world as China's stage—the opera also presents the world as a totalizable whole.

Microcosmically, it thus helps indicate how China's late Qing crisis-ridden situation came to be linked to a geographically far-off yet conceptually proximate imaginary of others perceived to be engaged in a shared contemporary moment of historical crisis and change. Indeed, in this general sense, the story of Poland's demise—territorially partitioned by foreign countries and literally wiped off the face of the world map, yet still present as an imaginary of a somewhere with a potential future being wrought in the present—lent itself particularly well to this type of dramatic treatment.

This chapter offers a reading of the opera text as a performative historical interpretation.[15] It introduces how an "everyday historiography"[16] of global space was textually produced out of an intellectual engagement with the cognitive and material concerns of its specific historical moment. In the course of the discussion, I unravel the interpretive conditions for the opera's particular rendering of Poland's demise at the unlikely hands of the Turks, while introducing the three overlapping themes central to this book. They are: how, through a recognition of the uneven global space of modernity, problems of state-people relations were identified in China's turn-of-the-century moment; what the parameters of the discursive formation of these identifications were; and how it was contradictorily proposed that these recognitions could be organized as praxes in late Qing China.

A Note on the Title and a Brief Synopsis

The title of the opera, *Guazhong lanyin*, literally translates as "Planting the Melon [or, Seeds of the Melon], Cause of the Orchid"; yet each character in the title carries double meanings that defy a literal—and even a literary—translation. *Gua* (melon) forms part of the compound *guafen* (cutting the melon) commonly used in early-twentieth-century China to refer to the partitioning of China by the Western powers and Japan after the Sino-Japanese War of 1895 and the Boxer Rebellion of 1900. *Zhong* (to plant; seed) appears in the compounds *zhongzu* and *renzhong*—*kind, people, race*—concepts not only central to the Darwinian language prevalent in Chinese sociopolitical discourse of the time, but pivotal concepts in the opera. *Lan* (orchid) is part of the compound used to transliterate *Poland* (*Bolan*) into Chinese; and *yin* (cause; consequence of) forms part of the compound *yinyuan*, a Buddhist-derived concept denoting an origin that produces lasting effects. Hence, embedded in the poetic vagueness of the title are a variety of contemporaneous concerns and new discursive usages in late Qing China.

At the same time, the title also evokes the melancholic and contemplative mood appropriate to a tragic drama. Highlighting this mood, Wang wrote in an epigram preceding the opera script, "In July, when the fragrance of a country is scattered like wild orchids, one can eat melons to cool one's blood. If causes are examined to understand effects, feelings will be calmed and the heart will remain unwounded."[17]

Guazhong lanyin—the first half of which (the only extant portion of the text) is translated and placed in the appendix to this book—concerns a war between Poland and Turkey, precipitated by an alleged insult dealt by the former to the latter. The insult is perceived and experienced through the performative (mis)interpretation by the Turkish ambassador to the Polish court of a term—*tongzhong* (same race/kind)—used by the Polish "emperor" to ritually classify his foreign visitors on the occasion of their visit to him for his thirtieth birthday celebration. The events dramatized in the opera flow from the consequences of this "insult": the decision by the Turkish "emperor" to invade Poland to avenge the insult, albeit only after he is convinced by his envoy that there *is* an insult to avenge; the "treachery" of an educated Polish commoner, who, dissatisfied by his treatment at the hands of Polish authorities, decides to betray them by guiding the massed Turkish army through Poland's secret defenses in exchange for personal gain; the arrogant complacency of the Polish general in charge of the country's defenses, who relies upon natural geographical barriers rather than a sound military strategy to fend off the Turks; and the disunity of Poland's aristocratic parliament combined with the ineffectualness of the youthful Polish "emperor." At the thrilling close of the first part of the opera the Turks have vanquished the Poles on the battlefield and Poland's demise seems assured. Punitive terms of a peace treaty are dictated and accepted in principle by Polish envoys to the Turkish encampment; back in Warsaw, parliamentary ministers bicker, unable to decide upon a course of action.

The second part of the opera—now lost to us—was evidently action-packed. According to a review in *Dalu* (The Continent), "there are scenes with a parliament, a church, dancing, treaties, spies, conspiracies, assassinations, patriotic associations, dare-to-die corps [*gansi jun*], etc."[18] Although we cannot be sure of exactly what happens, given that Wang Xiaonong was concerned with popular educational goals, there was undoubtedly instructional dramatization of resistance to partition and the creation of popular unity out of the seemingly fatal divisions within the ruling state and between the state and the people. That much can be inferred from Chen Qubing's review, in which he stated that the opera's major point was,

> to show that relying on foreigners will lead to perishing, and that relying on the government will also lead to failure. It intends to alert audiences to the evils and dangers of foreign relations and to the corruption of internal politics. Its final point is that failure to unite as a group [*jie tuanti*] and failure to pursue an uncompromising policy [*tiexue zhuyi*] will inevitably lead to the failure to survive.[19]

Chen added in a later commentary that the drama "revolves around the question of ethno-nationalism [*minzu zhuyi*]" and that "even those who are absolutely blind to current events can see that the performance is relevant to today's Russo-Japanese War: who represents the Koreans and who the Easterners [*dongfang ren*, i.e., the Japanese] is very clear."[20]

Yet, as Chen certainly knew, it was not just Korea (Poland) and Japan (Turkey) who were at issue in Wang's drama, since the mixing of metaphors and tropes also ambiguously indicates the identity of China with Korea/Poland and of Euro-America with Turkey/Japan. These correlations are at once transparent and opaque. What therefore needs to be explained is why Poland and Turkey came to be plausible substitutes for Korea/China and Japan/Euro-America; indeed, what makes the opera text interesting as a historical document—or as a text that produced and was produced by a particular type of historical context—is Wang's curious choice of presenting *Turkey* as Poland's modern partitioner. This choice—and choice it was: the textual bases for Wang's script correctly identified Russia along with Austro-Hungary and Prussia as the primary partitioners of Poland through the eighteenth and nineteenth centuries[21]—was not arbitrary. Nor, however, is the choice indicated by any necessarily homological or allegorical reading of the text; indeed, whatever the supposed correspondences, the dramatic action follows no actual chronology or set of events derived from Ottoman Turkish or Polish history, nor does it follow any chronology derived from Chinese/Korean/Japanese histories of interaction with each other or the world. Of course, given the wholly unhistorical nature of Wang's drama, and yet its radical historicity, it could be said that Wang's combining of contemporary concerns to construct a coherent operatic narrative was merely a strategy demanded by the exigencies of this art form, the need to create composites and to exaggerate situation and action to enable and enhance performative expressivity and dramatic presentation.[22] However, leaving the analysis at the level of operatic formalism reveals nothing about the new historical consciousness produced in and through the text.

Indeed, aside from drawing some well-worn analogies between Poland's modern fate (partition) and China's potential fate (imminent partition, or *guafen*), *Guazhong lanyin* transforms Poland's demise at the hands of the Turks into a sophisticated commentary on the multiple dimensions of the mutually constitutive relationship between the modern world and China. The drama does so by weaving certain strands of the growing domestic crisis to a global process with which it is linked, and by moving certain concepts to central or pivotal roles—primarily the concept of "race" (*zhong*). The following analysis unpacks the text/context produced by and in the opera; the three arenas of explication are, first, perspectives on popular participation in political and national transformation in the context of larger debates on state-people relations. With reference to the opera, the analysis examines histories of Poland circulating in China in the late Qing, the popularity of which reflected and exposed a perceived identity of historical situation between China and Poland, which not only helped spawn a minor intellectual obsession with Poland's modern fate, its history, and eventually, its literature, but also rendered "Poland" a ubiquitous metaphor for the modern world.[23] The second arena of explication is that of discursive usages that connected China to the world in new ways, central to which were notions of "race" and of "loss of state" (*wangguo*). As concerns the opera, the unfolding on the Korean Peninsula of the Russo-Japanese War ambiguously foregrounded the problem of *tongzhong*—or same race—in a modern global context of threatened state destruction (*wangguo*, or *mieguo*) and foreign intervention. A third arena concerns the potentials for a new popular politics, which, in the context of the opera's performance, reflected the explicit aspiration to connect current events to entertainment as part of a strategy of arousing popular consciousness and activism in the cause of sociopolitical transformation. Each of these arenas is discussed separately, yet each is present in the others; in other words, they do not stand in a causal or functional relationship to one another. Moreover, the discussion is not primarily focused on Wang's departures from "truth," but rather on his selection and his mode of relating issues to one another in an exemplary staging of the world of China's present.

Poland in late Qing China: Politics, the State, and the People

"Poland," as both proper noun and verb form, was, by 1904, a discursive fixture in Chinese texts about the modern world and China's crisis. First widely invoked in 1896 as a worst-case scenario indicating the perils of partition and the consequent desirability of top-down institutional reform to ward off such a threat, "Poland" was transformed after the 1898 coup into a one-word indictment of the insufficiency of such top-down strategies and, conversely, became an expression for the need for an elite-led popular struggle. By 1904, in one of its starkest incarnations, "Poland" became a verb substitute for the increasingly ubiquitous term for partition, *guafen* (cutting the melon): "to Poland me [us]" (*bolan wo*) efficiently expressed the centrality and imminence of the terror of "Polandization" (partition) in conceptualizations of China's precarious situation.[24] Below, these transformations in the "Poland" trope are brought into focus by paying specific attention to the changing perspective on politics, the state, and the people encoded within the use of the trope itself. Indeed, "Poland" is only significant as a *Chinese* trope if we see how it figures the problem of state-people relations in global context, a problem that had become a much-debated issue after the 1898 coup.

In 1896, Liang Qichao's account of the modern destruction of Poland, the subjugation and deportation of its people, and the banning of the use of the Polish language by Russian conquerors as a disciplining tool appeared in the third issue of his influential new journal, the *Shiwu bao* (Chinese Progress). Derived from a translation of Walter K. Kelly's *History of Russia from the Earliest Period to the Present Time*,[25] Liang's brief account blamed Poland's partition on the weakness of the Polish people and their rulers, as well as on the rapaciousness of their conquerors: the Russians, Austrians, and Prussians. In Liang's rendition, the collusion of the Polish aristocrat-rulers with the Russians, in the face of several abortive bloody popular rebellions against foreign rule, sealed its fate: Poland, the *guo* (state), was "lost" (*wang*) and its rulers were traitors. Written soon after the end of the Sino-Japanese War (1895) and after the disastrous terms of the Treaty of Shimoneseki that ended the war had been publicized, Liang's account of Poland's demise stressed state decline and failure to adapt as the major explanation for its perishing. This was precisely what Liang saw as relevant to China's situation at the time: "Alas! If a state (*guo*) is not competitive, it will be tied up in the other people's yokes and their tea will be as bitter as poison . . . In the mid-1600s, Poland was a great country of Europe. Then it didn't take care of its internal politics; its officials and the people . . . became weak and soft . . . [and the country was partitioned]."[26]

In the context of the 1898 reform period several years later, Kang Youwei, Liang's teacher and the intellectual leader of the reform effort, brought the example of Poland to Emperor Guangxu's attention. Like Liang's account, Kang's 24 July 1898 submission to the throne of a seven-volume work entitled *Bolan fenmie ji* (Account of the Partition and Destruction of Poland) emphasized the internal reasons for Poland's partition, which he identified as political corruption and incompetent leadership. He noted that in Poland the aristocrats were conservative and used their power to obstruct reform and suppress patriotic elites; the resultant stagnation in Poland's polity, he wrote, set the stage for Russia's manipulations, leading to open division among the Polish rulers and the eventual dismemberment of the country. Kang warned that if too much time was wasted in China over deciding about reforms, "then we will become like Poland; and will not those who preserve the old and obstruct reform be helping . . . divide themselves?"[27] Kang's emphasis on the corruption and stagnation of politics in Poland and on the forced exclusion of nonbureaucratic elites from politics accorded well with his advocacy of institutional reform for the Qing in 1898. That is, his concern with the closed system of the dynastic bureaucracy and its ritualized rule, the inflexibility of which precluded both a meaningful politics involving a larger cross section of elites as well as any significant improvements in commerce and industry, was reflected in Kang's rendition of the reasons for Poland's demise. His reading confirmed his own state-centered, elite-led institutional approach to reform and dynastic salvation.[28]

The condition of the state and its rulers (not of the people or society) was the major concern in these two early accounts of Poland. Indeed, the problem of state-people relations was neither well recognized nor articulated, and Poland's demise—and by extension, China's precarious situation—was squarely placed in the realm of the state, whose vitality, or lack of it, was deemed the determinant of survival and strength. Here, politics itself was understood narrowly: as pertaining and confined to the court/dynastic system, which defined the state (*guo*). The lesson emerging from this reading, no less for Liang than for Kang, was that the Qing could only avoid Poland's fate through judicious and timely change devised from within the institutional structures already in place, change that should be implemented by elites from outside the established bureaucracy (such as themselves). As such, prior to the coup in September 1898 that spelled the end to the reforms and that led to Kang's and Liang's respective fourteen years of exile abroad, and thus when confidence in the dynasty's ability to reform itself was still high, "Poland" was understood as a state that had been definitively "lost." It was a *wangguo* (perished/lost state). The Qing's hope and salvation lay in quickly reforming its institutions and widening its definition of politics so as not to follow Poland's path.

This relatively optimistic view of the immediate possibilities for the Qing, and its corresponding static fixing of Poland in an irrecoverable past-present of "lostness," was soon destabilized. After the reform movement of the summer of 1898 and the attendant collapse of confidence among many intellectuals in the ability of the dynasty to direct reform, the Poland code was transformed into a metaphor,[29] and "Poland" became a floating signifier. On the one hand, it remained an all-purpose locution that expressed the finality of lostness and partition: to be "Polanded"; on the other hand, it also received a new rooting in contemporary times, and came to express something much more ambiguous and hopeful: a "lost" state that nevertheless had an active "people" (*minzu*), who could recuperate not the state but the Polish nation.[30]

The metamorphosis of "Poland" became possible, on the one hand, as a number of new publications began to document the activities of the Polish elite and the Polish people in opposition to Russian rule (Prussian and Austro-Hungarian parts of Poland were generally ignored in these accounts). In the pages of the *Zhejiang chao* (Tides of Zhejiang) and *Jiangsu*, two major Chinese student journals published in Japan beginning in 1903, the Polish people's fight for ethno-nationalism (*minzu zhuyi*) was now extolled as an admirable example for Chinese to follow. Led by the Polish Socialist Party (*Bolan shehuidang*), whose very existence demonstrated the continued vitality of the Poles as a people, Polish activists, identified interchangeably as nihilists and socialists,[31] used a variety of ingenious methods to keep alive and promote opposition to the foreign occupation of their territory. Among these methods were popular rebellion, assassinations, and strikes, as well as the smuggling of newspapers published abroad into Poland for the purposes of mobilizing the consciousness of the Polish people.[32] Highlighting the relevance of these activities for China, Liu Yazi, a close associate of Wang Xiaonong's and Chen Qubing's, as well as an important figure on the Shanghai reformist literary scene, wrote in his preface to the Chinese translation of Shibue Tamotsu's *History of the Decline and Loss of Poland* (*Bolan shuaiwang shi*) that the book could "indicate to Chinese how to protect our people and how to maintain a spirit of opposition . . . It can be a mirror for us."[33] And, by 1908, Lu Xun's magisterial essay "On the Power of Mara Poetry" (*Molo shili shuo*) prominently highlighted Poland's premier poet of the nineteenth century, Adam Mickiewicz, as an exemplary nationalist figure who, in the absence of an existing state, foregrounded nationalism in his poetry, not as a political but as a populist emotive category.[34]

These new accounts of Poland mixed with changing emphases in China's political discourse of the time, where state-people relations had now become a primary subject of intellectual contention. It was through this mixing that, in the first several years of the new century, "Poland" emerged as a site of struggle. That is, it was recognized that while the Polish state was indeed lost, the people, or the ethno-nation was far from extinguished.[35] Key to the rearticulation of "Poland"—from *wangguo* to contemporary site of popular struggle—was the theoretical and conceptual distinction now being made between the people and the state, and the attendant incipient rearticulation of *guo* from "state" to "nation."

This is precisely the distinction that Wang Xiaonong's opera makes. In *Guazhong lanyin*, the absence of unity between people and state facilitates Turkey's victory. By the same token, it is precisely this absence of unity that harbors within it a different future. That is, the separation of the people from the state opens the possibility for the potential detachment of the people from the state that allows for a redefinition of the state/people relationship into a new type of politics and polity altogether. In the opera, Poland's state (exemplified by the tragicomical ministers, the divisive parliament, and the young, ineffectual emperor) is regarded by the people (exemplified by Wang Guonu, the educated commoner who betrays Poland) as bearing no relevance to themselves: "Poland" is a source of neither pride nor identity; it is merely the source of oppression and alienation. This irrelevance is signaled by and actualized in the "traitor" Wang Guonu's forsaking of any identification with the state's interests—"I will no longer pay any attention to this same race (*tongzhong*) idea," he says at a climactic moment of the drama—a decision that leads to his easy bargaining away of Poland's security for his own gain.

Wang Guonu functions here as a transparent symbol and symptom of the state/people divide. It is only in the context of such a divide that a "slave of a lost state" (*wangguo nu*)—a locution for which the character's name is a homonym—is possible as a modern historical type and that his betrayal of the state-defined *zhong* (kind; race; people) makes historical sense at all. By the same token, if we are to understand the trajectory of the drama, Wang Guonu and his treachery cannot represent any final historical moment of division. Rather, he is an essential part of the process of "the people's" conceptualization and actualization of *tongzhong* (same kind; race) unity, a new unity that cannot be premised upon the existing state and indeed must be constructed from outside the confines of the state. Wang Guonu, in other words, figures the final dissolution of an old people-state relationship and the beginnings of a new articulation of that relationship in modern nationalist terms.

It is this transformation that was recognized soon after the 1898 coup to be the precondition and premise for the reconstruction of China, the nation, in face of what clearly was state (dynastic) weakness. And it is in this context that the problem of "the people" and of how to reconfigure their relationship to the state became a particularly fraught issue in Chinese intellectual debate in the early twentieth century, for, part of the transformation in the concept of politics noted above precisely included asking the question of who participates in politics and how; or, of what constitutes politics and a potentially participating people. In these considerations, many intellectuals ambivalently discovered in "the people"—or, in the category of the "social" (*shehui*) or the *qun* (group), abstractly defined[36]—the necessary grounds from and upon which to build their new visions of the nation. Rarely untinged by an elite contempt and distrust for nonelites, this discovery nevertheless served to foreground the question of what place "the people" could occupy in new sociopolitical praxes. I take up these issues in greater detail in chapters 3 through 5 below.

In closing this first frame of discussion, suffice it to note that Wang's choice of "Poland" for his dramatic context and his particular interpretation of the Poland trope ingeniously reflects and precisely articulates some of the intractable problems that were of most concern in late Qing intellectual debates. For while the terror of partition and "loss of state" is unambiguously central to the dramatic action, the potential for "nation," as embodied in a transformed relationship between the people and the state, is moved to center stage. The portentous pronouncement at the end of the first part—that the loss of state is looming—signals that a new resolution to survival is on the horizon. That resolution, however, cannot reside in parliament—in nation qua state institutions—but rather in a new relationship forged between the people, their territory, and their culture. This combination of issues suggests why Poland was a logical site in which to situate a Chinese opera in 1904.

Japan, Turkey, Korea, and the Russo-Japanese War: Mobilizing "Race"

Most of the historical discussions of Poland in the late Qing gave a central role in the partitioning of the country to three interrelated factors: the instability of the system of electing kings; the aristocrats' stranglehold on politics, their corruption, and their contempt for the common people; and the reliance by different factions within the state upon foreign powers, Russia primarily, to prop themselves up. In none of the discussions does Turkey figure at all. In Shibue Tamotsu's volume, one major textual source for Wang's script,[37] Turkey is loosely identified as Poland's ally against Russia in the period leading to the first partition (mid-eighteenth century), but once Turkey has been vanquished by Catherine the Great's Russia, its role in Polish affairs ceases.[38] Thus, what is important, at least as far as this discussion is concerned, is Wang's choice of Turkey (not Russia) as the partitioner of Poland and, more specifically, the interpretive work this substitution does in rendering China's (and Korea's) turn-of-the-century situation visible. Indeed, both Japan and Turkey, in separate but linked ways, were ambiguous specters haunting Chinese politico-cultural discourse at the time, and these two improbable bedfellows were made to meet and were drawn into a relationship by Wang Xiaonong in the context of the Russo-Japanese War in Korea, begun in 1904 and concluded in 1905 with the defeat of Russia by Japan. The master trope that connects Japan and Turkey to each other and to China/Korea is *tongzhong*—or "same race/kind"—understood as a dispersed *geographical* and *historical*, not a static cultural or phenotypical, designation.[39]

Increasingly invoked in journal essays from 1898 onward,[40] *tongzhong*, in reference to Japan, often expressed the hope for Japanese assistance in staving off Western encroachment on China and in helping China reform from within the dynastic structure. As D. R. Howland has demonstrated, this was a hope for cooperation based upon a fanciful reading of past civilizational relations between China and Japan, the legacy of which was presumed to be transmitted, as cooperation between the two, into the present era of China's difficulty and Japan's growing strength.[41] *Tongzhong* in this figuration became part of one type of early-century pan-Asianism, which invented and articulated an Asianism of racial-cultural identity, with Japan at its geopolitical and geocultural center. This is discussed further in chapter 6. Here, suffice it to note that, from 1895 through the fall of the dynasty in 1911, the Qing officials who invoked *tongzhong* in reference to Japan usually referred to an ahistorically conceived civilizational commonality between Japan and China, which could be used in the present to legitimate the Qing emulation of some of Meiji Japan's state-centered reforms.[42] Meanwhile, many late Qing intellectuals—among them Kang Youwei and Liang Qichao as well as Huang Zunxian and Zhang Binglin (Taiyan)—tended to use *tongzhong* slightly differently. They used it as a historically affiliated spatial category that drew upon civilizational affinities between Japan and China but was not limited by and to them. This latter invocation of Japan's *tongzhong* relationship with China was often used to advance arguments for more far-reaching political-cultural transformation than those promoted by dynastic officials.[43] However differently it was used, by 1904 *tongzhong* was a well-established discursive fixture, albeit a still ambiguous concept, with reference to Japan.

In contrast to Japan's contemporary health and vitality and its purported lengthy past civilizational and now regional-spatial *tongzhong* relationship to China, *tongzhong* with regard to Turkey was an entirely new invention. Indeed, Turkey, as Liang Qichao noted in an early 1898 preface to a translated book on the Russo-Turkish War (of 1877), had only become a *tongzhong* with China recently, for, as Liang wrote, despite its religio-cultural dissimilarities from China, Turkey was a fellow "sick man of the East." It was Turkey's shared position in this new concept of a geopolitical "East," along with its shared contemporary problem of empire decline, that allowed Liang to appreciate Turkey's interdependence with China for modern survival. As Liang speculated, the only thing preventing Turkey from being destroyed by Europe, in the manner of a Poland, for example, was the existence of the second "sick man of the East," China.[44] In fact, the shared threat of extinction is what made Turkey "Eastern" and not "European" for Liang.[45]

The China/Turkey *tongzhong* relationship was also thoroughly explored by Kang Youwei in his book *Tujue xiaoruo ji* (The Demise and Weakening of Turkey), which, like the book on Poland, was submitted to the Guangxu emperor during the 1898 reform period.[46] Having noted in his second memorial to the throne (of May 1895) that Europe regarded China as "the

Turkey of the East,"[47] Kang underscored in his 1898 treatise to the emperor that, of all the countries in the world, Turkey was not only in its internal structure most similar to China—being an old-style empire—but it was also, in its global positioning, of "the same kind" as China (*er wu tongzhong ye*). Specifically, he wrote that Turkey in the past had been a strong empire that had "made the hearts and bones of Europe tremble and shake. But in modern times, Turkey has slowly become more conservative (*shoujiu*) and fallen behind; it has gone into decline and become poor. This process has been going on for a long time. If it does not lead to the loss of the state, then it will lead to an overturning (*tujue bu wangguo, ze geming*)."[48] Facing two such distasteful choices, Turkey's only alternative, Kang insisted, was to "stop the decline and weakness" with thoroughgoing state institutional reform. For Kang, it was in this contemporary reformist endeavor that Turkey's "sameness" with the Qing resided, a "sameness" that turned out to be China's good fortune, Kang speculated, as having a *tongzhong* ally in reform would be helpful to the overall efforts of both.

Turkey's relationship to China as presented by Liang and Kang—foisted upon China, as it were, via the European marginalization of both—was thus simultaneously seen as a shared "sickness" *and* a hopeful site for mutually dependent healing and regeneration through state reform. As such, the geographical and tropological *tongzhong* relationship between the two was configured out of a contemporary global and ostensibly similar state-imperial structure, made possible through the idea of "the East" (adopting European Orientalist designations), an idea that was turned slightly later into "Asia." Unlike the representation of the Japan *tongzhong* connection, however, the Turkey-China *tongzhong* connection was presented as a new product of modern uneven global space that spawned modern reformist imperatives.[49] It was, in short, explicitly seen as a product of modernity, and it was through this new lens of the uneven global space marked by the "East" that Turkey was made a plausible *tongzhong* substitution for Japan in Wang's opera.

By 1904, the civilizational/racial/historical/spatial conceptions of the "East" and of "sameness" were further complicated by the convergence on the territory of Korea of a set of circumstances that completely unsettled and reproblematized the issues altogether. One of Meiji Japan's rhetorical justifications for the Russo-Japanese War—as well as earlier, for the Sino-Japanese War of 1895, which also had been fought on Korean soil—was to save its *tongzhong* (J: *dōshu*) Korea from perdition (at the hands of either

China or Russia). This justification presented problems for Chinese intellectuals. Already in 1903 some Chinese students in Japan had suspicions about rhetorical appeals to China/Japan *tongzhong* relations, suspicions that broke into the open upon the publicizing of the 1903 Osaka Exposition's classificatory schema, in which China was classified by the Japanese organizers and exhibited in the same pavilion as the "raw barbarians" of Korea, the Ryukyu Islands, India, Hawaii, and so on.[50] Chinese students saw this classificatory maneuver as a deliberate insult: not only because of wounded civilizational pride, but because such cavalier Japanese attitudes echoed to them the types of discriminatory and condescending treatments they often suffered in Meiji Japan.

Nevertheless and contradictorily, despite the deeply felt insult and the brief student protest to both Meiji and Qing officials over the exposition, the furor was short-lived. Russia's threatened takeover of Manchuria and Korea in 1903–4 helped temper Chinese students' doubts about Japan, when it became clear that the Meiji leaders were prepared to rise to Russia's challenge and that the Qing leaders were not. Indeed, Russian threats to Manchuria and the Qing's refusal to confront them provided a large impetus to the radicalizing of Chinese student activities in Japan throughout 1903.[51] Thus by early 1904, Chinese students in Japan, stridently confrontational over both Russian ambitions and Qing compromise, were ready to find in Japan's warmongering a protective haven for China's integrity: Japan would save China/Korea/Manchuria from Russia and through this it would provide evidence of its true contemporary *tongzhong* relationship to China. By mid-1904, overseas student sympathies strongly favored Japan in the conflict with Russia; Japan was restored to Chinese students' good graces, and accusations about its would-be hegemonic striving (temporarily) were suppressed in many commentaries. By contrast, Chen Qubing's Shanghai paper, *The Tocsin*, which, as we have seen, was intimately connected to Wang Xiaonong, began in early 1904 to warn that Japan was poised through this war to become "just as predatory as Russia."[52] Rather than finding in Japan a repository for China's hope, as did many overseas students, the perspective in the opera instead reflects Chen Qubing's disquiet, as both Wang and Chen warned of Japan's unreliability as an ally. Indeed, they each in their own way exposed Japan's intent to twist *tongzhong* into an excuse for domination, rather than use it as a basis for equality and regional solidarity.

In the opera, the transformation of *tongzhong* into an expression of new divisive global power relations rather than of regional equality and solidarity is first established as plausible through the ambiguous spatially defined "sameness" of Japan and Turkey (both "Eastern"), which makes Turkey an intelligible stand-in for Japan. The specific deployment in Wang's opera of *tongzhong* indicates the interpretive twist. We are introduced to a young Polish emperor celebrating his coming-of-age thirtieth birthday, a celebration marked by the stamp of a traditional imperial *tianxia* (all under heaven) legitimacy, provided by the attendance at the event of emissaries from far and wide.[53] Secure in the supremacy and future longevity of his *tianxia* empire, Emperor Augustus confidently conducts the welcoming ceremonies for his guests according to accustomed ritual norms. In the process, he unintentionally offends the Turkish emissary. It soon becomes clear that the rituals are problematic, not inherently so but in their interpretive interaction with a particular historical moment. To signal this—in the pivotal act around which the rest of the drama flows (see pages 204–5 in the appendix)—Wang uses a doubled meaning of *tongzhong*.

In effect, Wang both conflates and distinguishes an older notion of civilizational sameness (*tongzhong* as it purportedly pertained to Japan) with a newer notion of regional-racial sameness (that *tongzhong* notion just explicated above in relation to Turkey), by transposing Chinese ritual norms of ranking emissaries from abroad according to their distance or proximity to China *in terms of civilization* into a ranking according to considerations of distance and proximity in terms of *geography and race*. Both the older and the newer meanings are efficiently conveyed by the term *tongzhong*, wherein the simultaneous differentiation and conflation of the two concepts, expressed in one and the same locution, allows Wang to render *region/race* rather than *civilization* as the new center of relationships among peoples and between states in the modern world. That is, the doubling, which depends for its performative intelligibility upon alternative interpretations of the same concept, enables Wang to simultaneously mobilize (false) notions of civilizational sameness (the Polish ritual usage), by filling these notions with newer meanings of "race" and difference (the Turkish interpretation).

As is clear from the dramatic causality set in motion at this point in the opera, the ritual is read as an insult precisely because of a performative (mis)interpretation by the Turkish ambassador that depends upon a particular global historical context, in which "race" itself is a meaningful category of unequal international relations when hitched to global power, or geography. In this sense, "Turkey" serves in the opera as a plausible site from which to denaturalize "civilization" as the structural basis of world relations (Turkey is civilizationally different, unlike Japan) while inscribing "race" and regional power as the new meaningful category of global ordering[54] (Turkey is both "same" and yet more powerful than Poland, thus deserving of better treatment). In this new matrix, the insult—which turns on the combining in the concept of *tongzhong* of contemporary notions of race and power, not on the appeal to past legacies of civilizational affinity—seems to be manufactured by an overly sensitive Turkish envoy. But it quickly becomes the normative basis for a crusading violence: the assault on and partition of Poland. It is thus at the very moment when the Polish emperor uses the concept *tongzhong* in a "traditional" ritual sense of civilizational sameness and the Turkish ambassador interprets this term in a modern sense of global power and racial difference that the historical moment of Wang's present is fully figured. In short, it is at this point that the concept *tongzhong* is recognized and authorized as a modern discourse of racial/power difference and as a pretext for global violence, and thus is rejected as a legacy of civilizational sameness and of contemporary cooperation. In this way, Turkey can stand in for both Japan (falsifying older concepts of *tongzhong* as civilization) and for Euro-America, for whom the combination of "race" and geography—translated as the notion of "the West" as hegemonic History—was a major pretext for violent assault.

Thus, in one simple scene and by virtue of a performative present historical moment, Wang links global power to the idea of *tongzhong*—understood spatially and racially as a category of modernity, not civilizationally as a category of the past—and renders race and geography (in their Darwinian universalist relationship) and *not* civilization (in its universalist imperial Confucian sense) as the pivotal concept of modern world ordering. Only when global power relations are centrally constitutive of its meaning is "race" (*zhong*) recognized as attaining its shattering historical significance.[55] In the opera, as in the modern world, the civilization/race confusion and conflation becomes the basis for the production of new meanings and for precipitating new consequences.

The pivotal concept of *tongzhong* hence works in the opera's context regardless of which analogical symbolisms are understood to be operative. If Poland is China and Turkey is Europe and the conflict is a China/Europe conflict, "racial" differences in the narrow sense of human phenotypes are clear and the China/Europe conflict can be seen as turning on and legitimated by this obvious difference. By the same token and reading with the contemporaneous commentators, if Poland is Korea/China and Turkey is Japan and the conflict is between Korea/China and Japan, "race" refers to the falsity of a locally situated same-civilization idea. Here, then, *tongzhong* is transposed into a geographical idea ("Eastern"), which, when linked to global power arrangements and a specific historical moment, then is transformed from sameness into difference. This transposition moves *tongzhong* away from being a basis of solidarity to being a cause for conflict and an excuse for domination; thus it not only exposes Japan's specific project in Korea, but also produces an understanding of the uneven global space of modernity.

In sum, Wang's use of Turkey (not Russia) for Japan in the context of conflict over Poland-Korea/China in 1904 reads multiple disjunctive aspects of modern modes of global interaction and modern figurations of global space into a historically synchronic and performative present. In the text as well as in the opera's expectations of its audience, the series of apparent incoherences are made to cohere in a provisional expressive totality that produces an interpretation of the new foundations of the modern world.[56] Turkey specifically allows Wang to provide this complex and compelling interpretation of the contemporary world, for it highlights—in a way that Russia could not (Russia is unambiguously European with relation to Japan/China)—the utter falsity of the purported *tongzhong* basis of the contemporary China/Japan—or Japan/Korea—relationship.

The Stage: Text, Context, Performance

The obvious concrete site for Wang's presentation was the stage. As the epigraph cited at the top of this chapter makes clear, Wang Xiaonong viewed the "stage" in both literal performative and abstract metaphorical terms. This double figuration was common by 1904, since one way that Chinese intellectuals had for articulating the concept of their new sense of an uneven global present in which China was participating was precisely through a rhetoric of performance and staging. Indeed, the twentieth century was often presented as a dynamic and dramatic stage, upon which were unfolding the histories-in-the-making of global actors, all performing in the same arena, but who rarely met or may never even have known one another.[57] This view was summarized by Liu Yazi in his introduction to the journal *The Great Stage of the Twentieth Century* (*Ershi shiji dawutai*), of which he, Wang, and Chen Qubing were co-editors:

> What we must do now is press the blue-eyes and purple beards [Westerners] into the garb of Jester Meng [Chinese drama] and set forth their history, so that the French Revolution, American Independence, the glorious revivals of Italy and Greece, and the cruel destruction of India and Poland may all be imprinted on the minds of our compatriots.[58]

This emerging sense of the staging of global and Chinese history—whether literal or figurative—emanated from and helped produce a new sense of temporal and spatial simultaneity, or a sense of synchronic historical time, of an "entire social world undergoing constant discontinuity, replacement and change,"[59] in active relation to other places.

The late Qing opera reform movement was one reflection and articulation of this new conceptualization of the world as stage and the staging of the world. Part of a much larger art and literature reform movement, which had received its first coordinated expression in 1902 with the publication of Liang Qichao's journal *Xin xiaoshuo* (New Fiction),[60] opera reform, as historian Li Hsiao-t'i has demonstrated, was a vital element in the widespread vernacularization of culture in the late Qing period.[61] Unlike literary reform, however, opera reform, as its founders articulated it, had the explicit intention and capability of going beyond the need for literacy presupposed by writing and reading. Indeed, by virtue of its very form and history in China, opera could and did reach deeply into the largely illiterate masses. Chen Duxiu, then editor of a journal in Anhui Province, noted this in his influential 1904 essay on opera and drama, in which he asserted that the performance venues for new-style operas—the teahouses—could become "schoolhouses," where even the blind or the deaf could "open their minds."[62] Chen continued that, of all the art forms, opera was the most suited to the task of "awakening the people," because people's attendance at performances was undertaken voluntarily and with great enthusiasm.[63] In a similar vein and specifically in reference to Wang's opera, others noted:

> From an artistic perspective, the detail in the staging immediately and strongly affects the audience; the musicians and actors also perform in good harmony. Those who might have been tempted to turn their backs on something different will, on the contrary, want to reject those old things that have accumulated in their hearts and give themselves over to the new sights and sounds; [they will want to] laugh and think about the myriad things that trouble and delight them.[64]

Wang Xiaonong's *Guazhong lanyin* was the most celebrated and written about "new-style" opera of the first decade of the twentieth century, but it was not the only one performed nor was it the only script reprinted in the journals of the day. From the far southwest in Yunnan Province—where, as one historian notes, "the majority of the scripts were actually staged and performed"[65]—to the cosmopolitan treaty port of Shanghai, opera reform was on the journalistic and performance agenda across the Qing empire. While it took different forms depending on different regional styles, a common theme of all new-style operas was the dramatization of current and foreign events for Chinese audiences,[66] although the sites that served in the dramas as loci for action were various: for example, in Yunnan, nearby Annam (Vietnam), colonized by the French, was the favored foreign site for the dramatization of local (Yunnanese), national (Chinese), and global concerns.[67]

While Shanghai was the original base for the launching of opera reform as a coordinated undertaking, the performance situation there was quite different from that in Yunnan and other places. For, by the early twentieth century, there was a large concentration of well-known Beijing opera actors as well as well-established sites for opera performance in the city.[68] As such, most of the operas performed in the major venues were drawn from the standard repertory, were written by established script writers, and featured famous actors. There was thus a considerable amount of resistance to new-style opera to be overcome in Shanghai. As the actor Xu Banmei recalled, by 1904 the notorious Xia brothers (Xia Yueshan and Xia Yuerun) had collaborated with the famous actor Pan Yuegao to stage new-style operas at the Dangui Teahouse, on Wuma Road; while over at the Chunxian, just down the road from the Dangui, Wang Xiaonong's "even more daring" experiment was to stage operas with actors in Western garb.[69] Yet, on Xu's account, sometimes the "outcome [of new-style dramas] was less than ideal," for these operas were "neither fish nor fowl; neither Western nor Chinese." Indeed, "some of the audience wanted these performances to be transformed into spoken drama . . . And a portion of the acting world was relatively dissatisfied with this type of drama; they thought that there was too much spoken and too little singing, that the gong and the drum were used too sparingly, and that it was too cold and bare on stage, almost disappointing to an audience."[70] Wang's opera was thus unique in having been performed in Shanghai, even while it was also exemplary of a whole trend of reformist practice.

By the same token, the connections that such intellectuals as Chen Qubing were hoping to forge through their promotion of opera reform were not only to bring to a Chinese public an awareness of the world and, thereby, a sense of conscious identification with the Chinese crisis. They also intended to bring to youthful elite-born social activists of the time an awareness of the necessity and urgency of expanding their mobilizational strategies to achieve social transformation. In his essay "On the Advantages of Opera" Chen Qubing openly urged these elite activists to involve themselves in drama, by connecting up with opera artists, and by writing and staging operas that appealed to the dramatic expectations of both audiences and actors alike. Chen added that "revolutionary opera could be far more effective than even such works as 'The Revolutionary Army' [*Geming jun*, by Zou Rong; published in 1903]."[71] These advocacies were repeated and extended in the Hong Kong journal *Zhongguo ribao* (China Daily), and they appeared to be realized in the performance of Wang's *Guazhong lanyin*.

Wang Xiaonong himself embodied the sociological and dramatic aspirations of the reform movement. He was an actor with many ties to the Shanghai intellectual elite of the time; as a former member of the bureaucratic gentry, his entry into this elite society had probably been easier than for most actors, because his elite origins were representative of only a tiny minority of actors, who were predominantly from the lower classes. (There was the added anomaly of his being Manchu among a majority of Han Chinese advocating reform/revolution, although this fact was never mentioned in the reviews of his opera at the time.)[72] Wang's literal connection of the lower-class society of actors to elite society—in both personal-sociological and revolutionary-activist terms—was deemed a good example of the possibilities for translating revolutionary programs devised at the elite level to the lower echelons, through mutual involvement in each others' affairs. Even more concretely, the mixing in the opera audiences of the representatives of the new student/intellectual groupings in opposition to the dynasty and the regular operagoers of indeterminate class also presented new possibilities for making connections between revolutionaries and revolutionary performances/performers in public sites, now transformed into potential spaces for the fomenting of popular activity.[73] These were at most desires, possibilities, and potentials. It is relatively clear in hindsight that the promise and potential of such programs was not fulfilled at this point.

Whether or not the movement was actually successful in fulfilling its aspirations for a welding of "the people" (audiences and actors) to the elite (intellectuals/reformers/revolutionaries), the opera reform movement does mark part of a new effort by intellectuals to productively combine text, context, and performance, with the purpose of producing a new set of cultural and national codes, metaphors, and tropes that could be mobilized for transformative action in the present.[74] In this sense, Wang's opera not only created one local (Chinese) discursive and practical terrain upon which the premise of global spatial simultaneity could be articulated in the late Qing Chinese context, it also specifically demonstrated how sociopolitical transformation might be achieved by mobilizing "Poland" directly into a Chinese interpretive and practical space.

Conclusion

There is no causal relationship between the "Poland" and "Turkey" tropes in Wang's drama and the larger context of late Qing thought and discourses on "the people," globality, revolution, or nationalism. Rather, the two types of discourses mutually informed and mutually constituted one other. Indeed, the very notion of "staging the world" or "the world as stage"—to which "Poland" and "Turkey" pointed both specifically and generally—relies upon a notion of simultaneity (not mere causation or comparison) and contemporary synchronicity, since without synchronicity, the "Poland" trope is ineffective as metaphor, the "Turkey" figure incomprehensible (or merely exotic), and the "China" figuration artificially and parochially limited. "Poland's" significance, then, is not limited to being an ahistorical metaphor for partition for it was also a concrete place with a contemporary history of struggle that foregrounded a historical divide between the state and people. This divide suggested that the ostensibly terminal fate of the "loss of state," abetted by foreign depredation, could potentially lead to a rediscovery of "the people" and a possible reconstruction by them of the nation. "Poland's" significance thus resides in its microcosmic figuration of one modern historical problematic of nationalism: the possibility for "the people" to construct the nation out of the ruins of the state within the global context of unevenness.

Meanwhile, "Turkey" also took on significance, by being transformed from occupying a completely "other" civilizational space from China—as in Liang's early 1898 rendition—to becoming a geographical (Eastern) *tongzhong* with China. Its significance as a trope thus resides not in its "otherness" but in its foregrounding of a transition from a reliance upon civilizational sameness to a dependence upon racial/geographical sameness/difference as the dominant principle for the ordering of modern global power relationships. While the "Poland" code was to continue, throughout the late Qing, to vacillate between the ahistorical tropological and the concrete historical figurations, Turkey, as discussed in chapter 7, reemerged in 1908 to become a model of multiethnic monarchical constitutionalism that Chinese revolutionaries rejected in favor of a monoethnic deposing of the Chinese dynastic system.

With such historicities in mind, it is now possible to see that it was neither accidental nor arbitrary that Wang Xiaonong chose Turkey as Poland's modern partitioner in 1904. For, however unhistorical such a choice was in the context of Poland's or Turkey's history, this choice effectively foregrounded how Chinese intellectuals extracted and produced new meanings and new sites for the forming of discourses of Chinese nationalism through new conceptualizations of the contemporary world, of modernity, and of China. How this became possible from 1898 to 1904 is the topic explored in part 2.

PART II

DETERRITORIALIZING POLITICS: THE PACIFIC AND HAWAII AS CHINESE NATIONAL SPACE 3

People call the twentieth century the era of the Pacific [*taipingyang zhi shidai*]; I call the twentieth century the era of big disorder [*daluan zhi shidai*].[1]

Historical geographers and historians of the "everyday" have long noted that place and space are concepts fundamental to historical experience.[2] Yet, however spatial all historical experience may be, the necessity to cognitively map situatedness within space—whether global, regional, national, local, or some other configuration—comes to the forefront of historical consciousness and contention and becomes particularly visible only at moments of acute rupture or historical dislocation.[3] The conflicted situation of late Qing China presented just such a moment for Chinese intellectuals. On the one hand, internal breakdowns fueled efforts at theorizing the gathering crisis in terms of a new people-state relationship; this theorizing, combined with the breakdowns, increasingly destabilized the claims of the dynastic system to represent the correct relational unity among politics, learning, and Chinese-ness. Indeed, the late Qing concern with specifying "the people," as many historians have recognized, required a reinvention of the very notion of "Chinese-ness." This reinvention partially conserved while also undermining the claims of imperial-Confucian and imperial-dynastic civilizational universalism, allowing new conceptual configurations of these vital relations to emerge.[4] On the other hand, after the 1898 coup, a considerable portion of Chinese nationalist theorizing and mobilizing took place outside the territorial bounds of the Qing empire, and the first direct targets of mobilization were often Chinese who resided outside of these boundaries. Given these two impulses, the rapid transformation in spatial consciousness that made the rendering of Chinese overseas into plausible and even central constituents of the Chinese "national people" (*guomin*) is impressive—and yet ill-understood.

Spatializing the problematic of "Chinese-ness" is particularly necessary precisely because "Chinese-ness" has generally been addressed by historians and others in reified culturalist-ethnic terms. As Prasenjit Duara, among others, has noted, within the newly posed problematic of "Chinese-ness" in the late Qing, there arose increasing contention over the incorporation of overseas Chinese into an incipient national narrative, a contention that was worked out between the dynastic state and its various critics concerning who and what properly embodied cultural-ethnic-national Chinese-ness. This contention, as he indicates, was enmeshed in a fiercely contested domestic political and economic arena, where different factions—the Qing state, reformers, revolutionists, among others—sought to claim the loyalties of Chinese overseas for often contradictory political and economic projects.[5]

Duara's account is illuminating, as far as it goes. Yet, it still begs the question of how Chinese overseas were recognized as "Chinese," a question that needs to be examined without a reification of the very category—"Chinese"—that must be explained. I argue here that "Chinese-ness" *first* became a global political topos and only after became a reified culturalist-ethnic one. This process was not simply a result of shifts in internal sociopolitical discourses and of the new mobility of Chinese intellectuals outside the Qing empire; it was intimately tied to the emergence of the Pacific as a contested space of modernity. This emergence brought to the fore of the theoretical conflicts over "the people" the possibility of a deterritorialized political praxis in and through this new global space. The conceptual efforts to substantiate the incorporation of overseas Chinese into a national political praxis via the Pacific discussed below thus focus particularly on the post-1898 emergence of concerns with creating an active and conscious "national people" (*guomin*) out of a presumed passive population of "slaves" (*nuli*) in China; these concerns were initially worked out in the recently colonized space of Hawaii, where many Chinese activists, including Liang Qichao, Sun Zhongshan, and others, went to raise funds for their respective efforts to overthrow or reform the dynastic state.[6]

Deterritorialization and Chinese Overseas

By the turn of the twentieth century, it was only a recent development that overseas Chinese could be considered likely targets of concerted incorporative endeavors. As K. Scott Wong has noted, the official Qing position as late as the 1850s held that Chinese residing abroad had forfeited their subject-hood in the Qing empire, and were deemed neither deserving of nor entitled to imperial assistance or protection.[7] This official attitude changed through the 1860s and 1870s, as efforts to investigate and regulate the abuse of Chinese laborers abroad, particularly in Cuba and Peru, resulted in the establishment in the late 1870s of Chinese consuls abroad, one of whose duties was to monitor Chinese laborers' conditions. It changed further in the 1880s, when, in the midst of the self-strengthening restoration years following the devastating midcentury peasant rebellions, the Qing state and provincial authorities began to vigorously and openly solicit the financial contributions of overseas Chinese for their various modernization projects.[8] In 1893, the legal prohibitions and stigmas against emigration were abolished and thus, by the end of the century, the juridico-legal as well as the sociopolitical and economic conditions of possibility through which overseas Chinese could be "captured" as political subjects for China had been established.

With his emphasis on national narrativity, Duara has called this process of incorporation inherently paradoxical, by which he means that he finds an inherent conflict between the territoriality of nation-statism and the deterritorialization of overseas Chinese—a conflict that appears to him as an antithesis between bounded state sovereignty and unbounded ethnicity. As Duara summarily states, "The deterritorialized nation is in many ways the precise antithesis of the formal conception of the nation-state in the global system of nation-states."[9] There is, however, no *inherent* conflict (there are multiple historical ones, of course), if one recognizes the ongoing twin reconfiguration in this process of national space and sociopolitical issues on the one hand, and the recognition of the embodied labor and capital represented in and through overseas Chinese on the other. That is, the problem appears differently if the concept of deterritorialization is rejoined to capital, as suggested by Gilles Deleuze and Félix Guattari,[10] and oriented away from its use in diaspora studies where deterritorialization is interchangeable with a reified ethnic notion of transnationalism.[11] For with this latter definition, as ethnic transnationalism, deterritorialization is stripped of its material links to capital and modernity, as uneven global regimes of power, and reappears merely as a moment in contested national (and transnational) *narratives.*

To be sure, superficially the late Qing moment seems to present the paradox that Duara identifies because of the convergence of several trends:

the mobilization of newly discovered potentials among Chinese overseas for political and economic purposes; the inevitable contested narrative invention and instantiation of "Chinese-ness" in the service of a contested statism; and the working out in overseas communities of political factionalisms originating in both Chinese and local politics and society. Yet, even though all of these elements are undoubtedly present, if this moment in the social production of national space, understood broadly, is tied to its properly global moment and thence understood in terms of the emergence of a relationship between national territoriality and the deterritorialization of capital and labor, the apparent "paradox" of bounded space/unbounded people, far from appearing paradoxical, instead becomes an integral or even an inherent historical dimension of modern nationalism, for China as elsewhere.

As Deleuze and Guattari have pointed out, "capitalism . . . is not at all territorial . . . [I]ts power of deterritorialization consists in taking as its object, not the earth, but 'materialized labor.' "[12] Moreover, it is a process that "provid[es] a universal subject and an object" for the potential construction of a modern state-form, itself the bounded organizing schema of capital, as both a global trend and as national desire.[13] In other words, nationalism, when seen as a historical problematic intimately tied to an uneven global modernity whose totalizing tendency is expressed in and through capital, is precisely *premised upon* de/reterritorialization (as a modern capitalist, not merely a diasporic, notion), and unboundedness, far from being the nation-state's antithesis, is one of its very foundations—for imperialist nations, just as for China, albeit in very different ways.

For imperialist nations, as any number of theorists and historians of colonialism have argued, de/reterritorialization was effected through a combination of colonization/imperialism, capital/primitive accumulation, and territorial expansion.[14] For China, the process of de/reterritorialization was incipiently effected through the recoding of Chinese abroad into a new national imaginary of "the people" and of their obligations toward the weakened state; this recoding process took place within the context of a Chinese state, society, and territory beset by internal social disintegration and capitalism in an imperialist form that was simultaneously eroding and maintaining the Chinese economy and social structure.[15] Thus unlike, for example, Meiji Japan—situated in the same global context of unequal treaties, albeit with a strong state, and where the process of de/reterritorialization took the form of contestations over internal legal reforms and the acquisition of regional colonies[16]—the extended moment of contestation over de/reterritorialization in China *appears* as an attempt to contain a diffused political subject/object as a culturalist essence. This appearance, and its quick reification into ethnicity (or natural ethnic feeling), however, should not obscure the material conditions established by the relationship between capitalism and nationalism that made such a containment, or recoding, possible. Thus, the historical problematic needs to be reconfigured: when the late Qing emergence of nationalism is explored in terms of how internal Chinese transformations came to be apprehended from within a new consciousness and experience of modern global space, it becomes clear that Chinese intellectuals figured what soon became articulated as a cultural-ethnic problem of "Chinese-ness" by *first* linking overseas Chinese to the emergent sociopolitical problem of "the people" as subjects/objects of national political and economic praxis, in an attempt to capture a universal political subject for the nation. While this process certainly raised issues of narrativity, the unboundedness of Chinese overseas was precisely the condition of possibility for the congealing of a concept and praxis of nationalism that initially centered on *them* as the primary active political and economic agents of national integration.

For this possibility to come into view, it was not the presence of Chinese abroad that needed to be recognized; after all, Chinese had been migrating from southern China for centuries already, their presence in the *nanyang* (Southern Seas) was well known, and their personal financial contributions to their families and localities were also well known. Rather, the characteristics of modern global space and its significance for a reconceptualized China needed to be seen and grasped as new premises for concept-formation and praxis. How this came to be is explored below in three moments: the arrival of King Kalakaua of Hawaii in 1881 in China, where the message of global transitions he bore to the Qing empire from the perspective of the immanently threatened space of Hawaii was roundly ignored; the arrival of Liang Qichao in Hawaii in 1899–1900, whereupon the overseas Chinese population helped him to view the relationship between colonization, nationalism, and popular political struggle differently than he had before; and the writings of Lin Xie, who brought the overseas Chinese and Hawaiian questions to a popular readership in his vernacular journalistic texts of 1901–2, in which he outlined the relationship of Chinese overseas to the Chinese people in China.

A Hawaiian King Visits China

In April 1881 the head of the Qing empire's *Zongli Yamen* (Foreign Affairs Office), Li Hongzhang, received a curious visitor at his office in Tianjin. King Kalakaua of Hawaii was stopping in China on his way around the world. Yet, unlike in Japan, where the king had just been received as a head of state with all the pomp and circumstance the Meiji leaders could muster,[17] Kalakaua's arrival in China had gone relatively unremarked by the Qing authorities. As William Armstrong, a member of the king's cabinet accompanying him on his tour, described it: "We arrived at Shanghai at noon . . . No royal salutes were fired as we entered the Woosung river . . . We dropped suddenly from the pinnacle of royal hospitality to its base, and the royal standard lay dejectedly in its canvas bag."[18] Despite the general lack of attention accorded the king, Li Hongzhang did hold a banquet for him in Tianjin, and Kalakaua later wrote, "Judging from what I have personally seen as regard [*sic*] China, and coming into immediate contact with the men that rules [*sic*] her destinies and have the power in their hands, I am impressed with the friendly feeling and good will they have towards us."[19]

Upon Kalakaua's departure from Tianjin, Li Hongzhang sent a bemused dispatch to the Qing court about the king's visit. It bears citing at length:

> [The king said]: Since ancient times, the world has been divided into three large continents: Asia, Europe and Africa . . . We [Hawaiians] are Asian, as are you [Chinese] . . . [The Europeans] settled Africa, which they have already completely swallowed up in their insatiable greed. Recently, they have also been nibbling away at Asia: Turkey, Sudan, Afghanistan, and India, as well as the western parts of Burma and the northern part of Mongolia are already engulfed. As of now, white people have settled four and a half continents, and Asians cannot even protect the half-continent that remains . . .
>
> Now, the strongest in Asia are, first, China, and then Japan. The remaining small states, such as Korea, Annam [Vietnam], Siam, and Burma are precariously balanced. If they do not reform their governments, then people from afar will rely on force to take them over. Hawaii is alone in the middle of the Pacific Ocean; our territory is small and our population sparse . . . Fortunately . . . for the moment we are at peace. But conditions are changing . . . We cannot be complacent. The past strength of brown peoples [Asians] is gradually declining. The reason we cannot arouse ourselves is because each country relies on its own

> past strength. We not only have failed to unite together to depend upon one another, but on the contrary, we are cruel to one another. This is a great pity. If we unite, we will be strong; if we persist in division, our energy will be dispersed . . .
>
> . . . We [Asians] should discuss affairs with sympathy for one another and united as one; it is unbearable that China and Japan have lost their good will [toward one another].[20] [I] have warned the Japanese emperor, and now [I] am cautioning you, Li: if we were able to unite so as not to leave foreigners a single opening, would this not be the best way to arouse our brown Asian peoples? I eagerly await for this to happen.[21]

Li noted, incredulously, two other things in his dispatch: that the king claimed that there were many Chinese on his island; and that Kalakaua had implored him to keep the purpose of his visit a secret, lest Westerners discover that Asians were plotting to unite against them.

As the chief foreign affairs expert of the Qing, Li Hongzhang had been, since the 1870s, an advocate for establishing Chinese missions abroad,[22] one of which was located in Honolulu. It thus may be unreasonable to believe that Li really had no idea about Chinese in Hawaii, or about the existence of such a place. Perhaps Armstrong was exaggerating when he wrote that Li was only informed about Hawaii by his secretary, a certain Li-Sun, graduate of Hamilton College in New York, on the day of the king's visit. However, it is not difficult to believe that Li may well have been bemused by Kalakaua's claim that Hawaii and China were both "Asian," that the Chinese and Hawaiians were of the same "race" (*zhong*), and that they should together initiate action against "Westerners." Nor is it surprising that Li would have found these claims and pleas not only presumptuous but outlandish. For clearly, Hawaii impinged little on Li Hongzhang's consciousness, and the islands in no way helped structure his thoughts about the world and even less about the Qing empire.

By the same token, it is more understandable why China—and broadly, Asia—*did* help structure King Kalakaua's thoughts on the world and on Hawaii in the 1880s, and why Kalakaua's sense of Hawaii's and his own precariousness was rather more urgent than Li's. In an immediate sense, the king was facing the calamitous decline of Hawaii's native population, who were being lost to disease. As a practical matter of repopulating his islands in order to continue the productivity of the very sugar plantations that were so threatening to his sovereignty and yet also so important to his government's revenue, encouraging Chinese (and Japanese) immigrant labor was a major factor in the king's calculations for the survival of his kingdom. Indeed, one major purpose for the king's visit to both Japan and China was to discuss "the emigration of their subjects from their territory to the sugar plantations of our islands."[23] Specifically, as Kalakaua noted in a letter written from China to his minister of foreign affairs in Hawaii, his purpose was "*First* . . . stopping if possible further immigration of Chinese to the islands, without carrying with them their wives, and *Secondly*;—To secure for our government the same privileges granted to the United States Government, the right at any time to restrict return, or remove, the large influex [*sic*] of Chinese to our Islands . . . On these two subjects our mission has been successful."[24]

Behind this immediate concern with labor and repopulation, longer-term global trends that threatened to swamp the Hawaiian kingdom were also preoccupying the king. Most urgent was the increasing intensity of assaults on the kingdom's sovereignty emanating from the expanding local strength of white plantation owners, who were intent on destroying the autonomy of the monarchy while at the same time agitating for United States annexation of the islands. The local strength of the planters was intimately tied to the extension of the overland American imperium toward the Pacific coast in the post–Civil War era, a trend that Kalakaua could hardly ignore.[25] And even though, up until 1898, support in the United States Congress for the territorial annexation of Hawaii was weak, nevertheless, in the economic and socio-cultural-religious realms, inexorably Hawaii was being integrated as an incipiently colonized space into the American imperium.

In face of this situation, Kalakaua had tentatively begun in the 1870s to counteract plantation capitalist and white missionary pressure by bolstering his kingdom's connections to Asia in demographic, cultural, and geopolitical terms.[26] As part of this effort, during his visit to Japan Kalakaua had attempted to enlist Japanese assistance against the United States by appealing to the Japanese emperor for the formation of "a grand Asian cooperative league, with Japan and Hawaii leading the nations."[27] The appeal fell on deaf ears. Indeed, the Japanese were harboring altogether other plans for "Asia" that, while still inchoate in the early 1880s, were certainly tending toward Japanese domination of, rather than cooperation with, other peoples and countries in the region.[28]

For entirely different reasons than in the Japanese case, Kalakaua's attempts to gain Li Hongzhang's interest in a movement of Asian solidarity were also rejected. Unlike the imminently threatened Hawaiian kingdom or the Meiji Japanese, for whom the expansion and instantiation of capitalist modernity (in the Hawaiian case, as a space of colonial difference, and in the Japanese, as a positive desire) were immediate concerns, the Qing empire—or, at least the bureaucratic stratum that Li Hongzhang represented—despite the partial loss of territory and sovereignty to foreign powers that had followed the Opium Wars, was still relatively secure in its ability to reassert its sociopolitical autonomy and its civilizational universality. Having recently quelled the internally threatening rebellions—the Taipings and the Hui, in particular—and having embarked on the restoration of the dynasty after these cataclysmic disruptions, Li Hongzhang, a major participant in both the quelling and the restoring, while certainly intent on raising the Qing's diplomatic profile on the international scene,[29] was nevertheless neither consciously concerned with nor susceptible to appeals for alliances that might question or disrupt the very dynastic and world orders that he was attempting to restore and/or join.

Moreover, even though in his diplomatic correspondence with counterparts in Japan Li had tentatively begun to adopt the Japanese-inspired phrase "*tongzhong*" (J: *dōshu;* same race/civilizational kind)—that very phrase that Kalakaua had used to exhort Li to an Asian solidarity with Hawaii—the "sameness" evoked by this concept for Li was not only imaginatively limited to the Confucian civilizational realm, but, because of the perceived historical subordination of Japan to China in that realm, *tongzhong* was hardly a strong or even plausible geopolitical principle conducive to broader alliances for Li or other Qing officials.[30] Indeed, unlike a decade and a half later, in the 1880s the concept *tongzhong* was far from possessing anything but the vaguest meaning for Chinese foreign affairs experts or Chinese elites in contact with Japanese counterparts—the preferred concept still being *tongwen* (same writing/civilization).[31] It certainly had no global/regional, racial, or supracivilizational connotations, nor any geopolitical significance that could have allowed for Hawaii to be conceptually included in its purview. One can thus well imagine that an appeal based upon such a concept could but seem fantastic to Li Hongzhang when proposed by King Kalakaua.

In Hawaii, the gathering storms of the 1880s that King Kalakaua had belatedly attempted to avert or partially subvert culminated in the deposing in 1893 of the next Hawaiian monarch, Queen Liliuokalani, Kalakaua's sister, who had succeeded him to the throne upon his death in 1891. As the agribusiness-dominated, white-settler republic was established in the monarchy's place, expansionists in the United States began to loudly claim Hawaii as the key to American "commercial and military control of the Pacific."[32] By the late 1890s and once the United States formally went to war with Spain in the Philippines in May 1898, the erstwhile attempts by the Hawaiian monarchy to maintain Hawaii as a sovereign kingdom collapsed. Hawaii quickly came to be overwritten by new narratives of belonging: in these, Hawaii was American, and the Pacific was claimed as "America's lake," with Hawaii at its strategic and paradisiacal center.[33]

By contrast, when Kalakaua had arrived in China in 1881 bearing his message of a shared threat to Hawaii and China alike, not only had the type of consciousness required for an analysis of global space that might render such a message meaningful in Qing China not yet emerged, there had also not yet emerged the social stratum from within Qing society that could and would seize upon such a consciousness to imagine and attempt to mobilize an alternative to the world and China as they appeared. This consciousness would grow within a short few years and from within a very different historical configuration. When it did, it is striking, although not entirely surprising, how closely King Kalakaua's pleas to Li Hongzhang articulate the very analyses of global trends that found so many proponents and that sparked so much urgent activity and rethinking in China after 1895.

After the Qing's defeat in the Sino-Japanese War in 1895, the problem of a differentiated but linked global spatiality within the context of a shared threatened local destruction was increasingly recognized in intellectual circles as an urgent conceptual and practical problem, so much so that the very global trends that had so preoccupied Kalakaua in the 1880s now came to preoccupy many Chinese intellectuals. And, as confidence in the dynastic state waned after 1898, proposed solutions to China's problems came to rest not upon state-dominated diplomatic internationalism, but upon deterritorialized politics that in effect laid claim to modern global space by linking its various localities through mobilizations of people for diverse national projects and into new nationalist imaginaries. It was in this complex environment that, by the late 1890s, Hawaii was transformed into and acknowledged by many Chinese intellectuals as a touchstone of "Asian," "Pacific," and world concern. No insignificant island in the middle of an inert ocean, as Li Hongzhang had thought it, Hawaii now appeared as a center of a newly emergent Pacific—a dynamic and contested region in formation—and thus as an important stage for the contemporary drama of the twentieth century. In this process, Hawaii, not being allowed to remain "Hawaiian," became "Pacific" and "American"; it also became (potentially) "Chinese" and "Asian" as well.

The Pacific as World Stage

The new awareness of the Pacific and Hawaii in China derived initially from the sharpening contestations in and over the region within the twin regimes of geopolitics and an expanding global capitalism, both trends that had so urgently propelled King Kalakaua eastward in the 1880s, and which became visible in China after 1895. The decisive reach of the United States over the Pacific through Cuba, Hawaii, Guam, and into the Philippines consolidated this visibility. By 1897 report after report in the new journals of the day kept readers informed about the repeated United States promises to *not* annex the islands, with the tone of the articles becoming more strident as evidence accumulated that the United States had every intention of going against its public word.[34] Most of these reports came from Japanese or British newspapers and international wire services expressing antagonism to United States plans.[35]

The outbreak of the war between Spain and the United States in mid-1898—initially in Cuba, and then extended to the Philippines—brought anxieties over proposed U.S. annexation of Hawaii to a critical pitch. The constant references in the Chinese press to stated American plans to station permanent troops in Hawaii (and Guam), to build permanent military installations in Hawaii to accommodate the occupation, to turn Hawaii into a coal depot for the growing American Pacific fleet, and finally the actual American involvement in the Philippines all helped articulate and reinforce the growing sense of an emerging Pacific region that stretched from the United States to China, and that was connected through the central nodes of Hawaii and the Philippines.[36] In characteristically insightful fashion, Liang Qichao summed up these trends in late December 1899, right before leaving Japan for the United States, when he observed in an essay for his Yokohama-based paper *Qingyi bao* (Journal of Pure Critique) that Hawaii was an important stepping stone for America to the Philippines, and thence to China in an overall strategy heralding a new era for China, Asia, and the world.[37]

A further summation of this point came in 1901, when the journal *Kaizhi lu* (Journal of New Learning) published an anonymous essay entitled "On the Development of Imperialism and the Future of the Twentieth Century World."[38] One of the first attempts to systematically define the new term *diguo zhuyi* (imperialism), the essay recounts the rise of the United States as an imperialist power and the emergence of the Pacific as the modern world's new contested stage. Designating this rise as constitutive of a new era, as well as a betrayal of the (supposed) American historical legacy, the author states:

> From the founding of the country, America has preserved republicanism and non-aggressionism [as its two basic principles] . . . And yet, in these past several years, it has emerged to swallow Cuba, annex Hawaii, defeat Spain, and take over Luzon [the Philippines]. It also recently participated in the allied troop assault on our country [during the Boxer Rebellion; 1900–1901]. In one blow, they have abandoned the memory of their esteemed founder, Washington, and the principles inherited from him in order to compete on the world stage with the other powers.[39]

Indeed, although obviously not located in the Pacific understood geographically, that is where Cuba was placed conceptually in the late 1890s through its linkage to Hawaii and the Philippines in the contemporary historicity indicated by American expansionism. Thus, integral to the sense of the Pacific as a new world stage were the 1896–1898 Cuban revolution, the Philippines, and Hawaii.

To be sure, many essays of the time understood the emergence of the Pacific as a product of a natural geographical expansionism translated into a geopolitical normativity. Yet, a certain "Monroe Lover" grasped more profoundly the implications of the relationship between deterritorialization and national territoriality in the new era of modernity. In his essay of mid-1903 published in *Zhejiang chao* (Tides of Zhejiang), a prominent Tokyo-based student journal, "Monroe Lover" explicitly tied the Pacific and modernity to a complete restructuring of temporal-spatial relationships, a development he explored through the changing reach and meaning of the Monroe Doctrine.

> [The Monroe Doctrine] has a fluid not a stable meaning . . . If one says it has no definition, then the definition appears; if one says it has a definition, then the definition is impossible to find. Its principles embody the spirit of the physical location of the American continent on which it concentrates. However, its principles also leak into those areas on

which the Doctrine has designs but which have not yet experienced it, and are not of the American continent and thus do not pertain to the historicity of the Doctrine's era. The Monroe Doctrine is just that sort of subtle thing that cannot be predicted.[40]

According to "Monroe Lover," the early nineteenth century (a temporal category) corresponded rather closely to a certainty of place, where the American continent was the specific location of the Monroe Doctrine's spirit, creation, applicability, and definition. By contrast, the twentieth century's spatiality could not be deduced from or limited to a stable place or temporality; indeed, the twentieth century was witnessing a temporal-spatial disjuncture, detectable through the doctrine's new applicability, which was no longer attached to any particular correspondence between time and place. Thus, while the original doctrine was devised as an anti-Europeanist (*paiOu zhuyi*) measure by a new American government ostensibly intent on protecting the American continent from European meddling, now it had become an abstract hemispheric (*banchoude*) measure, where there was no longer any predictability in its space of applicability. In effect, the doctrine had been set loose from territoriality, as was "America" itself. Further, as "Monroe Lover" was aware, it was precisely the doctrine's displacement, now onto the "clean territory" of Asia, which was not deducible from its original temporal-spatial-historical definition, that was crucial to understanding the fluidity, flux, and unevenness of global modernity.

As a geopolitical principle, the twentieth century thus signaled and confirmed the rise of two new powers, Japan and the United States, to prominence in a new global Pacific configuration. By the same token, as a contemporary historical principle, the emergence of the Pacific remained interpretively open: it could contingently provide opportunities for and challenges to those who could claim that space. Not only, then, did American expansionism into the Pacific (including Cuba) centrally help constitute an understanding of imperialism and a redefinition of the world stage in China, but to the extent that there arose simultaneously a potentially revolutionary national understanding of global space, the Pacific was rendered a potential stage for Chinese as well. It was, in the end, a breakdown in the notion of proper place—deterritorialization—signaled by an understanding of imperialist expansionism that made possible the very political praxes premised upon deterritorialization which allowed Chinese intellectuals to lay claim to the Pacific, through Hawaii, for Chinese *national* projects.[41]

Deterritorialized Politics and the Hawaiian Chinese

In late December 1899, Liang Qichao left Japan, where he had been in exile since the September 1898 coup d'état that ended the reform movement; he was headed to the United States to raise funds for his and Kang Youwei's recently founded organization, the *Baohuang hui* (Save the Emperor Society). Planning to stop only briefly in Honolulu before proceeding to the U.S. mainland, Liang was unexpectedly quarantined in Hawaii for six months because of the plague epidemic that engulfed that city's Chinatown.[42] He was recalled to Japan by Kang Youwei in mid-1900 before he could continue with his trip.

During his stay in Hawaii, Liang was not idle: he raised funds for the *Baohuang hui*;[43] started a newspaper in Honolulu entitled *Xin Zhongguo bao* (Journal of New China), for which he wrote editorials;[44] and kept up a busy schedule of public speaking. At the beginning of his stay, he also wrote a diary and many poems. Indeed, Liang's extended sojourn in Hawaii turned out to be fortuitous, as it helped him better understand some of what he had learned and observed over the past year in Japan, where, by his own account, his "mind had changed" and his "thinking and language had come to bear no resemblance" to what they had been before.[45] Indeed, the stay there seems to have made him aware, as no previous abstract theorizing had, of the worldliness of being Chinese at the dawn of a new century. As he noted in his diary of the period: "I was born twenty-seven years ago, but I have only recently begun to learn not only how to be a person of the nation, but also how to be a person of the world."[46] This new consciousness of the worldliness of being Chinese also made Liang aware of the potential Chinese-ness of the world.

The first entry in Liang's diary is for 19 December 1899, the day he left Japan; the last is for 10 January 1900. His notes from his first-ever transoceanic voyage reveal an excited state of mind, as the sea journey apparently gave Liang some time for reflection after what had been a hectic year and a half of activity.[47] Immediately after the opening passages that describe his sadness at leaving Japan, his "second home," Liang, in a combative spirit, defended his use of Western calendar dates for his diary entries: "Some might ask: Why do you, a Chinese, use Western dating in your diary? Is it because you do not love your country? My answer: Not at all. . . . Loving one's country resides in substantive action, not in empty words."[48] He further noted that a unified dating system was a small step to take toward integrating China and the world on one scale of time, a necessity in the current era, when people were in increasing contact with one another. The unity of the modern time he inhabited as a Chinese and as a person of the world having been established, Liang's entries for the remainder of the transoceanic journey are mostly notations on weather, eating and sleeping, and so forth.[49]

On December 31, Liang reached Hawaii, where he had to rely upon two American Christian missionaries who had lived in Gansu Province for some years and who spoke "the northern language" (Mandarin) to help him with the entry procedures. Upon disembarking, he heard that because of the plague epidemic that had begun in the Chinatown section of Honolulu, the Chinese in Hawaii were in strict quarantine. Unable to get in touch with his contacts, he went to a hotel (with which he was apparently not pleased), and then to find the Japanese consul on the islands.

In addition to the diary, on the trip over, Liang also wrote an open-endedly expansive short poem, entitled "Encountering Rain on the Pacific Ocean" (*Taipingyang yu yu*), in which the concrete possibilities that he later glimpsed and specified upon arrival in Hawaii are not yet evident: "One rain connects two continents / Cleansing waves wash the earth and flow East / They cannot wash everything away / For the embracing wind and thunder travel far."[50] By contrast, several days after his arrival in Honolulu, Liang wrote another poem, "Song of the Twentieth-Century Pacific," in which he waxed both melancholic and eloquent about the world as it appeared from those "eight dots lost in the middle of the ocean": "The middle of the Pacific is the horizon of the twentieth century. Whether the drama [of this century] will be a tragedy or a comedy, a drama of strength or one of cruelty, all are possible. We were born here and now, so how can it be other than our good fortune? Take a good look or two at the world! Great changes are afoot."[51] In the "Song," Liang evinced an ambivalence about the "drama" in which he was involved and about the changes that were afoot. It begins by locating Liang in the world: "On the continent of Asia is a man / His name is Rengong and his surname, Liang."[52] Synecdochically connecting him to "Asia"—*not* China—the "Song" goes on to meditate on the course of the modern world's transformation. At a particular point, it pauses in its lyricism to note some of the more disturbing consequences of this transformation: "The world has unexpectedly been united under one roof, because of greater and bigger competition, increased connections, and greater oppression and cruelty. I interrupt my song to pay respect to those who have shed their blood."[53] An extended note on the Hawaiian natives and the Australian aborigines commemorates those who have been sacrificed in the name of the modern world.

Continuing after the brief interruption, Liang notes that with the final phase of global spatial integration almost complete, the Philippines in the East and those "eight dots in the middle of the ocean" were being swallowed, turning the Pacific into an "inland lake (*lihushui*)," contested by the United States, Japan, and—Liang implicitly warned—China as well.[54] The basis for China's claims to the Pacific, Liang implied, lay as much in Hawaii as did the basis for U.S. or Japanese claims. For, in connecting Hawaii to China via "Asia" and the "Pacific," Liang was able to see this new world space not only as an abstract challenge or as a settled geopolitical principle, but as an opportunity to be taken up by purposive action.

He found this opportunity when, after several days of lonely wandering, during which he lamented the quarantine in Chinatown primarily because it prevented him from having a forum in which to give a speech,[55] Liang's contacts eventually came to find him. They were, Liang noted, "most enthusiastic to hear domestic news," and, Liang added, "seven or eight out of ten [of these Hawaiian Chinese] are indeed open-minded."[56] Their open-mindedness, Liang noted, had everything to do with their situatedness in Hawaii and recent events there. Indeed, Liang's diary provides a narrative of recent Hawaiian history, presumably gleaned from his Chinese contacts, in which he included those aspects that seemed to parallel or echo developments in China and elsewhere: that is, a history of foreign encroachment and colonization. He wrote that, even prior to the 1893 revolution, actual Hawaiian government power had already been in the hands of "white people" for some time,[57] a comment that resonated with Liang's growing anxiety about the seizure in China (and elsewhere) by Euro-Americans of strategic political and economic power. He continued that, since her overthrow in 1893, the Hawaiian queen had been in Washington, "in exile, while others occupy her territory,"[58] and he sympathetically compared Liliuokalani to the Song dynasty poet Li Houzhu, who had written prolifically on the "loss" (*wang*) of the Song to the Yuan dynasty in the thirteenth century. Through this parallel to Chinese history, Liang familiarized the situation in Hawaii, yet this familiarization did not lead Liang to reaffirm the

Song *wang* as the paradigm for Hawaiian *wang*; rather, it allowed him to shift his focus from a past notion of *wangguo*, which was confined to dynastic state overthrow, to modern notions of *wangguo*, which included the loss of cultural identity and the perishing of the Hawaiian race that was proceeding apace on the islands.

The shift in the conception of *wangguo* becomes even clearer in Liang's use of population tables, which demonstrated that the number of native Hawaiians was decreasing by a tenth at each census, and which, he surmised, gave Hawaiians at most one hundred years before "not one native is left."[59] Turning to language, he observed that because English was Hawaii's national language, over half the native children did not speak Hawaiian.[60] Bringing all these observations together, Liang concluded: "Of old, in the perishing of a state, the state alone was lost [*zigu zhi wangguo, ze guowang eryi*]. Today it is different: when the state is destroyed, the people/race follows it [*jinye buran, guowang er zhong ji sui zhi*] . . . From this we can know that the disaster of people/race extinction (*wangzhong*) is imminent."[61] The rearticulation of *wangguo*, now a modern process of racial, linguistic, cultural, and political annihilation, was to be repeated from this time forward as one of Liang's most incisive insights on the modern world and one of his most desperate cries for action in China.[62] Indeed, hereafter, in Liang's essays as in the essays of others, *wangguo* most frequently came to be used to point to the modern problem of colonialism.

The specification of *wangguo* as modern colonization in turn gave rise to one of Liang's most oft-repeated conundrums after 1900: how to make the Chinese people aware that the process they were undergoing was not merely a problem of state loss but a national problem. Indeed, Liang believed that the Chinese people only knew the emperor/dynasty and were unaware of the nation, and that their ignorance of the fact that China, the nation, was poised on the brink of *wang* at the hands of imperialist powers had prevented them from acting to save it. This line of analysis depended upon a prior transforming of the very notion of *guo* from (dynastic) state to (incipient) nation, a transformation that Liang had begun to undertake in systematic fashion in early 1899. In a synthesis of his understanding, Liang had written in October 1899, "The Chinese people do not even know there is such a thing as a national people [*guomin*]. After several thousand years, there have been the two words *guo jia* [state, family] but I have never heard the two words *guo min* [state, people] ever uttered." Liang explained: "*Guojia* is when one family [*jia*] owns the state [*guo*] as private property . . .

Guomin connotes when the state [*guo*] belongs to the people (*min*) as public property . . . This [*guomin*] is then called a national people."[63] Liang's distinction—terminological and conceptual—turns on word combinations: *guo* as state, *jia* as family, *min* as people, where *guojia* means family-state and *guomin* means people-state. In the latter, *guo* is constituted as the state of the whole people and no longer of just the family (i.e., dynasty), thus recasting the problem of *guo* from an emphasis on dynastic states to an emphasis on the relationship between people and polity—in other words, to nation. To prevent China's (not merely the Qing's) imminent *wang*, Liang proposed to mobilize the *min* (people) in the name of the *guo* (nation), although the specific ways in which he proposed so doing did not receive fuller articulation until his 1902 essay *Xinmin shuo* (On the New Citizen).

All these issues were just coming together in Liang's thought during his stay in Hawaii in early 1900, where Liang also began to think through the problem of making "the people" active participants in national affairs in light of the threatening global context. Notably, he did this in Hawaii by finding there a suitable "people" to mobilize for Chinese nationalist purposes. Here, Liang's positive evaluation of the Hawaiian Chinese led him to hope for their leadership, not merely in funds but in substantive spirit and action, in overcoming China's impending *wang* crisis. As Liang wrote in his "Song" poem: "I observe that the thinking of the island peoples [*haiguo minzu*; speaking of the Chinese, not the Hawaiians] is elevated and lively, and I hope that our compatriots too can take flight on the wind, can ride on the waves!"[64] His sense of the potential of the Hawaiian Chinese to act as the *guomin*, national people, who would save the nation was reinforced when he recognized, as he observed in his diary, that they were "much more advanced in political thinking than people in other places,"[65] an advanced thinking that was attributable to their experience of the recent decade of upheaval in Hawaii: the deposing of the monarchy in 1893, the establishment of a republic in 1894, the violent suppression of a promonarchical rebellion in 1895, and the annexation of the islands by the United States in 1898.

Indeed, Liang seems to have believed that the political experiences, or the experiences of politics, of the Chinese in Hawaii could become a foundation for and basis of China's own political transformation:

> In the past ten years, this capital [Honolulu] has seen three revolutions [*geming*], which brought down the old monarchy and raised up a new

> government. These events were witnessed by the people in my group and have been etched in their minds for eternity . . . One can thus well imagine how the ferment of the French Revolution could sweep Europe in less than ten years. It is certainly not inexplicable! One can also surmise how we must affect change in the minds of our people.[66]

The place-space linkages, no less than the global-national connection or the global historical narrative embedded in the above passage, are not only remarkable aesthetically, they also provide a crucial interpretive key to the historical condition of possibility for Liang's (and others') incorporation and appropriation of Hawaii into Chinese nationalist praxes.

In the above account, Liang situates the Chinese he met in Hawaii, the place, and defines their relevance for contemporary China via their experience of Hawaii's upheavals. These upheavals are significant events for the world and for China, not only because they point to the new process of *wangguo*, but because they had endowed the Hawaiian Chinese with an elevated political consciousness. These local upheavals with world significance are temporally-spatially universalized by Liang, when he resituates the Hawaiian Chinese experiences of Hawaii's revolution in the modern revolutionary historical trajectory signified through the French Revolution.[67] In a final move, Liang takes that moment of universalized revolutionary modernity, transformed now from its French meaning to its modern colonial meaning, and reattaches its transformative potential, via the Hawaiian Chinese, to a spatially distant China.[68] Thus were Hawaiian history, the Hawaiian Chinese, and revolutionary activity all rendered plausibly part of contemporary Chinese nationalist praxis.[69] In this seemingly unconscious and apparently natural process of historical narrativization, Liang effortlessly wove his new spatiality of experience, through which he was able to draw the newly encountered world of Hawaii and Hawaiian Chinese into a new horizon of meaning—the Pacific, modernity, global and Chinese change.

Liang's rendition of the Hawaiian events had little to say about Hawaiians, except that the latter would soon be extinct. Here it is the transformation of the Chinese in Hawaii into potential arbiters of and founding participants in the Chinese national future that is most striking. Indeed, the seemingly effortless historico-spatial maneuver that allowed Liang to connect the temporally distant French Revolution *through* contemporary Hawaii to a spatially distant China in a modern time-space of global (revolutionary) change also allowed Liang to link the Hawaiian Chinese—not culturally-ethnically, but politically—to China's national project, as an activated *guomin* who recognized the *guo* as a nation and its potential modern fate of *wang*. This recognition of theirs stood in stark contrast to Liang's frequent condemnations of the Chinese in China, who, according to him, lacked such an awareness. Thus, whatever the misrecognitions that animate the alleged correspondences between the French and Hawaiian events (misrecognitions that are, in any case, more usefully seen as interpretively productive readings of global history than as mistakes), what is noteworthy is how this global historico-spatial consciousness became possible, plausible, and soon enough "natural" for Liang in Hawaii.

By 1901, after his return to Japan, Liang's vision of *wangguo* as colonization was extended into a systematic review of the historicity of the modern world that had been forged through what he called the "New Rules for Destroying Countries" (*mieguo xinfa*):

> [Of old], when a state was defined by one person, or one family, those who would destroy it [*mie*] needed to capture its monarch, collect its officials, destroy its temples, and remove its large weapons. When that one person, that one family, was destroyed, then the state [*guo*] was destroyed. Today, it is not that way . . . If one really wants to destroy a people and a state [*ren guo*], the whole nation must be destroyed [*bimie qi quanguo*] . . . In the past, destroyers were like tigers and wolves; today, they are like foxes. Either they use commerce, or they use loans, or they train your soldiers, or they establish advisors [in your government], or they build roads, or they use the excuse of quelling [your] internal disorder, or they offer assistance to [your] revolution.[70]

These "new rules" and the era that they defined—which he explored through the historical examples of the modern colonizations of India, Egypt, the Philippines, the Transvaal, and Poland—constituted a set of practices that Liang elsewhere called "invisible dismemberment" (*wuxing de guafen*).[71] It was precisely this set of practices that was encapsulated by the transformation of *wangguo* into colonization.

Furthermore, Liang well recognized in 1901, when the disastrous terms of the Boxer Protocol had been dictated by the allied powers occupying Beijing, that *wangguo* did not need to be manifested in and through outright territorial control. For, as Liang understood, the situation in China was one of imminent destruction, precisely because the American-proposed Open

Door policy of 1901 called for keeping China territorially whole and nominally sovereign, while keeping it equally open to commerce for all. He noted in this regard that the Open Door policy was just a semantic cover for colonialism by other means; it was just one more "rule" of destruction: "Are not Shanghai, Hankou, and other [treaty ports] called concessions [*zujie*]? What are concessions but colonies [*zhimindi*]? If the whole country [under the proposed Open Door policy] becomes a free trade zone, then is that not equivalent to making the whole country a colony?"[72] Ending with a caution that China did not have to become a Hawaii, India, Egypt, Transvaal, or Philippines to be considered colonized, Liang drew attention to the multisided facets of colonization and imperialism and to its specific formation in China, later called "semi-colonialism."

Rey Chow has noted in her discussion of the detail as a mode of reading and of narrative rupture that it is necessary to recover the moment of rupture, before it is naturalized into historical inevitability.[73] Here, the historical rupture that is usually renarrated as naturalized Chinese ethnic solidarity makes it possible to specify how Hawaii allowed Liang to see the modern process of *wangguo* as a principle of colonial difference and thus as a marker of global modernity. Through this recognition and his fears for China's imminent fall to *wangguo*, and in the context of Liang's general condemnation of the Chinese people in China for their ignorance of their situation, Liang found the Chinese in Hawaii particularly promising candidates for an active national people who could save the situation. For *they* truly understood not only *wangguo* as a modern principle, but also the urgency of constituting themselves as a people, not for Hawaii but for China. Thus, in Liang's retelling, indebted as they may have been to the *place* (Hawaii) for their political awareness, these Hawaiians (Chinese) were to be political in a different *space* of action, that is, in China, now welded to Hawaii through a shared Pacific-ness and the shared modernity of their *wangguo* predicament. As such, Liang's abstracting of the Hawaiian Chinese from their locatedness in Hawaii, and his reattachment of them to China through their attitudes on and experiences of modern crisis and revolutionary action, consolidated for him the basis of their Chinese-ness (as a political topos); of their worldliness; and thus of their potential role in China's national political process.

Meanwhile, Hawaii's loss, while lamented, was left a historical casualty of the contemporary world. The islands were now overwritten not only by incipient narratives of American belonging, but also by Chinese claims to it as well. And there is no doubt that Liang left the Hawaiians behind. As he wrote in the last line of his diary: "But white people alone cannot destroy Hawaii, the Hawaiians must also destroy themselves."[74] It was precisely Hawaii's history of destruction that made real for Liang what the crisis of modernity was about; it also made possible for him the linking of Hawaii to China and of Hawaiian Chinese to the concept of "the people," as prospective and prescriptive political agents in a newly invented deterritorialized politics of the Chinese nation.

Bringing Hawaii to China

For those Chinese intellectuals not traveling or residing abroad, one challenge was to integrate the issues raised by globality into a material space of experience and practice in China. To be sure, linkages between Chinese in Hawaii and their kin in the southern provinces had helped serve from midcentury onward to map out a social geography of labor across the Pacific, and in social praxis if not in explicit articulation, the Chinese on both sides of this deterritorialized labor practice perhaps had a better sense of the contingencies of place and space than the more rooted intellectuals in China. It was only after 1898 that peripatetic Chinese activists such as Liang and Sun Zhongshan used these social geographies of labor and capital to map out for themselves new modes of political mobilization and nationalism. Once this connection was made, more and more often, overseas Chinese, officially and not, became the "focal point around which many Chinese rallied to express their indignation over abuses suffered by the Chinese."[75] The 1903–1905 movement to boycott American commodities in protest over the ill-treatment of Chinese in the United States is symptomatic of this connection.

How to translate these new efforts and their significances into a politics in China, through which sociopolitical geographies of labor could be connected to an expanding social space of popular praxis became a topic of particular import after the Boxer Rebellion. A long essay written by Lin Xie,[76] printed in one of the first vernacular papers in China—the *Hangzhou Vernacular Journal* (*Hangzhou baihua bao*)[77]—and published serially from December 1901 to January 1902, was one of the first attempts to make explicit for Chinese audiences at "home" how they and the Chinese abroad were linked. Lin later explained his commitment to vernacular journals, stating that "China's educated people are hopeless. The only ones in whom one can still have hope are those who plant the fields, make handicrafts, petty merchants, soldiers, and those small ten-year-old boys and girls";[78] his essay, entitled "An Account of the Sufferings of Chinese in Hawaii," is suffused with this hope.[79]

Lin's story of Hawaii—one of several he wrote at the time on *wangguo* histories[80]—was written in the wake of and with the backdrop of the burning of Honolulu's Chinatown during the plague scare and directly after the fiery destruction of Beijing by the allied assault that had ended the Boxer Rebellion (1901). The essay is thus mostly concerned with ways in which the Chinese people should constitute themselves as a "people" by understanding their current shared crisis and tasks, as well as with convincing his audience that state-centered solutions to China's problems were bound to fail. His narrative focus is, on the one hand, on the perfidy of American authorities in their handling of the plague scare,[81] which leads him, on the other hand, to emphasize the possibility and necessity for Chinese, at home and abroad, to cultivate self-reliance through an awareness of their common predicament and of their potential solidarity. He articulates the linkages between Chinese in Hawaii and those in China in terms of a shared crisis of socioeconomic subjectification. As with Liang, for Lin these linkages had little to do with ethnic or cultural essentialisms and everything to do with establishing a common experience of sociopolitical crisis in the modern context. And, as with Liang, for Lin, the Hawaiian Chinese made the Chinese "people," as a potentially active political category, intelligible, just as it was shared "statelessness" (*wangguo*) that made the modern world intelligible as a totality. Unlike with Liang, however, for Lin, the crisis is manifested not in an explicitly political consciousness, but in an awareness and experience of economic success and competition.

Lin begins his essay by warning his readers that there is nothing to be gained from hoping for foreign or state assistance in their current plight:

> I have no reason for narrating this piece other than to warn each and every one of you to take a deep breath of courage and to realize that it is impossible to demand that foreigners take us seriously these days. It is not now possible to look forward to a time when there will be someone who comes to protect us with all his might. There is nothing to demand, nothing to look forward to: we can only depend upon ourselves.[82]

The "ourselves" is the Chinese whom Lin wishes to create as a unified group; it does not refer to the state or its officials.[83] Lin's proposed method for people to build up their self-reliance is through the acquisition of knowledge (*kai zhihui*)—reading books and newspapers—not fussing over foreign religion and missionaries (this was after all right after the Boxers); and by respecting and actualizing Confucius's dictum that "all Chinese," from top to bottom, "love one another as brothers."[84] This prescription sounds familiar enough for the time, as the "acquisition of knowledge" was an oft-repeated proposed remedy by Chinese elites for what was usually condemned as the people's "ignorance." As Lin self-consciously commented after proposing these methods: "There are those who would say that these solutions of mine are awfully shallow. Xuanfanzi [Lin's pseudonym] responds: the reason I say these words here is to give people examples of what they can accomplish now. Of course, there are many things to be done; but we haven't the power to do everything at once."[85] Thus disaggregating the overwhelming magnitude of China's problems, Lin reorders the problems into a possibility for action in face of what would appear to be a time (post-Boxers) appropriate for resigned passivity. As such, it was not knowledge qua knowledge in which Lin was interested; rather, it was "knowledge" that would produce activity.

Lin explicitly linked his call for "knowledge" and "brotherhood" by Chinese in China to the Chinese in Hawaii:

> Hawaii was originally peopled by the Kanaks. In 1893, white people seized the territory and established a republic. In 1898, America took control.
>
> In the past, many Chinese merchants went to Hawaii to do business and they were treated quite well. Because the Chinese merchants got there earliest and obeyed the laws, the area they occupied was good and they named it "Tang people's street" [*Tangrenjie*] . . . Later, when the Americans arrived to do business, their area was not so advantageous and they did not conduct business completely legally.

For Lin, the problem of "legality" introduced the problem of whose claims to the space of Hawaii were more legitimate. Read backwards, then, the statement that "America took control" in 1898 is deviously linked to the illegality through which American merchants conducted their business. As such, for Lin, the defining marker of "Chinese" in Hawaii was entrepreneurial prowess, or, a spirit of self-reliance and an ability to form a community of interest and identity in a business-oriented Chinatown where American control is deauthorized.

With the ominous note of (American) illegality established, Lin continued:

> In the 25th year of Guangxu [1899], some Chinese from Chinatown got sick and died; several natives also got sick and died at the same time. Gentlemen! Look at human beings in this world: every day some are born and some die; there is nothing strange in this. [But] coincidentally at this time, ordinary American merchants and native merchants were witnessing the decline and failure of their businesses, while the Chinese businesses in Tangrenjie [Chinatown] were flourishing . . . So a rumor was set afoot: "Not good, not good, there is an epidemic coming from Tangrenjie and it is more contagious than electricity. If we don't think of a way [to stop it] immediately, we will not be able to guarantee our American lives . . ." So, they sealed off Tangrenjie and carried out an investigation.[86]

According to Lin, as the Chinese in Hawaii got stronger entrepreneurially, American (and native Hawaiian) merchants conceived a need to suppress them. As with the Boxers, mentioned obliquely earlier in the essay, so with Hawaii's Chinese businessmen: in the Boxers' case, a strong popular uprising against foreign missionary privileges invited suppression; in the Hawaiian case, superior Chinese entrepreneurial acumen invited illegal practices. In Hawaii, these practices, in combination with the arm of an alien state, were justified through one of the most natural of occurrences: death.

Rather than establish the Chinese in Hawaii as passive or ignorant victims of foreign power, as essays on *huaqiao* (overseas Chinese) and most intellectuals' pronouncements on "the people" more generally were doing at this time, Lin's narrative is premised on the opposite: that is, on the relationship between Chinese strength and foreign suppression. He foregrounds this relationship through an explicitly spatialized narrative, where the account establishes a place for Chinese business activity—Tangrenjie (Chinatown)—that, because of its purported impingement on the activity of American merchants, provokes an American effort to recontain the activity to its proper place, that is Chinatown. The sealing off of Tangrenjie with the excuse of an epidemic that, "like electricity," spreads contagiously and thus erases boundaries evokes the contemporaneous geopolitical struggle over Hawaii and the Pacific while also suggesting the deterritorializing impulse of commercial activity. Meanwhile, the moment of urgent recontainment is articulated in the story by Americans through their rhetoric of (Chinese) disease, a rhetoric that can be clearly linked to discourses prevalent in the United States at the time that presented Chinese as virulently diseased threats to the American body politic and the American people.[87] Thus, practically, the moment of Chinese expansion that invites suppression is figured by an affirmation of entrepreneurial prowess likened to electrical flows that transcend boundaries and thus mimic deterritorialized capital and potential national praxes; these then can be linked to a new global imaginary of "Chinese-ness" that is not only unbounded territorially, but also tied to a specific activity: self-reliant entrepreneurship.

Continuing with his tale, the suppression of Chinatown is particularly distressing to Lin:

> Ten days passed and several more [Chinese] got sick and died. Doctors came to have a look; some said it was the plague, others said it wasn't. But it didn't matter to the Americans whether the individual case was serious or not: anyone who was sick was immediately sent to the side of a pool, where their clothing was burned and they were forced into a bath . . . ; they were then forced into a disinfecting room to be fumigated and sent to a quarantine hospital . . . As a consequence, even those who would not have died, did die.[88]

When this cleansing was not effective in stemming the purported plague, Lin wrote, American authorities decided to burn Chinatown to the ground. In forcing everyone out—"Even women with bound feet were forced to take the wrappings off their feet and burn them; pity those small-footed women, who unbound their feet and then were forced to walk!"—American authorities, Lin implied, were intent on destroying the specific place and condition of Chinese success so as to reclaim it as rightfully American space.

"Alas," he concluded,

> most stateless people [*wangguo min*] in the world suffer in this way; most people with no officials suffer in this way; most tribes with no chiefs suffer in this way. Yet our China clearly has a state and clearly has officials: can it be that Americans don't know this? If we acknowledge that they don't know, how is it that everyone knows that England, France, Japan, and Russia have states and officials? [How is it that] they are

> uniquely ignorant about the fact that China has a state, that China has officials?
>
> Even those of us narrating this story don't know what the main reason is, or where it comes from. Some say it is the fault of the common people, [but] common people have no way of making a living in China, so they go abroad and suffer in extraordinary ways. How can it be their fault? Who is to blame? The narrator doesn't dare say.[89]

In this passage, Lin reintegrates the Chinese in Hawaii and the Chinese in China through their shared condition of "statelessness" and suffering. For, it was, on one level, the failure of the Qing state to protect both those in Hawaii and those at home (the Boxer rebels and their allies) that identified them all as "Chinese" and also as "stateless"; and, on another level, it was from within this shared statelessness, that the "brotherhood" Lin advocated in the beginning of the essay became the ideal of creating a self-reliant national people that bypassed the state altogether.

In this figuration, Lin ingeniously reflects the fact that *guomin* was coming into the wider political discourse of the day (1902) as the sociopolitical antithesis to the *wangguo min* (stateless people) and its concomitant, the *nuli* (slave). In conjunction with this new antithesis—between an active *people* and passive *slaves*—the common condition of "statelessness" was also becoming by the early 1900s a ubiquitous way of figuring China's shared global space with other colonized peoples, both as tragedy and absence (of power) and as opportunity to rebuild that power upon different bases (that is, through activity that took the state not as its premise but as its antithesis). For Lin, then, the intersection of these two processes through his reading of Hawaii facilitated the appropriation of Hawaii as a contested place/space of political and economic activity significant for Chinese in China; he also linked the Hawaiian Chinese, through their almost literal embodiment of the potential for the redefinition of the Chinese nation and the Chinese people, to the Chinese at home.

Conclusion

As an abstract tropological category, "the people" (*guomin*) became a major focus of sociopolitical discourses tied to nation (albeit not reducible to it) among Chinese intellectuals at the turn of the century. Almost from the beginning, this tropology introduced a complex and contentious new element into conceptualizations of the Chinese polity. For, in "the people," as a theoretical abstraction, was to be found a source of legitimacy and agency for the proposed reformulation of the dynastic polity into a nation; and yet at the same time, in concrete terms, this people was also deemed not quite ready—indeed completely unprepared—to take on the burden of its own historical representation and agency. In other words, while it was widely agreed that "the people," as an abstract topos, were a major factor in modern theories of society and politics, the *actual* people's potentially diverse imaginings of polity and social participation had to be contained and funneled through the interests and representations of a supposedly more common (elite-defined) social or political good.[90] With the theoretical certainty about the importance of "the people" but the practical distrust of the Chinese people in China, it was the Chinese abroad who came to occupy, in practice if not in explicit theorization, a privileged position in the construction of "the people" as actual sociopolitical subjects. In the end, in effective political practice, the overseas Chinese became metonyms for "the national people" (*guomin*), as mobilizable subjects of diverse late Qing national projects, understood as a praxis based upon deterritorialized politics.[91]

On this view, the linking of overseas populations in global space to a concept of the "people" helped produce and actualize a "national people" in the political realm. At the same time and by the same logic, these overseas populations were linked to efforts to reconceptualize the Chinese nation, not only politically, as demonstrated, but also economically, through their contributions to the national project and as models of self-reliant entrepreneurship.[92] The historical contingency of this process is most clearly seen through an examination of Hawaiian, not the more usual *nanyang* (Southern Seas), Chinese,[93] for the presence of Chinese in Hawaii was the direct or indirect product of nineteenth-century capitalist restructuring and of its attendant world markets in "free" labor, unlike the presence of Chinese in the *nanyang*, where southern Chinese had been emigrating for centuries and thus were not tied to this specific historical moment in the same way.[94] It was precisely from within this particular node of the new global space of deterritorialized and uneven modernity that new theorizations and praxes of "the people" could emerge.

This brief contingent moment of the articulation of Chinese-ness as a political topos became available for reified appropriation—and contradictory articulation—from this point on. These reifications took two dominant forms, which, while coming from different directions, reinforced one another. On the one hand, Chinese overseas were reified through the naturalizations of Western/Japanese geopolitical power and the attendant teleologies of Chinese state weakness. In these, overseas Chinese were "victims." On the other hand, they were reified ethnically through claims on their essentialized culturalist "Chinese-ness." In Chinese essays written after 1902–3, the naturalization of normative geopolitics and the reification of culture and ethnicity had by and large already taken place. Indeed, in journals as diverse as *Jiangsu* and *Hubei xuesheng jie* (Hubei Students' World), both considered revolutionary-leaning journals, or in the *Waijiao bao* (Foreign Affairs Journal), considered a reformist (albeit not dynastic-aligned) publication, the earlier moment of contingency had been sewn up, as it were. The "Pacific" was now articulated as a natural geopolitical space of big-power competition, and overseas Chinese as victims of the same.[95]

That the moment was fleeting and thus that it was quickly remade into historical inevitability and culturalist essence should not obscure the fact that the discovery of the Chinese in Hawaii from 1898 to 1902 helped inform open-ended new discourses on China and the modern world and produce a convergence of a social geography of Chinese abroad with a homological correspondence between these Chinese and emerging discourses on the "national people" as a political topos for China. As is evident, the seizing of the potential of Hawaii by Chinese intellectuals in this period emerged from some of the same types of analyses of global and local trends as those proffered by King Kalakaua in the 1880s to Li Hongzhang, albeit not from a perspective of state-state alliance, as the king had hoped for, but from a perspective of a deterritorialized politics motivated and activated by self-proclaimed agents of a new antistate national politics. This situation was rendered possible because it was in the post-1895 period that China's situation came to be viewed through the lens of modernity as uneven global space. Hawaii thus became a place of competitive organizational activity—for Liang, Sun Zhongshan, and others; it also became a sociohistorical space through which to conceptualize the modern world, the Chinese people, and the Chinese nation, not as paradoxical antitheses to one another, but as mutually constitutive of one another in a newly invented deterritorialized politics of the Chinese nation.

The outbreak of a revolution against United States's efforts to colonize the Philippines at this same time added yet more layers to the complex process of the formation of a discourse and potential praxis of nationalism in China. Indeed, the Philippine revolution was almost immediately considered relevant for China, not only because of the recognitions of global space outlined above, but also because of a concurrent recognition of a new global temporality of modernity, which suggested the relevance to China of the relationship between colonialism/imperialism and revolution as discursive and practical claims on history.

4 RECOGNIZING COLONIALISM: THE PHILIPPINES AND REVOLUTION

People who suffer from the same illness are sympathetic to each other.[1]

Yan Fu's "burst into print"[2] after 1895 with his translation of Herbert Spencer rapidly yielded a broad infiltration into Chinese intellectual discourse of a Social Darwinian historical universalism. However flexibly interpreted by Chinese intellectuals,[3] this new universalism strongly suggested that, in the metaphorical stream of time structured by an idealized late-nineteenth-century European temporal-spatial order, China's place was at best temporally downstream from and spatially peripheral to Euro-America. The resultant "backwardness" of China vis-à-vis a demonstrably stronger Euro-America seemed to fixedly stage the world, as it were, through a diachronic temporality dependent upon Euro-American centrality. Yet, just as this diachronic staging was coming into view, a synchronic staging of the world was also becoming visible. In this other staging, the very temporally displaced and spatially peripheral world to which China was seemingly relegated was recognized to be neither. Indeed, on this synchronic stage, the world appeared to be in temporal-spatial flux rather than in a fixed order. It was at this point that it became increasingly apparent to Chinese intellectuals that Chinese problems, while specifically Chinese, also shared features with other peoples' problems by virtue of sharing the twentieth-century world stage. On this stage, there was no centered "China" in contradiction to the rest of the world, but rather a "China" that was conceptualized in a mutually dependent relationship to the world, a mutual dependence most clearly illumined through the recognition of revolution as a modern principle and a shared mode of being for "stateless" or colonized peoples. As a 1901 essay on imperialism published in the *Kaizhi lu* summarized this point:

> Today, on the stage of the twentieth century, events are more important and more filled with cruelty [than in the nineteenth century] . . . Yet, even though the independence of the Philippines has been all but crushed, and the independence of the Transvaal confronts imminent disaster, and while imperialism [*diguo zhuyi*] is on the ascendant and independence cannot yet vanquish it . . . nevertheless, on the two continents of Asia and Africa . . . the furious struggle between imperialism and Independence[4] . . . will surely be many times fiercer than [the struggles unleashed by the] revolutions in Europe . . . Are not Asia and Africa the battlegrounds of the twentieth century?[5]

The view of modernity as synchronic uneven global space in a coeval temporality created three related, often contradictory situations that helped make visible both possibilities and further problems for China. First, as we have seen, there developed a noticeable rupture in bounded temporal-spatial ideas, which suggested how "China" was being transformed into a problematized national space within a changing world. Second, within this context, the Chinese *people* came to be considered to be not only "behind" Euro-American–Japanese people, who had seemingly grabbed the historical upper hand, but even more startlingly, they were also "behind" such actively united but previously despised or ignored peoples as the Filipinos and the Boers in the Transvaal. And, finally, China's modern national history came to be recognized through the terms of most such problematized spaces, temporalities, and peoples of the modern world, that is, in terms of colonial categories.

These situations and their relationships were incipiently articulated to one another through observations on the Philippines, which was erupting in violent revolution first against Spain (1895) and then, more visibly, against the United States (1898). The conceptual connections Chinese intellectuals made to the Philippine events from 1899 to 1903[6] helped Chinese intellectuals recognize revolution as a modern mode of being in the contemporary world, through which the intertwined topi of "the people," the nation, modernity, and history were specified. Indeed, the Philippine struggle brought revolution itself to the forefront of consciousness, while suggesting an isomorphism between the Chinese nationalist problematic and global anticolonial practice, even while the fit was not entirely apt. Ultimately it was this ill-fitting isomorphism that suggested a colonial paradigm for the Chinese nationalist project, a new paradigm that helped inform a Chinese revolutionary endeavor that, unlike the anticolonial revolutions with which it was self-identified, did not take *Western* imperialism as its primary foe (however much this was lamented and cursed), but rather, that reformulated the seventeenth-century Manchu conquest of the Ming dynasty as a modern colonial conquest of China and proposed revolution as the way to remedy this "colonial" situation.

Revolution as Transformative Topos

The acceptance among Chinese intellectuals of an equation between revolution and the construction of a new nation was far from automatic; and it is not attributable to a linear process of internal historical inevitability.[7] Prior to the 1898 reform debacle and for a time afterwards, the dominant influence in Chinese intellectual circles had been Kang Youwei's proposition that change be embodied primarily in institutional reform. Kang's 1897 work *Kongzi gaizhi kao* (Confucius as Reformer), a synthesis[8] of the prior efforts of the New Text (*jinwen*) school of Confucianism, had reworked the premises of the imperial (and literati) ruling tradition by reconfiguring Confucianism into an activist doctrine of practical statesmanship from a conservative doctrine of the status quo, and by re-presenting Confucius himself as the original institutional reformer rather than as the preserver of inherited forms. Kang's appeal to the authority of Confucius as the arbiter of Chinese history—past and present—was driven by his urgent conviction that only through thorough institutional reform within the context of the dynastic system would the Qing be able to stave off both foreign aggression and social disintegration.[9] The failure of the reform movement was followed, chronologically not causally, by the eruption and disastrous denouement of the Boxer Rebellion (1900–1901).

For critics of the dynasty, these two events demonstrated the inability of the Qing to embody either a modern definition of "China" or to contain social and intellectual challenges to its rule, and it was at this point that political revolution came to be seriously considered across the Chinese intellectual spectrum. As Arif Dirlik has pointed out, nationalism, "a product of China's plight at the turn of the century . . . produce[d] an intellectual orientation that discovered in revolution the key to China's survival—and the creation of a new world."[10] Indeed, by 1902 the accumulation of contemporary examples of revolutionary praxis from around the world could yield a guide to revolution that was seen as potentially adaptable to any place where deterritorialized political praxis was relevant. As Ou Jujia, a former student of Kang Youwei's and an early editorialist for Liang Qichao's *Shiwu bao* (Chinese Progress), summarized this guidebook approach in his pamphlet entitled "New Guangdong" (*Xin Guangdong*):

> Before the Cubans rose, their elites [*yishi*] secretly convened an alliance. They dispatched people from different groups to covertly unite comrades and to amass great sums of money. They also went out to spread the word about the cruel policies of the Spaniards and about the tragic conditions of the people on the island. Their proclamations could be seen all over the island; they angrily seized people and publicly declared: "We have taken an oath to seek independence and we will not give up unto death." Their courage was really that firm; their determination was really that great. So, they were able to resist the complete armed strength of Spain using only the small population of their island . . .
>
> Gentlemen! Gentlemen! Take a look at the relationship between our government and our people: can it come close to what the Boers did to England or what Cuba [and the Philippines] did to Spain?[11]

The major point of Ou's pamphlet was to propose that the Guangdongese were the best candidates for an autonomy that he saw as a necessary precondition to the launching of a revolution in China,[12] but, most interesting in the above passage for the present discussion is how Ou's account reads as a generic formula for anticolonial revolution in the contemporary period: a secret elite organization that crosses national boundaries, intensive propaganda, funding from abroad, and, perhaps, at a critical juncture, outside assistance.

Soon thereafter, in 1903, Zou Rong's classic of the Chinese revolution, *The Revolutionary Army* (*Geming jun*), splashed across the political scene of Shanghai and China. The publication of this pamphlet, which drew for its contemporary examples of revolution upon the Philippines and the Transvaal, also carried an inflammatory preface by Zhang Binglin (Taiyan), which contributed to the eruption of the *Subao* case in mid-1903. In Mary Rankin's assessment, this case was instrumental in opening "a gulf between revolution and reform" among Chinese intellectuals.[13] Substantially concealed prior to 1903 by conceptual confusions as well as a considerable overlap in the constituencies and interests of the various groupings of radical activity in China, Japan, and elsewhere, this breach widened after Zou's pamphlet and the ensuing public exchange of heated letters between Zhang, who refuted the validity of retaining the Manchu-Qing monarchy in any future plans, and Kang Youwei, who insisted on the continuing relevance of the emperor to China's future. The arrest, trial, and imprisonment by the Qing state of Zou and Zhang on charges of sedition further polarized the climate.[14] By 1905, the ideological split would take on organizational form, with the formation of Sun Zhongshan's *Tongmeng hui* (Revolutionary Alliance).[15]

Yet, Ou's piece and many others of the time demonstrate that it was not merely the Chinese situation that informed these conceptual and organizational transformations. However, of the places that Ou chose to highlight in his pamphlet, Cuba was only briefly significant in China,[16] whereas the Philippines and the Transvaal each refractively illumined crucial and problematic internal aspects of the Chinese situation, while lending concrete and contemporary meaning to the viability of revolution as a solution to China's problems.

Making the Philippines Visible

For all its importance to Chinese intellectual discourse from 1898 to 1903, the Philippines (or Luzon) had to be rediscovered in China, as the central role that Manila had earlier played as a site for the exchange of Chinese wares for Mexican silver had long been forgotten.[17] The initial wire reports in the Chinese press from 1896 to 1897 on unrest in the islands did little to suggest any necessity to pay closer attention, since, in these early years, growing rebelliousness there was generally characterized as *luan* (disorder), a word most often used in the official Chinese lexicon to condemn so-called heterodox actions of small or large proportions; the label thus suggested that the unrest was an internal Spanish problem of governance and that it was of an illegitimate nature. Numerous reports through 1899 and 1900 helped change this view: as information became more available and as interpretations of that information changed, disgust at the magnitude of the United States's betrayal—of itself and of its erstwhile Filipino allies—came to replace the original neutral tone of dispassion about U.S. assistance to the Filipinos in their efforts to detach themselves from Spain. The shift in interpretation was not immediate, for until June 1899 Liang Qichao's *Qingyi bao* (Journal of Pure Critique) and other papers regularly featured reports by Spanish missionaries who had fled to Japan and Hong Kong full of tales of terror about the "banditry" of the

"Aguinaldo Party" (Emilio Aguinaldo being the leader of the resistance) and of native-induced chaos.[18] Juxtaposed to those reports, the ninth issue of the *Qingyi bao* (March 1899) also devoted many pages to a reprinting of the Philippine declaration of war against the United States, which, in its Chinese rendition, bristled with righteous indignation over the American betrayal and with staunch commitment to the task ahead: "How can this island of ours, insignificant as it might be, be constrained in ways normally reserved for dogs and horses? So, the two armies will open fire and the destruction will be immense; but how could we allow them to enslave us, to not let us see the sun for the rest of our lives?"[19]

It was with the airing of these issues, after June 1899, that the "bandits" and their "*luan*" (disorder) were entirely reclassified: Aguinaldo, previously labeled the "chief bandit," became "general" or "leader"; his illicit "party of disorder" (*luandang*) became an army of "righteous seekers of independence"; American policy was named annexationism and colonialism; Americans were labeled "cruel";[20] and Aguinaldo was established as "the eminent hero of the South Seas."[21] When the nascent Philippine republic reached the first anniversary of its declaration of independence from Spain (summer 1899) still embroiled in a bloody war with its erstwhile U.S. allies, extracts from Aguinaldo's stirring speech to his army and people were prominently featured in the *Qingyi bao*,[22] free of competing interpretations of the events derived from missionary or others' tales. It was now recognized that the Philippines was involved in a revolution, a *geming*, and not merely a *luan*.

The shift in interpretation complete, events in the Philippines quickly spawned a number of in-depth commentaries and analyses in China. Yet, unlike with Hawaii, the Philippine events took on a wider significance not connected to the overseas Chinese there. This significance was underscored by the personal relationships forged in Japan and Hong Kong between leaders of the Philippine revolution and Chinese intellectuals in exile. Thus, at the same time as awareness grew of the potential for revolution to solve China's problems, awareness also grew of the Philippines, dominated by a foreign power yet actively forging a new path in history.

In observing the Philippines, it was learned that, not only had the Philippine revolution successfully ousted Spain, and not only was it now resisting the United States's attempts to transform it into an American colony, but the Filipino people were actively creating new modes of sociopolitical praxis for colonized peoples (*wangguo min*, or "stateless people") in the modern world. In helping tie questions emerging in China about the relationship between history, revolution, and nation to a contemporaneous global moment, the internal social relations and organization that seemed to have made the Philippine revolution possible also helped show a way of conceptualizing revolution in China, as both violent action and historical claim.

The Philippine Revolution and Activism

It is a rare turn-of-the-century political essay or editorial that does not include mention of both the Philippines and the Transvaal (Boers) as inspirational examples from which China could learn. I will discuss the Transvaal in the next chapter. Here, suffice it to note that both situations had both so seeped into the consciousness of Chinese intellectuals by late 1899 that the invocation of these two examples in the writings of the period are almost incantatory in their frequency. Moreover, these invocations are integral to the new theorizations in which they are embedded. Liang Qichao, for example, was consumed from the late 1890s onward with the philosophical and social problem of reconfiguring the relationship between the state and the people in his evolving views of nationalism. In one of his early essays (1899) on the question, he determined that the harbinger of the modern era was the power of the people in non-Euro-America, who, he claimed, were poised to overtake the Euro-American states. As he wrote:

> Thirty years ago, they [Western countries] encountered Japan; recently, they have encountered the Philippines and now the Transvaal . . . Thirty years ago in Japan, and now in the Philippines and the Transvaal, the respective struggles against these great countries have demonstrated that strength and weakness cannot be determined [by the state], for the sharp edge of Euro-America has been blunted and their rudders turned around in the encounters. This is because the power of the [Euro-American] people [*guomin*] has decreased relative to the power of those whom they have attacked in the modern competition among peoples.[23]

The potential "power of the people" (*guomin zhi li*) could be mobilized for China, according to Liang, only if the Chinese recognized that Asia, alone on the map of the world, had yet to be completely "dyed white." The essay thus concluded with an exhortation to the Chinese people to compare themselves to the people of the Philippines and of the Transvaal, for it was their ability to *qun* (group, unite) and to act that provided a compelling model for Chinese to emulate.

Not only for Liang but for many others, in the Philippine revolution was found the first proximate example of how a "stateless" people could turn their weakness and "statelessness" to strength and purposeful activity. This was one of the major points of the first full-length Chinese essay on the Philippines, entitled "On the Independence of the Philippine islands,"[24] written by Ou Jujia in 1899 for the *Qingyi bao* (Journal of Pure Critique). Ou, having fled to Japan with Liang and Kang after the 1898 coup,[25] set the vitality of the emerging Philippine events against what he saw as the demoralized and defeated Chinese political and intellectual milieu, whose fragility and timid reformist proposals compared unfavorably both to the surging Meiji Japanese and to the Filipino revolutionaries. Ou thus began his essay by setting the Chinese elites' response to defeat within a Poland/India paradigm of "lostness":

> The proof of China's present danger can be seen in Poland and India . . . and China could be a continuation of this. I would call attention to this as a warning to the Chinese people, but it would only dishearten them . . . After the Sino-Japanese War . . . [our former Chinese] arrogance almost completely disappeared. When discussing the state's peace and security, officials above and scholars below cried: "[all] will be lost, [all] will be lost" [*biwang*]. And when asked how to save [the country], they said that the Western military was strong and the Chinese military weak and in decline, and hence, there was no alternative but to submit to fate. If in the face of fear and dread such as this, you tell them the stories of the decline and perishing of Poland and India, they will say: "If Poland and India could not be a match for the Europeans, what hope can there be for China?"[26]

Not interested in merely exhorting through the negative finality of Poland's and India's *wangguo*, Ou proposed a contemporary model of action that could turn the "Poland and India" figure on its head. This model was the Philippines.

However, for these islands to become credible as a model, Ou knew that he first needed to overturn previous Chinese conceptualizations of them: "The South Sea islands are located in the middle of the ocean; they belong to the tropical belt and are all populated with people of the Malay race. From long ago, China diligently occupied them from afar, [while] seeing them as beyond the pale of civilization (*huawai*)."[27] This conceptual blindness was not, according to Ou, reduced by the steady stream of emigration of Chinese to Manila since the Ming dynasty; to the contrary, it was only strengthened as Luzon came under the commercial and then political sway of Holland, Portugal, and finally Spain, "when command of the seas became important for commercial strength, [and] the nibbling—the strategy of stateless settlement (*feiguojia youzhimin zhi zhengci*)—began." As Ou noted, throughout these transitions, Chinese paid no attention, merely despising the Filipinos for their primitiveness.[28] Even now, Ou wrote, when "the doors of Asia" had "Western feet inserted in them" but "those living in the rooms have yet to realize it," the Philippines still did not register in Chinese consciousness.

In drawing the Philippines—previously distant islands in the middle of the South Seas and beyond the pale of civilization—into a proximate "Asian" identification with China, Ou transformed them into a credible producer of meaning for China, while also indicating how the Philippines could show China a different way of thinking about their situation in the world:

> They [the Chinese elite] have lost all hope. The level of their thinking stops at a conviction that to be strong is sufficient for taking advantage of the weak; to be big is sufficient for taking advantage of the small; to be numerous is sufficient for torturing the few. They have no knowledge of the fact that strong and weak have no definite form; big and small do not define strength; numbers do not define principle; that self-reliance [*zili*] can turn weak into strong, self-strengthening can turn small into big, and the unity of the people can turn the few into the many.
>
> Just look at the small island of the Philippines led by native people to oppose the preeminent rising power of the world, America . . . So, what of our China, with its vast territory and huge population, which is thousands of times bigger than the Philippines? If the Philippines can be self-reliant, what is the logic behind the claim that China cannot be? Please, let us now consider the Philippines.[29]

Ou's challenge, via the Philippines, to the validity of such seemingly immutable categories as "civilization," "strong," "weak," "big," and "small" —a challenge that was repeated in essays and writings across the intellectual spectrum of the time[30]—located the Philippines in a sphere of transformative activity. The familiarization of the islands thus was not achieved, as in the case of Hawaii, by appropriating overseas Chinese as a national political force, but by marking out transformative activity in a global historical-temporal space that was intimately shared by China and the Philippines. The rendering of the Philippines into a model for China henceforth, albeit only ephemerally, helped disrupt an intellectual orientation that both Western colonial and Chinese civilizational discourses shared: that is, the distancing of other peoples and cultures by denying them "coevalness."[31]

What is striking therefore about the beginning of Ou's essay is how his explicit extension of coevalness to the Philippines led him to question not only inherited Chinese worldviews (by conceptually resituating the Philippines as important for China) but Western worldviews as well. In the latter case, in narrating the perfidy of American "assistance" to the Philippines, Ou noted that, when confronted with the U.S. betrayal,

> the islanders, angry and desiring independence, declared: "America wants to make our island into a colony. Had the people known this, would we have come to this today? We would sooner have settled with the Spanish government!" The leaders and the people . . . swore unto death to fight to the end with America, stopping only when they obtained their independence. But, after the American annexation of Hawaii and Cuba, the Americans knew of their intention to take the Philippine islands in order to open the doors of the Far East . . . They rallied the strong countries of the world to not allow this contemptible and insignificant place [the Philippines] to destroy their dynasty [American power] . . . Alas! From this one can know the techniques of the Europeans![32]

Designating American "assistance" an insidious "annexation," Ou demonstrated an astute awareness of the collusions involved in the U.S.-proposed Open Door policy of these years.[33] More pointedly, he also demonstrated great insight, following Liang Qichao's slightly earlier comments on the relationship between imperialism and ideology, into how American representations of the Philippines as "contemptible and insignificant" helped create the "reality" that allowed the United States to proceed with its colonization. As Ou saw it, the remedy to the representational problem—that is, the Philippines as a trope for primitiveness that authorized American conquest—and to the American betrayal of its own supposed historical legacy was action. Action not only would falsify the truth-claims of the labeling, but it would work to create a popular solidarity that could actually realize the very ideals of American history that the United States had now betrayed. In Ou's account, there is an almost mystical belief in the ways in which ideas of freedom and solidarity could and would motivate action, and an almost total blindness to both the subjective bases of knowing as well as to problems of social and revolutionary organization. His boundless enthusiasm and his blindness are understandable in the context of how very new revolution as a topos of proper intellectual discussion was in 1899; and his optimism about the prospects for Filipino success also probably rendered invisible problems of revolutionary organization.

Indeed, in August 1899, the outcome of the war was by no means certain (it had only really begun in earnest in February): American troops were suffering huge battlefield losses and other casualties related to tropical illnesses, all documented in the Chinese press, while the lengths to which the United States would go to assure an outcome favorable to itself were still not clear. Thus, in completely unmediated fashion, Ou echoes Aguinaldo's rhetoric, as it had been reported in the *Qingyi bao* earlier: "How can China, big as it is, fear the small, while the Philippines, small as it is, oppose the big?" And he added: "It is said that Asia is unable to promote independence, yet it has begun in the Philippines. The Philippine sea is close to us . . . the wind of freedom and independence [emanating from there] will blow over our whole country . . . and then our 400 million compatriots will cultivate patriotism in their hearts; and it will have been the Philippines that aided us in overcoming our precarious situation."[34] Ou's political point here is clear enough: to use the Philippines to goad his fellow elites to action. Yet, beyond this functional aspect, Ou's linking of the Philippines to China via a common contemporary historical and geographically spatial Asianness (for him, the Philippines [not Japan] was the first to actively defend independence for "Asia" in this new era), begins to reconfigure what the task of a properly Chinese—and Asian—nationalism might be. Revolutionary activism was central to this reconfiguration, even though what this meant concretely remained undertheorized and abstract as an organizational or Chinese-specific proposition.

Not all who were interested in questions of activism were as confident as Ou, nor as literal as he, about the self-evident relationship between ideas and action. The question hence remained of how to motivate action, and who would be the proper agents and targets of this mobilization. As suggested in Chapter 3 above, one answer to this question was the overseas

Chinese; there were others. And other intellectuals soon took up the question explicitly and critically.

Intellectuals and the Group

The issue of motivation, agents, and targets was taken up directly in Lin Xie's "A Record of the Righteous Uprising of the People's Party of the Philippines," published in 1901. Lin, as we have seen, was particularly devoted to communicating to a wider public, and, like his account of the Hawaiian plague incident, his account of the Philippine revolution was also published in the *Hangzhou Vernacular Journal*.[35] In any comparison of Lin's essay with Ou Jujia's, however, it must be noted that Lin's essay, although only separated from Ou's by two years, was situated in a very different context: internally, the Boxer Rebellion had ended in the final denouement of death, destruction, and the allied occupation of Beijing; meanwhile, the Philippine revolution was quickly moving toward defeat, a process documented in the increasingly pessimistic newspaper accounts of Aguinaldo's disappearance into the mountains, American gains on the battlefield, and mass native suffering on the islands due to quarantines, famines, and other American-imposed privations. The boundless optimism of mid-1899 had thus turned by late 1901 into a broad reassessment of possibilities for organization and to a skepticism about what an aroused revolutionary people might accomplish.

Yet, unlike other intellectuals who, as a group, repudiated the Boxers for their supposedly atavistic behavior, Lin Xie lent qualified affirmation to them through his narrative of the Philippine revolution. Lin was one of a minority in this regard, for in the essays of the time, the condemnation of the Boxers—surely an example of an aroused people—was often and yet paradoxically set alongside the valorizations of other peoples such as the revolutionary Filipinos. This contradictory attitude was opposed by only a few, such as the author of the retrospectively famous "Yihetuan yougongyu zhongguo shuo" (The Benefits of the Boxers for China) published in the *Kaizhi lu* in 1901. Even in this essay, as in Lin's, the Boxers were validated through a direct positive comparison of them to the Philippines and the Transvaal. As the *Kaizhi lu* essayist put it: "Here, we come full circle [in our account of the Boxers]. For the realization of a people's [*guomin*] responsibility is nowhere more visibly vigorous and evident, is nowhere more laid bare and flourishing, has nowhere revealed more starkly the banner of independence and rung the bell of freedom than in the battles between America and the Philippines, Britain and the Transvaal."[36] Lin Xie's affirmation of the Boxers via the Philippines was nevertheless different from the *Kaizhi lu* essayist's, and his affirmation of the Philippines was also different from Ou Jujia's earlier account. Indeed, rather than abstractly extolling popular revolution as such, Lin used his essay to raise crucial questions about the relationship of intellectuals or social elites to revolutionary process and organization.

Lin began his essay by infusing the terms in his title with a popular meaning, thus introducing new sociopolitical vocabulary and conceptualization to a popular audience unfamiliar with elite political discourse or global current events:

> The title of this piece is "A Record of the Righteous Uprising of the People's Party of the Philippines."
>
> The Philippines is a small island [*sic*] in Asia; a people's party is when a majority of the people of a country, all of whom love one another as brothers, unite together in a faction [*dang*], just as told in the *Romance of the Three Kingdoms* . . . "Righteous uprising" [*qiyi*] means, in accordance with natural justice [*gongli*], when [people] righteously take up arms, rely upon a righteous spirit, raise a banner of righteousness and gather a righteous army, fight against normally unrighteous states. This is the general principle [of *qiyi*]. It is not only completely sanctioned, it is dignified and correct, it is open-hearted and glorious.[37] Everyone embraces a leader and is unwilling to submit to others; by uniting the dispersed together, the principle of preserving the race is honored. (Note: race comprises those of our type, those of our tribe/clan [*zhongzu shi women jeyizhong jeyizu de ren*]).[38]

Locating the Philippines in "Asia" was relatively new, albeit by 1901, clearly already naturalized. As for Lin's interpretation of *qiyi* (righteous uprising), Harold Schiffrin notes that this concept traditionally "lacked any positive political content; [it referred] to popular protest movements of local rather than national scope."[39] However, Lin Xie's explanation deploys the word *qiyi* so as to change its meaning into something both "national" in scope and "political" in import. Indeed, when conjoined to the concepts of "people's party" and to "race" (*zhongzu*), Lin's notion of *qiyi* clearly takes on the modern meaning of revolution (*geming*): as both national and political. Indeed, the overall point of the essay precisely was to explicate the problem of *qun* (group; unity) in the contemporary moment, with particular reference to the relationship between elites and the people in the forging of the *qun* through revolutionary activity.

After the linguistic lesson, Lin's narrative makes the observation that while the people in the Philippines were originally "perfectly able to be independent," the lack of good leaders had driven them into ignorance and stagnation. The advent of Europeans—"each country dreaming of taking the Philippines as a dependency [*shuguo*]"—had thus resolved itself into foreign rule, imposition of cruel taxes, restrictions on politics, and the co-optation of Filipinos into the Spanish army as tools of Spanish "policies of torture." Filipinos were hence oppressed not only by foreigners, but "by their own people, their own race [*zhongzu*]." Lastly, Lin pointedly mentioned the role of missionaries, "who went everywhere spreading their lies—but I can't bear to speak of that!" (Presumably because this was published at the end of the Boxer Rebellion, which was sparked in part by the local divisiveness spawned by missionary alliances with local elites.)[40]

Having established the contours of the situation, Lin continued that resistance to the oppressive policies in the Philippines began with the formation of a "people's party" (*mindang*), which attempted to exercise "freedom of speech" through the publication of newspapers organized by those who had studied in Spain and who, upon return, had set up schools. It was through these new social institutions that "the people were gradually educated and gradually awakened to the principle of protecting their race and people." In addition, organizations such as the "bricklayer's righteous association" (the Freemasons) and the Katipunan (spelled phonetically; identifying the organization to which Aguinaldo belonged) also became vehicles through which a broader cross-section of people was incorporated into structures of opposition to Spain. By 1895, the Spanish governor-general began a crackdown on all these activities.

In speaking of the violent suppression of the organizations that lasted through 1897 and their consequences, Lin's deep ambivalence about elite-led reformism is clear. Questioning the nature and depth of the commitments of a reformist elite faced with state-sponsored suppression, Lin castigates this elite for running into exile to "chat and discuss," while leaving the brunt of the suppressions to be borne by the people left behind.

> Pity those elites! They were caught in the East and chased to the West, and some escaped to Hong Kong and Japan. (Gentlemen! You know:

most of these elites, even as they took up arms in the name of righteousness and patriotism . . . were afraid of losing their lives and sacrificing themselves . . . [Yet] if something is unsuccessful, is it not preferable to die [rather than escape]? . . . Those reformers [*weixin de ren*] want their deaths to have great significance; this is only because they think they can take on the world's burdens by chatting and discussing.) The Philippine elites escaped to Japan, just when things were at their most critical and dangerous . . . At precisely that moment, those who study . . . ideas on protecting the race and the people cut themselves off.[41]

These remarks allow Lin to suggest that elites alone cannot be counted upon to carry opposition to its final conclusion.

By the same token, in these remarks, the contours of Lin's attraction to the Philippines as an example becomes manifest. In one sense, the attraction was "natural," given Lin's revolutionary and populist temperament. But the appeal is more specifically attributable to what Lin perceived as being the similarities in the social and political structures of colonization and reformism in the Philippines and China. In the trajectory of colonization and administrative assimilation that Lin described for Spain in the Philippines is visible a critique of the Manchu conquest of the Ming and the Manchu assimilation of Han Chinese into their structures of rule. While this specific parallel was to become explicit a few years later, in his castigation of elite Filipinos, Lin simultaneously raised questions about those exiled Chinese elites who were both assimilated into and alienated from the structures of rule and who "chat and discuss" without having any contact with "the people" of whom and on whose behalf they purport to speak.

Indeed, Lin—in contrast to Ou Jujia and Liang Qichao, for example—clearly identified the problematic role of colonized intellectuals in popular organizing and revolutionary struggle, a problem that perhaps was most famously articulated by Frantz Fanon in the late 1950s.[42] Lin's critique, like Fanon's, figures an essential ambiguity about intellectuals, particularly foreign-educated ones, as a revolutionary class; like Fanon—albeit Fanon in psychological terms with which Lin is utterly unconcerned[43]—Lin was troubled by the possibility that intellectuals and elites would betray the very revolutionary process they mobilized. Here, however, there was a contradiction for Lin. On the one hand, for elites, "the people" remained a necessary if merely a rhetorical device; while, on the other hand, foreign-educated elites, whose peripatetic cosmopolitanism contributed to their ability to initiate struggle from an understanding of a wider context, initially played a progressive role in mobilizing people, even while it was precisely that cosmopolitanism that also facilitated their abandonment of the people and of reformism when their own lives were at stake. Lin's concern over the role of elites was thus not only tied to the ongoing changing status of the traditionally exalted scholar-elites of China, whose field of action was now both reduced and expanded through their advocacy of and yet refusal to engage in a popular politics. His question was also a completely new one, devised as it was out of a new social-political and global situation. In the end, for Lin, the question of the social hegemony of the cosmopolitan intellectual in a moment of national transition arose not only, or not merely, as a Chinese problem; it was a problem of the contradictory situation of intellectuals from the non-Euro-American world in general, for whom global space both enabled knowledge leading to action but was also potentially a space of national betrayal.[44]

The contradiction having been identified, a problem remained. For if the global had to be engaged and yet also was the site of betrayal, what constituted a more stable terrain and who were more properly the agents of activity? It was with these questions that the concept of *qun*, as an internal social manifestation of the "national people," was examined, not only by Lin but by Kang Youwei, Tan Sitong, Liang Qichao, and many others at the time.[45]

By the turn of the century, *qun* had become the centerpiece for programs of sociopolitical transformation by being radically redefined away from its sources in *jinwen* (New Text) Confucianism. In a previous guise, as Benjamin Elman has demonstrated, an attempt to reorient *qun* as a concept had been established by the Jiangnan literati groups in the eighteenth century, well before Kang, Liang, and others picked it up in the late nineteenth century and put it to different purposes.[46] In Elman's context, *qun* was mobilized to legitimate independent groups of scholars not tied to the bureaucracy; and, for all its potentially oppositional political content, *qun* was mostly a sanctioned designation for what were scholarly "lineage" or "kinship" groups—families of thought. By the turn of the twentieth century, Kang Youwei interpreted *qun* as the natural state of humanity: *qun* was what made human beings human—while Tan Sitong emphasized *ren* (benevolence; love; humaneness) as the moral basis of all human *qun*. Thus, both Kang and Tan used *qun* more expansively than did the eighteenth-century literati, as both included all of humanity in its purview. Yet they also took *qun* to be essentially given; for neither was it a problem that needed to be explained or a condition to be forged. Instead, it was the self-evident answer to the question of human society, the major problem being how to fortify an already existing *qun* in order to strengthen it and thereby the state. (Both were also concerned with how to create a transcendent *qun* of the world.[47]) Even Yan Fu's interpretation of *qun* via Spencerian Darwinism, as James Pusey has shown, was also particularly well-suited to the concept of an already existing community, for in Yan's explication, "struggle" was that which happened primarily *between* species, not *within* species.[48] As an already assumed polity, "China" constituted for Yan Fu a natural community of the *qun* (which included Han, Manchus, Mongols, etc.), and thus *qun* for him was not so much a historically evolved category as a primordial one. For this reason, Yan's tautological equation of Chinese *qun* with China as a self-evident given was politically debilitating, because, in the moment of crisis among those intellectuals who were troubled by what they called the passivity of "the people," questions inevitably emerged: how does the *qun* become one? How does it fall apart? How and by whom could it be reconstructed? Who should be included and why?

The idea of the naturalness of the *qun* gave way, then, not under the assault of Darwinism or the reinterpretation from within Confucian texts, but under mounting sociopolitical pressure to specify "the people's" role in constructing the nation. And with the questions posed, *qun* increasingly became not only an object of definition but the subject of theorization, contestation, and re-creation. One of the great late Qing theorists of *qun* was Liang Qichao, whose 1897 essay "Shuo qun" ("On Grouping") opened the concept to new approaches.[49] Although in his initial comments Liang affirmed the idea of an already existing *qun*—he began with the observation "*qun* is the essence and *bian* [change] is the means"—he soon achieved an explicit awareness of the need to reconceptualize *qun* as a political entity to be forged through action. As Hao Chang has noted in this regard, "With this view of *qun* as a socio-political organism, Liang's thought evinced a notable tendency to drift . . . toward an incipient idea of national community."[50] For Liang, however, the relationship between the putative mobilizers (the elite) and "the people" remained rooted in assumptions about the leading social role of elites, who were responsible for educating and informing "the people" on their proper roles. In Lin Xie's case, by contrast, the relationship of the people to elites in the forging of the national *qun* was a problem to be raised rather than a premise to be assumed.

After a detailed account of the battles between the Spaniards and the "People's Party" army in the Philippines, Lin opens a self-conscious "digression" in his narrative to highlight the problem of elites and the people. Foregrounding the role of José Rizal, famed novelist and poet of Philippine independence, who, upon his return to the Philippines after an extended stay in Spain, was exiled to the provinces, arrested, and then executed in 1896 by Spanish authorities, Lin noted:

> The Spanish government accused [Rizal] of having contact with the Masons, but they had not a shred of evidence to prove it. All they had were the several books Rizal had written, in which he had urged the people to stand up for themselves, just as we are telling the story of the uprising of the Philippine People's Party to urge everyone to stand up for themselves. But Rizal's books were of his own authorship, whereas ours is adapted from someone else's book. Those who hated Rizal could use his books against him and to execute him; those who hate us can only open their eyes, but have no other recourse.
>
> But, this is a digression.[51]

It is a digression with a purpose. Salvaging the role of the cosmopolitan intellectual who is connected to the world by virtue of his privileged position, Lin used Rizal's willingness to sacrifice his life as a model of a committed revolutionary elite.[52] As Lin showed, Rizal's sacrifice assisted in mitigating the social distance between the "people" and the elites, allowing him to become a heroic martyr. It was through this sacrificial act that the closing of the gap between peripatetic elites and a more rooted people could be achieved.[53] Indeed, it was the closing of this gap that, in Lin's view, would gradually produce a modern *qun* able to create a collective nation in the present moment.[54] Lin stipulated, rather romantically to be sure, that would-be revolutionary elites should be prepared to pay with their lives for their ideals, as it would only be through such sacrifices that the people and elites could be welded into a *qun* of the nation. With this ideal of the unified and activated *qun* in place, Lin moved at the end of his essay to ostensibly cite Aguinaldo so as to specify what this active *qun* might accomplish: "Aguinaldo has stated that he does not trust Europeans: 'White people in the past have discriminated against and insulted peoples of other races. We Filipinos should not concern ourselves with whether or not they are trustworthy, for there is only one sort of boundary between peoples [*zhongzu jiexian*], and it can be summed up in one word: it is called self-reliance [*zili*]."[55]

In the end, then, recognizing difference *between* peoples was not the most important boundary for nation-creation in Lin's view. The only "boundary" he recognized (via Aguinaldo) was the one that people asserted in their struggle to create themselves as a self-actualizing, unified *qun* within a world of many different *qun*. In this sense, the revolutionary process for him was not merely, or not only, reactive—the defining of the "us" against the "them"; rather, it was an act of creating the people who constituted the nation, defining who constituted the "us." On this view, *qun* was neither a primordial ethnic nor an ethnocentric nor a preexisting category. Rather, it was a historical one, which was problematized and made visible when set in a global context of conquest, colonialism, and difference.

Here, then, Lin not only took several steps away from Ou Jujia's 1899 ascription of a self-evident relationship between ideas and action, as well as away from the self-evidence of the *qun*; he also recognized that boundaries construed as "difference" merely served Euro-Americans as a way to legitimate their repressive colonizing policies. Within this nexus, he also raised the question of elites and people in a revolutionary national situation. Few subsequent essayists extended his insights, however—perhaps because the Philippine revolution was crushed shortly thereafter. Indeed, the problem of relations between the elite and the people was to remain undertheorized for many more years. What was extended out of these observations, though, was the recognition of the historical relationship between Euro-American promotion of a discourse of "difference" and their conquest and repression of non-Western peoples. As this relationship came into fuller view, a more complete understanding of the totalizing project of Euro-American imperialism also became visible. At the same time, it was at this point that attempts were made to fit the narrative of modern Chinese history into a colonial model that would contest this totalization from a specifically Chinese space as well as from a shared global space of colonial experience.

Revolution as Anticolonial Praxis and as Reclaiming History

As revolution and the internal creation and mobilization of the *qun* took on a concrete meaning for Chinese intellectuals, the impulse to make the Philippines speak directly to the Chinese situation required them to leap over or to erase some relatively significant differences in their respective historical situations. Those differences, for our purposes here, reside in the formal centuries-long experience of European colonialism in the Philippines, an experience that China lacked. As I discuss more fully in chapter 6, this lack of colonial experience, as it were, was soon filled by the increasingly persuasive historical rendering of China as a colonized space, albeit one colonized not by Euro-America but by the Manchus. The designation of the Manchus as fulfilling the modern task of colonizer was crucial to the conceptualization of China's trajectory of national independence as one requiring an anti-Manchu revolutionary *paiwai* (ousting foreigners). It was also crucial for another major historical argument mobilized against the Manchus—for which the early radical *guocui* (national essence) scholars, such as Zhang Binglin, were most well known—that is, that the Manchu usurpation had reduced "Chinese learning" to a set of narrow legitimating foundational texts and interpretations that, over the centuries, had stifled "true" and diverse learning in China and thus its "true" history.

This new consciousness of history and its relationship to a colonial discourse of modernity did not initially emerge as an internal problem of narrating the nation—finding a suitable past and present trajectory that posited the linear diachronic movement of the entity called "China" through time—but as a global problem of "weak people's" claiming the right to write their own history. Indeed, the whole issue of history and nation was first forcefully raised in relation to how "difference" was systematically produced and deployed by Euro-Americans in their conquest of the world. Two essays from 1903 on the Philippine revolution confront this problem; both drew extensively on the writings already mentioned above, as well as on the veritable flood of reporting about the Philippines that filled the Chinese and Japanese newspapers of the day.[56] They also drew heavily from a book written by Mariano Ponce, delegate to Japan from the Philippine Revolutionary Government, whom many Chinese residing in the Tokyo-Yokohama region met and knew well.[57]

Ponce's *History of the War for Philippine Independence*, written in Spanish in

1900, translated into Japanese in 1901 and into Chinese in 1902, was perhaps the single most influential text for post-1902 Chinese interpretations of the global and Chinese significance of the Philippine revolution.[58] Moving beyond the American and Japanese geopolitical arguments, Ponce directed Chinese attention to an experience of colonialism that spoke directly to Chinese intellectuals. Indeed, for Chinese intellectuals it was Ponce who first persuasively cast colonialism as a global discursive problem, a characterization that not only facilitated the universalization of the Philippine national experience well beyond its particularities, but one that endured well beyond the duration of the Philippine situation itself.

Ponce's *History* is the first official account of the Philippine nationalist movement and the revolution from the perspective of Emilio Aguinaldo's party,[59] and it establishes Aguinaldo's faction of the Katipunan as the central actors in the events. The leadership of the Aguinaldo faction was comprised of Spanish-educated elites and landowners, many of whom had studied abroad, unlike the rivals Aguinaldo had displaced, who were peasants and artisans led by Andres Bonifacio. Ponce's narrative thus presented a class perspective particularly congenial to Chinese intellectuals, who were, after all, of the same emerging and established social strata as Ponce and Aguinaldo. This shared class background made Ponce and his book credible sources for Chinese intellectuals.[60] Moreover, because of the narrative's suppression of the heterogeneity of Filipino society and of the conflicts within the Katipunan itself—of which Chinese then remained unaware—Chinese intellectuals could well imagine that Filipino and Chinese social structures were in many ways similar. This facilitated the familiarizations that were key to their taking Ponce as an authoritative voice[61] and to their imagining that the Filipino people were indeed as unified as Ponce claimed them to be, all of which also reinforced the unfavorable comparison between supposed Filipino unity and the purported lack of unity among the Chinese people.

In writing his book, Ponce wished to speak not only to Chinese but to Japanese elites as well. As the Japanese preface, written by Miyamoto Taira, noted, "Our group of friends knows next to nothing of the Philippines and thinks that their people are still in the dark ages; after reading this book, we can know how civilized and educated they are, and how courageous, with a spirit just like that of the samurai of ancient Japan."[62] Clearly aware of prior biases against the Filipinos held by both Japanese and Chinese, Ponce, who was in Japan attempting to garner Japanese government support for the revolution,[63] crafted a narrative strategy that aimed at capturing and reinforcing social elitism, by creatively inserting Filipinos into global elite status while rearticulating the social role of that elite from maintaining order and upholding the statist status quo toward promoting revolutionary struggle.

Under the Spanish, Ponce wrote, Filipinos were depicted in Europe and the world as "relics of the stone age." In exhibitions, the Spanish always put "tribesmen" on display with feathers in their heads and primitive bows and arrows in their hands; in books, Filipinos were also always described as "primitives." But the truth, Ponce asserted—busily erasing the complexity of Filipino society—was that Filipinos were full participants in European intellectual and scientific life, frequently appearing in their catalogs of famous scientists, writers, and artists.[64] What the Filipinos were doing through their revolution, Ponce declared, was showing the world that it was the Spanish and Americans[65] who were, despite their beautiful rhetoric, truly uncivilized:

> Neither the various primitive behaviors of the Spaniards toward the Filipino people . . . nor the subsequent exercising of the Filipino people's right to declare war against them were ever recognized by the world. Yet, according to the habits and customs of the "civilized" world, the latter actions are not out of the bounds of propriety. But civilized people and their cosmopolitan humanism [*shijie zhi rendao*] exist in a fundamentally uncivilized system.[66]

Repeating a line from a speech of Aguinaldo's that appropriated the Monroe Doctrine's rhetoric for new purposes, Ponce wrote, "Of old, Monroe, an American president, declared that America is for the Americas. Today, in that spirit, we declare that the Philippines is for the Filipinos! . . . What we seek is complete independence; nothing short of that will suffice."[67]

Ponce's rhetoric and version of events exerted a strong influence on Chinese thinking not only about the Philippines but about the ways in which colonial discourse and unevenness globally was produced and exploited by Euro-America. His rendition helped focus attention on questions of history, representation, and the modern as well as upon the unreliability of the Euro-American rhetoric of "humanism" and "civilization." These questions were taken up in mid-1903, when two essays on the Philippines specifically drew out the implications of Ponce's narrative for China and for more totalizing concepts of History in an uneven global context. The first, by Tang Tiaoding [Erhe],[68] was published in the Shanghai journal *Xinshijie xuebao* (New World Scholarly Journal); it reprinted the introduction and first two chapters of Ponce's text, accompanied by extended commentaries inserted at significant points.[69] The second, an essay in two installments written anonymously for the *Hubei Xuesheng Jie* (Hubei Students' World), one of the most influential of the exile student papers, essentially organized all available information on the Philippines into a comprehensive and coherent statement on the modern world situation.

Tang Tiaoding's first intervention into Ponce's text comes after the initial passage, in which Ponce describes the representations of Filipinos in Spanish books. Tang comments:

> Now I have finally understood the reasons for the distinguishing labels "civilization" [*wenming*] and "primitive" [*yeman*] . . . I have read this *History* and have shed many a tear; I have grieved for the Philippine people; I have stopped eating. I have . . . sighed over the Spaniards' calculating ambitions: . . . they spread a net of lies to cover the eyes and ears of the world, to prevent people from detecting their real plans . . . They take the profits, enslave the people, subvert their rights, deprive them of their identity, and yet that is not all. They use language to kill them, to humiliate them, to contaminate them. Alas! White people are indeed vicious . . .
>
> Since *jiawu* [war with Japan] and the allied assault [during the Boxer Rebellion], our China has perhaps been captured between book covers by those people, and they number in the thousands. How do we know that these books are not of the same genre as the Spanish books [on the Philippines]?[70]

In this outburst, Tang recognizes, via Ponce's suggestion, that historical representations, far from mirroring truth, were ideological statements that had material consequences for particular peoples while also producing an entire global structure that was reproduced by claiming itself as "history."

In this insight, Tang moved well beyond Ou Jujia's, Lin Xie's, and Liang Qichao's earlier recognitions about the relationship between expansionism and "European techniques." In the earlier statements, representations were understood as deliberately false manufactures tied to specific actions (targeted destructions of another country or another people), where the falseness could be disproved by demonstrating the inadequacy of their specific truth-claims. In these early critiques of "European techniques," opposition to domination rested—borrowing Robert Young's phrase—upon the conviction that the existence of a resistant singularity that defied the narrative closure of Western imperialist historicism was itself sufficient to defy imperialism.[71] By contrast, Tang recognized the more totalizing project of imperialist historicism. He recognized that this was a project not limited to any one episode of assault, but rather entended to a systematic and systemized mode of signification that enabled Euro-American claims and practices of domination to be called "history." Thus, in Tang's understanding (deriving from but moving beyond even Ponce's articulation), the single-axis binary of domination and resistance in one country was rendered into a systemic global principle. This transcendence was not achieved through what Homi Bhabha has called "mimicry" or "hybridity"[72]—which, as theoretical constructs, remain bound to place-based and binary categories. Tang's universalization was understood, rather, through and in the production of a universal subject of a different History altogether, a universal subject not necessarily bound to one place or one "nation." In the end, the recognition of the totalizing project of Western imperialist historicism emerged not merely from a binary view of confrontation, and thus not from a specific "place," but from the identification of China with the Philippines in a newly articulated world space of shared colonial experience that was everywhere, and thus that defined the modern itself.

Clearly, the purported universal subject of History in this non-Euro-American guise was actually a class-based one and depended on positing the (foreign) educated elite intelligentsia as the Historical subject par excellence. The subject thus turns out not to be so universal after all, and its historical possibilities are hence limited. Nevertheless, the potential project enabled by the production of this new subject of History was one that was rooted in a newly discovered shared colonial spatiality of experience,[73] an experience understood as constitutive, albeit not necessarily encompassing or exhausting the totality, of the experience of modernity. Whatever the "misrecognitions" and the internal and global class implications that such a construction involved (all of which had their particular as well as global consequences), the formulation of "colonial experience" as constitutive of the modern Chinese nationalist project via the Philippines contributed to the transformation of ideologies of the Chinese and global present in radical ways. Indeed, initially, this process transformed horizons of praxis, where the "national" project was apprehended as no mere internal problem of political systems, but rather as a cultural-political-historical problem that needed to be taken on at the global level. In the late Qing in particular,[74] this recognition facilitated a radical cultural politics of nationalism, which firmly entrenched the problem of "civilization" as not merely a *Chinese* problem but as a problem of global imperialist objectification. As Tang Tiaoding well recognized, historical-cultural representations far outlived their concrete locus and time of production, to engrave and reproduce enduring "truths" about peoples in the historical record itself.[75]

With this view, Tang Tiaoding posed the question: what could "civilization" possibly mean? He mused,

> I read white people's national histories [*guoshi*], and when it comes to the colonies they built up, they always decorate [their accounts] with glamorous rhetoric exaggerating their orderly rule by law. They provide plenty of indisputable evidence about the extent of native peoples' primitive customs and ignorance, as proof for why those people deserve to be conquered. This type of praise [for themselves] and condemnation [of others] is done with an eye toward the final judgment of history. Egypt, Poland, Cuba, India, South Africa, all these regions: just read the books on the history of the perishing of their countries [*wangguo shi*]! . . . In the past, I felt that the situation clearly demanded that these countries and peoples should perish . . . But now I know that these books were all written by white people, where truth and falsehood are confused.[76]

What provoked Tang's interest here was how European countries narrated the history of their colonization of others as an integral part of their own national histories; he was also interested in how the "primitiveness" of the natives produced and legitimated the claims to "civilization" in Europe. The mutual dependence of the constructions was not based on any equal ability to negotiate representation, as Tang recognized: while the Spanish were able to convince the world of their claim to "civilization," the Filipinos were condemned to "primitiveness" and thus to historical oblivion. (Tang even admitted that, prior to reading Ponce, he was susceptible to this view.) For Tang, the inadequacy of the specific representation radiated out from the specific instance of the Philippines to encompass the rest of the world, and he was led to automatically extend the insight on representation and history gained from the Philippines to incorporate Egypt, Poland, Cuba, South Africa, and now also China into the schema. Indeed, for Tang, it was no longer merely the historical fact of *wangguo* that was the most troubling aspect of the whole colonial process; rather it was the hegemonic language that indelibly fixed places and peoples as "natural" objects of "destruction" (*mie*) and subjects of "loss" (*wang*) for all time. This perspective was disturbing enough to make Tang call for a rethinking of the very relationship between history and "civilization," not in terms of specific political or cultural systems, but in terms of the global circulation of historical discourse.

In the next section of his commentary, Tang demolishes the arguments for constitutionalism and republicanism just then being debated vigorously in Chinese journals and political circles by charging that both political systems were premised upon the faulty logic that "rule of law" or "rule by law" somehow produced a civilized situation. He noted:

> Ever since there have been laws, colonies have been transformed into wastelands, and nobody ever cared. Laws are a matter of convenience for those of us who make them, but in their application in the colonies, what *we* call laws are merely our own customs and conveniences. Ever since there have been laws, the weak (*ruozhe*) have had nothing to eat: look at what England has done to India, Russia to Poland, Japan to Taiwan, Spain and America to the Philippines; they've taken territory and increased the number of officials, and it is all done in the name of the laws of civilization! Indians, Poles, Taiwanese, Filipinos: they all have had to abandon their original customs in order to "obey the law" . . . Yet, this "law" is merely other people's customs and interests that they force people to follow . . . This is the reason that anarchists [*xuwudang*] tear the web of law into pieces; this is the reason the Filipino rebels risk their lives.[77]

Despite his unlikely comparison between anarchists and the Filipino revolutionaries, Tang nevertheless observed that when "law" was merely an instrument of violence and domination, constitutionalism and republicanism were equally forms of barbarism. The impossibility of relying upon such state-centered solutions to the situation led Tang away from a consideration of any particular political system as the national-historical goal. Instead, he suggested that reclaiming "history" was the only basis for reclaiming civilization, globally and nationally.

Unlike the *guocui* (national essence) scholars, however, whose target was the internal dismantling of the Manchus' grip on Han Chinese history, and unlike Liang Qichao, whose interest in narrating the nation was in part at least to dismantle the hegemonic hold of the dynastic historical paradigm,

Tang Tiaoding's goal for rewriting history was aimed at the global arena, where "history" circulated as the discursive claim of the colonizers. This discursive claim did not leave China behind, despite China's lack of formal colonial structures. Indeed, as Tang pleads toward the end of his commentary, "Learned people of my country: are there any of you who are getting ready to write our history? Don't let white children, laughing behind our backs and clapping their hands with glee, take up their pens and paper [to write our history for us]."[78]

For Tang, then, it was the global battle over imperialist historicism that was the one to fight. In pursuit of this battle, Tang did not even pose the question of the contradictory role of the elite intellectual in revolutionary struggle, since, in his view, the arena of struggle was the discursive one of "history," not necessarily one of material organization. As he concluded: "The Filipinos have spoken for themselves and at least they can say this: the revolution was the real intention of the high-minded people [*zhishi*]."[79] It was the very "speaking" of revolution that appeared to Tang as the proclaiming of the Filipino as an agent and subject of history, and in this sense, for him, the actual failure of the Philippine revolution, mostly crushed by 1903, was not so relevant as the enunciative act itself.[80]

Tang was perhaps on one level elaborating a model of what one might call a revolutionary politics of authenticity, in the spirit of the early Japanese *shishi* (high-minded people), whose model of self-sacrifice was quite influential for Chinese in the late Qing, and with whose spirit many initially equated the self-sacrificing actions of nihilists, anarchists, and revolutionaries. But beyond this and at a different level, Tang also powerfully suggested that revolution was not merely an internal sociopolitical *event*, but, because of the discursive power of imperialist historicism, it was an event with a claim on and to the world: sparked to be sure and mobilized through specific revolutionary actions of specific peoples, but taken to the global stage, which was the only space, Tang felt, where history could be secured. Here the point for Tang, unlike for Ponce, was not so much to counterpose a "real" history against a white-manufactured fiction. Rather, by connecting the Chinese situation to the global situation through a discourse of imperialist historicism, Tang seemed to wish to destabilize the seeming structural certainty of the world system itself. In this sense, the eventness of the revolution was almost beside the point.

In contrast to Tang Tiaoding, the author of the *Hubei Student World* essay, also written in 1903 and entitled "Brief Outline of the Tragic Loss of the Philippines" (*Feilubin wangguo canzhuang jilue*), reached somewhat different conclusions, albeit also based upon an examination of historical representation. Written in what was emerging as a paradigm of *wangguo* histories[81]—the Hubei author twisted the paradigm to assert that the price of revolution, which in the present age was invariably failure and destruction (*wang*), was nevertheless worth the effort. Without such effort, one would become a mere slave (*nuli*), to the West and of History. As with Ou's and Tang's essays, the "Brief Outline" begins by setting the world stage for the "tragic loss of the Philippines." With Hong Kong taken by England and the Ryukyus (Liuqiu) and Taiwan by Japan, the author stated, the Atlantic was joined to the Pacific, with the Philippines, "the pearl of the Pacific,"[82] situated at the confluence of this convergence. According to the author, this convergence was heralded several years previously with "big waves in the *Nanyang* [Southern Seas]," which "awoke the world from its dreadful dream with a loud roar"; that dream was the false belief that the American Monroe Doctrine was confined to the American continent.

Upon this stage enter the main protagonists, who are "the first actors in the tragic play of our yellow people throwing off the shackles of white people in the name of freedom and independence: this was the war in the Philippines."[83] Echoing Liang Qichao, who had earlier written that the Filipinos were "the pioneers of independence in Asia; they are the first of the yellow race [to fight for] people's independence [*minquan*],"[84] this assimilation of Filipinos into "yellowness," along with the designation of the Philippines as "the first" or "pioneers" in Asia, signals not only the centrality of the Philippines to early Chinese constructions of race as a global conflict between "yellows" and "whites," but the ways in which Chinese intellectuals came to identify *themselves* as "yellow" and "Asian." If the Philippines was the avatar of "yellowness," then, Japan, as leader of the "yellow race" and of "Asia," appeared quite differently. As the Hubei author notes, in describing the Filipino refusal to be "bound in the shackles of the civilized people" of the United States:

> [The Filipinos] even asked a certain Chinese [Sun Zhongshan] to help them buy weapons from Japan, but this scheme was betrayed by an unreliable and immoral Japanese thief . . . Alas! These ever-perfidious Japanese speak constantly of a same-continent [*tongzhou*], same-civilization [*tongwen*], and same-race [*tongzhong*] Asian alliance; they even claim that

> Filipinos are related to them by blood.[85] These Japanese nevertheless engage in immoral trickery and have done nothing but help force Filipinos into horse and cow slavery forever. Alas! It is not heaven that oppresses the yellow people; it is yellow people who oppress one another! With such a race [*zhong*], I wish the world would just cease producing anything in the color yellow![86]

The betrayed politics of alliance with Japan was replaced by the more promising politics of "genuine" racial and Asian solidarity offered by the Philippines.

The distancing of Japan and the familiarizing of the Philippines is reinforced in a passage where the Hubei author seizes upon the relationship between historical representations and civilization brought up by Ponce and expounded by Tang:

> We know all too well now the ways of the green-eyed, yellow-haired ones: they declare themselves a first-class race and, the most arrogant under heaven, declare they thereby have a right to rule other races . . .
>
> They [Spain] wanted the world's countries to know that the Filipinos were primitives rooted in the stone age of prehistoric times, depicting them as a people who stuck feathers in their heads like unruly grass. They published much on this to feed the "civilized" people. Aroused to revulsion, it was unnecessary for civilized people to feel any connection to, or to reach any understanding of the Filipinos.[87]

This comment on Western "civilized" practices led the Hubei author not to a discussion of the West, but to a parenthetical aside that commented on the 1903 Osaka exhibit, "Exhibit of the Races of Man," over which Chinese students in Japan had raised a vociferous protest:

> The books that Americans write about the Chinese character say that one can devise a chart by dividing up the world's customs. They use our country's various bad habits as an inexhaustible source for constructing their categories and drawing their charts. Those who know no better and look at them [the charts] undoubtedly conclude that we Chinese are subhuman.
>
> This year in the Japanese exhibition [in Osaka], they wanted to classify Chinese people with various native peoples [*tumin*], as if we were all similar, and implying that we were all "uncivilized" in the same way.[88]

The interrelated problems of scientistic categories, representation, and visualism are understood here as a potential harbinger of Japanese designs on China.

To be sure, in the Osaka exhibition the Japanese organizers had grouped the "inferior races" of China, Korea, the Ryukyus, India, Hawaii, Taiwan, and Java under the heading "raw barbarians" (*shengfan zhong*) and once the plan was known, it was vigorously attacked by Chinese students in Japan.[89] While there is little doubt that the Japanese organizers intended the grouping as a way to inscribe Japanese superiority in Asia and Japanese scientific authority in classifying peoples, the Chinese students' response was not merely a protest against that specific episode, but rather is evidence of their heightened awareness of the actual and potential historical implications and material consequences of China's classification as "primitive" or "raw," consequences that were not merely a civilizational slap in the face, but which could lead to *wangguo*. Indeed, the outburst emerged because the Chinese students in Japan had understood the consequences of the representational practices of imperialist modernity;[90] were profoundly aware of the significance of the structures of meaning of visual organization;[91] and were also aware of the colonial world order into which Japan, it now seemed, wished to insert China. And it is at least in part for *these* reasons that the Osaka exhibition was perceived as such a problem, and not merely, as many historians have claimed, because of a Chinese racism or a civilizational Sinocentrism.[92] Thus, while the "Brief Outline" author was without a doubt upset at the classification of China with other "native peoples" (*tumin*), the source of the upset also stemmed from the recognition that the classifications authorizing this grouping presented no innocent production of knowledge. Rather, as he well recognized, it was precisely this kind of knowledge production that authorized "belief in the cruel treatment of people and in the extermination of other peoples as if they were not members of the human race."[93]

Leaving the Osaka exhibit and going back to the specific problem of the Philippines, the essay moves into a long account of the events that led to the Philippine revolution against Spain, to the defeat of that initial effort, and the escape of the leaders to Hong Kong, where the United States offered them an alliance, and where Aguinaldo, who had managed to break free of the Spanish shackles, "fell into the American cage."[94] The second installment of the essay is devoted to explaining the cunning construction of the "cage," and it is clear from the narrative that for the Hubei author, as for so many others at the time, the betrayal in the Philippines of the American self-representation as a "benign" country (in Benjamin Franklin's oft-quoted words),[95] provided the confirmation of the reconfiguration of global space.

In this context, revolution possessed an expansive global significance, not only because it was called forth and informed by the times, but because each transformation of a colony into an independent nation would contribute to the transformation of the globe, the times, and the discourses that produced the very world that had hitherto been foreclosed to the primitive other. Or, so it was thought. By the same token, it was also in this context that the Hubei author expressed his shame at comparing China to the Philippines, for the Filipinos, "rather than surviving by being someone's slave," had instead refused to submit, at the risk not only of their lives, but of *wangguo* itself.[96]

Conclusion

Within a short few years—from 1897 to 1903—the designation of the modern global and Chinese problem was being utterly transformed. Indeed, in 1897, the solution to China's problems had been discussed primarily in terms of recuperating "true" Confucianism, whereas by 1903 revolutionary transformation in conjunction with other colonized peoples of the world was seen as a viable and even necessary solution to China's problems. That is, while Liang, Kang, and others in 1897 theorized the possibility of challenging imperialist ideology from a uniquely Chinese space, by 1903 many now asserted that the only possibility for launching such a challenge was from a space of action and meaning-production not contained by a particularistic civilizational norm nor even to a territorial location. It was thus in 1903, with the example of the Philippines in full view, that the "utopianization of revolution"[97] found its full voice in Zou Rong's *Revolutionary Army*; this utopianization was not merely Chinese, but global.

In 1899, Ou Jujia understood this global reconfiguration through an emphasis on revolution (*geming*), that, having spread over the world—from the Mediterranean to America, to the Eastern Seas (Japan) and the Southern Seas (Philippines)—had now improbably reached what he called the "African seas" (*feihai*). In Ou's view, while the Philippine revolution signaled the rise of Asia, and the Transvaal "revolution" demonstrated the rise of Africa, both were harbingers of a new global and Chinese future.[98] A few years later, another author rendered this connection even more tightly: " I look at Europe and am afraid for Asia; I look at Africa and rejoice for Asia; I look at Africa's Transvaal and I am ashamed for China. I want to use the Transvaal to shame China; I want to use Africa to condemn Europe . . . It is possible to shame Europe; it is possible for China to rise; it is possible for the Transvaal to inspire."[99] Indeed, the gathering revolutionary cries of these years helped bring revolution to a level of global and national concreteness: "Africa for the Africans," Transvaal President Paul Kruger was reported to have announced;[100] "Philippines for the Filipinos," Emiliano Aguinaldo was often cited as saying; "Asia for the Asians," Japanese pan-Asianists were promoting; "Guangdong for the Guangdongese," Ou Jujia wrote in his 1902 pamphlet *Xin Guangdong*; "Hunan for the Hunanese," declared Yang Desheng in his 1903 pamphlet *Xin Hunan*. These cries did not merely echo the Monroe Doctrine's "America for the Americans"; rather, they created a new local and global language in and through which revolution, China, nationalism, and the world were linked in an interdependent, urgent global project of reconfiguration.[101]

On this view, the acceptance of revolution among Chinese intellectuals as a modern mode of being represents no mere linear move from "reform" to "revolution" as functional strategies of seizing state power; rather, it represents a rethinking of the modern world and of China based upon a completely altered understanding of both. Relatedly, imperialism and colonialism were not the already existing discursive premises and consciously grasped "reality" against which Chinese intellectuals formed their understandings of their late Qing historical situation; these categories of analysis came into being at the same time that Chinese intellectuals situated China within modern global history and modernity. In short, Chinese intellectuals produced a recognition of China's historical situation at the turn of the century from within an incipient colonial discourse that they pieced together from observing and identifying China with the Philippines, among other places. And, it was in the process of this self-recognition that a colonial paradigm for and discourse of modern Chinese history took hold in China in the late Qing. While at the time (and arguably, ever since) none of the issues raised was resolved—how to create and mobilize the *qun*, how to conceptualize the "people," how to negotiate the contradictory role of elites, how to reconfigure the relationship between "civilization" and "history"—nevertheless, all of these questions, intimately tied to specifying and understanding the mutually constitutive parameters of the

Chinese nation and of global modernity, were brought to the forefront of discussion.

Even after the Philippine revolution was decisively crushed, the significances found in the Philippines were detached from the particular events and reattached, via a new universalism, to the Chinese nationalist problematic. One consequence of this detachment was that when the Filipino struggle was defeated, their particular claims as a people were summarily forgotten by Chinese (to be rediscovered several more times over the course of the next century).[102] Another consequence was that in the same measure that the Filipinos were observed and established as model peoples of the modern world because of their ability to struggle—to demonstrate civilization not only through textual claims but through contemporary action—the unequal social relations within the Philippines could be presumed not to exist or assumed to have been overcome. Social divisions in China could not so easily be erased; they were, after all, part and parcel of Chinese intellectuals' own social experience and they were divisions that, on the one hand, intellectuals wished to preserve as part of their own privileged social position, but that, on the other hand, needed to be mitigated at least rhetorically in order for nationalist projects to make social, political, and intellectual sense. The inability of Chinese intellectuals to face this conundrum squarely often led to the displacement of their own roles in producing social division onto the figure of the Chinese "people,"[103] a displacement that facilitated the relegation of the Chinese people to a sorry state of backwardness for their ostensible failure to overcome social division.[104]

In this complex situation, the intertwining of the colonial paradigm with the problem of the people pointed to the need for reconfiguring the relationships of dominance established by the practice of historicism (globally and internally) and by modern colonialism and imperialism through revolution, understood as a global endeavor. However, it also increasingly pointed more narrowly to the possibility that an exclusive *minzu* (ethnos) was the bearer of *guomin* (national people) potential and of national meaning in China. This ethnicization of "the people" and its attendant incipient narrowing of the significances of revolution is the topic of the next chapter.

5 PROMOTING THE ETHNOS: THE BOER WAR AND DISCOURSES OF THE PEOPLE

If one were to try to explain things [in the Transvaal] by reference to world maps [it would be impossible, for] is not Africa black and without color? If one were to try to explain [the Boers] through reference to historical maps [it would be impossible, for] is not the Transvaal also black and without color?[1]

Efforts to theoretically specify what the concept of "the people" was and how they were to be transformed into an active "national" people gave rise to two major formulations of the problem. Often using overlapping terminology, these formulations were framed theoretically in terms of whether the people should be conceived primarily as a statist concept, a citizenry, or as an ethnic concept, an ethnos (*minzu*). The statist formulation came to underpin a political strategy aimed at transforming the dynastic state into a constitutional monarchy, through which "the people" would be defined in relation to the state; this yielded a variant of nationalism usually termed *guojia zhuyi* (nation-statism). The ethnic formulation, by contrast, underpinned the emerging discourse of anti-Manchuism, through which "China" and "Chinese"[2] were to be stabilized under a Han ethno-racial sign, and "the people" defined by the unitariness of the ethnos as actualized in the activity of *paiwai* (expelling others) aimed at the expulsion of the Manchus. This was usually termed *minzu zhuyi* (ethno-nationalism). These alternative conceptualizations did not represent any rigid divide and they did not inhabit separate discursive domains; these two forms did indicate different processes within the discursive formation of nationalism. Indeed, the efforts to differentiate the concepts were not merely semantic or academic, as the differentiation was intimately tied not only to how the process of nation-formation was conceived,[3] but also to what was deemed most important in China's and the world's modern history and contemporary situation; in this sense, the concepts represent different interpretations of the world and modernity.

While both *guojia zhuyi* and *minzu zhuyi* took the newly recognized modern significance of imperialism and colonialism as central to their formulations, the former saw the greatest threat to China as emanating from Euro-American imperialism, understood as commercial, territorial, and political expansionism; whereas the latter understood colonialism, rather than imperialism, to be the major problem of modernity, with colonialism in China represented by the Manchu usurpation of the Chinese state. Ethno-nationalists, such as Sun Zhongshan, thus posited the need for an "anticolonial" Han revolution against the "real" colonizers of China, the Manchu Qing. An irony of this moment, therefore, is that the coming into being of an incipient colonial discourse of modern Chinese history yielded the possibility for a globally as well as nationally relevant revolutionary discourse to grow in China, yet it was in fact the "reformist" intellectuals, exemplified by Liang Qichao, who were more anti-imperialist, and it was the more "revolutionary" intellectuals who were relatively less so, albeit more anticolonial. This latter outcome was a consequence of the claimed historical equivalence between Manchu and Western colonial power. Another irony is that the recognition of imperialist historicism and colonialism as problems of global modernity in need of global solutions also led to a narrowed recentering of "Chinese-ness" around ethnicity, which allowed for "the people" to be specified *not* through either political consciousness or revolutionary activism but through an essentialized ethno-racial designation. This recentering, in fact, relieved Chinese revolutionaries of the responsibility for politically mobilizing "the people" because they could claim a naturalized anti-Manchuism as the basis for revolution.

Thus, from 1898 to 1903, at the same time as Chinese intellectuals discovered deterritorialized politics and the need to reinvent the *qun* through revolutionary activism, they also began to determine more particularly the relationship between a *minzu* (ethnos) and a *guomin* (national people). This issue was elaborated just as the Boer War, which erupted in late 1899 and lasted to 1903, provided them with a compelling opportunity to observe how an ethno-nation came to actualize itself in the contemporary world. Indeed, in the Boers' efforts to instantiate themselves as an ethno-nation in relation to the establishment and defense of the Transvaal against British efforts at domination, many Chinese intellectuals found a congenial model for how a "backward" people could lay claim to modernity and to ethnonationalism.

Guomin and Minzu as Historical Topoi

From 1895 to the turn of the twentieth century, the two concepts—*minzu* and *guomin*—were generally undifferentiated and were merged into an overall discussion of the *guojia* (state).[4] Yan Fu, the most systematic modern theorizer of the relationship between people and state in the immediate post-1895 period, posited in 1895 that the construction of proper democratic state structures was a prerequisite to the fostering of a loyal and patriotic people. In his proposals for state reform, Yan called for the inauguration of a national assembly that would "instill in the people loyalty and love";[5] he posited that the direction of reform needed to be from the state downward. Until after the 1898 reform movement, which itself was premised upon a state-centered view of change, this top-down version was the dominant way of understanding the problem of sociopolitical transformation.[6] However, with the crushing of the reforms, more radical understandings of state-people relations came to the fore; in these, "the people" emerged as a potentially important prior category of nation: prior, that is, to the state. It should be noted that this new emphasis on the priority of the people was no mere reiteration of *minben* (primacy of the people) derived from Mencius, for in *minben* doctrine the state-form was assumed (as the imperial state) while in the articulation at the turn of the century, it was precisely changes in the state and its relationship to the people in the new totality now called "nation" that was at issue.

It was Liang Qichao who began to alter systematically the terms through which the state-people problem was discussed, when, in 1899, he began to emphasize and deploy the term *guomin* in a sense that was not coterminous with either *guojia* (state) or *minzu* (ethnos). Indeed, *guomin* seems to have mediated for him the opening gap he was coming to perceive between any self-evident correlation between a *minzu* and the state. By the first years of the twentieth century, in Liang's emerging view, "nation"—also termed *guojia*—could be encompassed neither by the notion of a singular ethnos nor by the state alone; it was at this point that Liang came to posit, via the category of the *guomin*, a dynamic mutually constitutive relationship between *guojia* and "the people." Unlike Yan Fu, then, Liang recognized the need for an interdependent formative relationship between the state and the people in the very definition of a modern nation-state.

By 1903, the conceptual detachment of the people from the state in theoretical terms, combined with the observations of change in the world around them, had led to a broad acceptance by many Chinese intellectuals of a reversal of the process that had, up until 1898, been taken for granted as constituting the relationship between people and state: that is, a reversal of the previously accepted idea that the state (*guo*) exclusively defined "the people" (*min*) and that the modality of historical change should and did emanate from the former to the latter. Indeed, there was a recognition that the posited ideal *min* in the accustomed top-down formulation was a *shunmin*, an obedient people; yet it was precisely this ideal of obedience in the post-1898 period that was being conceptually transformed into the global figure of the slave (*nuli*). In its "slave" version—as *wangguo nu* (slave of a lost country)—the obediently passive people was the terror-filled portent of modern oblivion rather than an ideal fulfillment of statist strength.[7] As one essayist put it, "*guomin* should be taken as the opposite of 'slave.'"[8] It was in this process of reversing the ordering of these concepts in specifications of the direction of historical change (now that the state should be a reflection or expression of an active people rather than the passive people being obediently determined by the state) that the problem of the relationship of "the people" to the state was elaborated.

The initial raising of the conceptual problem of historical change did not mean that the relationship among *guomin*, *minzu*, and *guojia* was theoretically foreclosed, nor that one category was immediately privileged over the other, nor yet that any of the terms or the processes to which they pointed singly or in relation to one another were even well understood. Indeed, coming to an understanding of the relationship among them was a major topic of debate at the time. And the debate was joined with direct reference to the actualization of the abstract categories on the contemporary world stage, a stage upon which Africa was just then playing a starring role through the unlikely figures of the Boers.

Refiguring "Africa"

There was great optimism engendered by the discovery that "Africans" (as the Boers were designated) were engaged in the most modern of activities—revolution. This optimism, however, also provoked the familiar anxiety about the Chinese being left even further behind. Chen Tianhua expressed this anxiety in his celebrated 1903 pamphlet *A Bell to Warn the World* (*Jingshi zhong*):

> Are the Chinese people any less capable than are the people of the Transvaal? . . . [The Transvaal] is only as big as one prefecture of China, and its population is only as large as one district in China, [yet] it battled with the world's greatest power, England, for three years . . . This event happened before everyone's eyes, and is known to all . . . Now, how could such a small country go to war with such a large one? . . . [It is] because the people of the Transvaal have an unshakable spirit, and all of them are prepared to die on the battlefield, unwilling to become the slaves of others.[9]

The Boers thus revealed the modernity of Africa just as the Filipinos revealed the modernity of Asia, both convincingly demonstrating their abilities to *qun* (group; unite) and to struggle. Indeed, their activities, while indicating the optimistic potentials for China and the world, also reinforced anxious narratives of the present, through which China was also connected to the colonized world in an association of terror, threatened territorial partition, and racial extinction. These connections put into stark relief the difference between slaves and people: "The strange thing is that our Chinese people see England and Germany as emperors of the heavens and don't dare resist them. If our people properly emulated the events in Africa, who knows how strong England's and Germany's positions in their dependencies would remain. But our people don't know how to oppose; our Chinese people's strength is much below that of the black slaves. How ashamed I am for the Chinese people!"[10]

The "black slaves" figure is crucial here, as the fear and "shame" of comparing China to Africa was even more profound than that of comparing China to the Philippines, for Africa—geographically distant and historically unconnected to China in any discernible way—had been assumed since the mid-nineteenth century to be the last truly unhistorical space of the modern world, an unhistorical space peopled, moreover, entirely by "slaves." This view of Africa as irrelevant to the historical world—as a place of "slaves"—had emerged in China in large part from the geographical blackness and historical blankness of Africa as specified often through Euro-American missionary designations[11] of Africa as a "dark continent" and a benighted site for the "production of slaves," in Wei Yüan's succinct phrase.[12]

Wei and Xu Jiyu, both mid-century historical geographers and Qing officials whose works served as the starting point for knowledge of the world in nineteenth-century China, had drawn their unflattering pictures of Africa from a small reservoir of earlier Chinese accounts as reinterpreted through the organizing supplements of Euro-American racialist discourses. Since Chinese had few sustained or direct contacts with Africa until at least the 1880s (through increasing trade) and then particularly after 1903, when, in the wake of the Boer War, a wave of Chinese contract labor was drafted for gold mining in South Africa and their abusive treatment began to be publicized in the main journals of the day,[13] Africa impinged little on Chinese consciousness through the end of the nineteenth century, when other peoples, more directly aggressive in China, commanded rather more attention.[14] As such, while both Wei and Xu were aware that the Ming dynasty eunuch Zheng He had made his way in the fourteenth century to the east coast of what was now identified as Africa; yet, as both also knew, this contact had borne little historical significance for Chinese, as Africa never had entered into what Enrique Dussel calls a "planetary system."[15]

Thus marked by geographic disadvantages as well as by the lack of discernible sociopolitical structure (understood as a strong state), the dark invisibility of Africa and Africans was established at mid-century and the region was thence largely ignored until after the Sino-Japanese War of 1895 and the full-scale introduction of Social Darwinism. At this point, Africa—the continent and its people—reemerged, albeit only to be refixed at the bottom of the new global hierarchical order. As the blank spaces on Wei Yüan's and Xu Jiyu's mid-century maps of Africa came to be filled in, albeit with names pertaining to European countries, "black" and "white" (as well as "yellow") increasingly took on global historical meaning. This infusing of skin color with sociohistorical and geographical significance allowed for the construction of a set of equations that, while hardly remarkable for the time (replicating as they did white Euro-American equations), were nevertheless new in their significance for China: white (race) = Euro-America (historical space) = civilized (people) versus black (race) = Africa (unhistorical place) = uncivilized (slaves). With these equations firmly fixed from 1898 onward, the binaries of historical/unhistorical space and of people/slave became epistemologically structuring distinctions.

Yet, just as Africa was seemingly pushed to the far margins of historicity and world historical significance, it was also drawn conceptually closer to China, as the conjoining of discourses of "slavery" in its new colonized (*wangguo nu*) form with the benighted image of Africa in another of its primary late-century guises—as the site for European territorial partitioning—made the terror of "Africa" manifest as yet another mirror to China's potential modern fate. The maps of Africa, figuring as they did a specular absence of Africans and an overabundant presence of Europeans, when set alongside the maps of China that indicated territorial concessions to Europeans, thus made for a dramatic visual and visceral comparison,[16] in whose terror-filled cartographic prism Africa's "blackness" was overfilled with contemporary meaning. In this composite image "slavery" came to be seen as the result of "enslavement" (*nu*) and of "slavishness" (*nuli xing*), while partitioning (*guafen*) and the threat of colonization (*wang*) also were seen as the result of a people's basic lack of consciousness: that consciousness that now divided the civilized from the uncivilized; the historical from the unhistorical; a "people" from "slaves."[17] These distinctions were honed by Yan Fu as well as by Liang Qichao, each of whom wrote in separate treatments that the world stage of history—past and present—had no enduring place for "slaves," who were but potent specters haunting the world, reminding those not yet enslaved of their potential future.[18]

By the turn of the century, the "slave" trope—as *wangguo nu* (colonized slave), as *heinu* (black slave), or in other forms—had become both a metaphorical and literal expression for the historical depth to which any people could sink,[19] and Africa was firmly attached to this tropological figure. An educational ditty of the time summarized this starkly:

> Westerners are good at calculating,
> They use troops for partitioning,
> From which they arrive at enslaving.
> Others perish, others die;
> New methods of destruction are yet nigh.
>
> Now let's consider Africa,
> Peopled entirely by black slaves.
> Also ponder the two Americas
> Today merely Western-hegemonized enclaves.
> Native peoples there were not strong,
> And look! Now the red race is half gone.
> (Native people of the American continents are of the red race.)
>
> There is yet a country called Poland;
> Partitioned by three others with no end.

(Russia, Prussia, and Austria carved it up three times.)
And even such a place called Egypt,
Which, for lack of foreign currency, was gypped.
Their people became poorer by the day,
In the end, even for food there is no way.

And Annam there below Guangxi,
Now is France's dependency.
While today it yet has a sovereign,
Its people still greatly suffer under the foreign.

. . . .

Worst in the world are the Indian fools,
Who destroyed their country with their own tools.
Accepting money offered by foreign troops,
They put the same race idea [*tongzhong*] into a pot to cook;
Indians don't know how to protect their race,
So see how they've now been gnawed to death?[20]

Through the Boers, however, Africa was made visible in yet a different guise: through them, "Africa" seemed to be contesting its enslavement and its representation as "slavish," thereby making a full claim on modernity and historicity.

The Boers and History

Before general historical and modern significance could be generated out of the Boer War, the complex situation leading to the war first had to be unraveled. This entailed settling the historical narrative of the Boers and of what their conflict with Britain was about: state politics or ethnonationalism. Prior to the outbreak of war in October 1899, building tensions in the Transvaal region were generally understood as emanating from British/Dutch conflicts, in which the Boers were seen as Dutch proxies. Soon, however, the conflict came to be understood according to the British justification for their attack on the Transvaal: that is, that Uitlanders (citizens of other countries, primarily Britain, residing in the Transvaal) deserved the right to participate in Transvaal state politics, and that the Boers' refusal to allow Uitlander participation had forced the British to come to their aid through military means. In this (British) understanding, the Uitlanders and the Boers were construed as two politically defined peoples (*guomin*) inhabiting the same territory with equally legitimate claims on the Transvaal state. The question was thus not one of Boer sovereignty as an ethno-nation but of equal political representation in the Transvaal state.[21]

With the war's inception, this British-dominated justification was quickly discredited. As the *Yadong shibao* (East Asian Times) stated in November 1899, a month after the war began: "The Dutch in South Africa are called Boers. Boer means farmer. They cultivate land for a living and are frugal and simple people. The Boers have gone to war with England numerous times in order to shake off the shackles of English constraint. They often proclaim: 'Our people are courageous and have no enemies in this world.'"[22] The report went on to note that the farmer Boers, in the course of their short history, had been confronted not only with Britain's military might, but recently with the power of other European mine owners, an influx that had brought the episodic military confrontations to a new level: "The majority of the mine owners are wealthy English, German, and French businessmen . . . Their [respective] governments [originally] disallowed them from participating in [local] politics . . . The English government then established an African Company . . . to buy up all the mines in the territories . . . and then they [the British] complained that the Boers were discriminating against them."[23] In this view, the ostensible conflict over Uitlander participation in Transvaal politics was unmasked as a British bid for economic domination over the Transvaal and in competition with other European powers. Thus, by the end of 1899, the Uitlander demand for political participation was reinterpreted as a British bid for colonial power.

This interpretation further revealed that the British and the Boers were two different ethno-peoples; and that two such ethno-peoples living in one space were not equally justified in their pursuit of political representation. In other words, the Boers came to be designated not a *guomin*—as a statist concept—among other legitimate *guomin*, but a separate *minzu* historically attached to the Transvaal (the place, not the state), with an exclusively legitimate right to that place. By the same measure, the British and Uitlanders were understood as alien peoples and thus as political interlopers. The war thus turned out to be about the defense of Boer *minzu* sovereignty rather than the enforcement of political justice within the realm of the state, and the potential change from Boer control to Uitlander control of the machinery of state through Uitlander participation in politics came to be seen as a qualitative change—a potential *wangguo* (lost nation) situation—rather than simply a quantitative change in political representation (as the British had it).

The rapid shift in interpretation over the nature of the conflict—from one of Britain correctly defending the Uitlanders' right to political representation in the Transvaal state, to one of the Boers' defense of their ethnonational sovereignty—immediately led to a shift in views on the Transvaal president, Paul Kruger, who in early 1899 had been characterized dismissively as "nothing but a savage [*yeren*]."[24] By the end of 1899—in a shift that paralleled and echoed the re-viewing of Aguinaldo in the Philippines—Kruger was designated the heroic leader of a civilized "ethnos." This new designation yielded a new view of the whole situation. As Du Shizhen, an editorialist for the Shanghai-based *Xinshijie xuebao* (New World Scholarly Journal) and a classmate of Tang Tiaoding,[25] noted in 1902:

> Western biographies of Kruger, even though they admit that his commitment to independence is admirable, nevertheless just defame him . . . They call him a dictator, one who could only act by using weapons [i.e., not a diplomat], one who had no education and was ignorant. I sincerely doubt their words and believe them to be exaggerated excess . . . For is it not in the English character to always praise themselves while disparaging others? To always confuse truth with falsehood?[26]

In a wider sense, then, these shifts led to an alteration in historical understanding. With the placement of Kruger and the Boers in the modern context of anticolonial revolution and imperialist historicism, both appeared to Du (and many others) not only as civilized, nor even only as modern, but also as universally and historically significant for the current age in which China was embedded.

Chinese were not alone in their assessments of the Boers' significance; indeed, a century ago the Boers were widely acknowledged as the repressed conscience of British imperialism and as those who would begin to bring the newly-consolidated British imperial system as well as the History written in its name to its knees. For, although most contemporaneous observers considered Paul Kruger, president of the Transvaal from 1883 to 1900, an extreme example of closed-mindedness, narrow religiosity, and crudeness,[27] he and the people he led nevertheless were often seen as righteously crusading warriors defending themselves against British economic and military might.[28] To J. A. Hobson, the most famous British dissenter from the war, which he scathingly criticized in his dispatches to the

Manchester Guardian as precipitated by the discovery of gold in the Pretoria region in 1886, the conflict was an unmitigated economic, moral, and political disaster for Britain. While Hobson was no admirer of Kruger, the man, he nevertheless, in *Imperialism: A Study* (1902), synthesized his views as they had been crystallized through his critique of the Transvaal war to write despairingly of the deleterious consequences of Britain's post-1870s "new imperialism."[29] Indeed, Hobson's critique of this "new imperialism" was in large part responsible for altering the very concept of imperialism, hitherto considered a healthy sign of strength and as a mode of intra-European rivalry, in the direction with which we are most familiar today: as European action against and in the third world.

The pro-Boers, an oppositonal movement emanating primarily from the Irish and Scottish portions of the British Empire, were also concerned with how political grievances within the Transvaal were used by Britain to further the interests of exploitative mine owners. By contrast to Hobson's critique, pro-Boer opposition was mounted not in the name of preserving a smooth liberal capitalist order at home, but rather as a critique of the expansion of "capitalism, the bloodless soulless rule of Companies" into the communities of the Boers—"simple in their lives, loving their land, their cattle, their homes."[30] Resonating with critiques of the practices of British colonial power in Ireland and Scotland, and specifically, with critiques of the enclosure movements that had destroyed Scottish and Irish farmers a century earlier, the Pro-Boers saw in the Boers figures of their own past and future.

At the same time, in tsarist Russia the *Bulletin of World History (Vestnik Vsemirnoi Istorii)* also proclaimed that "in the history of the spread of British supremacy in the world, this is perhaps the first time the victim, which has already been earmarked by the British lion, deafens the voice of reason and hastens to accept the challenge."[31] Like the Pro-Boers, Russians condenmed the war not simply because it signified a debasing of British moral authority but because Russians also identified with the Boers as rural victims of the global forces of capitalist restructuring,[32] forces that the tsarist government was hardly heeding.[33]

Similarly, the focus in many Chinese commentaries on the Boers, after the interpretive lines of the conflict had been settled, was initially on the Boer claim on History. This latter point was made in a mid-1902 essay in the reformist *Waijiao bao* [Foreign Affairs Journal],[34] which noted: "England is by far the strongest power in Europe . . . but the Transvaal, in the mean and rustic region of Africa, has been able to struggle and to fight with them for several years now . . . Only after a long time has it been possible to determine victory and defeat."[35] For the *Waijiao bao* author, however, the significance of the Boers did not reside in the survival or perishing of the Transvaal state but in how this survival or loss would reverberate in the world:

> If England were to vanquish the Transvaal, then in Western history books it would be recorded that in such and such a year . . . the English utterly defeated South Africa and that the latter would never rise again. [However] if England were defeated, then the Transvaal would gain independence and England's overseas dependencies in Africa . . . would subsequently become restive . . . I am certain that England's dependencies around the world will undergo big transformations in the twentieth century, and one of the origins of this can be located in . . . Africa.[36]

For the *Waijiao bao* author, then, the consequences of England's victory resided in European discursive claims to superiority as encoded in Western history books; yet, the fact that these claims were limited to Western texts reflected not universality but the parochialism of the claims. By contrast, the consequences of a potential Boer victory resided in the stirring of unrest in other colonies, that is, in the transcendence of the present by colonial peoples that would belie the parochial claims to superiority of the Europeans. In this sense, Britain spoke to Westerners while the Transvaal spoke to the world.

For Du Shizhen, Kruger's and the Transvaal's universal modernity was evidenced in their supposed resistance to statism, the most advanced form of *minzu* consciousness yet available. As Du noted: "Since the eighteenth century, every country in Europe has experienced ethno-nationalism (*minzu zhuyi*), which has spread like fire, like a stream, like wind, like electricity, wildly covering more places than any expansion of the past several centuries." With nationalism came ethno-national-imperialism (*minzu diguo zhuyi*), which, through its seizure of colonies, "provided the measure of an ethno-nation's rise or decline." Yet, according to Du, Kruger had gone beyond even this phase, and had "assisted in the advancement of civilization in the modern world."[37] Kruger's claim to "civilization" and history was thus based upon what Du understood to be the Boer desire to "organize an independent civilization," the overriding feature of which was an effort to "establish a nation with no government [*wuzhengfu zhi guo*]." This achievement, Du noted, would be "so glorious as to make the Boers unique in history. It would make them a completely unique *minzu* in the world."[38]

In Du's conception, the constitution and actualization of a *minzu* could be premised not upon the unifying structures of the state, but rather on a unified community of individuals without any necessary form. Accordingly, in Du's history of the Transvaal Republic, the state became a problem for the Boers because, "although the desire [for this new stateless civilization] was great, the reality of it was hard to attain." This was because of the need to defend against British designs, a necessity that had pushed the Boers into forming a "republican polity," which Du considered a "regression" and a major "tragedy of the modern world."[39] Indeed, it was the British-induced establishment of a state form for the Transvaal that was now being contested by the Boers. Kruger's brilliance, according to Du, was to triumph over the internal conflicts generated by statism by turning the whole logic of the nation not toward internal rule (the elaboration of statist forms and institutions) but toward the goal of expelling foreigners (*paiwai*). Thus, while Du saw the state and territoriality as alien impositions on the essence of the *minzu*, and while he also recognized that the state could be used for the purposes of protecting the *minzu* against foreigners, he nevertheless saw the state as the primary reason for the eventual disunification of the *minzu* and for historical regression. In Du's assessment, then, Kruger's success as well as his failure stood at the convergence of these elements: having seized the reins of the state in order to protect the Boer *minzu*, he lost the Transvaal to the British: "Even though outwardly the small and weak Transvaal won a [moral] victory, in reality, they were defeated."[40]

In his rejection of the state, and in his reification of the *minzu* as its own historical justification, Du perhaps took these issues further than most at the time.[41] Indeed, his tautological valorization of the *minzu* marks an extreme version of the grounding of the nation entirely in a mythically conceived ethnos. Nevertheless, his rescue of Kruger and the Boers as local forms of knowledge about the formation and defense of a *minzu* disconnected to a state did succeed in establishing a mutuality between the particularity of Kruger and the universal historical significance that could be derived from his failed endeavor. On the one hand, this mutuality was part of a broader reassessment of the very ideological markers of universality and historicity—previously signaled by the existence of a state and of textual civilization—that had been inherited from Chinese tradition and that were now being imposed in new modernizationist form by Western imperialist practices and ideologies. On the other hand, it also led to a type of understanding of imperialist historicism similar to that gained through the Philippine revolution.

The Boers, Modern Civilization, and Militarism

Because the Boers were initially known as uneducated farmers who resided in the "unhistorical" space of Africa, their claim on civilization could not be substantiated through a version of civilization that took technological, textual, or economic advancement as primary markers.[42] Admiration for the Boers thus had to be constructed out of different materials than was admiration for the Filipinos, whose claims to modern civilization were credible in part because they were based on terms familiar from both Euro-American and classical literary Chinese criteria: that is, upon the culturally valorized repeatable signs of "the workings of the mind" in textual form.[43] The inclusion into a notion of modern civilization of the Boers, who emerged onto the world stage for Chinese intellectuals through essentially the same process as the Filipinos[44]—that is, through their pursuit of an improbable struggle against a major world power at precisely a time when Chinese relations with those very same powers had hit their nadir—was based entirely upon evidence of a nation-building process that relied upon the "spirit" of a *minzu* ready to resist "slavery" at all costs through non-state-centered social militarization. Indeed, explanations for the formation of the Boer ethnos had little to do with their self-constitution vis-à-vis the African populations they had displaced or slaughtered: among the dozens of essays on the Boers, few mention prior "native peoples,"[45] and the few that do merely figure these peoples as part of a landscape that is quickly repressed.[46] Instead, the dominant explanation began from the premise that the Boers had earlier emerged racially through the mixing of several European types, and that politically and socially they had constituted themselves in opposition to the expansionism of the British. This narrative of becoming most emphasized what were seen as the characteristics that formed the bases for Boer claims on modernity: their singular *minzu* essence and their social militarism.

At the beginning of the war, the military aspects of the battles drew attention, in China and Japan, because of the startling reversals suffered by the British army in the first six months. These reversals prompted the Meiji

Japanese state, interested in British military strategy, to send observers to South Africa,[47] where they attributed British difficulties not so much to Boer prowess—as was later seen to be the case—as to the British use of troops raised from their colonies,[48] or to the ignorance of the British commanders about the conditions in which they were fighting.[49] It was soon recognized, however, that British difficulty, whatever its military provenance, was compounded by the militarized structure of Boer society. As one commentator wrote:

> The standing army of the Transvaal is five hundred troops . . . This corps has received German and Dutch training and their technique is refined. They are stationed in Pretoria and Johannesburg . . . Aside from this regular army, everyone in the country is a soldier. All males from the age of ten [*sic;* actually sixteen] and over have the duty to serve as soldiers. Each Boer must own a horse and a gun; once an order is given, they must mount their horses and pack tins of dried meat in the sidebag . . . Most troops act without hierarchical commands . . . so the columns are quite disorderly and the uniforms are not standard. But their shooting and accuracy are astounding . . . The Boer military strategy is primitive [*yeman*] and follows no logic [*wu yiding zhi guilu ye*].[50]

In addition to this social structure, which made it possible for every individual Boer to resist every British soldier, the Boers' supposed imposing physiques also impressed both Chinese and Japanese commentators. The characterization provided in 1900 by the Japanese journalist Fukumoto Nichinan,[51] who contributed much to Chinese views of the Boers, was particularly breathless in this regard:

> The mixture of one or two peoples [*minzu*] yields a new national people [*guomin*] when they suddenly leap out onto the world stage. Even though in ancient times there was no shortage of this type of phenomenon, in the past few millennia, it is unprecedented. If it has occurred, it is only with the Boers in today's South Africa . . . Customs, mores, tastes, language, religion have all combined into one people-type [*renzhong*] and this ethnos [*minzu*] is very unique: [they combine] Dutch determination and stubbornness with French heroism and zeal . . . [It is said that] Boers are six feet tall and have steely physiques . . . Ah! With character and bodies like that, if one were to add good education and trained intellects . . . who in this world would be able to challenge them?[52]

Soon, then, for Chinese, it would be primarily the militarization of Boer social structure that was most intriguing, especially when this imagined social structure was combined in the imagination with the outsized figure of Kruger as the epitome of a warrior and with the Boers as a unified, physically imposing *minzu*. Many came to see this combination of factors not only as the key to the Boer ability to resist the English, but as one important—if not *the* most important—component of a modern *minzu*.

In this context, the difficulties faced both by the Americans in the Philippines and by the British in the Transvaal not only alerted the Americans, British, and Japanese to the fact that warfare in the colonies was not exclusively about superior firepower; it also helped make Chinese aware that combatting incursion by a superior power was possible if the *minzu*, as self-conscious individuals and as a consciously formed collective, were willing and able to defend themselves. For at least one observer, Sun Zhongshan, this was the most striking lesson of the Boer War,[53] and from 1900 onward, Sun repeatedly invoked the Boers in his speeches and pronouncements as exemplary people-warriors, a model modern *minzu*, from whose example of social militarization the Chinese could learn. As Sun wrote in the 1903 essay that marked his "modest debut as a pundit for the [Chinese] student world in Japan,"[54] the character of the Boer resistance provided "evidence" that, should the Chinese learn from them, then "on the day of division [of China by the Western powers], more than half the Chinese could be mobilized and the Powers would not know another day of calm."[55]

Far from being taken as a condemnation of the Boers as uncivilized or regressively primitive, then, the image of a whole social structure consisting of fiercely loyal, quasi-mythical marksmen, savage in their practice and willing to die not for their state but for their *minzu*, and led by a crusading warrior (Kruger), resonated powerfully in Chinese circles. Indeed, this image of the Boers combined well with and reinforced the revival of interest at the time in knight-errant figures (a stock character in many Japanese and Chinese popular stories, dramas, operas, and histories).[56] These figures were increasingly being mobilized into current political contexts, while also being conjoined to a burgeoning Chinese fascination with the Japanese "men of will" (J: *shishi*) of the Tokugawa-Meiji transition period—those whom Liang Qichao in 1897 called *dongxia*, or Eastern knights.[57] The imaginary combination of the militaristic Boers, the knights-errant, and the *dongxia* as modern "men of will" mutually redefined one another. In this redefinition, the knight-errant was reconfigured from its literary form, where it appeared as an individual quality, and reappeared as a potentially new national social type.

This reconfiguration is evident in a comparison of how the knight-errant figure appears in an 1897 essay by Mai Menghua, an associate of Liang Qichao's, with its transposed reappearance in another essay by Mai in 1900. In the earlier essay, Mai praised the abstract virtues of the knight-errant by emphasizing the individual heroic qualities of this most extraordinary type;[58] by 1900, Mai's conceptualization of the knight-errant was explicitly linked to and informed by the Filipinos and the Boers. Indeed, in the later essay, Mai urgently called upon the Chinese people as a collective to recognize that the globally valorized *xia* type was exemplified by peoples "who rise" like the Filipinos and Boers, and not by "those who fail," like the Indians and potentially the Chinese. The reason for this global valorization, he stated, "is that modern nations recognize that the *xia* spirit of the people (*minzu*) is essential to the nation."[59] Here, then, when read through the Japanese men of will,[60] and thence through the Filipino and Boer warrior figures, *xia* became a compelling modern national type rather than merely a heroic individual.[61]

Many essays of the time thus prominently featured the Filipinos and Boers in an effort to emphasize the necessity of popularizing *wu* (militarism) along with *xia* as social and national virtues,[62] a new emphasis that underpinned the growing interest among Chinese intellectuals after 1901 in militarism as a positive rather than a negative necessity for a modern people.[63] It is unsurprising, therefore, that the interest in the Boers, *xia*, and men of will coincided with and contributed to conceptualizations of the "military citizens education" (*junguomin jiaoyu*) movement among Chinese students in Japan, a movement that began, as historian Sang Bing has shown, with the 1903 formation of the Society for the Education of a Militant Citizenry (*Junguomin jiaoyu hui*), which had emerged from the prior Anti-Russian Volunteer Corps (*Ju E yiyong jun*), itself organized to pressure the Qing into confronting Russia's move into Manchuria.[64] It is worth noting in this regard (although Sang Bing does not) that from 1901 onward virtually all of the essays on militarism and on the proposed military citizens education movement prominently refer to the Boers as a contemporary example of precisely the type of militarized *minzu* that China should emulate and mobilize. Moreover, a large number of the direct and indirect participants in the various movements—Tang Tiaoding, Wang Xiaonong, Chen Qubing, and so on—were also heavily involved in producing Chinese meaning out of the Philippine and Transvaal events.

Following the collapse of both the Boer/Filipino revolutions in 1902–3 and the military education movement in its organizational form after 1903,[65] there was a turn by many participants toward anti-Manchu activism and the rewriting of modern Chinese history under the colonial ethnonationalist sign. These developments were rhetorically animated and historically located primarily through the idea that the Manchus—as a *zhong* (race) and as a *minzu*—were alien "others." When added to the supposed demonstrable benefits of *minzu* cohesion through the Boers, this new understanding of the Chinese historical situation began to turn to a reification of the ethnos as the exclusive basis for the nation.

Ethno-nationalism and Anticolonialism

The reification of the ethnos in the Chinese case was particularly instantiated through the last of the Boer War's interpretive guises, which held that the war was a manifestation of the natural right and historical obligation of a *minzu* to actualize itself in the world.[66] As we can recall, the Uitlanders were now seen as agents of the British state as well as of the capitalist restructurings of the Transvaal that were stripping the Boers of their *minzu* sovereignty. This interpretation was fully elaborated in early 1900 analyses that attributed the war's outbreak to the pursuit of the Transvaal people's autonomy rather than to political arrangements internal to the Transvaal state. As one commentator cogently remarked: "The problem of sovereignty is the foundation of the conflict . . . ; electoral rights are merely a symptom."[67] In this guise, the Boers spoke to the proposition that "nation" was no mere problem of state arrangements but rather a problem of a prior *minzu* formation, where "sovereignty" lay in the *minzu* and not in the state.

A series of essays in early 1900 by Fukumoto Nichinan, essays later collected into a book published in China in two different translations in 1902 and 1903,[68] clarified this issue. Fukumoto presented the war as an antimodernist affirmation of a fast-disappearing agrarianism threatened by industrial-capitalist destruction, and he asserted that "the origins of the war can be identified as residing in a struggle between . . . peasant-shepherds and merchant-workers."[69] Informing Fukumoto's perspective was his attitude toward Japan's late Meiji situation, where the disruptive and socially disorganizing effects of industrial capitalism were already quite manifest, not least in his own birthplace, Fukuoka.[70] The dissolution of village life had led Fukumoto to recuperate a Japanese "national essence" (J: *kokusui*; C: *guocui*) from a position that asserted the uniqueness of Japan's *minzoku* (C: *minzu*; ethnos).[71] For Fukumoto, then, the Transvaal war echoed and confirmed the lamented trend toward the disappearance of agrarian life in the face of capitalism, and the consequent erasure of the *minzu*, as an ethnos and a way of life, from its putatively proper sociopolitical position of centrality.[72]

Like Fukumoto, many Chinese commentators also saw in the Boers a historical confirmation of the possibilities of a *minzu* actualizing itself on the world stage. But the Boer struggle reverberated for Chinese differently from the way it did for Fukumoto, as antimodernist tendencies rooted in rural communities were not major concerns for most Chinese intellectuals at this point, apart from some anarchists.[73] (To be sure, Sun Zhongshan did take seriously the plight of the peasants as part of his overall plans for reconstructing the Chinese nation; yet, Sun's early program for *minsheng*, or people's livelihood, was less antimodernist than it was designed to facilitate socioeconomic modernization.)[74] Chen Zhixiang, the Chinese translator of Fukumoto's *A History of the Establishment of a New Nation in South Africa* (*Nan A xinjianguo shi*), did not even allude in his prefatory remarks to Fukumoto's antimodernist anxieties, nor did he betray any misgivings about modernization in his summation of the lessons to be derived from Fukumoto's book. As Chen explained Fukumoto's main point: "Any *minzu*, big or small, that has a sense of shame can be strong," and this "sense of shame" is demonstrated by a *minzu*'s unwillingness to be "slaves," an unwillingness exemplified by the Boers who, when threatened, took on the British—the "strongest empire in the world"—even though they were aware that to fight would mean almost certain death.[75] Chen concluded that national spirit (*guoqi*) was synonymous with a warrior spirit (*shiqi*), and if the latter were strong, then the *minzu* would flourish; if it were weak, the *minzu* would perish.[76]

Thus, what Chinese interpreters took from Fukumoto's account was not his defense of rural life, and even less his perspective that a *minzu*'s essence was located in an ideal and natural rural community. Rather, they formed the conviction that the mode of laying an historical claim to modernity was through the realization of the *minzu*, a particular historical endeavor. Indeed, annotations to an essay entitled "Brief Biography of Kruger, Hero of South African Independence," translated from the Japanese and published in the *Youxue yibian* (Overseas Students Translation Magazine),[77] directly confront more statist approaches to the problem of nation-formation. The essay's translator/annotator begins with an attack on Liang Qichao (who remains unnamed) and on the course of elite-led reform; he particularly condemns Liang's *Ziyou shu* (Book of Freedom) for its transformation of Rousseau's emphasis on popular sovereignty and general will into a conviction on the necessity of asserting state interests over and against society.[78] The annotator then reviles Liang for his former willingness to "shed hot blood" and his current retreat into "empty chatter" or "pedantry." Chattering pedantry, the annotator asserts, could never give rise to the kind of heroism needed in today's world, for,

> while heroes and courageous people [*yingxiong yu haojie*] can benefit from learning and it can augment their heroic or courageous methods, if a person is not born a hero or a courageous person, then no matter how abundant his new ideas, no matter how many books he has read, he can be considered nothing more than having been born in a modern era [*wenming shidai*].

As he further explains, when the era is a modern one, "all people are heroes and courageous men"; yet, when the era is not a modern one, individual heroes have a particular sociohistorical role to play. Most important to his analysis, "in the places they [heroes] are produced, the state [*guo*] need not be a modern civilized one, the people need not be wise and educated . . . [Heroes] do not flow naturally from wisdom and education."[79] On this view, a heroic age is an "age of transition" (*guodu shidai*) located at the intersection between barbarism (*yeman shidai*) and modernity (*wenming shidai*).

Thus using Liang and reformism as his foil, the annotator disparages attempts to unify China—either internally or with the global system—under a statist sign, since for him the globally differentiated "age of transition" indicated a differential historical time for colonized peoples. Kruger was meaningful, then, because of his very situatedness in a particular time within the universal albeit uneven space of modernity, where lack of education and lack of textual civilization were, rather than barriers to progress, the preconditions to it. Kruger, in fact, illumined that age and those conditions as no other "hero" hitherto had. And, as the annotator noted, the same conditions as Kruger's and Africa's were abundantly present in East

Asia, where, if the "many primitive countries" wished to progress, they needed to dispense with such people as Liang Qichao and embrace men of action.[80]

By way of conclusion, the annotator further noted that seeking ships and technology as a measure of modernity was "superficial," for it was "patriotism" (*aiguo xin*)—not a statist but a *minzu* category—and "strength of unity" that were of primary import at the current juncture. Ending with an inevitable comparison between the Boers and the Indians, who were "slaves" and already a "people of a lost country" (*wangguo zhi min*), and thus with the inevitable question—"Do we [Chinese] really want to wait around to become another India?"—the annotator urged Chinese to stop seeking the outward signs of modernization, to stop chattering, and to concentrate instead on *minzu* formation, heroism, and struggle.[81]

At first glance, what is perhaps most curious about this formulation, implying as it did the Chinese people's passivity as compared to the Boers' activity, is that it emerged just after the Boxer Rebellion had raged across northern China and in the midst of ongoing local and regional peasant resistances to the restructuring of their world by semicolonial capitalism.[82] As mentioned previously, Chinese intellectuals, with rare exception, excoriated the Boxers and condemned the participants for being "slaves," in large part due to their alliance with the Qing state (itself coming to be labeled a "slave" or "puppet" (*kueilei*) of foreign countries)[83] and to the perceived superstitious qualities of Boxer beliefs. Chinese intellectuals were similarly not very sympathetic to peasant uprisings in general. What explains the apparent illogic, then, is the perceived difference between the Boers as a singularly unified *minzu* in comparison to the putatively Manchu-controlled Boxers and/or the supposedly atavistic, non-national-minded peasants in the localities. That is, the Boxers were condemned for failing to recognize the "otherness" of the Manchus, and thus their own *minzu* essence (as Han Chinese); as such, even though the Boxers certainly gave evidence of struggle, theirs was not a modern *minzu* struggle at all. Peasant activists, by the same token, were condemned for their conservative, unmodern, and essentially limited imaginations.

To be sure, the unitary singularity of the Boers was an illusion, and this illusion certainly clouded Chinese views of the Transvaal and the Boer War. More important, however, the emphasis on the *minzu* that was derived from these views quickly turned, on the one hand, into a reification of the nation in terms of a primordial *minzu*, and, on the other, to an ongoing condemnation of the Chinese people in general. In 1904 this dual orientation was reflected in an essay entitled "On Ethno-Nationalism" (*Lun minzu zhuyi*), wherein the editorialist differentiated between two types of nationalism in the modern period: one unified the same race and same people (*tongzhong, tongzu*) and was carried out through the consolidation of states as exemplified in Italy, Germany, Belgium, and Hungary; the other was an attempt to free one's people from another people, as exemplified in Poland, Finland, Ireland, the Transvaal, and the Philippines. The former type had been successful; the latter, as contemporary events demonstrated, had been singularly unsuccessful. Relating this to China's situation, the editorialist lamented that, historically, China had adequately developed a "same race/same people" (*tongzhong*) consciousness and a state to go with it, but had woefully neglected the other form of modern nationalism, that is, the formation of a strong *minzu* consciousness that led to "expelling foreigners" (*paiwai*). Ignoring the historically constitutive relationship between the one type and the other, the editorialist concluded that the *paiwai* form of activity was the most crucial element of contemporary nationalism, and thus was the one that needed to be fostered in China.[84]

As we shall see in chapter 7 below, within a few years (by 1910), the two concepts *tongzhong* and *minzu*—the racial and the ethnic notions—were made into synonyms through a sleight of hand: they were firmly imputed to the Han Chinese as a people-race, and in that form were made *predictive*—rather than productive—of the Chinese nation-state. This sleight of hand allowed for the continued rhetorical appeal to the *minzu* as the basis of the nation, and the absolute displacement of "the people" from the actualization of the nation-state.

For the moment, and by way of summarizing the emergence at this point of a *minzu zhuyi* orientation linked to its global moment, Sun Zhongshan's naturalization of the relationship between *minzu* and nationhood in 1906 points to how these unstable conceptualizations very soon came to be taken as the premise for the Revolutionary Alliance's project:

> Ethno-nationalism [*minzu zhuyi*] does not mean hostility to other states [*guojia*], but the prevention of other states' seizing the sovereignty of our *minzu*. We Han people cannot claim that we have a nation [*guo*], because we have long since lost our sovereignty [to the Manchus] . . . We are a people of a perished nation [*wangguo zhi min*]! . . . [Yet] an ethno-nation [*minzu*] called the Transvaal in South Africa consisting of only

> 200,000 people engaged the British for three years before succumbing . . . Han people, shall we take our subjugation lying down?[85]

Here, then, the *minzu*/nation conflation is completed by being firmly hitched to the colonial narrative of modern China figured in terms of the Manchus as colonizer. That is, Sun fully equates the Manchus with modern-day Western colonizers and thereby inscribes them as originary colonizers of the Chinese people, no less so than the Westerners observed to be "enslaving" everyone from the blacks to the Indians, Filipinos, Vietnamese, and Egyptians. The "facticity" of this historical narrative yielded the conviction that the only way out of this colonization was an ethno-national revolution against the Manchus, an undertaking that was thus fully convergent with the anticolonial revolutionary tenor of the times.

Statist-nationalism and Anti-imperialism

This very same set of events and issues also gave rise to a very different set of conclusions. Indeed, others concluded that, because of the *failure* of the Boer and Filipino struggles, what China needed was not an ethno-national revolution, but rather the development of an active *guomin* in conjunction with and indeed under the thumb of a strong state. Liang Qichao, as the primary proponent of this version of nationalism, thus came to precisely the opposite conclusion from Du Shizhen and other *minzu zhuyi* nationalists in his observations of the Transvaal. While Du concluded that the state was a major problem for the Boers and the Transvaal—and thus that the state was a historical obstacle to *minzu* progress—and while other *minzu zhuyi* nationalists concluded that state-led reform was at best a chimera and at worst a further "enslavement," Liang concluded that the Boer failure was actually attributable to their lack of a strong state, and thus, that the state was the most important protector of a people or a nation.

As we have seen, statism was a position that Liang came to gradually after the 1898 reform movement, and his observations of events in the rest of the world after 1902 powerfully informed this gathering tendency, just as during the 1898–1901 period precisely those same events had led him initially to question the centrality of the state. Liang's lengthy essay of mid-1901, "On the New Rules for Destroying Countries" (*Mieguo xinfa lun*), marks a watershed in this regard. Among other things, in this essay Liang stressed that the presence in South Africa of the European mine owners formed part of a pattern of "destruction"—understood as economic infiltration into native structures—visited upon non-Euro-American peoples and countries by Euro-America. Placing the Boer War alongside Poland, India, the Philippines, and Egypt (his other examples of the "new rules for destroying countries"), and comparing them all to China's contemporary situation, Liang fully explicated the pattern of destruction with relation to the problems of state sovereignty, private property, and national territoriality through his reading of Transvaal history.

Liang began the Transvaal portion of the essay by noting that the Boers "are a strong people [*minzu*], and today they are fighting a war with the British. For the past century, they have repeatedly been compelled by the English to move inland." He continued with a brief narrative of the establishment of the Transvaal and the Orange Free State—two loosely organized "republics" founded upon cooperative family agriculture, herding, and hunting (not upon a self-evident *minzu* identity, but upon a state plus a style of life). As Liang wrote, the Boers were "leading a carefree, calm, and quiet life" (the battles the Boers waged against native peoples are ignored), until Europeans discovered gold and began systematically accumulating wealth and territory. "Within twelve years [from the discovery of gold in 1886] . . . they created companies, [and snatched profits], and a formerly deserted area suddenly became a densely populated city: Johannesburg," the city of gold. Liang proceeded to catalog the various British attempts to undermine from within the indifferently organized state structures of the Transvaal and Orange Free State, efforts that included repeated attempts to stack the parliament with British company men, as well as British state support for the mine owners' demands for increased administrative control over economic policy in the region. "The British changed their previous plans to swallow the country by military means into a strategy of invading it with wealth," wrote Liang, even while the Jameson Raid of 1895 pushed the confrontation into "barbaric violence." The issue of Boer political autonomy broke out anew in 1899 over another Uitlander appeal for British support: "The British government, relying on its big-power status, used strong-arm methods" to enforce this appeal, Liang commented, although "this had little immediate impact." And yet, as Liang noted, "it did bring up the question of state sovereignty; [because such participation] would have rendered the Transvaal into a de facto British protectorate."[86]

The first and most obvious lesson Liang drew from this account was that it fit into a pattern of *fa*—rules, methods, ways, means—that Euro-

Americans used to destroy other peoples in the world; it was thus one of many modes of imperialist conquering.[87] This mode Liang then compared to the recently signed Boxer Protocol, and he cautioned: "To those who claim that opening mining, railroad, and concessionary rights to foreigners is not harmful to the sovereignty of the whole, I advise you to read the history of the Boer War."[88]

More broadly, however, Liang's articulation of the lessons of the Transvaal represents quite a different interpretative appropriation of the war for China than seen above. That is, for Liang the war was clearly an imperialist effort, understood in terms of territory, property, and state sovereignty, whereas for the *minzu zhuyi* nationalists, the war represented a colonial effort to enslave a *minzu*'s essence. Thus Liang, rather than narrate the war as the substantiation of the Boer *minzu*, emphasized that the increasing strength of foreigners within the economy was eroding the autonomy of the state. For Liang, then, it was state autonomy—and the state as bearer of sovereignty—rather than *minzu* autonomy—and the *minzu* as bearer of sovereignty—that was of primary importance. Transposing this observation to China, Liang noted that the erosion of economic and political sovereignty was also occurring there, all the while undercutting the ability of the Chinese people to protest this erosion effectively. He queried: "Are not Shanghai, Hankou, and other [treaty ports] called concessions (*zujie*)? What are concessions but colonies (*zhimindi*)? If the whole country [under the proposed Open Door policy] becomes a free trade zone, then is that not equivalent to making the whole country a colony?" In Liang's view—where, in contrast to what we saw in Liang's work on Hawaii, colonization was now understood primarily as a form of economic and political imperialism rather than as a form of ethnic control—the effectiveness of this "invisible" method of colonization would be most manifest if a people thus indirectly colonized protested their treatment. That is, as he observed, when people protest harmful actions perpetrated directly by foreigners, they are widely praised as patriots; by contrast, when the government is essentially a puppet of foreign powers, if people are aggrieved by foreigners indirectly through their own government and take up arms to protest, they are labeled anti-government insurrectionists and traitors.[89] The corollary to this dilemma for Liang was that China's major problem—as with the Transvaal—was overcoming "nibbling" Western incursions on autonomy and state sovereignty by overcoming state weakness and state puppetry.

In short, Liang's view of the constitution of the Chinese nation in the contemporary global situation rested upon a dimly perceived albeit passionately felt suspicion about the capitalist world-economy, whose hierarchically organized political forms and methods of capital accumulation established inherently uneven relations of unequal exchange and domination at the global level. The particular historical form that these uneven relations of unequal exchange took—in the Transvaal as in China—necessitated for him a rearticulation of the state form that could take on global unevenness at what Liang considered to be its ultimate source: the political state's hegemony over the polity and the economy.[90] This concern soon evolved for Liang into a theory of nationalism that took the strengthening and protection of the state as the key to the production and survival of the nation.

Through this state-centered theory of nation, of which Liang was China's most eloquent and tireless exponent after 1903, Liang not only repudiated some of his previous more radical tendencies that focused on a bottom-up movement of nationalism; he also substantially rethought the theoretical relationship between state and society. Indeed, Liang's previous philosophical and practical analyses of the proposed new relationship between the *guomin* (people; citizenry) and *guojia* (nation-state)—through which he had come to the conviction that a *guomin* and a *minzu* were not one and the same thing—were now turned into an unambiguously statist philosophy. And while, throughout this period and to the end of his life, Liang resisted the temptation to displace anxieties over the construction of a social totality ("the nation") onto *minzu* antagonism—which is what the *minzu zhuyi* nationalists were to do—Liang did encapsulate his idea of historical dynamism (*dong*) in his concept of *guomin*, or, what he was calling by 1902 the *xinmin* (new citizens). This led, by 1903, to a growing "overriding concern with the rationalization of the state,"[91] which led him to make a sharp distinction between *minzu* and *guomin*, with the state becoming not only the mediator—or interpreter—of those two terms, but their very means of actualization in the world. Indeed, it was at this point that Liang determined that the state—not the people—was the bearer of national sovereignty, and that *minzu* was but one of several factors composing the *guomin* (citizenry) in a "nation-state" formation. This reformulation increasingly led Liang to emphasize the destructiveness of revolution and popular struggle (as Xiaobing Tang has explored), and to posit the need in China, not for *minzu* conflict, but for the building of an autonomous, stable, and temporarily absolute state,[92] where the people were to be taught to uphold the state as a precondition to their participation in the nation.

In the terms I have been using, then, Liang, having been the original architect of the framework for a colonial narrative of modern Chinese history—through his rearticulation of the problem of *wangguo*, for example—soon rejected the consequences of one version of this narrative—its colonial form—as they were taken up by ethno-nationalists. That is, Liang did not go along with the Manchu-as-colonizer mode of analysis that emanated from this colonial narrative; instead, he became a major proponent and promoter of *guojia zhuyi* nationalism, or statist nationalism, one major internal goal of which was to define "the people" in terms of the category of "citizen" by dependently articulating both to the political state. The major external goal of this statism, then, was not to conceive the nationalist project as an idealist *minzu* or anticolonial one, but rather to conceive it as "primarily an effort to meet the challenges of foreign [that is, Euro-American] imperialism."[93] Thus the resolution to the contradiction Liang came to see between a Rousseauian internal equalization of rights and the need for a state that could project strength outward increasingly yielded a philosophical position that subordinated the interests of society to the interests of the state.[94] It is in the context of Liang's working out of his statism that the "rules" essay, the Transvaal, and the other examples of peoples subjected to destruction are situated.

In sum, the view of modern world dynamics and global restructurings of space through Euro-American economic incursion and political insinuation—imperialism—helped bring Liang closer to a recognition and conviction that the only way to "save" China was to build a stronger state. What marks Liang's passage to a *guojia zhuyi* variety of nationalism most clearly, as it evolved out of the early period (1898–1902) and out of his early concern with Boer and Filipino revolutionary action as models of the revolutionary process of *guomin*-formation, is that Liang's solution to the possibility of antagonism between the state and the people, as to the possibility of antagonism among the people, was conjoined to his concern about the consolidating strength of imperialism. This produced a theoretical orientation that privileged the state over the people in order to assert, preserve, and protect the state's autonomy in the global sphere. It was after the Boxer debacle in 1901, the failures of the Boer and Filipino struggles, and then fully by 1903 that Liang essentially left behind the Filipino and

Boer struggles as exemplars of a people-centered modernity and nationalism, even as he had extracted from these events a lesson on imperialist modernity and on the dangers of revolutionary failure that led to a statist concept of nation. As such, while Liang saw the Anglo-Boer conflict as an instance of the worldwide "competition between national peoples" (*guomin jingzheng*)—an interpretation that ignored Japanese antimodernist claims; rejected the British claims that the war was about internal political "justice," "freedom," and "equal rights"; and repudiated the claims about *minzu* essences—this recognition led not to a utopianization of *minzu* as the exclusive definition or basis of a nation—internally or globally—but rather to a vision, through analogy, of the imminent danger of the final breaching of China's precarious integrity and state sovereignty that could only be shored up through state-centered solutions.

Conclusion

One of the more remarkable things about the Boer emergence in China was how it contributed vitally to a language change, in Joseph Levenson's sense. That is, in the numerous biographies of Kruger and the citations to Boer pronouncements, the Transvaal, and the Boers—not to mention Kruger himself—were placed into a new language-space, through which they were familiarized and mobilized in the Chinese context. This familiarization was not accomplished through *tongzhong* racialist or Asianist perspectives, but rather through the promotion of a new sociopolitical language that underpinned, articulated, and reinforced China's shared contemporary historical space with other colonial peoples understood in *minzu* terms. In this sense, the transformation of the Boers into subjects of their own particular history and of a global history was intimately linked to the modern transformations with which Chinese intellectuals were theoretically and practically grappling in their efforts to specify who the "Chinese people" were, what the basis of their specification as a national people should be, and upon what basis "China's" claims on modernity should be articulated.

In one version of this language change, to cite one commentator, "If people do not [submit like] Egypt [to] a strong enemy, then what could emerge is Boerized Egyptians."[95] Here, we can recall the fearful rhetoric of China being "Polanded"; the opposite of being "Polanded" was to be "Boerized": that is, to develop a fierce *minzu* consciousness that would inform a death struggle, even if the struggle that emerged therefrom were a failure. Indeed, better to fail numerous times as a "Boer" than to never fail at all and be "Polanded" and enslaved like the Egyptians or Indians.

A larger issue in this language change was whether "the people" should be conceived with the *minzu/guomin* understood as multiply constituted within an overarching teleology of statism; or whether it should emanate from an instantiation of a presumed *minzu* essence, whose imaginary unity would wholly define the ability of the *guomin* to actualize itself on the world stage.[96] As we have seen, Liang Qichao was increasingly taking a state-centered approach to this problem. And while others were, like him, also making a distinction between the terms *minzu*, *guomin*, and *guojia*, their distinctions led not to a reification of the state but rather to a reification of the *minzu* that, in the late Qing, took the particular historical form of anti-Manchuism. Thus, just when Liang was resisting the temptation to displace China's modern social dislocation and crisis onto a posited internal "other," such intellectuals as Zhang Binglin, Sun Zhongshan, and Liu Shipei came to formulate this dislocation in cultural/racial/ethnic terms. Prior to 1904, this was at most a tendential potential; by that year, however, the split between *guojia zhuyi* (statist nationalism) and *minzu zhuyi* (ethnonationalism) became more apparent and more insistent.

At the same time as *minzu zhuyi* nationalists posited a primordial *minzu* essence that could be mobilized, these very same commentators continued to lament the Chinese peoples' "backwardness." However enabling this new *minzu* recognition was as an elite nationalist proposition, therefore, the anxious displacement of China's problems onto the figure of the people was reinforced. Two tendencies thus became visible: on the one hand, intellectuals' own claims to social status in terms of literacy was potentially being displaced by a new modern necessity to struggle and militarize, for which literacy was not necessarily a relevant social marker. On the other hand, the very social divisiveness that was produced and reproduced by elite practices was also displaced onto "the people," who were condemned for being unable to accomplish the requisite "grouping" in comparison with others just as unlettered as they. In this fatal conjunction and double displacement, the admiration lavished upon the Boers and Filipinos contributed negatively and contradictorily to Chinese intellectuals' evaluations of the Chinese people, and the tension between the "backwardness" of the Chinese people and the necessity to devise national solutions that included these very same people—if not as primary agents, then as primary subjects—was reinforced. The working out of this problematic and this contradiction has informed ever since a large part of twentieth-century China's historical passage.

That said, it is important to note that even *minzu zhuyi* nationalism was not internally unified, as the emphasis on *minzu* could be read as a dynastic culturalist position just as it could be understood as an anti-dynastic racial/ethnic position. Indeed, the actual politics of the major late Qing promoters and proponents of *minzu zhuyi* nationalism—Kang Youwei, Zhang Binglin, Liu Shipei, and Sun Zhongshan, among others—were in many ways starkly different. For example, Kang Youwei's emphasis on New Text Confucianism as the cultural marker of "Chinese-ness" led him to support the dynasty as the primary and indeed only conceivable cultural producer of "Chinese" meaning. That is, for Kang, the Chinese *minzu* could only be constituted through cultural Confucianism and its proper socio-political manifestations, of which the dynasty was the only possible guarantor. In contrast, Zhang Binglin's and Liu Shipei's version of *minzu zhuyi* was premised upon the political-cultural accusation that the Manchu Qing had suppressed the true diversity of Chinese learning, a recuperation of which they advocated through their *guocui*, or national essence, scholarship.[97] This led them to the political corollary of the need to overthrow the Qing and to reassert an authentic Chinese ethnoculture that could isomorphically produce national meaning.

In the wider global context, there was good reason for such evolving anti-Manchu revolutionaries as Zhang Binglin, Sun Zhongshan, Liu Shipei, and the others discussed above to seize on and recognize (even if it was a misrecognition) in the Boer struggle the living actualization and affirmation of a *minzu* claiming its essence and battling on the contemporary world stage for its ethno-national autonomy. In one immediate sense, this tie to the world made anti-Manchuism not merely an abstractly intellectual proposition, nor a mere harking back to a Ming loyalist past, and nor even an unintelligible culturalist position; rather, anti-Manchuism became part of an emerging modern global civilization, and as such was situated squarely in the mainstream of modern anticolonial activity.[98] With this new situatedness, the conjoining of the fearful slavery/people binary with a colonial paradigm of Chinese history was completed, a synthesis that enabled, produced, and helped popularize a new interpretation of the Chinese and global situation. In its Chinese manifestation—which, to be sure, recuperated, drew on, and was often articulated in terms of scholarship and debates both from within Chinese classical textual traditions and from outside the imperially codified traditions (such as from within Buddhism)[99]—the Manchus were designated China's primary colonizing "others," and the "enslavement" of the Chinese people was said to date not from concessions to Western powers in the 1840s but rather to the seventeenth century (the Ming-Qing transition). Meanwhile, as an interpretative instantiation of modernity, China's situation was firmly connected to others around the world, whose individual and collective struggles would help redefine that world, and thus, perhaps, the unevenness of modernity as well.[100]

In sum, from 1898 through 1903 a newly constituted recognition of and concern with what was often called "national imperialism" (*guojia diguo zhuyi*) or "expansionism" (*pengzhang zhuyi*) gave rise to the emergence of an understanding of the relationship between "nationalism" and "expansionism" that made it possible for Chinese theory and practice to be premised upon a nation ideal—alternatively founded upon the idea of the primacy of the state or the primacy of the ethnos. This new theoretical and practical orientation drew for its conceptual energy and indeed for its very language—not its vocabulary, which obviously enough came from Japan—from the global situation of the colonized world. An initial combination of *tongzhong* (same race) and *wangguo* (lost country) into a modern global temporality informed by a recognition of the modern production of global spatial unevenness allowed for the articulation of the decentering of the experience of modernity that permitted the Pacific, Asia, and Africa to emerge into view, not as inert geographical designations diachronically ordered, but as material sites for the production of new global, national, and local meanings, practices, and histories on a synchronically understood world stage. This decentering shift allowed Chinese intellectuals to appropriate world events and places for a reconceptualization of China that was both of and in the world, both of and in modernity.

After 1903–4, when the global and domestic situations both hit bleak new lows, there grew considerable anxiety across the ideological spectrum that China's situation required yet another rethinking, the third in the space of less than a decade. In this new rethinking, the open-endedness of the previous formulations needed to be sewn up, and Chinese intellectuals proceeded to rework their expansive and unstable formulations into more stable organizational forms. The post-1905 period thus saw the creation of two very different types of organizational conceptions: the first was a radical Asia solidarity that attempted to substantiate the region as a site for a non-state-centered politics from which to launch a pan-Asian revolution. In this effort, China's revolutionary endeavor remained intimately tied to a global configuration, although the space of its imagination—Asia—was more limited than the previously expansive moment of worldwide revolutionary spatiality. With the collapse of that effort, and now from within Sun Zhongshan's Revolutionary Alliance, Chinese revolutionary energy was recreated even more narrowly, and the discursive formation and organizational form of early-twentieth-century Chinese nationalism was unstably completed. It is those two moments that the next two chapters elucidate.

PART III

PERFORMING ON THE WORLD STAGE IN ASIA 6

So long as there are nation-states [*guojia*], we must uphold nationalism [*minzu zhuyi*] . . . We are concerned not just for our own Han race, but for other victimized nations, whose lands have been conquered, rights usurped, and people enslaved . . . A true nationalist is one who extends his sympathy to others who have suffered from the same [national] excruciation. — Zhang Taiyan[1]

The emergence of specific discursive formations of Chinese nationalism, as we have seen, was intimately intertwined with the conceptual linking of China to the modern world: China became thinkable as specifically national at the same time as, and only when, China became consciously worldly. In his 1901 introduction to what he hoped would become a full-fledged revisionist history of China, Liang Qichao indicated how completely this worldliness had seeped into his historical consciousness.[2] In the conclusion to his outline for his long-term project, Liang proposed that the traditional dynastic divisions of Chinese history be discarded in favor of a tripartite periodization derived from European historical writing. According to Liang's new schema, China's "antiquity" was defined by the empire's political unification (in the Qin, 220 B.C.); the "medieval" period — to the Qianlong reign of the Qing (late eighteenth century) — was characterized by a history of "China in Asia" (*yazhou zhi zhongguo*), during which "the Chinese related to, had business and competed most intensely with various peoples of Asia [*yazhou ge minzu*]"; and the "modern" period (post-Qianlong) was marked by a "China in the world," during which "the Chinese people [*zhongguo minzu*] united with all the Asian peoples [*quan yazhou minzu*] in struggle and competition with Westerners [*xiren*]."[3]

Without going into the significance for Chinese historiography of this essay,[4] suffice it to note here that what is most interesting is not Liang's choice to impose Western historical periodizations on China but rather that it is only from the view of the modern period—China-in-the-world—that both Asia and China emerge as relevant formations. That is, despite his narrative, Liang's conceptualization of "China" is symptomatic of a prior understanding of global space, since his "China" could only emerge as an articulated historical process concurrently with "Asia" and the world. This is clear if we dwell for a moment on the elision between Liang's two concepts of Asia. In his "medieval" period, Liang's list of the "peoples of Asia" with whom the Chinese had business includes only those successfully incorporated into the Qing empire (that is, the Tibetans, Mongols, Tongus, Xiongnu, Manchus, and the Han), a concept that corresponds to the territorial extent and constituency of what Liang was figuring as the modern Chinese nation. By contrast, Liang's modern Asia encompasses an entity whose boundaries transcend the Qing, since it is the "Chinese" (the combined "Asians" of the prior period) along with other Asians (a formation distinct from "China") who are posed against "Westerners." Liang's first "Asia" was soon dropped as a historical category and normalized as "China"; whereas the second "Asia" became the modern region that, in Liang's view, was tied together—to each other and to China—in a historical identity because of its difference from and struggles with "Westerners."

By 1902, for Liang Qichao, "Asia"—which the year before still appeared as a historical contingency—became a geographical fact. In a series of four intertwined essays he wrote that year on the relationship between civilization/ modernity (*wenming*)[5] and geography, Liang presented a metatheorization of the relationship between historical progress—understood as the arrival of the modern world order—and the connections among the histories and geographies of Europe, Asia, and China.[6] As regards Asia, Liang provided a historical review of the different civilizations (*wenming*) developed in the region, where Asia no longer was the "medieval" construct that had become "China," but rather a diverse set of individual states and cultures.[7] While Liang provides no explanation for why this diverse set of states in "Asia" is "Asian," he does note that "the world's oldest states [*guo*]—India, China, the Jews, Assyria—without exception all emerged from this territory; and all the literature, philosophy, aesthetics, and technology of the West have their origins largely in India, China, Assyria, Babylonia, Phoenicia, Persia, Arabia, etc . . . Europe is undoubtedly the descendant of Asia; this is true not only of the past, but of modern times as well."[8]

Here, then, as Liang had come to understand it, "Asia" is a geographical region akin to the geopolitical "Orient" of European invention or to the Meiji Japanese *toyo* construct.[9] And by the end of the essay on Asia, what Liang had demonstrated in the previous essays in the series as being the permeability of Europe's topography as the explanation for Europe's current ascendance was seen as only a temporary—or contemporary—condition. Indeed, for him, the older relationship of geography and civilization was being transcended by a newer relationship between globality and modernity now marked by the coexistence of modern global unification and the simultaneous division of the globe into nation-states. In this context, Japan was highlighted by Liang for its ability to remain independent—"Japan is the hero of today's world because its independence is due to its own strength."[10] Yet, despite Japan, Liang asserted that "the reason Asia will be for the Asians does not lie in the present, but in the future." This, he explained, is because, while the other remaining independent states of Asia (Persia, Siam, Korea, and China) are now so threatened that it may no longer make sense to speak of them as independent, the motive force for a future "Asia for the Asians" cannot emerge from Japan, since Japan had allied itself with European expansionism. Rather, "Asia for the Asians" must emerge from the tensions between a unifying modern world and the forces of disunity unleashed by this very process.[11] An independent Asia thus could only emerge as an alliance among independent states.

For many intellectuals through the late Qing, "Asia" increasingly appeared, as it did for Liang, as a mediating conceptual and historical structure—a space—that helped link "China" and the world; it also became the concrete place where many intellectuals could mobilize the previous decade's conceptual linkages into performing on the world stage. Rather than only conceptually staging the world, then, Asia became the world stage upon which Chinese intellectuals were able to perform their national and global drama. However, the meaning of "Asia" was not stable: it was and has remained a highly contested category of global, regional, and national significance. Through the combining of the racial, cultural, geographical/geopolitical, historical, and politically radical impulses that had emerged over the 1895–1905 period, "Asia," as a historically specific region in a connected world, was created in 1905 to provide a concrete site for that political activity. And, from that time onward, the struggle for the creation of Asia as a regional imaginary and a political reality, along with the firm identification of China as Asian, was purposively taken up by a variety of late Qing intellectuals, albeit for various purposes and with different goals in mind.

1905: *Temporalities and Spatialities*

In 1905 Japan defeated Russia in the Russo-Japanese War, a victory that confirmed Japan's rise to power in the East, if not in the world. The celebration of this rise by the Meiji state and by others in many parts of Asia, who hailed it as proof that Asians were not inferior to Westerners, was not uncontested within Japan. For, just as the Japanese state was mobilizing its populace for industrialization and territorial expansion, the tensions that these endeavors produced were also yielding a significant amount of social and intellectual unrest. Nevertheless, initially attracted by Japan's growing national strength, a number of students and activists from around the region, including Chinese, gathered in ever-increasing numbers in Japan to study, exchange experiences, and learn from one another. There, many turned to radicalism and began to organize themselves for various political activities.[12] By the end of 1905, Japan's recent victory in the war had rendered it, indisputably but also contradictorily, not merely a new center of Asian capitalism and state-centered national strength, but also a new metropolitan node in a spatially dispersed but increasingly interconnected world system of radicalism. It thus simultaneously became a site for the production of new would-be hegemonic conceptions of "Asia" with Japan at its center, as well as a site for the production of other discourses on Asia and the world that produced contestatory praxes often aimed at displacing Japan's (and Euro-America's) proclaimed centrality in the region.

It was also in 1905 that the Qing government in China abolished the millennium-old civil service exams, which had served to bind classically educated Chinese elites to the state through bureaucratic service and sinecure. This move confirmed what had been at least a half-century-long process of the disarticulation of the Chinese elite into fragmented new social categories. From this fragmentation, and particularly after 1898, had grown the Chinese intellectual groups, which were more cosmopolitan and mobile, and thus less tied to the state than the gentry-elite of the past. By 1905, then, not only in social reality and discursively but in policy as well, social disjunctures and divergent intellectual activities helped confirm the disaggregation of what had hitherto been conceived of as an integrated sociopolitical order. In combination with the disjunctures in the global order—visible through the revolutionary uprisings detailed in previous chapters—the decade of organizational incoherences and fluid ideological searchings that had been spawned by and were responding to these various disjunctures came together under the umbrella organization of the Revolutionary Alliance (*Tongmeng hui*). Formed in 1905 in Tokyo, the Revolutionary Alliance for the first time articulated a relatively integrated program that fused revolution and ethno-nationalism into both prospect and project for China's modernity.

The year 1905 thus marks both a break from and a continuity with the decade just past (1895–1904), when the global situation, the Asian situation, and the Japanese and the Chinese situations had all moved into a different phase. The legacy of the revolutions and discursive appropriations of the previous years helped inform how 1905 was viewed, particularly in the conceptualizations of China's own revolutionary nationalist project as part of a worldwide revolutionary tide that, while now at low ebb, could be reignited through concerted Chinese activity. It is here, across the 1905 divide, that the craven character in Wang Xiaonong's 1904 opera—Wang Guonu (Slave of a Lost Country)—could be transformed into a utopian national figure: the "slave" reborn from his terror-filled immanence in China into a proactive ethno-national, neither subjugated slave nor obedient state subject, but rather, man of China who was also man of the world in a linked project of revolutionary activity. This possibility emerged from the specificities of China's position and the perceived commonalities between that position and the position of others; from 1905 onward, this possibility was grounded firmly in a newly historicized "Asia."

Discursive Filiations: "Asia" as Language and History

The initial term in Chinese for Asia—*yaxiya*—was a phonetic transcription, introduced to China in the seventeenth century by Jesuit missionaries.[13] Yet *yaxiya* as a classificatory schema was not widely used in Chinese histories or geographical treatises until well into the nineteenth century; it was simply not relevant. Even in the first modern world geography published in China, written by Wei Yüan in 1844 immediately following the first Opium War, there is no category for Asia. Rather, Wei's multivolume work is divided according to the traditional classificatory "seas" (e.g., "southeastern seas island states"; "Five Indias of the southwestern seas"; "States of the Ouluoba [European] Continent of the great western seas"; etc.).[14] In his discussion of India in the second volume, Wei does mention that "India . . . is in Asia (*yaxiya*)," but he does not elaborate and rushes on to discuss other matters.[15] By contrast, in the 1848 geography by Xu Jiyu, in part based on Wei Yüan's work, the classification *yaxiya* is used; Xu notes, in clarifying the unfamiliar designations used in his work, that these names were mostly transcriptions from English and Portuguese. As regards Asia, Xu states: "Asia is the name for what, in ancient times, was called Turkey Minor. Westerners call everything east of this Asia."[16] He elaborates: "Russia's territory is 6/10ths in Asia; however its capital is in Europe . . . Turkey's eastern and central territories are in Asia; however its western territories are in Europe."[17] And so on. Whatever its "accuracy" in reflecting the state of knowledge then being produced in Europe and transmitted to China, this convoluted explanation was of little epistemological consequence in China at the time, and it was probably all but meaningless to the majority of Xu's readers—highly educated elites themselves. Thus, despite the fact that both Wei Yüan and Xu Jiyu remapped the world and China's place in it in very significant ways, in the mid-nineteenth century, Asia as a category had little significance in Chinese conceptualizations of the world or of China.

By the late nineteenth century, as we have seen, the situation had changed completely. Indeed, at this point another word for Asia emerged alongside the first one: unlike *yaxiya*—a phonetic transcription—this second word, *yazhou*, implicitly connoted a region that was part of a multicontinental globe, in which there were several *zhou* (continents), of which *yazhou* (Asia) was one.[18] As historian Zhao Junyi notes in this regard: "*Yazhou* and *yaxiya* as words at the time [turn of the century] implied the meanings 'non-Europe' [*fei ouzhou de*] and non-Western [*fei xifang de*]; at times, they were rendered and deployed . . . as terminological opposites of *ouzhou* and *ouluoba* [both "Europe"] . . . So, at the turn of the twentieth century, 'Asia' did not solely and simply designate a geographical area or concept; rather, it incorporated quite an abundant coloring of politics."[19] Zhao's comment is suggestive. Yet it would be misleading to see China's new Asia merely as a binary opposite of Europe. For, in addition to being a term of geographical negation ("non-Europe"), and of resistance or reaction to Europe ("anti-Europe"), Asia also became a more fluid concept, with multiple contingent meanings and political possibilities. The contingency of these meanings, and the potential political radicalism of some of them, hinged on how issues of race/ethnos, geography, history, and civilization were combined. Rather than reinstantiating any notion of Sinocentricity, the new Asia represented the invention of a region from within modern circumstances. By the turn of the twentieth century, *yazhou* was an accepted term as both place and space; and it was conjoined to and also came to contain the "Pacific" category noted in chapter 3 above. In this guise, "Asia" became mobilizable in a newly reconfigured late-nineteenth-century global, regional, and national politics.

By the same token, the contradictory need demonstrated by Liang Qichao to connect China's Asia to Japan's growing strength, while also distancing it from Japan's expansionism, continued to be a factor in the rise of Chinese Asianisms of the turn of the century. Indeed, before "Asia" could be understood by Chinese intellectuals as a historical-cultural region that encompassed more than the Japan-China dyadic relationship and yet was still tied to it, the newly emerged discourse on global commonality (*tongzhong*) had to be detached from its predecessor, the discourse of "shared civilization" (*tongwen*). As D. R. Howland has demonstrated, prior to the mid-1890s the Chinese rediscovery of China's connections to Japan via the notion of *tongwen*—a "shared civilization" idea that presumed that Japan's history of cultural borrowings from China confirmed its subordination to China—came just at the time when Japan was busy distancing itself from China and the rest of Asia by marking out a national space of its own, in which China was subordinated to Japan.[20] By the late 1890s, from the Chinese perspective, quite the opposite tendency occurred, as it was only by drawing the world closer to China that Chinese nationalism—as a discursive formation—grew.

As we have seen, the new global linkages increasingly were phrased not in the language of *tongwen* (shared civilization), but in the language of *tongzhong* (same race/kind). Indeed, in 1898, as a principle, *tongzhong* was publicly promoted by Zhang Zhidong, a leading Qing dynastic official known for his work in education, to refer to Chinese affinities with Japan,[21] and in 1897, by the classical scholar Zhang Binglin (Taiyan), who was to become one of the leading voices for ethno-nationalism in the first decade of the twentieth century, also in a narrow dyadic sense. Yet, even while confirming the dyadic relationship, both Zhang Zhidong and Zhang Binglin reversed the usual emphasis on China's civilizational superiority to emphasize contemporary Japanese global leadership.[22] That is, in these early formulations, both Zhangs—albeit from very different directions—construed *tongzhong* and Asia as substantially contained by China's relationship to Japan and, following the Japanese, elevated Japan above China.[23] By 1903, however, *tongzhong* had been widely linked to the rest of the world—as a shared discursive claim on modernity. Following upon this expansion of *tongzhong* identity, the notion of "Asia" also expanded beyond its China-Japan containment.

It is in this altered context that Asia came to be fashioned out of peoples previously ignored in China (Filipinos, Siamese, Indians, Burmese, etc.), and of places that had in the past been gathered into different conceptual rubrics altogether (such as the *nanyang*, or Southern Seas). Like nationalism, then, early-century Chinese Asianism was explicitly aimed at connecting China more closely to its neighbors, rather than distancing it, historically or otherwise; it was precisely this historicization that allowed and even forced Chinese intellectuals to develop conceptual linkages to neighboring peoples and that permitted the production of new types of globalisms, Asianisms, and nationalisms. These connections required an initial discovery of the dynamism among peoples around Asia; they were followed by a rediscovery of historical linkages between China and others, linkages not dependent upon either Japan's current centrality, a previous Sinocentricity, nor on a mere acceptance of Western orientalist and geographical designations (as Liang's above-cited essay seems to do).

In its most well known Chinese guise, this new Asia was facilitated by the formation of the Revolutionary Alliance, which, under Sun Zhongshan's leadership, helped promote the primacy in Asia of what could now be identified as *the* Chinese revolution. That is, in Sun's new organizational view, Asia was to be functional to China's revolutionary endeavor. Indeed, because Sun's turn-of-the-century vision of Asia derived many of its conceptual formulations from Japanese pan-Asianism, Sun's "Greater Asianism" (*da yazhou zhuyi*) is the most familiar as well as the most often discussed of the early-century Chinese Asianisms.[24] (Even while Wang Jingwei's wartime-collaborationist version, demonstrably derived from Sun's earlier vision, remains the most universally condemned.)[25] Yet, while Sun's sometimes uneasy combination in a functional framework of pan-Asianism, Japanese centrality, and his Chinese revolutionary endeavor marks one point of Chinese Asianism along a jagged continuum, there was in the late Qing a host of other discourses of "Asia" that were neither China centered nor Japan centered, but rather specifically rooted in non-state-centered practices and in non-national-chauvinist culturalism. These radical Asianisms represented an attempt to create a politicized cultural regional formation that was as decentered as it was utopian. Just as with Sun Zhongshan, the proponents of this other, more radical Asia emerged from the moments of expansive globalism detailed in previous chapters. In substance, they attempted to take that moment further, by rendering the conceptual globality into organizational form; yet unlike Sun, they did not take any one national endeavor (the Chinese) to be more central than any other. Indeed, in collaboration with various exile "Asians" residing in Tokyo at the time, such figures as Zhang Binglin (Taiyan) and Zhang Ji attempted to salvage the mutuality of political activism that had been promised in the previous decade of discursive globality.

The "Asia" concept that resulted from their activities and rethinkings was shaped by, albeit not limited to, two simultaneous structures of knowledge and experience: the ongoing attempts to subject Asia (and the world) to a Euro-American-Japanese–dominated economic and geopolitical world order; and, internal state-dominated concepts of national, cultural, and regional formation. Seeking to contest internal state dominations and to provide a bulwark against Euro-American-Japanese depredation, they linked the substantive content of their Asia concept to the plurality of cultures and contemporary practices in the region embedded in the historical flows of people, not in state-centered activities. Made possible by a complex conjuncture of events, histories, and intellectual influences, their new vision of Asia was explicitly intended to subvert, rather than confirm, both the Euro-American imperialist and the Qing/Meiji statist status quos.

The organization through which this radical "Asia" was actualized was the short-lived Asian Solidarity Society (*Yazhou heqin hui*), established in Tokyo in 1907 by Chinese intellectuals with Japanese socialists and exiled Indians, Filipinos, and Vietnamese. While the actual efficacy of their intervention was negligible and their activities were soon suppressed, their rethinkings nevertheless helped bring together the conceptual relationships established earlier among geography, race, culture, and history, and their organizational aspirations also required these conceptual relationships to be attached to concrete people, rather than to abstract notions of others. In this sense, their substantiation of "Asia" in organizational form, on the one hand, represents a retreat from earlier globalisms, even while on the other hand it simultaneously represents a mutation of that globalism into concrete politicized form.

Indians: "Slaves" or "People"?

There were strong countervailing currents to the dynamic model of the world's people that had developed through the 1895–1905 period. The most prominent of these can be found in the numerous references to inert and passive people who are complicit in the "lostness" of their countries through their "slavishness" or inability/unwillingness to act. Of all the world's peoples, aside from "black slaves," it was the Indians who conjured for Chinese intellectuals the most dire image of passive "lostness"; indeed, China's "enslavement" to the Manchus and the terror of imminent "enslavement" to Westerners was most often articulated in terms of India's "enslavement" to the British. As an essay in the semivernacular journal *Tongzi shijie* (Children's World) succinctly put it in 1903: "There is no difference between [Indians] being the slaves of foreigners and [Chinese] being the slaves of the Manchu government"[26]—although Liang Qichao had already confirmed in his 1901 essay "On the New Rules for Destroying Countries" that, of the five cited examples of modern "destruction" (*mieguo*) (Poland, Egypt, India, South Africa, the Philippines), India was by far "the strangest case of all."[27] As Liang put it, "I have heard of countries destroying other countries, but I have never heard of a noncountry destroying another! . . . [Yet] India . . . was taken over by 70,000 small capitalists of the East India Company."[28] In Liang's account, this was possible because the "small capitalists" had trained Indians to be soldiers, and these Indians were then used to supervise their own people and to implement British policies on the local level: "Is this called using one's own country to destroy oneself, or is it called not being destroyed?," Liang queried, deciding in the end that it was both: for, he blamed the Indians—as a people (*minzu*)—for being "cruel to their own race" (*zhong*) and for fawning on foreigners (*meiyi*), as well as the British for being greedy and unmindful of other peoples.[29]

The Indians' perceived complicity in their own colonization was, by 1904–5, quite well established in China. A number of books were published from 1901 to 1905 on the issue, and each asserted that the Mughuls, upon their takeover of India, had crushed India's fine cultural legacy, sending the country into division and decline, thus making it ripe for British—or East India Company—picking by the late eighteenth century.[30] Numerous stories and essays repeated these "truths" without much further analysis, albeit with much horror. And, since the red-turbaned Sikhs used by the British as policemen and menials were so readily visible in the international settlements of the treaty ports and in Hong Kong, the "truth" of Indian "slavery"/"enslavement" was no mere abstraction, but felt as viscerally real.

In 1904 the popular Tokyo-based Chinese journal *Jiangsu* published a short story that nightmarishly evoked the kind of horror that Indian "enslavement" awakened in Chinese intellectuals. The story tells of an encounter between an unemployed and indolent Chinese man of letters, named Huang Shibiao (literally, Representative of Yellow Elites), and a mythical old man who appears to Huang in a daydream. The old man leads Huang (Mr. Yellow) on a brief foray into the near future. In this displaced time, they walk along the streets of Shanghai, whereupon they encounter a military formation marching toward them. There is a white person bringing up the rear.

> Shibiao looked closely at these people and they all had faces black as coal. They were wearing a piece of red cloth around their heads like a tall hat; around their waists, they wore a belt holding wooden clubs. Shibiao asked the old man: are these Indians? The old man said, yes, the English use them as police . . . Shibiao asked, why do they not use an Indian as the chief of police? The old man answered: who ever hear of that! Indians are people of a lost country [*wangguo zhi min*]; they are no more than slaves![31]

Later in the story, Shibiao and the old man are at a streetside food stall; a man wearing a red turban approaches and orders some tea. Shibiao notices that he has a yellow face and a short, squat stature. Curious, Shibiao inquires after his origins. The "Indian"—that is how he is identified—answers that he is Chinese. The man explains: "Don't you know? Now the English want us Chinese to . . . dress like Indians. They posted a decree three days ago: upper-class people have three weeks to comply; middle-class people have two months; and lower-class people have one hundred days. Although I cannot be considered upper class . . . I thought I'd change immediately nonetheless."[32] As they leave the stall, Shibiao observes disbelievingly that everyone on the street is now wearing red turbans. His guide, the old man, informs him that only four years has passed.

Resuming their stroll, they pass an elementary school, and Shibiao notes that English is being taught from textbooks identified as "India readers." He is now thoroughly shaken, for these readers were British-missionary-designed textbooks, and were already widely used in British-run schools in India. In 1896, Young J. Allen, an English missionary in China, had written an essay for the journal he edited, the *Wangguo gongbao* (Review of the Times), entitled "Twelve Advantages to India's Subordination to England," in which he had advocated, among other things, the introduction of these readers into Guangdong and Fujian on an experimental basis. The "India model" of colonization and education for China was vigorously promoted by Allen and other missionaries,[33] and in 1898 the newly founded Commercial Press in Shanghai had commissioned Xie Honglai, a Christian with connections to the missionary-run Society for the Diffusion of Knowledge (SDK; *Guangxue hui*),[34] to translate these primers, which were then sold under the name *Huaying chujie* and *Huaying jinjie* (China-English Elementary Reader; China-English Intermediate Reader).[35] This history of "India readers" was evidently well enough known for the story writer to drop it into the story without further explanation. The story continues with Huang Shibiao being summarily informed by the principal of the school where the readers are being used that all instruction is now in English, that Chinese-language instruction has been outlawed, and that a recent decree has mandated that within twenty years all communications—even private letters—must be written in English.

The story disappeared unfinished from the pages of the journal. Given the anti-Manchu stance of *Jiangsu*, the journal in which this story was published, it is very likely that the "loss," despite the story's projection into a near-future, also referred to the situation of Han Chinese in Manchu-ruled China. (The concern with head dress [the Indian turban standing in for the Manchu queue], language anxiety, racial leadership, etc., all make such an interpretation possible.) Yet, anti-Manchu or not, one does not need to look far for echoes of "lost" Indians. Indeed, even in Manchu-dominated publications, "Indians" were used in almost every conceivable way to point to the direst consequences of inaction or complacency. For one among many possible examples, in 1908 the relatively conservative *Beijing nübao* (Beijing Women's News), published and read by Manchu court ladies, launched a critique of "superstitious" beliefs, using India's enslavement and loss as its primary example of the evil of such beliefs:

> You thought that India was just fine, huh? Then why did it invite destruction [*heyi yaowang ne*]? It is because they only knew superstition . . . When the British arrived in the cities, they [the Indians] just sat around praying to Buddha . . . praying that their city would not be destroyed. What do you think: are these Indians foolish, or what? Do they deserve to die, or what? After not too long, they became slaves of the British, and they're still resting there in their dreams . . .

> Ah! Compatriots [*tongbao*]! I would like to ask you if you want to be citizens [*guomin*] of a great and independent nation, or if you want to become slaves [*nuli*] of a lost state? If you want the latter, then I've nothing left to say; if the former, then you should throw away those Bodhisattva statues modeled of clay . . . and you should give that money used for burning incense to your children for their education . . .
>
> If you don't believe me, then just watch: those red turbans will soon be wrapped around your heads, too![36]

In whatever forum, then, the terror of the doubling—the immanence of Chinese as a "lost people" evoked by the fearful plausibility of the interchangeability of Chinese and Indians—thus exerted a powerful pull on the imagination. Indians became the quintessential "lost people" (*wangguo zhi min*), and, along with the Poles, were metaphorically evoked—in the oft-repeated phrases "Indian and Polish slaves" or "Indian and Polish horse-and-cow slavery"—as terror-filled examples of a threatened Chinese fate.

That Indians were so rendered is not surprising as there was no revolutionary activity discernible from those quarters. Thus, unlike "Poland," which vacillated in late Qing discourse, "India" was inscribed firmly as exemplar of lostness and slavery. As one commentator succinctly summarized in late 1903, if China did not quickly and deliberately develop the same spirit of "independence" (*duli*) as the Philippines and the Transvaal, then its precarious sovereignty would soon vanish, and pressures for "slavery" (*nuli zhi yali*) would be impossible to overcome; indeed, without this spirit, "there will be no way to avoid slipping into the same cage as India, or the same horse and cow slavery of Poland," both of which were, the commentator noted, a kind of "death without death" (*qiu si bu si*).[37]

However, when Chinese intellectuals met Indians in Tokyo in 1905 and after, Indians became a different type of figure altogether, for there they met educated Indians who were vigorously involved in the incipient elite-led anticolonial struggle against the British. Rather than embodying the "lost" figures of subordination typified by Indians in the abstract or Indian servants of the British in the treaty ports, the activist Indians in Tokyo came to suggest for some Chinese intellectuals that Indians not only were not passive, but that there was a promise for a political-cultural revival in India based upon a rediscovered Buddhist-derived culture.[38]

Vietnam Rediscovered

The discovery of dynamism among Indians had its parallel in relation to Vietnam. In the 1895–1905 period, the French move up the Indochinese peninsula had rendered Vietnam an area of modern concern for Chinese intellectual-activists. While, clearly, Sino-Vietnamese relations go back much further than the modern period and are vexed in complicated ways the simultaneous increase in French demands for territory and concessions in the Qing empire's far southwestern regions at the turn of the century rendered Vietnam a modern concern rather than an old issue of tributary relations and thorny military confrontation. Rarely identified (at least not in the late Qing periodical press) as a *tongwen* (same-civilization) country and people, despite its impressive history of cultural borrowing from China, Vietnam was rediscovered by both Liang Qichao and Sun Zhongshan in 1905 through their separate encounters with the elite anticolonial activist Phan Boi Chau.[39]

Arriving in Japan in 1905 after fleeing Vietnam, Phan traveled to Yokohama to meet Liang, whose essays he had read in Saigon.[40] With a similar class background, elite education in the Chinese classics, anti-imperialist sentiment, and commitment to monarchical constitutionalism, Liang and Phan got along well. They were able to communicate with one another through brushtalking (*bitan*), a type of communication that depended upon sharing what D. R. Howland has called a civilizational "written code."[41] Phan's impassioned account of the cruel treatment of the Vietnamese by France so impressed Liang that he suggested that Phan write a "serious literary presentation" of Vietnam's plight.[42] Liang's suggestion was soon followed by the appearance of *The History of the Loss of Vietnam* (Ch: *Yuenan wangguo shi*; V: *Viet-Nam Vong Quoc Su*), transcribed into Chinese and furnished with a preface by Liang, and published in Shanghai in late 1905.[43] The volume was widely read in China and it soon went through five printings. Liang's moving preface and parts of the narrative itself were transformed into a drama script, entitled *Yuenan hun* (The Spirit of Vietnam), which was reprinted in journals and in various vernaculars around the country.[44]

Suffused with a sense of extreme melancholy, Liang's preface on the one hand laments the loss not only of the country of Vietnam but of the classical language that had tied Vietnam to China, or at least to the Chinese elite textual traditions. Along with this melancholy, however, the preface also celebrates the rediscovery of a new shared language of global commonality, through which the historical losses could be understood, commemorated, and acted upon in the present. And while Phan's account of the elite-led opposition to the French, of which he was a major motivator, resonated powerfully with Liang's own experience, Liang nevertheless resisted the temptation to assimilate the one to the other and maintained a careful distance from Phan's sense of "lostness." In other words, at the same time as Liang commented sarcastically on the "so-called civilization, the so-called humanity" of the French as demonstrated in Vietnam, he did not acknowledge that China's situation was quite so dire as Vietnam's.[45] Even so, for Liang, Vietnam's and Phan's loss were transformed into an elegiac opportunity for personal and national affinity.

Phan, apparently not fussy about ideological divisions,[46] also went to meet Liang's foe, Sun Zhongshan, with whom he debated the relative merits of reform and revolution as well as regional priorities. In the course of the encounter, Sun tried to convince Phan that the Chinese revolutionary endeavor he headed through the Revolutionary Alliance needed to take precedence over the Vietnamese anti-French project; and, Sun promised that, when he was successful in displacing the Qing, the Chinese would turn to help the Vietnamese. Phan, by contrast, predicted earlier success for the Vietnamese effort, maintaining that it would be easier to recover Vietnam from the French than it would be to carry out a successful revolution in China. With the success of Vietnam's endeavor, he promised, the northern part of his country could provide a good base from which Sun could destabilize China.[47] Part of the issue in their discussions was Sun's (correct) determination that Vietnam's colonization by the French was not easily reversed; yet part stemmed from Sun's conviction that China, too, was colonized—albeit by the Manchus and not by the Euro-American powers or Japan. In this sense, Sun and Phan were speaking past one another, each with a different idea of "loss" (*wang*). Thus, while Sun turned Phan's and Vietnam's loss into a recognition of commonality, he did so only by assimilating Vietnam's to China's situation and by rendering the commonality into an opportunity to promote China's revolutionary centrality. While Phan's prediction for Vietnamese success was sadly off by almost three-quarters of a century (during which Vietnamese-Chinese relations have been far from smooth, fraternal support),[48] by the same token, even though Phan and Sun did not agree on revolutionary priorities, they nevertheless remained on good terms. Indeed, Phan went on to join the Asian Solidarity Society in 1907 (he may even have been a co-manager)[49] through introductions facilitated by Sun to Chinese radicals involved in both the society and in Sun's Revolutionary Alliance.

Manchus, Colonizers, and Modern Global History

Just as many around Asia were being rendered into *tongzhong* (same race/kind) in a historically negative unity of *wangguo* (lost country) turned to contemporary positive purpose, the Manchus were increasingly figured as aliens to and disruptors of this unity. As early as 1901, through the journal *Guomin bao* (China Journal), which he co-edited with Qin Lishan, Sun Zhongshan and others had been concerned with establishing the historical basis for placing the central datum of China's modern colonization in the Ming-Qing transition of the seventeenth century. Soon, Zhang Binglin (Taiyan) became one of the major voices for this interpretation. One of the primary promoters of the late Qing "national essence" school (*guocui*), Zhang began at the turn of the century to differentiate between the exclusivity of Confucianism as an ideology of rule and the heterogeneity of historical Chinese schools of learning which had been suppressed in order for imperial Confucianism to secure its hegemonic ruling power. Decentering imperial Confucianism from its position as the exclusive definition of Chinese-ness (as it had been mobilized for bureaucratic rule), Zhang found in the space opened between the civilizational state and a plural heterogeneous culture a political-cultural basis upon which to oppose the Manchu Qing.[50]

This rediscovery of a plural culture led Zhang in two directions simultaneously. On the one hand, it led him into a racialized anti-Manchuism, in which *zhongzu*, or race/kind, became the marker of the Manchus' unalterable difference from Han Chinese and thus also the marker of the illegitimacy of their claims to rule Han China. The new orientation is most clear from his 1901 essay entitled "On the Correct Hatred of the Manchus" (Zheng chou Man lun), which concludes: "Both the Manchus and the Japanese belong to the yellow race, but as can clearly be seen from history, the Japanese are of the same type [zu] [as the Han Chinese], while the Manchus are not."[51] In its combining with the colonial discourse on modern China discussed in previous chapters, Zhang's cultural understanding rendered the Manchus not only political but cultural racial usurpers of China's national essence and essentially outsiders to "Asia." On the other hand, the rediscovery of cultural pluralism, rather than merely turning Zhang inward, also led him to an internationalist culturalism, through which he was able to reestablish China's links to India through a common Buddhist heritage, both sites of which had been suppressed by foreign invasion.[52]

By separating culture from civilization—or, by historicizing culture and divesting it of its dependence upon the dynastic system[53]—Zhang was thus able to articulate a new relationship between culture and politics in the global realm. His political activism henceforth took on an increasingly cultural-racial hue, while also taking him further into international alliances with those—such as Indians—whom he designated as being of the same "cultural-racial" kind. Thus, by 1905, just after arriving in Tokyo upon his release from Qing prison, where he had been incarcerated for two years for his role in the Subao case in Shanghai, Zhang had come to the conviction that *tongzhong* was primarily a cultural-racial category that encompassed not just China and Japan (as it had for him a decade previously), but a much wider selection of peoples. Zhang's cultural-racial understanding was actualized through his vigorous participation in the Asian Solidarity Society and his promotion of the Indian independence movement in Japan.[54]

Coming from a slightly different angle, Liu Shipei, another "national essence" scholar, who was not merely an anti-Manchu revolutionary but also an anarchist, understood the relationship between the Manchus, an alien people, and the Chinese in an unabashedly modernist historical-political mode. In an essay written in 1905, Liu wrote: "England destroyed India so that it no longer belonged to the Mughuls; England and France enslaved Egypt so it no longer belonged to Turkey; America plucked off the Philippines so it no longer belonged to Spain . . . In my opinion, had there not been the Manchu invasion of China, there would not have been the White invasion."[55] Liu here demonstrates how to renarrate world and Chinese history in light of the modern categories of imperialism and colonialism. That is, for Liu, the prior presence of an "alien" power facilitated and indeed made inevitable the modern "white" invasions of the present day. However implausible such a narrative may be, Liu's reading later allowed him to conjoin this global historical narrative to actual political organizational practice through the Asian Solidarity Society, in which he participated enthusiastically.

As for other society participants such as Su Manshu and Zhang Ji, each came to their participation in yet other ways. Su, primarily known as an aesthete, poet, and a founding member of the *Nanshe* (Southern Society)

(1909), whose parentage was ambiguous but who almost certainly was half Japanese and had grown up mostly in Japan, had spent a large amount of time in Siam, where he taught English and learned Buddhism and Sanskrit. He also reportedly became a Buddhist monk there. Later he gained entry into a variety of expatriate Buddhist circles in Japan and served for a time as a translator and teacher for the Sanskrit Study Society. He translated from English into Chinese the William Jones rendition of the Indian classic *Kalidasa*, as well as the poetry of the Indian poetess Toru Dutt. It is quite possible that the other Chinese members of the Asian Solidarity Society—such as Zhang Taiyan, with whom Su was on intimate terms—were introduced to the Indian members of the society through Su.[56] Su thus came to the society almost exclusively through a cultural conviction, for, despite his close friendships with many Revolutionary Alliance members and many anarchists, there is little evidence that he possessed a firm political stance.

Meanwhile, Zhang Ji, a prominent anarchist, had spent a good amount of time in Java, where he translated from English the portion of the *History of Java* that dealt with the overseas Chinese (*huaqiao*) resistance to Dutch rule. His translation was published in the *Zhongguo ribao* (China Daily), which was edited in Hong Kong by Feng Ziyou and functioned as the main Revolutionary Party mouthpiece until the founding of the *Minbao* (People's Voice) in 1905. Zhang's research into Javanese anti-Dutch politics and his work among anti-Dutch overseas Chinese reinforced his radical political involvements in Tokyo.[57] He was, along with Zhang Taiyan and Liu Shipei, one of the moving spirits behind the Asian Solidarity Society.

Mobilizing a Cultural Region: The Asian Solidarity Society

Just as Chinese intellectuals were involving themselves in new types of political activities in far-flung places, and just as they were settling upon a firm narrative of the Manchus as the equivalent modern colonizers of China to Euro-Americans in other places, they developed a new basis for building commonality, founded upon a respect for the very internal and regional cultural pluralisms (at least as these appeared in the historically documented elite spheres) that existing statist and imperialist missions had eroded or were threatening to corrode completely. Indians, Vietnamese, Koreans, Filipinos, and (oppositional) Japanese all gathered within this new anti-state political-culturalist "Asia" rubric, although there is some evidence that Koreans refused to participate because of the unwillingness of the Japanese participants to condemn the occupation of Korea by Japan. The "Asia" that emerged from these connections thus appears as a combination of previous global *tongzhong* discourses, newer "cultural essence" (*guocui*) discourses, radical anti-statist politics, and newly discovered historical affinities in religion, culture, and population flows. These were organizationally combined in the *Yazhou heqin hui*—the Asia Solidarity Society—in 1907.

In mid April 1907, Indian students in Tokyo—who numbered perhaps twenty[58]—convened a commemorative meeting for Shivaji, a seventeenth-century rebel who had initiated an uprising to overthrow the Mughul empire. Some Chinese attended the meeting. Zhang Taiyan, in particular, was quite moved by the occasion and in the beginning of May he published a stirring report on the meeting in the *People's Voice*.[59] Soon after, the Chinese and Indian activists formed the *Yazhou heqin hui* (generally translated as the Asian Solidarity Society); official English name the Asiatic Humanitarian Brotherhood; Japanese name the *Ashū washinkai*.[60] The society's stated goals were to establish the principle of mutual assistance among any and all peoples who were engaged in struggles for national and cultural independence in Asia. The only explicit criteria for joining were opposition to imperialism (*diguo zhuyi*)—defined broadly—and commitment to "protect solidarity" (*zibao qi bangzu*).[61] The founders of the society included Zhang Taiyan, Zhang Ji, Liu Shipei, the anarcho-feminist He Zhen, among others.[62] They were joined by at least two and perhaps as many as six Indians, whose names are now lost, but all of whom had been involved in the Shivaji commemoration[63] and all of whom were also connected to Shyamaji Krishan Verma, organizer in London of the first Indian anticolonial center of activism outside India.[64]

In order to attract members, the society's constitution was written in both Chinese and English,[65] and was printed as a pamphlet for distribution in Tokyo's lively radical circles.[66] The founders intended the society to include not only Indians, Chinese, and Japanese, but also Koreans, Vietnamese, Siamese, Filipinos, Burmese, and Malaysians. The pamphlet thus presumed an English lingua franca for those peoples colonized by Britain or the United States, and a classical Chinese education for the rest.[67] The society's first meeting was held at the India House in Tokyo's Aoyama district[68] and was attended by Indians, Chinese, and Japanese. All of the latter two groups were socialists and/or anarchists connected to the Socialist Lecture Group.[69] At the society's second meeting, held at a Unitarian church in Tokyo's Kudanshita district, these initial members were joined by some Vietnamese and Filipinos.[70]

The society fell apart eighteen months after its founding,[71] and its practical accomplishments were few.[72] Despite the brevity of its existence, the society's formation brought to fruition the accumulated experiences of the previous decade. Indeed, in the context of their mobilizational activity, the activists discovered and elaborated a history of cultural sharing as a premise for regional political solidarity. As the society's constitutional preface notes, historically there had been a diversity of religious and cultural traditions among India, China, Persia, and the "Southern Island" countries of the Malay Peninsula and beyond. Aside from India's Buddhism and Brahmanism, there were Persia's Zarathustra and the Sanskrit cultures of the "Southern Islands," not to mention China's Confucianism, Moism, Daoism, and so on. These cultures, it was asserted, had lived in mutual respect and peace for centuries, maintaining separate identities and rarely bothering one another.[73] Deeply aware that there was little unitary cultural legacy to hold these disparate places together, the author(s) of the preface nevertheless asserted that there was great political urgency to the formation of a society, or brotherhood, to unite this diversity under the banner of the modern category Asia. The reason for this urgency was stated in the preface:

> In the past several hundred years, as Europeans have drifted Eastward, Asia [*yazhou*] has become increasingly weak . . . India was first lost, and China followed at the hands of the Manchus. The Malaysian island group [comprising Malaysia, Indonesia, etc.] was taken by whites; Vietnam and Burma were subsequently swallowed up. The Filipinos, who began under Spanish control, gained independence only to be annexed by the United States. Only Siam and Persia still stand independent, and that cannot be for long![74]

Asia appears here as a historical cultural formation, where cultures are plural and where plurality can be seen as potentially unified only through a synchronic spatio-temporal narrative of common historical experiences of modern imperialism. In other words, the cultural heterogeneity suggests nothing inherently "Asian" about these various places; it is only by presenting the individual states that comprise the region in terms of a "century of

European drift" that it is possible to name Burma, Vietnam, Siam, etc. as regional formation and to mobilize it as such.

On such a view, Asia is not constituted by Europe, yet it is only possible to constitute it as a cultural-regional formation in light of European drift. The distinction is important, for, in contemporary theory, the common assumption that the "third world" can be, in Aijaz Ahmad's words, "constituted by the singular experience of colonialism and imperialism" has been disputed because, among other things, such a designation ignores internal class differentiation within those individual societies. Ahmad in particular has argued, cogently, that it is inadequate to view societies as being defined by their "unitary 'experience' of national oppression."[75] In the case of the Asian Solidarity Society (as with the Filipino and Boer moments before it), there is no doubt that differences in the internal organizations of the various national units were elided by those seeking to form conceptual or organizational solidarities across boundaries. There is also no doubt that these erasures not only facilitated the formation of these solidarities but also made it more likely that the sense of radical solidarity would disappear when the urgency passed. Indeed, there is plenty of evidence to indicate that this disappearance is precisely what happened, especially after the success of the 1911 revolution in China, which helped reconsolidate a notion (among Chinese historians and actors, at least) of revolutionary China's centrality in Asia, a centrality that thereby served to demote historiographically, at least, other Asian revolutionary movements to cameo moments on China's stage.

However, and with these caveats in mind, the brief Asian Solidarity Society episode nevertheless does demonstrate that, on occasion, non-Western peoples' perceptions of shared experiences of oppression (no matter where it came from) led *them* to construct for *themselves* global blocs that were independent of existing states, blocs that allowed them to link up for radical political purposes so as to construct regional solidarities out of their perceived global structural commonality. That these formations were based upon a shared class position and thus an ability to "speak" to one another in a shared cultural and social-elite language of aggrieved power—and thus on the suppression of internal heterogeneity—there can be no doubt; nevertheless, the significance of the self-constitution as an "oppressed people" need not be erased merely because it was "incomplete."

In contrast, then, to popular representations in the Chinese press, where, for example, Indians appeared as paradigmatic "slaves of a lost country" and as a people from whom Chinese should distance themselves with all due speed, in the Asian Solidarity Society's rendering, the commonality of "loss" was precisely the condition of possibility for the discovery of solidarity with Indians. In the society's view, this condition was made visible by understanding the history of each people individually and of all collectively in terms of a global historical trajectory. In the society's constitutional preface, this trajectory is most clearly illustrated by the figuring of the "loss" of India as predating the "loss" of China. That is, the central datum of loss for India is the Mughul takeover of the sixteenth century rather than British conquest, while the Manchus' overthrow of the Ming dynasty in the seventeenth is the central event dating China's "loss," where both moments are fully part of the society's understanding of modern imperialism, and where the understanding of *wangguo*, suffered at the hands of Euro-America, is now read back in time to figure *wangguo* as an event tied to Manchus/Mughuls that predates the arrival of Euro-America.[76] Indeed, in the preface, the Mughuls are blamed for crushing India's fine cultural legacy and sending the country into division and decline (making it ripe for British picking), while the Manchus in China are blamed for stifling the true Chinese tradition of cultural contention and diversity. Chinese-Indian commonality, then, is visible in light of the Euro-American moment of *wangguo*, which is the condition of possibility for their contemporary linkage in global space.

By the same token, the *wangguo* moment is merely the condition of possibility for a rediscovery of culture and history that produces a cultural reading of Asia in which "loss" is figured as a common internal state suppression. Thus, however tenuous the equivalence being drawn between the Mughuls/Manchus and Europeans, it is evident that the spatialized global historical consciousness forged in the course of the previous decade had, by 1907, enabled the emergence of a politicized cultural Asia, which could only be discovered by historicizing the plurality of cultural traditions within the context of the contemporary globalized world, and by asserting itself as an Asia-in-the-world through purposeful unified organizational activity in the context of global cultural-political struggle.

This point was underscored and elaborated by Liu Shipei, who published a lengthy essay entitled "On the Recent Trends in Asia" in November 1907, evidently as further analysis of the issues taken up in the Asian Solidarity Society's constitutional preface.[77] Beginning with an uncompromising statement of the problem, Liu notes: "Today's world is a world of brute force. And the territory of Asia is a ground upon which the white race uses its brute force . . . [W]e must eliminate their involvement in Asia."[78] Liu soon includes Japan in the "white race" category, and states that Japan is part of the problem, not the solution.[79] After an extended discussion of the various precarious situations in which India, Korea, the Philippines, Vietnam, Persia, Burma, Siam, etc., find themselves as a consequence of this "brute force," and a similarly long discussion of their respective impressive efforts to combat their problems, Liu ends the first section of the essay with the conclusion that it is only with the solidarity of the "weak peoples" (*ruozhong*) of Asia that China and the rest of the region can escape the dual clutches of Japan and the West.[80] Yet for Liu, "Asia" is Asia not merely because of its common experience of Western-Japanese domination and its common experience of struggle against this domination. More important, "Asia" is Asia because of the popular flows of culture and people that had fostered borrowings and communications through the centuries and that would allow a solidarity to form and take hold. Placing these cultural flows in the context of a utopian "one-worldism" (*datong zhuyi*), Liu says:

> Korea and Annam [Vietnam] were once within the Chinese sphere; their written language and customs are similar [to China's] . . . Siam's and Japan's written language is also based upon China's.[81] This would make it easy for East Asia to unite together. India is the source of Buddhism, which has flowed all over Asia . . . Islam entered from the Arab countries and is popular in Persia, and when the Persian Muslims were dispersed in their encounter with Arab incorporation, they spread all over India. Muslims and Indian Brahmins also went east from India and are now all over the Southern Seas [*nanyang*]. Today, Indians and Filipinos are familiar with British and American culture and this too makes it easier for western and southern Asia to unite.[82]

Liu's gentle account is a rendition of the construction of a region, in which the interplay of the past and the present establishes both historical dynamism and contemporary relevance. His emphasis on the flows of culture that are dispersed with the movement of people, along with his deemphasis of the state, explicitly elevates people's mobility to a central position of cultural-historical agency. And that this "popular" agency and the Asia constructed out of it significantly includes the appropriation of language and culture from imperialist expansionism poses no problem for

Liu, as he is not concerned here with establishing an ontological authenticity to cultural Asia, but rather in establishing a basis for contemporary political solidarity. This generously inclusive view lends Liu's vision its radical potential and significance.

Linking Liu's views with those of the Asian Solidarity, it is possible to see that, despite what is often seen as this period's conservative revival of "culturalism," or, in a different sense, the Chinese imitation of statist Japanese pan-Asianisms, both Liu and Zhang Binglin, by attaching culture to people rather than to the state or to bureaucratic elites, in effect were attempting to enable a radical politics forged of a regional-global solidarity. Indeed, as Arif Dirlik has pointed out in a different context, their inscription of native ideals (Buddhism, Confucianism, etc.) upon the new global situation "expressed a new cosmopolitanism that would ultimately rephrase those ideals in the language of a global political discourse."[83] Part of this rephrasing was the historicized discovery of a politicized cultural commonality and the mobilization of this commonality in a new regional formation that was explicitly *not* state centered. Indeed, this formation depended for its vitality and plausibility on *displacing* would-be hegemonic states and ideologies, as well as on contesting the emerging hegemony of Western-Japanese power.

Conclusion

A radical Asia idea emerged in Chinese thought and political practice after there had emerged a synchronic globalized sense of China in the world. It is this global space that suggested to Chinese intellectuals the contemporary cultural significance and political potential of the category Asia. The reformulation of culture as a non-state-produced set of practices, whose regional integrative properties were dispersed through people's historical mobility and contemporary revolutionary activism, was crucial to this Asia's radical political potential. Indeed, because the conjunctural condition for transcultural organization was the actual gathering in Tokyo of various nationalists, revolutionaries, cultural activists, and radicals from far-flung places around the region, it was *their* mobility, and the fungibility of *their* (elite) cultures within a new global context that enabled a radical Asianism to flash up among them at this particular moment in history. What is perhaps most striking about this radical Asia construct, despite its ephemerality, is the dynamic and critical role it played at the time in articulating relationships among a cluster of concepts that had come into being during the previous decade and that have remained central to modern Chinese nationalist historiography to this day. These concepts—culture, geography, race, history, imperialism, colonialism—singly and in relation to one another have endured as uncertain political and discursive legacies.

On the one hand, then, and in contrast to subsequent evocations of "Asia" specifically, the radical formation of Asia at the turn of the century did not conceal its construction out of a heterogeneous cultural/geographical space and claim for itself some ahistorical essence or unity. Rather, it acknowledged the historicity of space by *emphasizing* the temporal and structural contingency of relationships among cultures and races and by proposing to bridge this contingency through political commitments to activism. It was, in short, in the dialectical relationship forged between discourse formation and organizational activity that Asia as a place for performance on the world stage and Asia as global historical space were rendered meaningfully by and for Chinese intellectuals at the time.[84] This was a temporary culmination, as it were, to the previous period's searchings.

On the other hand, this radical Asia was flawed in many ways. At the very least, it was flawed by the fact that embedded within it was an acceptance of the very epistemological foundations that were its condition of possibility: that is, the partitioning of the globe from a Eurocentric perspective.[85] It was also flawed by the fact that, however much "the people" were invoked as the bearers of culture, they remained an abstraction, while the culture of which they were purportedly the wellspring remained essentially text-based and elitist. The Asia actualized here was, then, also based upon an ideal construct that undoubtedly had little to do with how a heterogeneous "people" in a wider sense of the term lived their lives. These flaws are perhaps most apparent when we consider the fate of "Asia" in the ensuing century: for as cultural discourse and political site, Asia was soon reified and appropriated for various distinctly unradical purposes. Thus, while "Asianism" has been a recurrent theme of twentieth-century Chinese (and "Asian") history, far from always including the same configurations of peoples, cultures, and states, it has been mobilized for very different purposes at different times. It has reappeared, in Chinese thought at least, in the guise of the 1930s culture debates that linked India and China in an "Eastern spirituality versus Western materialism" confrontation; it has also reappeared as the pan-Asianism of Sino-Japanese sameness advocated by both Japanese and Wang Jingwei's Nanjing government during the Japanese occupation of China in the late 1930s and early 1940s; and in the guise of Mao Zedong's revolutionary rhetoric of third worldism. Most recently, "Asianism" has emerged in the context of contemporary China's joining and promotion of the so-called "Confucian capitalist" network, which is based upon a narrow, statist, and teleologically culturalist and essentialist view of the region.[86]

Nevertheless, whatever the longer-term fate of "Asia," in the form explored above, modern Chinese history as it was narrated through the revival and rearticulation of anti-Manchuism in this period was made particularly relevant through the cultural-political reading of Asia that the global history of imperialism and colonialism had made visible. In this new historicization and in the concreteness of Asia as a site for performing on the world stage, the connectedness of China, Asia, and the world was rendered both the consequence and premise for global and national reconfigurations. Indeed, it was this very connectedness that also permitted the conceptual and activist delinking, as it were, of China from a historically constitutive idea of "Asia," which was displaced by a functional rendering of the region. As the endeavor to carry forward China's revolutionary task of overthrowing the Manchus was on the eve of success, "Asia" and the rest of the world increasingly became functional to China's national project rather than constitutive of it. Indeed, the initial years of the integrative role that expansive globalism played in the constitution of Chinese nationalist discourse were almost at an end by 1907–8, and the years of a more narrowly conceived nationalism—whose conceptual formation owed much to the global expansiveness now being left behind—had arrived.

7 RE-CREATING CHINA'S WORLD

One look at the Persian revolution will prove that revolution does not necessarily invite territorial partitioning; that revolution is not a prelude to partitioning is what our party has been saying all along. One look at the Turkish revolution will convince anyone that there was no move toward partitioning [in its wake]; the European nations were bystanders and watched it from afar.[1]

In 1908, news of the abdication of the sultan and the promulgation of a new constitution in Turkey (*tuerqi* or *tuerji*, indicating both the Ottoman empire and the specific fraction of the Empire that was Turkey) reached revolutionary-minded Chinese in Tokyo and stirred quite a bit of excitement. For, by 1908, these intellectuals were just arriving at the end of a three-year-long divisive debate—carried out in the pages of the two largest exile journals of the time, the Revolutionary Alliance's *Minbao* (People's Voice) and Liang Qichao's *Xinmin congbao* (New People's Miscellany)—about the future course of China. Ostensibly centering on the choice between a revolutionary overthrow of the dynasty in favor of a republican-style government and the retention of the dynasty under a constitutional monarchical system, one of the most critical points of the debate was over whether revolution would invite further partitioning by the imperialist powers. As such, the debate also ramified into and resonated with fundamental questions of what defined "change" and what defined a "nation" in the modern world.

Unlike the open-endedness of the previous decade, however, by the time of the debate (1905–1907), the basic terms and conceptualizations for processes of change and nation definition were more or less settled. Therefore, rather than help constitute the very terms of conceptualization, the Turkish revolution—along with the Portuguese and Persian revolutions[2]—was immediately instrumentalized in the service of already formed political and ideological positions. The Turkish revolution of 1908–1910 was thus dominantly written about by Revolutionary Alliance members, and it was seen against the backdrop of two interrelated concerns. In global terms, it was counterposed to Egypt's previous efforts at reform in the 1820s through the 1840s and was construed as the global historical denouement of the struggle between reform and revolution that all colonized or almost-colonized societies faced in the era of modernity. Because the Turkish revolution seemed to confirm the necessity for revolution as against reform, in domestic Chinese terms it was seen as an affirmation of the correctness of the anti-Qing revolutionary path guided by ethno-nationalism. It was thus narrated into a newly settled (albeit no less contested for its settledness) teleology of the relationship between modernity and nationalism, the essential components of which now centered on a *necessary* rather than contingent historical relationship between revolution and ethno-nationalism.

The Failure of Egyptian Reformism

Egyptian modernization efforts had been discussed widely in the pre-1905 period. These discussions usually subordinated the problematic relationship of mid-nineteenth-century Egypt to the Ottoman Empire, while evaluating Mohammed Ali's state-led reform efforts from the 1820s through the 1840s within the context of British and French incursions into the region. They thus mostly concluded that, in the age of imperialist modernity, state-led modernization was an illusory path, one doomed to historical failure. These Chinese readings were, however, at odds with the Japanese texts upon which they were based.

The best-known work on modern Egypt, translated from the Japanese and serialized in Liang Qichao's *Qingyi bao* (Journal of Pure Critique) from June 1900 to March 1901, centrally figured Mohammed Ali as a failed hero of modern Egyptian nationalism.[3] For the Japanese author Shiba Shiro,[4] Ali's heroism signaled Egypt's civilizational revival after a long period of decline, and thus Egypt's national hopes for the future. While various Chinese commentators also appreciated Ali's heroic efforts, for them the role of British/French intervention loomed larger.[5] Even Liang Qichao in 1901 derived a pessimistic conclusion about the prospects for Qing China's state reforms based on his reading of the history of Ali and Egypt; unlike Shiba's text, Liang downplayed (while lamenting) the notion of civilizational decline and instead focused on the contemporary global environment as an explanation for Egypt's failure. Liang's extended comments on Egypt in his essay "On the New Rules for Destroying Countries"[6] primarily condemned Britain and France for having lured Ali, Arabi Pasha, and Egypt into incurring an enormous foreign debt, which was then used as an excuse to place British and French advisors in the Egyptian government. Soon thereafter, according to Liang, Britain and France used the excuse of the popular unrest that arose in opposition to this incursion to usurp completely Egypt's political sovereignty, all the while proclaiming the Egyptians unfit to govern themselves. For Liang, Egypt's fate was an object lesson on what could happen by allowing foreigners to become advisors in the government, and his commentary functions as a thinly veiled critique of the Qing's drift toward foreign debt and foreign advisors after the 1901 Boxer Protocol. Indeed, as we have seen, this 1901 essay marks an ambivalent break for Liang: situated between his most radical period and the moment at which he finally decided on a statist nationalism, his review of Egypt (as with the other "destroyed countries") confirmed for him that Western imperialism was the primary foe in the modern world.

Kitamura Saburo's *Aiji shi* (History of Egypt), translated and annotated by Zhao Bizhen in 1902–1903,[7] also placed Egypt in the context of civilizational decline, but, unlike Shiba Shiro, Kitamura focused on the failure of Ali to harness the "people's" (*guomin*) active support for and participation in reforms. Yet, even here, the translator Zhao Bizhen's editorial comments indicate his dissatisfaction with Kitamura's interpretation; for, while Zhao admitted the shortcomings of the Egyptian people's spirit (*guomin jingshen*) and the failure of Ali to properly harness the power of the people, he nevertheless blamed British and French interference for Ali's failure.[8] Indeed, as Zhao interprets Kitamura's narrative of the exploits of Ali's successor, Arabi Pasha,[9] the lesson of Egypt becomes a condemnation of the European rhetoric of justice and equality rather than a condemnation of Arabi Pasha's policies or of the Egyptian people themselves:

> [The Europeans say:] "We will only remain so long as it takes for you to progress a little, and then we will leave the country for you to administer." The years pass and one hears nothing of progress; debts accumulate like mountains and the interest on them becomes unmanageable; finances collapse, people's energy is dissipated . . . And then, if and when they return the country to your hands, it is in such a mess that there is nothing you can do about it. Then others come in to attack

> and take advantage of your weakness, prompting the original ones to intervene again to "save" you.[10]

Despite, then, the insistence by Japanese authors that the lessons of Egypt were primarily about civilizational decline or the failures of the Egyptian people, Chinese commentators interpreted the Egyptian case as a problem of imperialism and thus of the complexities of the unevenness of modernity.

In a masterful statement of this complexity, Zhang Yüanji, then editor of the Shanghai-based Commercial Press, wrote a preface to the 1903 translated version of Shiba Shiro's volume in which he carefully drew out the significance of the temporal and spatial problem inherent in Ali's endeavor. As Zhang noted, Egypt's strategic geographical position at the confluence of Asia, Africa, and Europe made it only a matter of time before Europeans took a concerted interest in the place. As such, when Ali attempted his reforms, he was not only isolated temporally—being the only reformer in the non-Euro-American world at the time—but his area was the object of desire by an expanding Europe, a convergence that gave Europeans the luxury to concentrate their forces against him before events in other colonies dissipated and divided that energy while providing mutual support for would-be revolutionaries and reformers.

This historical conjunctural problem helped clarify for Zhang that Ali was neither a victim of his own nor of the Egyptian people's inadequacies, but rather a victim of contradictions within modernity as a global problem.[11] As Zhang pointedly lamented, Ali appeared to do everything that "Europeans welcome and praise most" in his efforts to modernize Egypt: he learned from Europe by implementing European banking and administrative techniques; he supported industrialization; he rationalized the bureaucracy and restructured Egyptian society; and so on. However, the result was that Egypt had "its national vitality exploited and ended by having its sovereignty stolen. Once Europeans gained control, they turned around and blamed Egypt, loudly condemning its endeavors."[12] Beyond the specificity of Egypt, Zhang Yüanji figured the conjuncture that structured Ali's efforts and his failure as a universal principle of contemporary times:

> Europe has two new nouns: one is imperialism [*diguo zhuyi*] and one is ethno-nationalism [*minzu zhuyi*]. These are words of political scholars and should probably be respected. Alas! Once one knows these two words, then [one knows] all about the Europeans annexing and

> swallowing weak countries and exterminating different peoples [*jianchu yizu*].
>
> Imperialism takes as its premise the expansion of power and influence; it does not oppose using intimidation to oppress the weak. Nationalism takes as its purpose the separation and division of different types [*zonglei*], and thus does not oppose mobilizing the unity of sameness in order to punish difference.[13]

For Zhang, then, the relationship between European expansionism and its ethno-nationalism not only structured the particular story of Ali's Egypt but provided the universal principle of the relationship between imperialism, European nationalism, and emergent nationalisms the world over. While Zhang was no proponent of ethno-nationalist revolution for China, he nevertheless perceived the vexed ways in which "identity" and "difference" were made into normative assumptions of European expansionism and the modern world it wished to create.

The interpretive lines established—here with reference to Egypt—between "internal" and "external" factors precisely constituted the parameters of the interpretive and practical problems Chinese intellectuals faced in designing appropriate concepts and modes of action for the transformation of Qing China. Egypt provided the best proximate example of reformism gone awry because of imperialism. Yet, while Liang Qichao soon thereafter concluded that, in the face of such an imperialist world system, the only true choice for China was internal consolidation around a state that could be made strong enough to stand up to the global powers more effectively, others, such as Revolutionary Alliance spokesman Hu Hanmin and his fellow *Minbao* (People's Voice) editorialists, drew different conclusions. For them, China's problems, however intertwined with the global imperialist system, could only even preliminarily be addressed by overthrowing the Manchu Qing, an analysis that depended completely upon the prior incorporation of imperialism and colonialism into a renarration of China's modern history that turned the Manchus into the modern colonizers. The correctness of these conclusions seemed to be confirmed by the Turkish revolution of 1908.

The Young Turks: Constitutionalism, Revolutionism, Ethnos, and the Military

The first long essay on the Turkish revolution (in contrast to the various reports filtered through Western wire services and Japanese newspapers) focused rather narrowly on the new Turkish constitution that resulted from the Young Turks' revolt. In this mid-1908 essay, Zhang Zhongduan, editor of the Tokyo-based Revolutionary Alliance-affiliated journal *Henan*, registered his qualified praise for the Turkish events.[14] Placing Turkey's recent transition in the now-accustomed framework of "Asia," Zhang explained that, aside from Japan, there were three types of situations that prevailed in the region: the already colonized (*yi wang*) (India, Burma, Vietnam, and Korea); those almost fully dependent on foreign protection (Siam, Persia, Afghanistan); and those who were still suspended between revival/survival and loss (Turkey and China). Zhang understood the current options for China by deriving his conclusion from the Japanese exception; in other words, it was constitutional government that defined for him the boundary between "loss" and "survival." For Zhang, then, Turkey now had tipped the balance toward its own survival by promulgating a real constitution and moving toward constitutional rule.

In analyzing the situation in Turkey, Zhang noted that, although previously Turkey had had a constitution (of 1876), the country had been riven by assassinations, popular unrest, and other disturbances in the ensuing decades because of the abrogation of that constitution by the sultanate. By contrast, at the present moment and in the wake of the revolution, stability seemed to have been ensured by the abdication of the sultan and the capture of Istanbul and other cities by the constitutional forces. The sultan's abdication "proved," according to Zhang, that monarchs were not needed for constitutional rule in such situations as Turkey's and China's (ignoring the fact that Japan had an emperor but scoring a point against the constitutional monarchists in China).

What also impressed Zhang was that the "Young Turks Party" emerged from "the people." In Zhang's recounting of the revolutionary process, he emphasized that the Young Turks, as a political organization and political party, had forged links to laborers—whose strikes had assisted the rise of the party—and, to Zhang's great surprise, was also connected to ordinary women, who had joined the party in unprecedented numbers. This popular political mobilization was further enhanced, in Zhang's view, by the

Young Turks' ability to harness the progressive elements in the military to their movement.[15] For Zhang, then, the Turkish revolution correctly combined the elements essential to a proper nationalist task in the current era: revolution, constitution, popular political mobilization, and militarism. Moreover, that amorphous category called "the people" gained some bit of specificity through his sociological identification of particular groups who could be counted on to form the backbone of a popular movement: laborers, women, the military.

There was, however, one aspect of the Turkish situation that caused Zhang some consternation: the ethnic and religious inclusiveness of the constitutional forces.

> The Turkish people have experienced the monarchy's coercion and the co-opting of officials through the high-sounding rhetoric proclaiming the unity of the empire and that the "Arabs" are equal. (Arab people are in Egypt and were destroyed by Turkey; this affair is reminiscent of the recent one in China, when the People's Party [*Mindang*] proclaimed that, once a new government is established, the Manchus will be treated like the rest of the people.) Yet, what is the enduring basis for the impartiality, motivation, and spirit of the lack of conflict between Muslims and Christians? This all remains extremely volatile, and I will be watching closely to see what happens next.[16]

Zhang thus reserved his final evaluation of Turkey's revolution because of what he presumed to be the inherent instability of a multiethnic, multireligious national formation, particularly one that retained, without any compensatory strategy, a rhetoric and practice of unity among ethnicities/religions that derived from a previous imperial formation. Proceeding with a jab at his political-ideological opponents, those, such as Liang Qichao, who maintained that once a dynastic-sponsored constitution was promulgated in China, Manchus equally with the Han should constitute the "people" (*guomin*) of the Chinese nation, Zhang foregrounded the uneasy and unstable compromise between Muslims and Christians in Turkey as proof of the need to exclude the Manchus from any political settlement in China, and to stabilize "China" in terms of the Han *minzu*.[17]

Despite his caution about the Turkish experiment, however, toward the end of the essay Zhang included the by now obligatory unfavorable comparison between China's current immobility and Turkish activity; between the lack of spirit on the part of the Chinese people and the evident spirit of the Turkish people; the uprightness of the Turkish military and the corruption in the Chinese military; the passivity of Chinese laboring people and of Chinese women and the activism of Turkish laborers and women. He concluded: "How can we arouse ourselves to this level? The only way is to organize and unify. But the biggest pity is that those [in China] who claim themselves to be enlightened [*ziming wei kaitong ren*], and who rhetorically proclaim the need to 'save the people and save the nation' are precisely those whose behavior is like a bleeding and ulcerous cancer."[18] In the larger picture, then, Zhang congratulated Turkey for having surged ahead of China—"with limits only itself can set in the future"—while lamenting that China continued to sink into further stagnation, with the Qing-sponsored National Assembly Party factions—part of the dynastic proposal for a move toward constitutionalism—unanchored in popular support and working only for their own and the Manchus' selfish interests.[19]

Indeed, at the very point when the Turkish revolution erupted, the constitutionalist solution in China had become particularly vexed, enmeshed as it was in arguments between the supporters of ethno-nationalist revolution/republicanism and the promoters of political reform that would result in monarchical constitutionalism. These arguments had been considerably aggravated after 1906 by the dynasty's own grudging support for convening a constitutional assembly (itself an effort to forestall its crumbling legitimacy among provincial power holders and local entrepreneurial interests).[20] Dynastic support for a constitution and its apparent dovetailing with the desires of monarchical constitutionalist factions abroad was consistently accused by the Revolutionary Alliance of being a crass, last-ditch effort by a dying dynasty to retain power. After the Turkish Revolution, in fact, the proposed Qing constitutional efforts were often compared to the 1876 Turkish constitution, with both varieties labeled "puppet instruments of the monarchy."[21] Nevertheless, as the Revolutionary Alliance supported constitutionalism—albeit in the form of a republican government rather than under the aegis of the monarchy—the Turkish solution of 1908 at first powerfully recommended itself for emulation, since it had apparently forced the abdication of the sultan and his replacement by a form of popular rule led by an elite party supported by significant fractions of the population along with the military.

Skepticism about the Young Turk revolution was not absent from the discussion, and while ultimately it was the ethnic "issue" that required most explanation, the revolutionariness of the revolution was questioned by the most radical Chinese: anarchists. Anarchists characterized the "so-called Young Turks Party" as a moderate faction within the spectrum of Turkish politics, and labeled their "so-called reform" laughable.[22] In praising the Turkish laborers for striking, anarchists noted that the involvement of the Young Turks Party in these strikes, far from being a salutary influence, had been a moderating brake on labor radicalism. Even while they conceded that anarchism could not be accomplished overnight, anarchist commentators nevertheless lamented that the strikers were not permitted to press their demands to a radical end, but rather were forced to succumb to the "political pragmatism" promoted by the Young Turks.[23] In their assessments, the seizure of state power by the Young Turks was merely putschist reformism, not a revolution.

By 1910, among nonanarchist Revolutionary Alliance members, the "success" of the Turkish revolution also came to be qualified. Rather than condemn it altogether, however, commentary on the Turkish events essentially took two directions. On the one hand were meticulous analyses of the organizational structure of the Young Turks Party and the ways in which their movement had grown. These focused on the movement in exile, the journalistic campaigns waged by exiled intellectuals, the efforts of the sultanate to infiltrate the organization with spies, the mobilization of internal forces (laborers and women) to support the exiled leadership, as so on. The most complete of these analyses[24] details the imperatives of underground and exile organization—where no one person can know too much; where revolutionary propaganda is passed through strictly policed organizational nodes in order to create "webs" of information not traceable to any one source; where women are enlisted to carry out some of the most vital and delicate operations (despite the rigid separation between men and women in Turkish society), and so forth—and it reads almost like a textbook guide to deterritorialized revolutionary political praxis that extended the 1902 revolutionary guide spun by Ou Jujia out of the Boer, Cuban, and Filipino struggles into a more concrete structure.[25] It also follows Zhang Zhongduan's earlier essay in sociologically searching for the portions of the population who could be identified as allies in revolutionary mobilization.

Another set of commentaries on the Turkish revolution, on the other hand, focused on the importance of establishing strong revolutionary goals, which, it was recognized, the Young Turks had not done. These commentaries also narrowed the sociological field of "the people" to the military. Thus, even while these latter commentaries continued to applaud the revolution as a gesture, they also used the shortcomings of the Turkish events as an opportunity to discuss specific problems and propositions faced by the Revolutionary Alliance in fomenting revolution in China and in specifying its goals and sociological scope.[26]

As a representative *Minbao* essay of 1910 asserted, revolution "must first have clear goals and then take place," because an "indulgent" (*guxi*) revolution (one without clear goals) would inevitably dissolve. As was demonstrated by the Turkish revolution, the essay noted (in an ominous prefiguring of the Chinese case), if revolutionary action was not decisive from the outset, repeated revolutions would be necessary to thoroughly transform the situation; it went on to assert that a revolution could not compromise with established authority and it could not emerge merely from the designs of a revolutionary party. Rather it had to be uncompromising and emerge from "the consciousness and sufferings of common people [*shi you yiban renmin zhi liangxin yu tongku er fasheng*]."[27]

On the first question—strong revolutionary goals—the problem with the Turkish revolution was its compromise with the institution of the sultanate, as a brief history of Turkish politics from 1908 through 1910 noted. According to Min Yi, the composite *Minbao* author of this latter essay, the Young Turks Party initially "had no desire to directly punish Sultan Hamid II, but rather [they supported] either waiting until the sultan was dead [to deal with the problem of the sultanate], or using the sultan to oppose the Mohammedean faith and then [forcing him] to resign his throne in favor of his son."[28] Such a strategy of "indulgence" was doomed to failure, and in the event, it resulted in Sultan Hamid II's co-opting of the revolution and the rapid resumption of the imperial dictatorship. This regression had necessitated a second revolutionary action, in which Sultan Hamid II himself was vanquished and deposed, even though the sultanate remained. This outcome, the essay claimed, was no different from what would happen were the proposed solution of the reformist constitutionalists to be taken, and it represented no real change whatsoever.[29]

However, the essay went on to explain, the political configurations in China and Turkey were actually different, and this difference meant that the Turkish revolution was instructive only on some issues, and not on others. Indeed, Min Yi noted, Turkey could already be called a constitutional monarchy, which meant the revolution was not a revolution merely for constitutionalism. By contrast, in China, it was "the ethnic problem [that] obstructs [constitutionalism]."[30] Revising the earlier skepticism about the multiethnic character of Turkey, the essay then asserts that the "ethnic problem" in Turkey had been solved by the prior break-away of the Ottoman Empire's national fractions. In other words, according to Min Yi, the difference between Turkey's and China's situations inhered in the fact that, in Turkey, "those who hold the sultanate dear are Turks" just as those who "promote revolution are also Turks," and since Turks are the majority people in Turkey, the Turkish revolution could be considered an internal affair between people (*guomin*) of the same ethnicity (*minzu*). It was a problem of political representation in a national state, and in that sense, it could not compare to the problem in China, where:

> Those who hold monarchical power dear are Manchus, and those who seek a constitution are Han [Chinese], not Manchus. This differs greatly from the revolutionary obtainment of a constitution in Turkey, because the main revolutionary motivation in Turkey is from Turks, supported by Macedonians, whose intention is merely to be a minority people supporting a majority people in order to secure their own survival. How could the [majority] Han even dream of supporting the [minority] Manchus so as to ensure their own survival?!
>
> If one calculates the position of the Han [in China], it is similar to the Greeks' plotting for independence [from the Ottoman Empire] . . . The Greeks were a civilized people who were compelled into submission to Turkey, just as the Han were compelled into submission to the Manchus. During the period when Greeks were subjected to the oppressive rule of Turkey, they knew to plot for independence and to not rest their hopes on a Turkish constitution. It is only because the [Greek] people had such intentions that they finally achieved independence. This is really exactly the same as the intentions of contemporary China's Revolutionary Party . . .
>
> [In Turkey] it was not just the Greeks, however. Bulgarians, Slovenians, Romanians, Montenegrins: all were peoples [*minzu*] subjected to Turkey's rule and all reacted in exactly the same way as the Greeks . . .
>
> How can the Han ignore this and follow the lead of the Macedonians?![31]

In short, according to this essay, the only true basis for a cohesive national state was ethno-national purity, which the Turks had already achieved. Moving the discussion away from state institutions as such, this figuration concluded that while the Turkish situation was still unstable and incomplete, Turkey's path toward stabilization was cleared, because the ethnic problem had been resolved. In this light, the issue in China was *not* merely one of promulgating a constitution—as an instrument of state; thus it was not the state qua institutions that was at issue—for, so long as constitutionalism was not based upon displacement of the Manchus, ethnic "difference" would remain a fundamental barrier to genuine nationhood.

Despite the incoherence of the ethnic argument as stated here, and despite the conflation of imperial formations with nation formations—in both the Ottoman and the Qing cases—the above analysis of the Turkish situation and of the difference between Turkey and China became a standard one. Indeed, Hu Hanmin took it as the premise for the essay he published in the same issue of *Minbao,* in which he discussed the proper relationship of "the people" to the military in revolutionary situations. Asserting that the major task of a revolution was to fundamentally alter the relationship between the people and the rulers, Hu claimed that the military had to be a key factor in this transformation, for only the military could mediate relations between those in power and those on the ground, the people. As such, he wrote, while the military in China had no shortage of soldiers who preyed upon people and exploited them, nevertheless their "ethnic feeling is the same as that of the ordinary people." This putatively shared "ethnic feeling" could be demonstrated, according to Hu, by reviewing the many incidents of hostility precipitated by encounters between the Han Chinese new armies and the Manchu Banners over the past decades.[32] This review led Hu to the conclusion that ethnic feeling between the Han military and the people needed to be fostered and encouraged, in order to render the military into a true force of popular revolution.

Here, it is noteworthy that the previous decade's need to historically substantiate *minzu* as a relevant category of national analysis had been completely naturalized. Thus, despite the recognition that Han Chinese soldiers in no way *acted* upon common ethnicity (*tongzhong*) in dealing with ordinary people, Hu still asserted that an objectively defined common ethnicity was the only operative category of national cohesion. It is also interesting to note that "the people" now were no longer displaced onto the figures of the helpless or the overseas Chinese, but rather subsumed by the figure of "the military," which was posited as the agent par excellence of ethno-nationalism.

In trying to recuperate the disjuncture he himself noted between the actual activity by the military that divided the people and the supposed ethnic cohesion that was to be the basis of action, Hu took a major detour to discuss the positive or negative positions of militaries in recent foreign revolutions—in the 1905 Russian Revolution (negative), the successive French revolutions (where in 1848 the military finally played a positive role), the English Revolution (positive), and so on. From this world historical tour, Hu concluded that only troops that opposed the state (in other words, not putschist troops) were truly revolutionary, and that no revolution could take place without the integral participation of and bloodshed by an army of co-ethnics.[33] Thus moving away from the abstract romanticism of the Boers, for example, and having "proved" that the military *could* play a positive role in domestically defined revolutions—so long as it was ethnically aligned with "the people" and not politically aligned with the state—Hu rhetorically asked what in fact prompted the Turkish military, which was historically so thoroughly wedded to the government, to finally choose to side with the revolutionary party, the putative voice of the people. In the absence of actual details about this—details, Hu complained, that were ignored in the newspaper accounts he had seen—Hu surmised that such a choice could only have been prompted by the magnitude of injustice perpetrated upon the people by their avaricious and dishonest rulers. It was this, Hu maintained, that the Chinese military and the Revolutionary Alliance could and should learn from Turkey.[34]

This observation leads Hu into a long disquisition on the relationship between violence, the creation of a citizenry, and the critical role of the military in both responding to and fostering sociopolitical transformation, a disquisition that he concludes with the observation that the only meaning that "preserving the nation" could possibly have is "protecting the people."[35] In other words, the "nation" was "the people" ethnically conceived and the military was both to reflect and protect its co-ethnics rather than be loyal to the state. From this point on, Hu's essay is most concerned with establishing the proper realm of action for the military, and with the necessity for the military to break free of its loyalty to corrupt governments. Again falling back on the notion of co-ethnicity, Hu comments that troops in general protect people of the "same race" (*tongzhong*), where the locution refers unambiguously to an internal, or *minzu* (ethnos), category, not to the previous expansive global category. Hu nevertheless notes that troops were often used to suppress people's resistances to oppression, whether the people were of the same ethnicity or not. This occurred often, he noted, in France and Germany, where troops were used to put down strikes and suppress worker's unions, which was the wrong way for the military to mediate between ruler and ruled.[36]

Hu's introduction of the problem of "loyalty" among and between people, military, and government, and indeed his whole discussion of the distance between actual behavior and putative ethnic solidarity opened a gap in the synonymy between "the people" and "ethnic sameness"—*minzu* understood as an internal *tongzhong*. This was a gap that Hu could not resolve in either theoretical or practical terms, particularly as the synonymous nature of these two terms had already been rendered a normative notion in Manichean colonial guise as an analysis of China's internal situation by the time. And, as was often the case in *Minbao* essays, when confronted with such a theoretical or practical conundrum, the essayist quickly moves into a jeremiad against the Manchus to conceal the illogic and problem. This is precisely what Hu did. For, in the end, Hu concluded, the "only way to get rid of dictatorship is through the military," even while this necessary condition was not sufficient to achieve total success. Indeed, he wrote, it was clear that even while the "Turkish revolution represents progress, it was not completely successful"; nevertheless, in comparison to the cynical training of Han troops by the Manchus for their own self-protection—equivalent, Hu wrote, to the British use of Indian troops and the French use of Vietnamese troops—the revolutionary troops of Turkey deserved congratulations and encouragement for their protection of the Turkish people.[37]

In sum, then, despite its apparent shortcomings, the Turkish revolution came to confirm for Chinese revolutionaries that the only proper mode of change and nation formation in the current period was "popular" ethnonationalist revolution, where the "popular" content was to be supplied by a military, whose loyalty had been detached from the state and reattached to co-ethnics. Politically, upon that basis alone would the promulgation of a constitution lead to a fundamentally new form of political rule and a new form of state-people relations: a genuine nation-state. The crucial category that objectively defined "the people"—ethnicity—was here understood as the sole legitimate basis for the nation, but not necessarily as an organicist idea; rather, it was understood and elaborated in terms of colonial categories of "otherness." And this understanding of ethnicity, *minzu* understood as a historical ontology defined by an exclusively internal *tongzhong*, not only allowed the breakup of the Ottoman Empire to appear similar to the perceived urgent necessity of the Han to rid China of the Manchus, but it completed the previous decade's tendential conflation of old-style imperial overlordships with modern imperialism in the new context of the move toward nation-states. With this conflation complete, ethno-nationalism also came to be separated from the previous expansive global understanding of *tongzhong*, which had linked different peoples of the world together in a politically understood category of "sameness" welded together by the threat of *wangguo*, or colonization, and was now reduced in scope to a specifically internalist proposition that indicated *tongzhong* and *minzu* as the sole proper foundation of separate nationalisms worldwide. In this final guise, *minzu* became the basis for modern Chinese nationalism—as discourse and practice.

The second point to emerge from this final moment revolved around the complete subsumption of "the people" into a sociological and institutional form embodied by the military. To be sure, the growth of "new armies" in the late Qing (those armies that were less incorporated into the old Manchu Banner system) along with the better quality of the new army soldiers (in terms of professionalization and education) seemed to offer precisely the opportunity for military detachment from the state that was supposed to be operative in the Turkish case. Also contributing to the valorization of the military, as detailed in chapter 5 above, was that militarism itself had come to be seen as a positive social virtue through these years. Yet, most crucially, the military, as a social institution and not merely as a social virtue, was now understood to be the key bearer of the "popular" revolution itself. This emphasis on the military as the perfect modern expression of popular revolutionary agency and of popular sovereignty, particularly when these were combined with an internal *tongzhong* solidarity read as an assumed *minzu* identity and unity, thus completed the displacement of the actual people from agentive activity, even while it retained the rhetorical appeals to "the people" and to their centrality, which had previously been established as necessary components of nationalism.

In the actual event, the "new army" did indeed become a crucial basis for the 1911 revolution (albeit almost accidentally), although their success at forcing the abdication of the last emperor did not lead to the long-term outcomes for which Hu and the Revolutionary Alliance members might have wished. Even less did the "new armies" reflect any broad-based support or unitary popular revolutionary will or ethnic cohesion. Nor even did the ethnic exclusionism of the alliance's nation-statist rhetoric endure much beyond the abdication. But the post-1911 collapse of the new republican state and the ensuing decades-long process of searching for ways to rebuild and reunify China is too well known in its narrative form to need recapitulation here.

Conclusion

In his book *All That Is Solid Melts into Air*, Marshall Berman writes: "Modern environments and experiences cut across all boundaries of geography and ethnicity, of class and nationality, of religion and ideology: in this sense, modernity can be said to unite all mankind. But it is a paradoxical unity, a unity of disunity . . . To be modern is to be part of a universe in which, as Marx said, 'All that is solid melts into air.' "[38] Berman's phrase "unity of disunity" pinpoints well the necessarily conjunctural nature of any specification of the intersection between global and local historical experiences and discursive formations. It is no accident that ethno-nationalist revolution came to be a unifying concept taken up within imperialist modernity—as a solution, it could be said, to the unity in disunity that is produced and represented in and by the unevenness of the global space of modernity—even while it was also perforce a primary factor that disunified the world by turning each people in on itself and shutting the door to more expansive global political solidarities. It was, however, not an inevitable path; rather, it was a path that needed to be discovered and forged anew by each people and each nation undergoing the process in their own particular ways. In China's case, it was forged from within the actually existing global and local circumstances as perceived by Chinese intellectuals over the last long decade of the Qing dynasty.

In the specific terms of this study, the incoherent lessons derived from the Turkish revolution by Chinese intellectuals represent an instrumentalizing of global events for the purposes of a recently constructed set of ideological and political programs in the Chinese context. Thus, rather than exploring the global and local structural conditions of the Turkish events and finding in them the essentially limited aspirations of the Young Turks, Chinese revolutionaries, who were now set on their path, focused merely on the eventness of the revolution (its instrumental and institutional outcomes) and not on the open-ended global historical process that connected modernity with revolution as constitutive topoi of their contemporary era and as potential global solutions to their local dilemma.

Nevertheless, despite, or rather because of, this narrowing of vision, the essential components of a Chinese nationalist discourse and practice were established by 1910–1911. Indeed, the conceptual and historical conflations, no less than the displacements onto the figure of "the people" of China's weakness and the subsequent attempt to reconstitute that people in institutionally containable form via the military, provided the immediate possibility for the anti-Qing revolution to achieve "success." The nationalist discursive synthesis, no less than the actual revolutionary conceptualizations and practices that informed it, has continued to inspire and plague Chinese intellectuals and the Chinese people for the entire century that has ensued.

CONCLUSION

In 1904 Chen Duxiu, then editor of a journal in Anhui province and later a co-founder of the Chinese Communist Party, asked himself why China was being encroached upon:

> The more I considered [China's problems], the more I thought, and then the more I grieved: the reason that our China is unlike foreign countries [*waiguo*] and indeed is bullied by these countries must have a good explanation. So I went to investigate [the histories of] other countries, and guess what? China is not the only country in this world being bullied by foreign countries! Look at Poland, Egypt, the Jews, India, Burma, Vietnam, and so on: they have all already been destroyed and turned into dependencies [*miezuo shuguo le*].[1]

Chen's insight is broadly representative of the insights of his transitional generation of intellectuals:[2] that explanations for China's modern problems transcended the West/China dyadic relationship. This insight led Chen to seek the answer to his anguished musing on China not only in China's past, nor in foreign countries' (*waiguo*)[3] present relationship to China alone, but rather in China's shared global situation with the "other countries" of the world. This shared global situation, initially concealed from view because of the treatment that China seemed to uniquely suffer at the hands of stronger powers, was rendered visible to Chen when the world was revealed to be a patterned whole.

At the turn of the twentieth century the understanding of globality as a shared historical condition on a shared world stage was quite new. It was from the vantage of this newly apprehended space and idea of globality, as it was put into dynamic relationship with the vexed situation in China—marked on one end by the Chinese defeat in the Sino-Japanese War of 1895 and on the other end by the Republican revolution of 1911—that Chinese nationalism, as a discourse integrally tied to a complex global historical moment and as a set of practices tied to the specific situation of China at the time, was formulated. Indeed, I have argued that contemporaneous events rendered modern global structure, or modernity as uneven global space, visible to Chinese intellectuals, and that the view of modernity these events illumined brought into particular relief certain central concepts of nationalism for Chinese intellectuals. The synchronic historical consciousness that emerged in the late Qing period thus both reflected and produced an awareness of the global structural conditions as well as the constraints of the contemporary moment. Together, these marked a Chinese intervention in the world—or, a multisided argument with the world "as is"—even while they were also a concession to the world as it appeared—a world cut in two, a colonized and a colonial world.[4]

The premise throughout this study has been that, as derivative as Chinese nationalism in its nation-statist form may ultimately have been, inquiries into the historical process of the discursive formation of nationalism are diminished if an essentially derivative or modular statism—that is, if the state as tyrannical narrator of nation is always posed as the central problem of nationalism—is taken as a substitute for broader inquiry. For, not only do such inquiries reduce the complexity of the time and space of global modernity to a linear, bounded narrative plane, they also contain historical process within an a priori national space defined by a retrospectively constructed state or reified cultural essence. Such inquiries thus inadequately acknowledge the diffuseness with which modernity and nationalism were experienced and apprehended within the very would-be totalizations created by capitalist expansionism across the globe; they also do not take into account the complexity of Chinese nationalism, which owed at least some of its innovative vitality and dynamism to the global problematic in which it was embedded and by which it was informed.

As a consequence of the study's dual focus on globality and discursive formations of nationalism, the questions with which it has been concerned have not had to do with distinguishing between state forms and native cultural content, since this way of formulating the historical problem posits a functional dichotomy between "external" and "internal" sources of change and definition, or between universal and particular contents of local nationalisms, dichotomies that are really little more than a historical and historiographical trap. Rather, the process of the discursive formation of nationalism in China is explored in this study from a perspective that takes immanent historical totalization as a recognized problem of global modernity: that is, as a totalization that was desirously and tendentially posed from a Euro-American hegemonic perspective while it was vigorously worked through—albeit only partially so—by Chinese intellectuals at the turn of the century. One point of the discussion has been to demonstrate that Chinese intellectuals considered this problem of immanence—of carrying only values that are produced through praxis—not from a position of centrality, nor of peripherality, and nor of culturalist/statist essence; all of these posit an objectivism upon the situation that poses a false sense of unity on the period and thus pose an obstacle to historical inquiry. The inquiry has focused, rather, on how Chinese intellectuals considered the problem of immanence from a position of incipiently recognized globality, for it was the centripetal trajectory of Chinese intellectuals' experiences of modernity, if we look at it *not* from a Western perspective nor from a putatively "pure" Chinese perspective, but from a shifted global perspective, that initially opened for them a truly global space of imagining informed by a modern time-space construed as a world stage of synchronic historical praxis. The study has consequently insisted that what the Chinese made of this stage, as a consciousness and as a new logic of political praxis, needs to be explained not merely by reference to hypostatized internal cultural contestations as captured and congealed in political forms and institutions, but by the material historicity of the rise of nationalism as a historical problematic in and of modernity.

The conceptual traversing of global space engaged in by Chinese intellectuals during the last long decade of the Qing dynasty enabled them to link *difference* and *identification* into a provisional synthesis that helped indicate the trajectory of Chinese nationalism. This trajectory was both eminently and universally modern—anticolonial and anti-imperialist—as well as specifically Chinese—anti-Manchu and antidynastic. It was also trapped by its allegiance to those universals and particulars. That the specific Chinese outcome—the overthrow of the Manchu Qing—represented a much reduced imaginary of nationalism from what was initially made possible from the originally expansive globality of the 1895–1905 period consequently can be explained not by the necessary reassertion of a Sinocentricity or a teleological cultural model of Han chauvinism, but by the overdetermination of the very posing of a nationalist problematic in the age of modernity.

As a historiographical or theoretical proposition, to make visible this part of modern Chinese history and the history of modernity as intertwined global and local experiences, it has been necessary to dispense with the idea that the only "worlds" that made any difference to late Qing Chinese—as intellectual or material bases for their imaginings and conceptualizations—were those of "the West," "Japan," or some authentically construed continuous Chinese past. Thus, while the study presents a specific discussion of Chinese history, its broader goal has been to look at modern global history in a different way, so as to begin to rethink theoretically and comparatively two prevalent and debilitating historiographical consequences to the exclusive structuration of the modern world as a relationship only or primarily to the West-Japan or to the native past.

First, in general writings on global history, the struggles and discourses in any particular site are usually seen, at best, as connected by the retrospective view of the scholar in an artificially constructed comparative framework.[5] Despite an implicit (and sometimes explicitly comparative) awareness that many processes happened at the same time (i.e., synchronically), modern global history is nevertheless generally written as the succession of individual moments in diachronic temporal relation to one another and in spatial relationship only to the West, rather than also in synchronic relation to other parts of the globe.[6] Indeed, as David Harvey has noted in this idiom, in the colonial global system of the nineteenth and early twentieth centuries, "the world's spaces . . . were deterritorialized, stripped of their preceding significations, and then reterritorialized according to the convenience of colonial and imperial administrations."[7] In that process, Frederick Buell points out, "the center was strongly bounded and the peripheries were splintered in order each to be linked separately with that core, in circuits as exclusive as possible."[8] These tight bilateral bindings of "core" and "periphery" as a structure of colonial relations were and remain, in altered form, real; they have, however, blinded historians to other types of historical consequences to the destructions of "preceding systems."

This study has endeavored to show that it is precisely in the recognition by Chinese intellectuals of China's shared world stage with other peoples and countries that the temporal/spatial problem inherent in a modern global history, the problem that poses all histories as a series of moments linearly and causally linked through the West, can and should be modified. In the present figuration, global and Chinese history become a multisided process of dialectical interaction—at the turn of the century, mostly conceptual interaction—among what are usually figured as different and separable parts of the globe in individual dyadic relationship to (Western) History.

Second, while a recent world-systems approach to global history has clarified that various parts of the world have interacted economically for a very long time, and that China was not only more "advanced" economically than the presumed world center (Europe) up until the eighteenth century, but that it also was more central to the emerging world economy than has generally been acknowledged, this approach is still limited by its focus on economism and statism. To be sure, on one level, the new positive spotlight on China is as gratifying for historians of China as it might be for Chinese in general, demonstrating as it does the centrality of a formerly peripheral China to the modern world of global trade and transformation. Yet, while such revisions undeniably have opened many new avenues of inquiry on Chinese socioeconomic history and on Chinese relations with non-Chinese over the centuries, thus making possible a rethinking of numerous issues that hitherto had remained mired in older paradigms informed by isolationism or Sinocentricity, nevertheless, the central structuring question for most of these inquiries remains wedded to answering why Europe rose and China did not. In posing (and attempting to answer) such a question, China can only be doomed to failure as "modernity" nears; or, in a new, more optimistic version of agentive historicity, China can also appear to have historically enacted an "alternative modernity," one that nevertheless still takes some putative homogeneous Western version of modernity as its standard as well as a putatively standard History—as determined by capitalist modernization—as its basis and goal. These lines of inquiry, as currently conceived, it seems to me, are intellectual and historical traps.

By contrast, the approach to global interaction here—admittedly delimited in time and space to the late Qing period and even further delimited to a small group of intellectuals, disproportionately influential though they and their conceptualizations of the Chinese nation may have been—has been to track interaction through a history of intellectual appropriations and admixings that circulated through other channels. Overdetermined many of these appropriations surely were, particularly when they were redissolved into a statist quest, or into what Hegel noted in a different context as being a dialectic of institutional life that seeks to ensure the unitary institutional perpetuation of the accidental convergence of multiple historicities.[9] Nevertheless, looking beyond and behind this unilinear logic, one can find another historical trend, whose dynamic possibilities were strong and which has reemerged consistently over the past century.

As a final gesture, it is important to note—lest anyone think this study has attempted to recuperate a new version of a history that imposes homogeneity upon the "third world," that is, a history that conceals contradictions—that at the same time as the uneven global space of modernity undoubtedly opened sources of imagining for Chinese intellectuals that were not directly from Euro-America or Japan, these imaginings and appropriations were suffused and enabled by global power relations over which Chinese had little direct control, which Euro-America and Japan directly dominated, and in which many Chinese intellectuals also wished to join. This space of imagining was thus often construed as a negative space of backwardness. As such, these imaginings were as rife with contradiction as any. Indeed, in large part because of this double-sidedness and the overdetermined nature of global modernity, Chinese intellectuals' positive identifications with the colonial world in the late Qing were both ephemeral and shot through with ambiguity, making it possible and indeed very easy for Chinese revolutionaries to turn their backs on these identifications when new historical conditions seemed to warrant it. And turn their backs they often did, particularly when the intertwined projects of state-building, of economic modernization, and of cultural renovation in the post-1911 period became all-consuming.

Yet, they did not turn their backs permanently. For global identifications have episodically reemerged throughout the course of the past century in China and these reemergences cannot easily be dismissed as naive, impossibly utopian, ideologically dictated, or historically irrelevant—although many Western as well as contemporary Chinese scholars have rejected twentieth-century China's revolutionary past and third world identifications as all of those. To the contrary, it seems clear that in the late Qing moment discussed in this book can be found the historical and philosophical (if not also the political and cultural) origins of a recurring leitmotif in twentieth-century Chinese history and Chinese nationalism: that is, the episodic and contradictory Chinese self-identification with the "oppressed of the world" (*bei yapo minzu*, as Sun Zhongshan was to put it on his deathbed in 1925); or the third worldist solidarities that were so central to Mao Zedong's and Zhou Enlai's foreign and domestic practices in the 1950s and 1960s; or, even, the Chinese pan-Asianism that informed Wang Jingwei's collaborationist government with the Japanese.

The claim here is not that the collaborators', Mao's and Zhou's, practices, or even Sun's sympathies trace a single line of lineage from the turn of the century moment, nor that all of these articulations *meant* the same thing. Far from it. The assertion is merely that, as a prosaic historical observation, it can be noted that, at those times of the greatest upheaval in modern Chinese history over the past century, a particular vision of modernity that breaks with the Western version of capitalist linearity and that reconstrues modernity's central historical problematic as the production of unevenness on a global scale repeatedly has come to the fore as an integral part of Chinese redefinitions of themselves and of the world. The origins and initial articulation of this historical leitmotif came in the late Qing, during the first extended moment when the conscious articulation of a global Chinese nationalist discourse and praxis became possible at the same time as the world as a structured totality became visible.

That the multiple alternative global solutions indicated by these identifications—amorphous and underarticulated as they always remained—came to be swamped again and again is, to my mind, not testimony to their historical irrelevance or lack of significance. It is merely testimony to the greater domination of capitalism and "the West" over the enduring possibility of imagining and fashioning futures that are not made in their own images.

APPENDIX
THE TEXT OF *GUAZHONG LANYIN*

Scene One: Ceremonies[1]

(Four servants, eight foreign soldiers, eight ambassadors. The eight ambassadors introduce themselves out loud.)

"Ambassador from Turkey, Fafuhan."
"Ambassador from Tartary, Duoerhan."
"Ambassador from Japan, Yoshi Taro."
"Ambassador from Persia, Weilin."
"Ambassador from 'King of the Sea' [England], Nelson."
"Ambassador from 'Country of Freedom' [France], Bijiali."
"Ambassador from the United Countries [Austro-Hungary], Pusai."
"Ambassador from the 'Two-headed Country' [Russia], Liefeiren."

(All speak together and to each other.)

"Gentlemen, ambassadors! Today is the thirtieth birthday[2] of the Polish emperor. Our respective emperors have ordered us to submit official congratulations and to offer precious gifts to him. We must proceed together to the palace. Let us go!"

(All exit together.)

Scene Two: The Birthday Celebration

(On stage: *Sheng:* Wuruniji; *Jing:* Bonusiji; *Sheng:* Kesixiusike; *Chou:* Zuosilisiji; *Sheng:* Keluoke; *Chou:* Suosunni; *Jing:* Lanniwei'er; *Sheng:* Suoerdike; four eunuchs; one head eunuch; *Xiaosheng:* the Polish Emperor, Augustus[3])

POLISH EMPEROR (*chang*)[4]: "These buildings, decorated with dragons and phoenixes,[5] are ancient and have endured for centuries."

(*Shi*): "This country, my Poland, has been passed down through many outstanding generations; it cannot be called mine alone. In fact I was publicly elected emperor; since that time, we have enjoyed many years of peace and prosperity."[6]

(*Bai*): "I am Augustus, Emperor of Poland.[7] I have accepted the honor of being elected the emperor of all Poland. During my reign, there have been no disasters and the country has been stable and at peace. Today is my thirtieth birthday and ambassadors from various countries have come to celebrate it. Open the dragon doors to them!"

(The eight ambassadors come on stage [and stand at doorway].)

AMBASSADORS: "Your majesty! We have come to greet you on your birthday!"

POLISH EMPEROR: "I do not deserve your honor and respect; I am unworthy to receive you, my elders."

AMBASSADORS: "You are deserving!"

POLISH EMPEROR (speaking to the head eunuch): "Pass the emperor's message: Ask those of the same race [*tongzhong*] and the same [religious] teachings [*tongjiao*] as we to enter first; and those of a different race [*yizhong*] and different [religious] teachings [*yijiao*] from us, to enter afterwards!"

(Eunuch repeats the message down the line.)

AMBASSADORS (step forward and together): "Your majesty! Felicitations on your birthday!"

POLISH EMPEROR: "Please, gentlemen, do not stand on ceremony!"

AMBASSADORS: "Our respective emperors command us to offer you these precious gifts in honor of your birthday!"

POLISH EMPEROR: "Thank you very much." (To the head eunuch): "Pass my message: Those from countries of the same race and same [religious] teachings as we, sit in the seats at the front; those from countries of a different race and different [religious] teachings from us, sit in the seats to the back."

(Eunuch passes message down the line.)

POLISH EMPEROR: "Gentlemen, please drink!"

TURKISH AMBASSADOR (mutters): "How irritating! how irritating!"

(He sits in a seat in the back.)

POLISH EMPEROR: "Gentlemen, please drink up!"
AMBASSADORS: "We have been sated with drink."

(Ambassadors leave; Polish Emperor and everyone else exit.)

Scene 3: Taking Down the Flag[8]

(Four soldiers and the Turkish Ambassador)

TURKISH AMBASSADOR (*chang*): "How irritating! How hateful! How could the Poles dare to distinguish between same race/same religion [and different race and different religion]! How dare they consider us Turks worthless! This incident is an insult to my country's dignity and is no small affair. It will be impossible to avoid calling in the troops to give battle!"
(*Bai*): "What a gutsy one this Emperor of Poland is! I obeyed my emperor's orders to come here to celebrate his birthday; then the Pole made that distinction between same race/same religion and different race/different religion! My great Turkey is a world power [*shijie qiangguo*], yet I was asked to sit in the seats in the back. If I were to ignore [this insult], it would be extremely undignified; it would be akin to permitting the Poles to look with contempt upon my country. I now cannot avoid taking down the flag and going home to call for the army. They will surely redress this wrong!"

(Four soldiers take down the flag; Turkish Ambassador departs.)

Scene 4: A Surprising Incident

(Eight ministers; four eunuchs; Polish Emperor)

POLISH EMPEROR (*chang*): "Yesterday was my thirtieth birthday. Ambassadors from the various countries brought their emperors' messages to me at the palace in honor of the event. I hope my people will enjoy peace; I and the aristocrats [*guizu*] will work together to defend our interests."
(Crier enters and says): "Your majesty! The Turkish Ambassador has taken his flag down and returned home!"

POLISH EMPEROR (to his ministers): "Gentlemen, what should we do, now that the Turkish Ambassador has taken his flag down and returned home?"

KESIXIUSIKE:[9] "Since the Turkish Ambassador has taken his flag down and gone home, the most that could mean is that there could be war. Our country should hence hurriedly train an army and collect funds to support it, in order to meet them on the field of battle. There is certainly nothing to be afraid of."

BONUSIJI:[10] "Your majesty! Do not listen to Kesixiusike; following his path would result in the disaster of war. You see, Turkey has a brave and strong army. We should not consider going to war with them without giving it very serious thought. In my opinion, we should avoid war."

WURUNIJI:[11] "You coward! [It is] your advice that will lead the country to disaster! As far as I know, victory in war always belongs to those with justice on their side. The Turkish Ambassador is making trouble for no reason; how can we possibly give in? Let us quickly amass an army and prepare for a big battle with them!"

SUOSUNNI:[12] "Your majesty! Do not listen to him! Turkey is a great country; they are disciples of Mohammed. The people are brave and fierce. We are certainly no match for them. In my opinion, let us quickly prepare an official letter of state and send a noble minister as ambassador to apologize in the hope of avoiding a big mistake and an even bigger disaster!"

KESIXIUSIKE: "How shameful it would be to write a letter of apology!"

SUOSUNNI: "That is not my fault. It is the only option open for a weak country [*ruoguo*] such as ours. There is nothing shameful about it."[13]

WURUNIJI: "He is really hopeless!"

POLISH EMPEROR: "Actually, I am not an incapable or humble person; I must fight to the death with Turkey. Pass the word! Ask the crier to come to the palace."

(Crier arrives.)

POLISH EMPEROR (to his servant): "Pass my command! I order Marshall Liske[14] to lead the army to defend the Mianjiang River. When the Turkish army arrives, a strong attack will be waiting for them. These are my orders!"

(Crier leaves.)

POLISH EMPEROR: "Since we have initiated a war, each of you, senior ministers and aristocrats, must go collect funds for the army."

WURUNIJI: "I will speak with the other senior ministers to make arrangements for these funds."

(All exit.)

Scene 5: The Provocation

(Four eunuchs plus the head eunuch; Turkish Emperor)

TURKISH EMPEROR: "We have battled with Europe nine times; when will we finally be able to prevail?"[15]

(*Shi*): "Our religious teaching is mighty Islam. Our country is the powerful Turkey. No one in the world can truly defeat us. At times we win and at times we lose."

(*Bai*): "I am the Emperor of Turkey. This morning I will hold audience. Servant! Pass my message: If there are memorials to the throne, ask them to be submitted as soon as possible."

TURKISH AMBASSADOR (arrives): "I, Fafuhan, present myself to your majesty, the Emperor."

TURKISH EMPEROR: "Fafuhan, why are you not in Poland?! Why have you returned?"

TURKISH AMBASSADOR: "My Emperor! I obeyed your orders and took the letter of state to Poland to celebrate the Polish Emperor's birthday. How could we have known that he would make a distinction between same race/same religious teachings and different race/different religious teachings, and that he would ask us—the great Turkey, a world power—to sit in the back seats among the other common ambassadors? I thought that if I were to ignore [this insult], it would injure the dignity of our country and permit them to look with contempt upon us—a great country! That is why I have taken the flag down and returned home.

I suggest, my great Emperor, that we avenge ourselves through war against them!"

TURKISH EMPEROR: "This is surely a trifling matter! It is not necessary to go to war over it?!"

AMBASSADOR: "An insult to a country's dignity is no trifling matter. If we do not go to war, none of us will ever be willing to go to Poland as an ambassador in the future."

EMPEROR: "Why not?"

AMBASSADOR: "Since Poland's emperor is clearly so arrogant, the Polish people, too, will certainly make trouble. Incidents such as insulting and expelling foreigners [*paiwai*] will unavoidably multiply. This would be an evil beyond words!"

EMPEROR: "Very well! We must act according to your suggestion. You are dismissed.

"Servant! Ask Jialuomasidebu to come in."

(Jialuomasidebu [hereafter, Jia] arrives.)

JIA: "After many long years of waging war, I have gained much fame for my wisdom and bravery.

I present myself, Jialuomasidebu, to you, great majesty!"

EMPEROR: "Rise!"

JIA: "Your majesty has called for me: is there an important matter of state?"

EMPEROR: "Poland has grievously insulted our country; I order you to lead 50,000 troops to Poland on a [punitive] expedition. There should be no delay!"

(Turkish Emperor leaves.)

JIA: "I have received an order to go to war. I am resolved and beholden to destroy [*mie*] insignificant Poland [*xiao Bolan*]."

Scene 6: Carrying Out Orders

(Four generals; four servants; four horsemen; Liske [Polish general] arrives)

LISKE: "We are brave, we are clever and we are prepared to wipe out our enemy. I, Liske, have obeyed my orders and gathered the troops. I believe Turkey is merely an uncivilized tribal people [*manzu*]; they have no sense of the significance of this war. I think I need not take this campaign too seriously!"[16]

(Others say): "General, perhaps it is best for you to make some preparations."

LISKE: "I do not think you know anything about it. Let me tell you: along this river, there are two natural barriers: one is Huizhouji;[17] the other is Lanjiangyan.[18] Even with thousands of soldiers, outsiders cannot possibly pass. The Turks are certainly just coming here to die."

(*Chang*): "I have led an army for decades and have won great fame in Poland. Even if Turkey sends millions of soldiers, they cannot possibly pass Lanjiangyan."

Scene 7: Confronting Danger

(Jia leads soldiers in red uniforms; they are sitting in boats.)

JIA: "Officers and soldiers! Men! Let us break through the mouth of the River!"

(All cry "yes" in unison and proceed. Surprise and fear. Some boats sink; there is chaos.)

JIA: "We must withdraw!"

(They retreat, defeated, and in broken ranks.)

WANG GUONU:[19] "The Emperor and the ministers are all people devoid of ideas; they have traded in their policy of expelling foreigners [*paiwai*] for a policy of fawning on foreigners [*meiwai*]. I think the loss of our country [*wangguo*] is approaching.

My surname is Wang, my given name is Guonu. Previously, I was a student of Warsaw Academy, but because I was disciplined by the authorities, I was unable to graduate. Now I am doing nothing and just wandering around at loose ends. Is it not absurd that from top to bottom the leaders of my country are all ignorant [*meng*]? The aristocrats hold power. I have heard that Turkey has initiated a war with us recently. The officers and soldiers of our army, not to mention the naval officers, are all susceptible to seasickness: even before the war began, ships collided with each other and many were shipwrecked before a shot was fired.[20] Indeed, no sooner do they spot an enemy ship than they turn around and run away with the wind. Upon their return [to land], they make a lot of excuses: either that the ship's engines broke down or that they had insufficient coal, or something.

As for the field army officers, they say they have one thousand soldiers under their command and if in fact they even have five hundred of those said thousand, they will be seen as good loyal officers.[21] When they carry out military exercises, they don't give a hoot for foreign guns; all they care about is smoking their pipes.[22] In the garrison, there are no good military officers; but at home, they have numerous good concubines. They buy one after another, and even a dozen concubines is not sufficient. Yet, is there any wonder that the feathers on their caps regularly change from blue to red, from red to green?[23] With such soldiers and such officers, how can we possibly go to battle?

We do have Marshall Liske, who is sophisticated, but he is rather too proud. They say that recently he has taken to relying upon the two natural barriers in the river without devising a good defense strategy. Perhaps Heaven is on our side for now, so Turkey suffered a major defeat and lost a number of soldiers.

The common people say that this is an affair of state and has nothing to do with them. Ha, ha! They have no idea: although this is an affair of state and ostensibly has little to do with common people, we commoners can still find opportunities to make fortunes in this country. People often say that when you see profit, you forget righteousness. I think I will just follow that example. For now, it is I who can criticize them [the leaders]: the Emperor simply wants to extend his autocratic powers; the aristocrats just want to defend their vested interests; the religious leaders just want to promote the power of religion for their own ends. So why should I, just a commoner with no rights of equality, have to die of starvation for them? Starting from today, I will no longer pay any attention to this same-race [*tongzhong*] idea; I will be a traitor and betray secrets to Turkey. For, if they can successfully navigate the river and win victory, I can be wealthy for the rest of my life.

This is thus my decision: I will betray my compatriots in order to make a fortune!"

(Wang Guonu exits.)

Scene 9: Encounter with the Enemy

(Four Turkish soldiers; Jia)

JIA (*chang*): "At the mouth of the Mianjiang River, we suffered the loss of men and boats; many brave soldiers died in the water. The Polish defenses are so good that it is possible that I will end this campaign without a single gain!"

(Turkish soldiers enter with the captured Wang Guonu.)

JIA: "How bold you are to come here to spy on us and to gain information. Come! Behead him immediately!"

WANG: "Stop! I have come with good intentions, yet you accuse me of being a spy. Only an idiot wants to be a spy!"

JIA: "Why then did you come here?"

WANG: "I came specifically about the matter at the mouth of the Mianjiang River."

JIA: "Speak!"

WANG: "Unbind me, then I will speak."

JIA: "Unbind him!"

WANG: "I cannot speak standing up."

JIA: "Give him a seat."

WANG: "What will you give me if I speak?"

JIA: "I will appoint you to an official position."

WANG: "I don't want to be an official; the people would curse me."

JIA: "I will pay you a fortune."

WANG: "I don't want that either. If I betray Poland to you, the Poles will hate me forever. They will destroy my home as well as the tombs of my ancestors. They will kill me. Even a fortune would be useless under those circumstances."

JIA: "Do not worry. From now on I will allow you to join with us in the religion [*tongjiao*] of our country and I will protect you."

WANG: "Thank you. Now I will speak.

The mouth of the Mianjiang River has two strongholds. One is Huizhouji and the other is Lanjiangyan. Both are very dangerous, but if I lead you, you will be able to enter the river without problems."

JIA: "How?"

WANG: "Why did you not send a reconnaissance team ahead of your army to make a map? It would have saved you a lot of trouble!"

JIA: "You are correct.

Generals: advance the troops to the mouth of the Mianjiang River."

WANG: "I have successfully sold my country down the river [*maiguo*]!"

Scene 10: Turmoil at Court

(Four eunuchs; eight ministers; Polish Emperor)

POLISH EMPEROR (*chang*): "Turkey is waging battle against us without reason. It appears they are simple warmongers. I have given orders to defend against them. The results of the war are unpredictable."

(Crier arrives and says): "Your majesty! The Turks have crossed the Mianjiang River. Liske has sustained a disastrous defeat. He has asked for reinforcements."

POLISH EMPEROR: "Ministers and generals! It was you who encouraged me to start this war. We have now suffered a terrible defeat. What should we do next?"

KESIXIUSIKE: "Victory and defeat are common occurrences in armed affairs. This is a long-standing principle of warfare. Why not mobilize the whole country to join the army in order to fight the Turks to the last man!"

BONUSIJI: "If we were still not to win, what would we do then?"

WURUNIJI: "The book of military principles says: 'if the soldiers' backs are to the wall, they will fight to survive [*zhizhi sidi erhou sheng*].'[24] Let us fight them to the death! We will undoubtedly win the war!"

SUOSUNNI: "No, no! In my opinion, using force is an evil idea. We will certainly lose the war; it is better to send a messenger to sue for peace."

KESIXIUSIKE: "You coward! How dare you say that? The shame of your words will certainly be recorded in history."

SUOSUNNI: "Losing a war and suing for peace: this is the only option open for weak countries such as we. There is no shame in it."

KESIXIUSIKE: "There is! If we knew the shame of it, we would prefer to die on the battlefield."

POLISH EMPEROR: "It is better for us to try to sue for peace."

WURUNIJI: "This is a matter for the parliament to decide. We cannot reach a decision here and now."

POLISH EMPEROR: "I intend to sue for peace. Who dares speak for war? I order Bonusiji to act as plenipotentiary minister and to go negotiate for peace."

BONUSIJI: "If I go alone the people of the country will curse me. Please send another to share the calumny with me."

POLISH EMPEROR: "Suosunni can go as your deputy. You may withdraw."[25]

(Everybody exits.)

Scene 11: Suing for Peace

(Four servants; eight Turkish soldiers; Jia)

JIA: "Finding a thousand soldiers is never any trouble, but finding a traitor is most difficult. Now that Wang Guonu has led my army through the mouth of the Mianjiang River and we have inflicted a great defeat upon Liske, we will soon reach the interior of Poland. What joy this gives me!"
(An offstage voice): "Ambassadors from the Polish court have arrived to negotiate for peace."
JIA: "Ask them to come forward."

(The two ambassadors enter and sit down.)

JIA: "For what purpose have your excellencies come?"
BONUSIJI: "Obeying my emperor's orders, we have come specifically to seek peace and to avoid more loss of life."
JIA: "Turkey has millions of brave soldiers and thousands of excellent generals; there is nothing to negotiate. We plan to fight our way to your capital, Warsaw. Then and only then will we talk about peace."
SUOSUNNI: "Your excellency, please do not agitate yourself. We came not to negotiate for peace, but to sue for peace."
JIA: "All right, how do you want to begin?"
BONUSIJI: "You are a minister of the victorious country; you should first lay out your terms."
JIA: "Our first demand: We began this war because Poland insulted our emperor. As a consequence, Poland will have to pay for this expedition. The total indemnity will come to 300 million taels."
BONUSIJI: "The people of Poland are poor. How could we possibly collect such a sum? Please reconsider the amount, your excellency."
JIA: "Very well. Since you are so pitiful, we can deduct 100 million taels.[26] But when will you give it to us?"
BONUSIJI: "We can pay it in installments over the course of ten years."
JIA: "If you cannot pay it in one lump sum, you must put down some collateral."
BONUSIJI: "What would make appropriate collateral?"

JIA: "We will take three provinces of Poland as collateral. After you have paid off the whole sum of the indemnity, we will return them to you."

BONUSIJI: "Poland only has eight provinces, how can we possibly cut off three provinces to give to you? Please do not joke with us. We could give you one province as collateral."[27]

JIA: "If we were to take three provinces through a clear victory in war, you could not argue. If someone were to come along to annex them through other means, what could you do about it?"

BONUSIJI: "Dare I ask what the second demand might be?"

JIA: "In Poland many groups make trouble; they threaten to disrupt the peace and stability of the country. Turkey thus wants to station 30,000[28] troops in the capital so as to maintain the peace."

BONUSIJI: "Stationing troops in our country without reason is too big an insult to us. I cannot possibly agree to this demand."

JIA: "You do not agree? Then let us resume the war."

SUOSUNNI: "Your excellency! Please be patient. This demand is an extremely weighty matter; we must first report to our emperor before we can give you an answer."

JIA: "That is reasonable."

BONUSIJI: "Are we permitted to leave?"

(They depart.)

JIA: "Did you see how weak and spineless the plenipotentiaries of Poland are? This insignificant country will doubtless be destroyed by our Turkey. Ha, ha!"

(All exit.)

Scene 12: Surveying the Scene with Great Emotion

(Desk with a bell and a pot of orchids on it; a rattan armchair)

TU'ERSIJI: "This desperate situation changes as rapidly as does the spring. In Poland, dedicated ones shed blood that is then scattered by the wind; the blood becomes like peach blossoms covering the dust.

I am the head of the state religion and of the House of Lords; my name is Tu'ersiji. Unfortunately, the Polish Emperor and his ministers are all ignoramuses; from top to bottom, all of them are blind, yet they preoccupy themselves with their struggles for power. When Turkey initiated trouble, the ministers supported going to war. Since the war began, Liske has been proud and arrogant; as a consequence, his army suffered a disastrous defeat. Now, we have to sue for peace. The Emperor arbitrarily decided to send ambassadors [to negotiate peace] without the approval of the House of Lords. The peace treaty will undoubtedly be injurious to our sovereignty [*guoquan*]. When I arrived today at the Senate to ask for news of the treaty, there was no information. I am so worried! I am so thirsty!"

(He rings the bell; a servant enters.)

TU'ERSIJI: "Cut open a watermelon [*kai yige xigua lai*]."

(Servant leaves.)

TU'ERSIJI (picks up a document): "So, the draft of the treaty has arrived."

(Servant brings the melon and cuts it open.)

TU'ERSIJI: "Just leave it on the table over there; I will eat it after I finish reading the treaty."

(Servant puts melon on the table; Tu'ersiji sits down in the armchair and reads the treaty aloud.)

TU'ERSIJI: "Article One: In order to avoid further loss of life, Turkey agrees to stop the war and sign a peace treaty.

Article Two: Poland has agreed to pay an indemnity of 200 million taels to Turkey in installments spread over ten years, and to use one province as collateral.

Article Three: As Poland has many groups of troublemakers that threaten the peace, Poland has agreed to allow 3,000[29] Turkish soldiers to be stationed on its territory to preserve the peace."

(He almost faints.)

(*Chang*): "After seeing this treaty, I am no longer myself; I am shocked, my blood is rising. All of a sudden, I have opened my eyes and looked around. It is so obvious: they are cutting the melon [partitioning] of our insignificant Poland. If we allow Turkey to station soldiers in our country, other countries will demand similar treatment and a share in the profits.[30] If one country stations 3,000 soldiers, the other will also station 3,000. The loss of my country [*wangguo*] is before my eyes."

(*Bai*): "Alas! I think this treaty will cause great damage to our country. Payment of an indemnity and the seizure of territory, these are acceptable. But the third article: they want to use the excuse of troublemakers to station 3,000 soldiers in Poland's capital. This is obviously using naked power [*qiangquan*] to interfere in the internal affairs of our country. Other countries will join in this treaty, and they will also station their armies. If things proceed along that path, my beautiful country will be cut like a melon [*guafen*]!

This is a very important matter. I will call for the convening of the House of Lords to discuss it. Come! Quickly send out notices: tomorrow noon we will meet at the House of Lords. Do not delay!"

SERVANT: "Yes."

(Exits.)

TU'ERSIJI (*chang*): "Tomorrow we will convene the House of Lords; we will certainly not permit Turkey to station an army of 3,000 on our territory. I have sent out notices in haste; there is no time. We must defend against foreigners who use their power to rob us of our rights and interests."

Scene 13: Convening [the House of Lords]

(Eight ministers; other members of the House of Lords; Tu'ersiji)

TU'ERSIJI: "Have you read my notice?"

ALL: "We have; please speak!"

(Tu'ersiji mounts the speaking platform.)

TU'ERSIJI: "Gentlemen: There are three reasons for the decline of Poland. They are:

First: The system of the election of kings. Since 1570, the King of Poland has been elected by the dukes. This person, moreover, cannot be from Poland, but must be from another country. What a terrible mistake! If the king is not chosen from this country, how can he be loyal and patriotic? If he is selected from another country, how can he not be an opportunist? When we welcome a king from country A, it is because country A is powerful; if we elect a king from country B, it is because country B is powerful. Having a monarch of a different people [*yizu*] rule over our people has not been advantageous, but rather extremely disadvantageous to Poland. This is the first reason for Poland's decline.[31]

Second: The people are not permitted to participate in politics. Even though Poland has a system of electing kings and also has a parliament, the so-called public elections are really just elections by aristocrats. The common people are not allowed to participate. As a consequence, the common people look upon the country as if it were external to themselves; they pay no attention to the country's safety or danger. Times of prosperity are times of prosperity for the aristocrats; times of decline are times for the aristocrats to begin to worry. The common people think all this has nothing to do with them. It has been customary in our country for civilian officials and generals to take care of domestic and foreign affairs, yet those who engage in affairs of state are all aristocrats, not commoners. We should understand that the common people are actually the foundation of the state. If there is a disaster in the country, the whole country suffers; indeed, it is the people who suffer; there is no such thing as a country suffering abstractly. But, as our common people know little about the affairs of state, the foundation of the country has been removed. In such a circumstance, how can we possibly defend ourselves against enemies who are as cruel as wolves? This is the second reason for Poland's decline.

Third: The reliance of each government faction upon a foreign power. Poland is a country that has the most factions in the world: there is the aristocrats' faction; the parliamentary faction; the monarch's faction; the empress faction; and the foreigners' faction.[32] Some of these factions may be good and some may be bad; some may be fit [*you*] and some may be unfit [*lie*].[33] But the worst thing is that some of them rely upon foreigners and have no independent nature of their own. For example, if one faction relies upon country A, country A will attack our sovereignty; if another faction relies upon country B, country B will attack our sovereignty. There are also those who are willing to be lackeys [*weihu zuo changzhe*]. They injure their compatriots. How hateful they are! And yet, there are also good and brave people willing to shed their blood to recover the sovereignty of the state. But, as they chase the tiger out the front door and slam the gates, they open the back door to let the wolf in. What a pity it is that so many people have sacrificed their lives and that we have still lost. This is the third reason for Poland's decline.

Take the case of negotiations with Turkey: there are two articles in the treaty about ceding territory and paying an indemnity. This is the price a defeated country is compelled to pay. But, as to the third article, Turkey wants to station 3,000 soldiers in our capital. This is my greatest concern. If other countries demand equal rights to act in this way, they too will station soldiers in Poland, and Poland will face the disaster of being carved up like a melon. And if foreign armies enter our capital, they will undoubtedly interfere in our domestic affairs and suppress our people. This will be unavoidable.

Now, I have called this meeting to discuss this latter problem. Please advise me."

(Steps down from the platform.)

WURUNIJI (steps up to the platform): "Gentlemen! When we decided to go to war, we were being brave. We did not expect that today we would have to sue for peace. This is a shame that cannot be expunged. We can never agree to the article that permits the stationing of soldiers in Poland. In my opinion, we senior members of the aristocracy should use the principles of international law to convince Turkey to abandon this article."

TU'ERSIJI: "You are correct. But in today's world, who even talks about international law?! If Turkey uses force to station their soldiers in Poland, how can we even talk about justice? They have already set international law aside; if we were to use its rhetoric and written principles to dispute their actions, I am afraid we would not have a chance of winning."

(Wuruniji steps down from the platform.)

KESIXIUSIKE: "I think that Turkey wants to station their soldiers in Poland for no other reason than to control our monarch and interfere in our domestic affairs. In my opinion, we should leave the emperor in the capital as a caretaker and move the parliament and government to another province. In this way, they would counterbalance one another. This will make it impossible for Turkey to interfere completely in our domestic affairs, even if they do station soldiers in our capital. It would render their troops an empty threatening gesture."

TU'ERSIJI: "This might be a good idea, but the problem is that I don't think we are able, or that we dare, implement it. If we move the parliament and government to another province, Turkey will surely use their autocratic power to gain control of our monarchy, thereby destroying our republican form of government. The disaster would be enormous and Poland would undoubtedly collapse."

(Kesixiusiki sits down.)

SUO'ERDIKE: "I have a plan to defend Poland: if Turkey stations 3,000 soldiers in the capital, we can train 15,000 soldiers to prevent Turkey from daring to make trouble."

TU'ERSIJI: "There is a proverb: 'A good general is a clever general, not a brave general; a good army is a refined one, not a large one.' Even if we were to train one million soldiers, they would be useless. In Poland today, many generals have this or that kind of bad habit to which they are heavily addicted;[34] soldiers are good at fighting for themselves, but not for the public good. Such generals and soldiers would at most be like lambs to the slaughter. It is totally useless. Your words do not reflect any understanding of the nature of our country and people [*guomin*]."

(Suo'erdike sits down.)

ZUOSILISIJI: "Gentlemen! Our people [*guomin*] are much weaker than Turkey's. In my opinion, we should make an alliance with a bigger country in order to defend against Turkey beyond the boundaries of our country. I think this is definitely the best idea."

TU'ERSIJI: "You idiot! You are speaking like a slave! If we rely upon others, we will lose our independence. Besides, as we are chasing the tiger out the front door, we will be letting the wolf in the back door. Even if Turkey were to depart under such circumstances, a stronger power than they would install itself. The disaster would be that much greater. Such humble words as yours pollute this space; get out of here!"

(Zuosilisiji leaves in shame.)

TU'ERSIJI: "I have an idea, but I don't know what you gentlemen will think of it.

The Turks are disciples of Mohammed. They are greedy and cruel. If we tempt them with profits and money, it might be possible for us to negotiate with them to accept our conditions. We could agree to pay 100 million additional taels in order to abolish this hated [third] article.

Using clever diplomatic means and words, perhaps we can save ourselves from this article. Do you agree?"

(One half of the members of the House clap in agreement.)

TU'ERSIJI: "One half has agreed. Without the approval of more than one half, this policy cannot be implemented. Please go home now to think about it; we will discuss it again tomorrow."

(Everyone leaves; Tu'ersiji leaves while singing.)

TU'ERSIJI (*chang*): "If the factions do not give up their individual interests and unite together, whatever we do will be useless. Tomorrow we will meet again. The country's loss is looming on the horizon!"

(He exits.)

[End Part 1]

NOTES

Chapter 1. Introduction

1 Jacques Rancière, *Disagreement: Politics and Philosophy*, trans. Julie Rose (Minneapolis: University of Minnesota Press, 1999): 26.

2 I use *totality* in the sense explored by Fredric Jameson (*The Political Unconscious: Narrative as a Social Symbolic Act* [Ithaca: Cornell University Press, 1981]), as a textual and representational multiplicity that is "to be reunified . . . at the level of its process of production, which is not random but can be described as a coherent functional operation in its own right" (56).

3 *Immanence* is used in the Marxist sense of carrying no values that are proper to it, but rather only those values that are produced and reproduced through praxis.

4 Fredric Jameson, "Foreword" to Liu Kang and Xiaobing Tang, eds., *Politics, Ideology, and Literary Discourse in Modern China* (Durham, N.C.: Duke University Press, 1993): 1, 2.

5 Zhang Zengqun, "Jindai zhongguo yu shijie: jige youguan wenti de kaocha" (Modern China and the World: Investigations on Several Relevant Questions), in Chinese Academy of Social Sciences, ed., *Zouxiang jindai shijie de zhongguo* (China on the Road to the Modern World) (Chengdu: Renmin chubanshe, 1991): 55.

6 For a recent example, see Xiaobing Tang, *Global Space and the Nationalist Discourse of Modernity* (Stanford: Stanford University Press, 1996). Tang's account convincingly demonstrates the untenability of an older Levensonian paradigm of modern Chinese history that posed a "Western" universalism irremediably against a "Chinese" particularism; it is nevertheless premised upon a "global space of modernity" whose expressive presence is found in a unitarily understood "West."

7 The historiographical turn to "insider" or "internal" histories of China, called for by Paul Cohen in *Discovering History in China* (New York: Columbia University Press, 1984), provides numerous examples of this tendency.

8 Ernst Gellner, *Thought and Change* (London: Weidenfeld and Nicholson, 1964): 169.

9 See Gellner, *Nations and Nationalism* (Ithaca: Cornell University Press, 1983): 1–7.

10 Benedict Anderson, *Imagined Communities*, 2d ed. (London: Verso, 1991).

11 Partha Chatterjee, *The Nation and Its Fragments: Colonial and Postcolonial Histories* (Princeton, Princeton University Press, 1993). Also see his essay, "Whose Imagined Community," in Gopal Balakrishnan, ed., *Mapping the Nation* (London: Verso, 1996): 214–25.

12 Chatterjee, *The Nation and Its Fragments*: 5.

13 As David Harvey has pointed out (*The Condition of Postmodernity* [London: Blackwell, 1989]: 264), in this general restructuring "the world's spaces were deterritorialized, stripped of their preceding significations, and then reterritorialized according to the convenience of colonial and imperial administrations." While the process of de- and reterritorialization was only partial in the Chinese case, since China was never fully a colony of anyone's, the general contours of the process had nevertheless, by the late nineteenth century, contributed to the broad rearrangement of domestic, regional, national, and global trade routes, cultural patterns, and population flows.

14 The words are from Peter Osborne, *The Politics of Time: Modernity and Avant-Garde* (London: Verso, 1995): 16; also see Naoki Sakai, *Translation and Subjectivity: On "Japan" and Cultural Nationalism* (Minneapolis: University of Minnesota Press, 1997): chap. 5.

15 Johannes Fabian, *Time and the Other: How Anthropology Makes Its Object* (New York: Columbia University Press, 1983): chap. 1.

16 As Tang puts it, this is the dilemma produced by "the modern subjugation of uneven spaces to homogeneous time," which "contributes to the subordination and reduction of other historical realities outside European and Western modernity" (*Global Space*: 7).

17 Mediation and mediating structures are understood here according to Fredric Jameson's articulation: "The invention of an analytic terminology or code which can be applied equally to two or more structurally distinct objects or sectors of being . . . What is crucial is that, by being able to use the same language about each of these distinct objects or levels of an object, we can restore, at least methodologically, the lost unity of social life, and demonstrate that widely distant elements of the social totality are ultimately part of the same global historical process" (*The Political Unconscious*: 225–26).

18 In Chinese historiography on modern Chinese history (*jindai shi*), this process is particularly occluded, in large part due to the conceptual blockage erected by the Maoist formulation of modern Chinese history as "semi-colonial and semi-feudal." Mao Zedong, "The Chinese Revolution and the Chinese Communist Party," in *Selected Works of Mao Tse-tung* (Peking: Foreign Language Press, 1967), 2:305–33. The "semi-semi" formulation has foreclosed historicization of these categories of thought and action by designating all instances of sociopolitical

unrest and transformation after 1840 as automatically anti-imperialist or anti-feudal.

19 For the relationship of paradigms to ideology, see Thomas Kuhn, *The Structure of Scientific Revolutions* (Chicago: University of Chicago Press, 1970).

20 James T. Seigel, *Fetish, Recognition, Revolution* (Princeton: Princeton University Press, 1997): 6.

21 V. Y. Mudimbe, *The Invention of Africa: Gnosis, Philosophy, and the Order of Knowledge* (Bloomington: Indiana University Press, 1988): 15.

22 Rey Chow, *Woman and Chinese Modernity: The Politics of Reading between West and East* (Minneapolis: University of Minnesota Press, 1991): 62.

23 See Michael Greenberg, *British Trade and the Opening of China, 1800–42* (New York: Monthly Review Press, 1951).

24 *Haiguo tuzhi* (Treatise on Maritime States) (Taipei, 1967), juan (volume) 17:1011.

25 Wei's proposed global approach centered on the *nanyang* (Southern Seas; now known as Southeast Asia), where he hoped to find a unified response to external threats that neither China nor the individual *nanyang* states could adequately meet. In Wei's account, the *nanyang* thus appeared as a new core in a newly glimpsed transitional world order. For a different interpretation, see Jane Leonard, *Wei Yuan and China's Rediscovery of the Maritime World* (Cambridge: Harvard University Press, 1984), and Wang Jiaqian, *Wei Yuan nianpu* (A Chronological Biography of Wei Yuan) (Taipei: Academia Sinica, Institute of Modern History, 1964), who see Wei's *Treatise* as a resuscitation of a traditional concern with the *nanyang*—in effect, as a return to a traditional Sinocentric world order. Here, they conflate the significance of the trade and tributary networks between the *nanyang* and the Ming dynasty with Wei Yüan's rediscovery of its importance within the context of a new crisis in the mid-nineteenth century.

26 This opening process, as socially revolutionary as it proved to be for some, did not work to even incipiently create a quasi-Habermasian ideal of a democratic public sphere. (See Joan Judge, *Print and Politics: "Shibao" and the Culture of Reform in Late Qing China* [Stanford: Stanford University Press, 1996] for a persistent conflation of journalism and public sphere/ democracy.) That is, the print media—its owners and its journalists alike—was not socially neutral. To be sure, there was much contention within and among the journals of the time; nevertheless, the most that can be said about the growth of the print media and its attendant opening out to a new conceptualization of politics and political participation is that it expanded a new field of legitimate social power to previously excluded or marginalized elite groups.

27 See H. D. Harootunian, *Things Seen and Unseen: Discourse and Ideology in Tokugawa Nativism* (Chicago: University of Chicago Press, 1988). As Harootunian notes, the difference between reading texts as *productivities* rather than as functional reflections of reality resides in "interrogat[ing] texts for their conditions of

production and their corresponding ideological effects," and "to propose that knowledge is given is to say that the text's object is already constituted and fixed, that the text knows itself" (13–14).

28 "Lun Zhongguo zhi jiangqiang" (On the Future Strength of China), *Shiwu bao* 31 (30 June 1897); collected in Liang, *Yinbingshi heji-wenji* (Collected Writings from the Ice-Drinkers Studio—Collected Essays) [hereafter YBSWJ; essays cited by *juan* (volume) number] (Taiwan: Zhonghua shuju, 1984), juan 2:11.

29 For Darwin in China see James Pusey, *China and Charles Darwin* (Cambridge: Harvard University Press, 1983).

30 See Hu Fengyang and Zhang Wenjian, *Zhongguo jindai shixue sichao yu liupai* (Modern Chinese Historiographical Trends and Schools) (Shanghai: Huadong shida chubanshe, 1991): 240–44. Also see Yu Danchu, "Zhongguo jindai aiguo zhuyi de '*wangguo* shijian' chukao" (Preliminary investigation into Modern Chinese Patriotic "Mirrors on the History of Lost Countries"), *Shijie lishi* 1 (1984): 23–32.

31 Many of these books were often called world history (*shijie tongshi*), even though they were, as Liang Qichao complained in 1899, actually merely histories of Western countries. See Liang Qichao, "Dong ji yuedan" (A Critique of Japanese Booklists), YBSWJ 4:82–102.

32 The political-territorial understanding of imperialism that made nationalism relevant to late Qing China can be compared to the New Culture–May Fourth period (1915–1925), when, as Arif Dirlik has shown, a new understanding of capitalism became the basis for a local recognition of capitalist incursion in China, which helped make relevant a radical Marxist or Marxian politics aimed against capitalism as a global schema. See Dirlik, *Origins of Chinese Communism* (London: Oxford University Press, 1989): 71.

33 For the problem of derivativeness, see Partha Chatterjee, *Nationalist Thought and the Colonial World: A Derivative Discourse?* (Minneapolis: University of Minnesota Press, 1993).

34 For two representative samples of this orientation (which characterizes the field in general), see, Gellner, *Nations and Nationalism*; Etienne Balibar, "The Nation Form: History and Ideology," in Balibar and Immanuel Wallerstein, eds., *Race, Nation, Class* (London: Verso, 1991).

35 This is true even when "local" studies carefully note that "locality" is a relative construct. See, e.g., Edward Friedman, "Reconstructing China's National Identity: A Southern Alternative to Mao-Era Anti-Imperialist Nationalism," *Journal of Asian Studies* 53.1 (February 1994); Lowell Ditmer and Samuel S. Kim, eds., *China's Quest for National Identity* (Ithaca: Cornell University Press, 1993); Prasenjit Duara, "De-constructing the Chinese Nation," *Australian Journal of Chinese Affairs* 30 (July 1993): 1–26.

36 Prasenjit Duara, *Rescuing History from the Nation: Questioning Narratives of Modern Chinese History* (Chicago: University of Chicago Press, 1995).

37 As Arif Dirlik has noted, the historiographical insistence in the China field on "internal" or "insider" history falls prey to "separating the text (of Chinese history) from its context (in global history)" Arif Dirlik, "Reversals, Ironies, Hegemonies: Notes on the Contemporary Historiography of Modern China," *Modern China* 22.3 (July 1996): 243–84; cite on 265–66.

38 For the consolidation of the narrative of the Republic, see John Fitzgerald, *Awakening China: Politics, Culture, and Class in the Nationalist Revolution* (Stanford: Stanford University Press, 1996).

39 On historical emplotments, see Hayden White, *Metahistory* (Baltimore, Md.: Johns Hopkins University Press, 1973): 9.

40 Li Zehou, *Zhongguo jindai sixiangshi lun* (Essays on Modern Chinese Intellectual History) (Beijing: Renmin chubanshe, 1986). This paradigm has proven popular in numerous studies of post–May Fourth history, e.g., Vera Schwarcz, *The Chinese Enlightenment: Intellectuals and the Legacy of the May Fourth Movement of 1919* (Berkeley: University of California Press, 1986).

41 For a recent work that affirms this position, see David Der-wei Wang, *Fin-de-siècle Splendor: Repressed Modernities of Late Qing Fiction, 1840–1911* (Stanford, Calif.: Stanford University Press, 1997). For an indicative critique, see Gan Yang, "A Critique of Chinese Conservatism in the 1990s," *Social Text*, no. 55 (summer 1998): 45–66; Wang Hui, "Contemporary Chinese Thought and the Question of Modernity," trans. Rebecca E. Karl, *Social Text*, no. 55 (summer 1998): 9–44.

42 Jacques Rancière, *The Names of History: On the Poetics of Knowledge*, trans. Hassan Melehy (Minneapolis: University of Minnesota Press, 1994): 11, 22.

43 This point derives from a central insight of Arif Dirlik, *Anarchism in the Chinese Revolution* (Berkeley: University of California Press, 1991). Dirlik demonstrates that, while the radicalism of anarchism cannot be reduced to the political projects of early-twentieth-century nationalists, anarchism was nevertheless enabled as an intellectual/practical orientation by the larger context of nationalism.

Chapter 2. Staging the World

1 The Chunxian Teahouse was one of several opera venues on Wuma Lu (today's Guangdong Lu) in Shanghai's foreign concession area.

2 Born into a Manchu Banner family, Wang took his *jüren* degree at age twenty-two and, through his father's intervention, was appointed clerk to the magistrate in Taikang District, Henan. After an altercation with local gentry, he was dismissed from his post. Despite family and social pressure, he renounced bureaucratic life, changed his name to "Xiaonong" ("to laugh at myself"), and embarked on a career as an actor on the Beijing opera stage. In the wake of the 1898 coup, Wang left the stifling Beijing environment for the relative free-

dom of Shanghai, where he helped found and promote the late Qing opera reform movement. See *Zhongguo chuqi huaju shiliao* (Historical Documents on the Beginning Period of Chinese Spoken Drama) (Beijing, n.p., 1980), 1:1–12; and *Xinhai geming shiqi qikan jieshao* (hereafter, QKJS; Introduction to Periodicals of the Xinhai Revolutionary Period), 5 vols. (Beijing: Renmin chuban she, 1982), 1:499–503. For reminiscences by those who met or acted with Wang, see Da Yunwan, "Wang Xiaonong de mingming" (Wang Xiaonong's fate and reputation), *Jiangsu xiju* 12 (1980): 38; and Zhou Xinfang, "Qianyan" (Preface), in *Wang Xiaonong xiqu ji* (Wang Xiaonong's Collected Dramas) (Beijing: Zhonghua xiju chubanshe, 1957).

3 See Wu Qianjie, ed., *Ershi shiji zhongguo xiju wutai* (The Twentieth-Century Chinese Drama and Stage) (Shandong: Qingdao chubanshe, 1992): chap. 2. Also see note 11 below.

4 *Jingzhong Ribao* (hereafter JZRB; The Tocsin), 14 and 16 August 1904.

5 Zhang Guyu, "Shanghai Jingju Yiwang" (Reminiscences of Shanghai's Beijing Opera), in *Shanghai wenshi ziliao xuanji* (Selected Documents on Shanghai History) (Shanghai: Renmin chubanshe, 1989), ser. 61, vol. 1, 211–25.

6 The performance was first advertised in *Dalu* (The Continent) on 2 and 3 July 1904.

7 Cited in "Guazhong lanyin," *Dalu* 2.5 (3 July 1904).

8 JZRB, 14 August 1904.

9 The reprinting appeared in the "miscellany" section (p. 4) of the JZRB from 20 to 31 August 1904; it was also serially published in Chen Duxiu's journal *Anhui suhua bao* (Anhui Vernacular Journal), 11–13 (10 September, 24 September, 9 October 1904) in a special section. The two texts are identical.

10 Advertisements for the volume appeared on the front page of the JZRB beginning on 23 October 1904 and ran in every issue for several months. There seem to be no surviving copies of either this volume or of the playbill (referred to in JZRB, 16 August 1904). Apparently, a fire in 1970 destroyed surviving material on Wang Xiaonong, including many of his opera scripts. Ren Wuji, "Wang Xiaonong yu *Guazhong lanyin*" (Wang Xiaonong and *Guazhong lanyin*), *Suibi* 9 (1980): 98–99.

11 See Colin Mackerras, *Chinese Theater: From Its Origins to the Present Day* (Honolulu: University of Hawaii Press, 1983); Su Yi, *Jingju erbainian gaiguan* (An Overview of Two Hundred Years of Peking Opera), 3d ed. (Beijing: Yanshan chubanshe, 1989): chap. 5; William Dolby, *A History of Chinese Drama* (New York: Harper and Row, 1976). Also see Li Hsiao-t'i, who places opera reform as part of an overall vernacularization of culture in the last decade of the Qing. *Ch'ing mo te hsia-ch'eng she-hui ch'i-meng yun-tung*, 1901–1911 (Lower Class Enlightenment Movement in the Late-Ch'ing Period, 1901–1911) (Taipei: Academia Sinica, Institute of Modern History, 1992).

12 On Chen Qubing (1874–1933), see Yang Tianshi, "Xinhai geming shiqi de Chen Qubing" (Chen Qubing in the Xinhai Revolution Period), *Jindaishi yanjiu* 3 (1984).

13 JZRB, 14 August 1904.

14 JZRB, 14 and 16 August 1904.

15 The concept of "performativity" as an everyday practice partially derives from Pierre Bourdieu, *Outline of a Theory of Practice*, trans. Richard Nice (Cambridge: Cambridge University Press, 1977). However, Bourdieu does not adequately deal with the production of new meanings in the interplay between performance and context, nor with the discontinuities and disjunctures that performance necessarily leaves open. Thus, following Angela Zito, I take the relationship between performance and text as "processual moments in a discursive formation." *Of Body and Brush: Grand Sacrifice as Text/Performance in Eighteenth-Century China* (Chicago: University of Chicago Press, 1997): 53–57; cite on 56.

16 Michel de Certeau, *Heterologies: Discourse on the Other*, trans. Michael Massumi (Minneapolis: University of Minnesota Press, 1986): 205.

17 Originally in *Dalu* 2.7 (30 August 1904); rpt. in A Ying, *Wanqing wenxue congchao: xiaoshuo xiqu yanjiu juan* (Anthology of Late-Qing Literature: Novels and Dramas) (Beijing: Zhonghua shuju, 1960), 9:624–25.

18 *Dalu*, 30 August 1904.

19 JZRB, 6 August 1904.

20 JZRB, 16 August 1904. On *minzu zhuyi* as ethno-nationalism, see chap. 5.

21 The primary sources were Liang Qichao's *Bolan miewang ji* (Record of the Destruction of Poland), which served as the preface to Kang Youwei's seven-*juan* work *Bolan fenmie ji* (Record of the Partition and Destruction of Poland). Kang's book, a submission to the throne in the 1898 reform movement, was never published, although Liang's preface was. Another source was Shibue Tamotsu's *Bolan shuaiwang shi* (The History of the Decline and Loss of Poland), published in China in 1904 (translated by Xue Gongxia). For more discussion on these sources, see below.

22 For indications on how historical narratives were adapted and altered for dramatic impact in Beijing operas in general, see Colin Mackerras, *The Rise of the Peking Opera, 1770–1870* (London: Oxford University Press, 1972), and his *Chinese Theater*; William Dolby, *A History of Chinese Drama*; and Tanaka Issei, "The Social and Historical Context of Ming-Ch'ing Local Drama," in David Johnson and Evelyn Rawski, eds., *Popular Culture in Late Imperial China* (Berkeley: University of California Press, 1985).

23 For more on the literary aspects, see Irene Eber, "Poland and Polish Authors in Modern Chinese Literature and Translation," *Monumenta Serica* 31 (1974): 403–45. Lu Xun and his brother, Zhou Zuoren, were enthusiastic translators

of Polish (as well as Hungarian) literature—from the German—in the first decades of the twentieth century.

24 See "*Ai Jiangnan*" (Alas, Jiangnan) in *Jiangsu* 1 (27 April 1903), in which the author writes: "If China does not stand up, then 'Poland us' ('*Bolan wo*') . . . ; if China does become independent, then 'America us' [*Meilijian wo*], 'Germany us' [*Deyizhi wo*]."

25 Kelly's book was translated by Xu Jinglo, and was available in China under the title *Eshi Jiyi* (Collected Translations on Russian History) in four volumes; it was subsequently collected into a compilation edited by Zhang Yinhuan, entitled *Xixue fuqiang congshu* (Compendium of Western Studies on Wealth and Power). Zhang, a former Qing minister to the United States, Spain, and Peru, was, along with Li Hongzhang, one of the two main forces in the *Zongli yamen* (Foreign Affairs Bureau) after 1895. He was a friend of Kang Youwei's and was partially responsible for bringing Kang to the emperor Guangxu's attention. For more on Kelly's book in China, see Irene Eber, "Poland and Polish Authors," and Don Price, *Russia and the Roots of the Chinese Revolution, 1896–1911* (Cambridge: Harvard University Press, 1974): 75.

26 Liang Qichao, "Bolan miewang ji" (Record of the Loss and Destruction of Poland), *Shiwu bao* [hereafter SWB] 3 (29 August 1896): 139.

27 Cite from Jian Bocan, et al., comp., *Wuxu bianfa* (The Wuxu Reforms), in *Zhongguo jindaishi ziliao congkan* (Anthology of Materials on Modern Chinese History) (Shanghai: Renmin chubanshe, 1953), 3:10. Kang's book was never published, as it was ordered destroyed before it could be printed and distributed by the *Datong yishu ju*, the publisher founded in 1897 by Kang's brother, Kang Guangren, and responsible for printing most of Kang's reform-era work. Excerpts from the work—one copy of which is in the Beijing Palace Museum Archives—are printed in Hu Fengyang and Zhang Wenjian, *Zhongguo jindai shixue sichao yu liupai* (Trends and Schools of Modern Chinese Historiography) (Shanghai: Huadong shida chubanshe, 1991): 240–41; and Tang Zijun, *Kang Youwei yu wuxu bianfa* (Kang Youwei and the Wuxu Reforms) (Beijing: Zhonghua shuju, 1984): 250–60.

28 As many others have noted, Kang's approach to institutional reform was mobilized and legitimated through his rereadings of the classical Confucian texts, through which he argued that Confucius was actually a reformer of institutions, rather than a preserver of them, and thus that Confucianism could be used for reformist and not just preservationist purposes. See, e.g., Hao Chang, *Chinese Intellectuals in Crisis Search for Order and Meaning* (Berkeley: University of California Press, 1987); Tang Zhijun, *Kang Youwei yu wuxu bianfa* (Kang Youwei and the Wuxu Reforms) (Beijing: Xinhua shuju, 1984); Hsiao Kung-ch'uan, *A Modern China and a New World: K'ang You-Wei, Reformer and Utopian* (Seattle: Univer-

sity of Washington Press, 1975); Li Zehou, "Kang Youwei sixiang yanjiu" (Study of Kang Youwei's Thought), in *Zhongguo jindai sixiang shilun* (Historical Essays on Modern Chinese Thought) (Beijing: Renmin chubanshe, 1979): 92–181.

29 I use "metaphor" in the sense that Joseph Levenson ascribes to *jingtian* (well-field system) in Confucian discourse. He says, "After centuries of having a literal Confucian significance, as simply a social system which Mencius described . . . (*jingtian*) turned into metaphor. It *stood for* things, values or social theories which were not Confucian at all." (Levenson, *Confucian China and Its Modern Fate: A Trilogy* (Berkeley: University of California, 1965), 3:17.

30 It is a rare essay of the period that does not invoke "Poland and India" or just "Poland" to make some point about the consequences of inaction in the contemporary situation. Yet, the "India" code generally pointed to the passivity of the Indian people, whereas the "Poland" code pointed to the corruption of the state. For more on India, see chap. 6 below.

31 For the confusion of socialism and nihilism in China at the time, see Don Price, *Russia and the Roots of the Chinese Revolution*.

32 From "Zuijin san shiji dashi bianqianshi" (History of the Major Events and Transformations of the Last Three Centuries), *Zhejiang chao* 3, 6, 7 (17 April, 12 August, 11 September 1903).

33 Published in China in 1904 and translated from the Japanese by Xue Gongxia (who joined the Revolutionary Alliance [*Tongmeng hui*] in 1905), this book is considered the textual basis for Wang's opera. See QKJS 1:482.

34 Lu Xun's essay was originally published in *Henan zazhi* (Henan Journal) 2 and 3 (February and March 1908) under the pseudonym Ling Fei.

35 It should be recalled here that "Poland" as such did not exist in this period, and had not since the late eighteenth century. In other words, what is being discussed here is literally a "nowhere" at the same time as being a potential "somewhere" rooted in a particular location indicated through historical activity.

36 See Hao Chang, *Chinese Intellectuals*, for an account of the "social" in late Qing thought. And, for the problem of the "social" in the late Qing debates on revolution, see Arif Dirlik, *Anarchism*. Also see chapters 3–5 below for more on the *qun*.

37 See Xu Banmei, *Huaju quangshiqi huiyi lu* (Recollections on the Initial Period of Spoken Drama) (Beijing: Zhongguo xiju chubanshe, 1957): 6; Ouyang Yuqing, "Huiyi chun liu" (Recollections of the Spring Willow [Society]), in *Ouyang Yuqing quanji* (Collected Works of Ouyang Yuqing) (Shanghai: Shanghai wenyi chubanshe, 1990): 176–77; and Su Yi, *Jingju erbainian gaiguan* (An Overview of Peking Opera's 200 Years), 3d ed. (Beijing: Yanshan chubanshe, 1989): 93–94. None of these commentators notes the substitution of Turkey for Russia.

38 See Shibue Tamotsu, *Bolan shuaiwang shi* (The History of the Decline and Loss of Poland), trans. Xue Gongxia (Zhilong) (Shanghai: n.p., 1904): chap. 2, pt. 4; chap. 3, pt. 1.

39 See chapter 6 for another discussion of this term in a different context.

40 As scholars of diplomatic relations between Japan and China in the pre-1890s period have noted, the term comes up relatively frequently. I am interested in its popular usage, not its diplomatic usage.

41 D. R. Howland, *Borders of Chinese Civilization: Geography and History at Empire's End* (Durham, N.C.: Duke University Press, 1996).

42 This commonality was also figured by the compound phrase *tongwen tongzhong* (same civilization; same race). For Meiji Japan and the Qing reforms, see Zhao Junyi, *Xinhai geming yu dalu langren* (The Xinhai Revolution and the "Mainland Ronin") (Beijing: Zhongguo dabaikeshu chubanshe, 1991).

43 For Huang Zunxian's views on Japan, see Zeng Hailin, *Huang Zunxian yu jindai zhongguo* (Huang Zunxian and Modern China) (Beijing: Sanlian shudian, 1988); and Howland, *Borders*: chaps. 4–5.

44 "E tu zhanji xu" (Preface to "Russo-Turkish War"), SWB 51 (22 January 1898), in Liang, *Yinbingshi wenji* (hereafter YBSWJ) 2:33–34. Also see Liang's essay "Lun Zhongguo zhi jiangqiang" (On the Future Strength of China), SWB 31 (30 June 1897), in YBSWJ 2:11.

45 Turkey was often called in Europe at the time the "Sick Man of Europe"; Liang's designation of Turkey as "of the East" thus brings it conceptually closer to China.

46 The book, as with the Poland book, was never published and was destroyed in the 1898 coup. The preface is reprinted in Tang Zhijun, ed., *Kang Youwei Zhenglun ji* (Collected Political Essays of Kang Youwei) (Beijing: Zhonghua shuju, 1981), 1: 298–300. *Tujue* refers here to the Ottoman Empire, and not merely to the fraction of that empire named Turkey; it does not refer specifically to the Turks as a race/people nor to the *tujue* as the once-strong, albeit now incorporated non-Han people residing in the northwest of the Qing empire.

47 Cited in Jung-pang Lo, *Kang You-wei: A Biography and Symposium* (Tucson: University of Arizona Press, 1967): 81.

48 Tang Zhijun, ed., *Zhenglun ji*: 299–300. I do not translate *geming* here as "revolution," since that term only acquired the meaning of "revolution" slightly later.

49 In the final chapter of this book, I revisit Turkey in connection to the 1908 Young Turks movement. As we will see, Turkey gained a much more substantive and an utterly different meaning at that point.

50 See the *Zhejiang chao* 2 (March 1903) for an untitled essay venting student outrage about the exposition.

51 The "Resist Russia Volunteer Army" (*JuE Yiyong jun*) of 1903 was a major rallying point for Chinese students in Japan. Chen Qubing joined the "Volunteer

Army," as well as the organization that succeeded it, the *Junguomin jiaoyu hui* (Military Citizenry Educational Association). In Shanghai, the daily broadsheet *Eshi jingwen* (Urgent News on Russian Affairs), founded in early 1904 to give voice to the anti-Russia movement, was quickly closed down by the authorities; the JZRB succeeded it, and Chen returned to Shanghai from Japan to take over as editor-in-chief. By this point, however, the editorial policy of the newspaper was not only to oppose Russia but also to not put too much faith in Japan. For more on these organizations, see Sang Bing, *Qingmo xin zhishijie de shetuan yu huodong* (Societies and Activities in Late-Qing New Intellectual Circles) (Beijing: Sanlian-Harvard Yenching, 1995): 238–72. Also see chapter 5 below.

52 Mary Rankin, *Early Chinese Revolutionaries*. (Cambridge: Harvard University Press, 1971): 99, 101.

53 For discussion of the role of ritual and of *tianxia* in emperors' birthday celebrations in China, as well as of the participation of Inner Asian Lords in such events, see James L. Hevia, *Cherishing Men from Afar: Qing Guest Ritual and the Macartney Embassy of 1793* (Durham, N.C.: Duke University Press, 1995): chap. 2.

54 For a different account of "race" in late Qing China, see Frank Dikkoter, *The Discourse of Race in Modern China* (Stanford: Stanford University Press, 1992).

55 For more on this issue, see Rebecca E. Karl, "Race, Ethnos, History in China at the Turn of the Twentieth Century," in Peter Osborne and Stella Sandford, eds., *Philosophies of Race and Ethnicity* (London: Athlone Press, 2002).

56 "Expressive totality" refers to the Hegelian/Lukácsian aesthetic project of seeing a work as an organic whole, where the critic's task is to "seek a unified meaning to which the various levels and components of the word contribute in a hierarchical way" (Fredric Jameson, *The Political Unconscious: Narrative as a Socially Symbolic Act* [Ithaca: Cornell University Press, 1981]: 56). Here, by adding "provisional," I wish to indicate that the organicism of the whole (world structure) is but contingently and discontinuously accessible at the moment of the performative present.

57 Any perusal through essays from the early twentieth century will yield a large number of titles evoking this "twentieth-century stage" metaphor. Examples are too numerous to cite here.

58 Cited in William Dolby, *A History of Chinese Drama*: 176–77.

59 Tetsuo Najita, "Introduction: A Synchronic Approach to the Study of Conflict in Modern Japanese History," in Najita and Victor Koschmann, eds., *Conflict in Japanese History: The Neglected Tradition* (Princeton: Princeton University Press, 1982): 7.

60 For Liang and the late Qing "literature reform movement," see Xia Shaohong, *Jueshi yü chuanshi: Liang Qichao de wenxue daolu* (Enlightenment and Eternity: Liang Qichao's Literary Path) (Shanghai: Renmin chubanshe, 1991); and Leo Oufan Lee and Andrew Nathan, "The Beginnings of Mass Culture: Journalism and

Fiction in the Late Ch'ing and Beyond," in Johnson and Rawski, eds., *Popular Culture in Late Imperial China*: 360–95.

61 Li Hsiao-t'i, *Ch'ing-mo hsia-cheng she-hui*.

62 Chen Duxiu, "Lun Xiqu" (On Drama), first published in *Anhui suhuabao* 11 (10 September 1904); rpt. in Chen Duxiu, *Chen Duxiu zhuozuo xuan* (Selected Important Works of Chen Duxiu) (Shanghai: Shanghai renmin chubanshe, 1991), 1:86–90; cite on 89. Not coincidentally, Wang Xiaonong's opera script was reprinted in this same journal beginning with this same issue.

63 Chen Duxiu, "Lun Xiqu": 89.

64 JZRB, 16 August 1904.

65 Yang Ming, ed., *Dianju shi* (History of Yunnan Drama) (Beijing: Zhongguo xiju chubanshe, 1986): 103.

66 See Wu Qianjie, et al., *Ershi shiji Zhongguo xiju wutai* (The Twentieth-Century Drama and Stage) (Shandong: Qingdao chubanshe, 1992): chap. 2, for a summary of developments in this regard.

67 The contents of the two major Yunnan journals of the time—*Yunnan* and *Dianhua* (Yunnanese Journal), both published by students from Yunnan in Japan—contain a number of opera scripts about Vietnam (and one about Poland [*Jiemei tuojun*; Sisters Join the Army], in the second issue). According to historian Yang Ming, most of these scripts were not written by professional actors or scriptwriters. Rather, they were generally products of students returned from or still in Vietnam, most of whom had been or remained active in organizations tied to either Vietnam's early-century resistances to French colonization or to China's incipient anti-Qing revolutionary movement. Yang Ming, *Dianju shi*: 101–2.

68 Colin Mackerras, *Chinese Theater*: 145–82.

69 Xu Banmei, *Huaju*: 1–2.

70 Ibid.: 6–7.

71 JZRB, 21 August 1904.

72 Another leader in the movement of the time, Ren Tianzhi, was also Manchu—reportedly the empress dowager's illegitimate son adopted by Japanese parents and raised on Taiwan (Xu Banmei, *Huaju*: 23–24).

73 Xu Banmei, *Huaju*: 7–8.

74 Here it must be distinguished from popular-level uses of drama and local opera, such as that used by the Boxers or other so-called "heterodox" sects, whose practices appear similar.

Chapter 3. Deterritorializing Politics

1 "Shijie zhi xinshi" (A New History of the World), *Jingshi wenchao* 3 (1902).

2 See David Harvey, *The Condition of Postmodernity* (New York: Blackwell, 1989);

Neil Smith, *Uneven Development: Nature, Capital, and the Production of Space* (New York: Blackwell, 1984); Edward Soja, *Postmodern Geographies: The Reassertion of Space in Critical Social Theory* (London: Verso, 1988); Kären Wigen and Martin Lewis, *The Myth of Continents: A Critique of Metageography* (Berkeley: University of California Press, 1998); Michel deCerteau, *The Practice of Everyday Life* (Berkeley: University of California Press, 1986).

3 "Cognitive mapping" derives from Fredric Jameson's clarification of an individual's relationship to "totality" and the possibility of a politics that emerge from this relationship, which he describes as the process of locating oneself in a complex environment whose parts become signposts to a structured whole. In effect, cognitive mapping marks a consciousness of the political unconscious. See Jameson, "Cognitive Mapping," in Cary Nelson and Laurence Grossberg, eds., *Marxism and the Interpretation of Culture* (Urbana: University of Illinois Press, 1988).

4 Joseph Levenson, *Confucian China and Its Modern Fate: A Trilogy* (Berkeley: University of California, 1965), demonstrated this turn. Also see Lydia Liu, *Translingual Practice* (Stanford: Stanford University Press, 1995): chap. 9.

5 Prasenjit Duara, "Nationalists among Transnationals: Overseas Chinese and the Idea of China, 1900–1911," In Aihwa Ong and Donald Nonini, eds., *Underground Empires* (New York: Routledge, 1997).

6 I do not discuss the specific organizational activities in which Chinese activists engaged, since there have been many studies of these activities. See, for example, L. Eve Armetrout Ma, *Revolutionaries, Monarchists, and Chinatowns: Chinese Politics in the Americas and the 1911 Revolution* (Honolulu: University of Honolulu Press, 1990); Marius B. Jansen, *The Japanese and Sun Yatsen* (Stanford: Stanford University Press, 1954); and C. E. Glick, *Sojourners and Settlers: Chinese Migrants in Hawaii* (Honolulu: University of Hawaii Press, 1980), chap. 12.

7 K. Scott Wong, *Encountering the Other: Chinese Immigration and Its Impact on Chinese and American Worldviews*, 1875–1905" (Ph.D. diss., University of Michigan, 1992): 44, 46.

8 See Zhang Guotu, *Zhongguo fengjian zhengfu de huaqiao zhengce* (The Policies of China's Feudal Government towards Overseas Chinese) (Xiamen: Xiamen Daxue Chubanshe, 1989): 140–41; Prasenjit Duara, "Nationals among Transnationals": 42–43; and for Zhang Zhidong's efforts in regard to overseas Chinese in the Philippines, see Andrew Wilson, "Zhang Zhidong and the Manila Consulate-General: A Study in Methods and Motives," *Papers on Chinese History*, Harvard University, vol. 3 (spring 1994): 116–34.

9 Duara, "Transnationalism and the Predicament of Sovereignty: China, 1900–1945," *American Historical Review* 102.4 (October 1997): 1031.

10 Gilles Deleuze and Félix Guattari, *A Thousand Plateaux: Capitalism and Schizophrenia*, trans. Brian Massumi (Minneapolis: University of Minnesota Press, 1986);

also see Antonio Negri and Michael Hardt, *The Labor of Dionysus* (Minneapolis: University of Minnesota Press, 1991).

11 Duara, "Transnationalism and the Predicament."

12 Deleuze and Guattari, *A Thousand Plateaux*: 454.

13 Ibid.: 452–53.

14 For a concise theoretical exploration, see Neil Lazarus, *Nationalism and Cultural Practice in the Postcolonial World* (Cambridge: Cambridge University Press, 1999): chap. 1.

15 For an excellent discussion, see Kathy Le Mons Walker, *Chinese Modernity and the Peasant Path* (Stanford: Stanford University Press, 1999).

16 See Mark Anderson, "The Foreign Relations of the Family State: The Empire of Ethics, Aesthetics, and Evolution in Meiji Japan" (Ph.D. diss., Cornell University, 2000): introduction.

17 Maraji Marumoto notes that Kalakaua was the "first reigning monarch and incumbent chief of state to visit Japan," and thus the Meiji was eager to demonstrate its grasp of Western-style ceremonials. "Vignette of Early Hawaii-Japanese Relations: Highlights of King Kalakaua's Sojourn in Japan on His Trip around the World as Recorded in His Personal Diary," *Hawaiian Journal of History* 10 (1976): 53–62. While in Japan, the king offered to sign an equal treaty with Japan, in contrast to the unequal treaties Japan was forced to sign with the Western powers. The Japanese rejected the Hawaiian offer, apparently for fear of antagonizing the United States and Britain. Jon Halliday, *A Political History of Japanese Capitalism* (New York: Pantheon, 1975): 52.

18 According to Armstrong, the son of Calvinist missionaries in Hawaii, who, prior to departure from Hawaii, had been appointed commissioner of immigration, the king was visited by the American consul-general upon arrival in Shanghai; the consul "urged him to visit Peking and be the first of foreign kings to enter the Forbidden City." See Armstrong, *Around the World with a King: The Story of the Circumnavigation of His Majesty King David Kalakaua* (Rutland, Vt.: Tuttle Publishers, 1977 [1904]): 88–89. The king never got to Beijing.

19 Richard A. Greer, "The Royal Tourist Kalakaua's Letters Home from Tokyo to London," *Hawaiian Journal of History* 5 (1971): 79.

20 King Kalakaua is referring to the partially resolved Ryukyu disagreement (1870s), in which Japan forced the Qing to relinquish suzerain claims to the islands; he is also perhaps referring to the confrontation between Japan and the Qing over Taiwan. For the Ryukyus incident, see Edwin Pak-wah Leung, "Li Hung-chang and the Liu-ch'iu (Ryukyu) Controversy, 1871–1881," in Samuel Chu and Kwang-Ch'ing Liu, eds., *Li Hung-Chang and China's Early Modernization* (New York: M. E. Sharpe, 1994): 162–75; for the Taiwan incident, see Key-Hiuk Kim, "The Aims of Li Hung-chang's Policies towards Japan and Korea, 1870–1882," in ibid.: 169–87.

21 *Zongli Yamen* archives, Academia Sinica, Taipei, Taiwan, box 01–21/20–6.

22 This had emerged a decade earlier as an acute problem, with the accumulation of abuses in Cuba and Peru. In 1874, the Chinese sent the Cuba Commission to those places to investigate the abuses; the commission published a report on their findings in 1877. The Cuba Commission was a joint Sino-American mission. For a summary of the history and a full reprint of the report, see *Cuba Commission Report: A Hidden History of the Chinese in Cuba* (Baltimore, Md.: Johns Hopkins University Press, 1993 [1877]).

23 Hawaii's Queen Liliuokalani, *Hawaii's Story* (Boston: Lothrop, Lee, and Shepard, 1895): 77. She adds: "It must be remembered that at this date [1881] . . . the question was to find some class of laborers who would not suffer in our tropical climate at field labor" (78).

24 Letter dated 6 April 1881, in Greer, "The Royal Tourist": 78–79. Immediately after the king's visit, there was a large upsurge in Chinese emigration to Hawaii: in 1864, there were only 700 Chinese while by 1884 there were over 18,200. Some of this increase can be linked to the passage of the first exclusion laws in the United States in 1882, which led many Chinese to disembark in Hawaii rather than continue to the mainland. For the demographics, see Eleanor C. Nordyke and Richard C. R. Lee, "The Chinese in Hawaii: A Historical and Demographic Perspective," *Hawaiian Journal of History* 23 (1989): 196–216.

25 Richard Drinnon, *Facing West* (New York: Schocken Books, 1990).

26 In the 1870s, Kalakaua began sending Hawaiian boys to Asia to learn Asian languages, culture, and commerce; he also began a process of "discovering" Asian influences in Hawaiian native culture. In the 1880s he published a book of Hawaiian mythology that contains a legend about Japanese fishermen landing in Maui before Captain Cook's time, a mythic way of establishing an Asia/Pacific link prior to the Euro-American arrival. (I thank Rob Wilson for bringing this information to my attention.) For another perspective on the demise of Hawaii's sovereignty, see Haunani Kay Trask, *From a Native Daughter: Colonialism and Sovereignty in Hawai'i* (Monroe, Maine: Common Courage Press, 1993): 1–28.

27 Armstrong, *Around the World*: xxiv.

28 See Yumiko Iida, "Fleeing the West, Making Asia Home: Transpositions of Otherness in Japanese Pan-Asianism, 1905–1930," *Alternatives* 22 (1997): 409–32; Victor Koschmann, "Asianism's Ambivalent Legacy," in P. Katzenstein and Takashi Shiraishi, eds., *Network Power: Japan and Asia* (Ithaca, N.Y.: Cornell University Press, 1997): 83–110.

29 For Li's diplomacy and foreign affairs posture in the 1870s and 1880s, see the various essays in Chu and Liu, eds., *Li Hung-chang*. For his attitude toward the United States, see Michael H. Hunt, *The Making of a Special Relationship: The United States and China to 1914* (New York: Columbia University Press, 1983): chap. 4.

30 See D. R. Howland, *Borders of Chinese Civilization: Geography and History at Empire's End* (Durham, N.C.: Duke University Press, 1996); Yumiko Iida, "Fleeing the West." For more on *tongzhong*, see chapter 2 above and chapter 6 below.

31 See Howland, *Borders*: chaps. 1–2.

32 Alfred T. Mahan, "Hawaii and Our Future Sea Power," *Forum* 15 (1893): 7.

33 For more on this American appropriation of Hawaii, see Rob Wilson, "Blue Hawaii: *Bamboo Ridge* as 'Critical Regionalism,'" In Arif Dirlik, ed., *What Is in a Rim? Critical Perspectives on the Pacific Region Idea* (Boulder, Colo.: Westview Press, 1993): 281–304.

34 Hawaii was known by various names in Chinese: *Buwa*, derived from a Japanese name for the islands; and *Tanxiang shan* ("sandalwood mountain"), so named for the sandalwood trade between Hawaii and China brokered by American merchants in the early part of the nineteenth century, discontinued by late century because the forests were depleted. Hawaii soon became *Xiaweiyi* or *Xiawei*. I assume all of these were recognized as "Hawaii" by readers and commentators alike.

35 For the role of international wire services in late-nineteenth-century Chinese news reporting, see Fang Hanji, "Zaoqi de xinwen dianxun" (Early News Wire Services), in Fang, ed., *Baoshi yu baoren* (Journal History and Journalists) (Beijing: Xinhua chubanshe, 1991): 218–19.

36 See, for example: "Lun Meibu hebing zhi gu" (On the annexation of Hawaii by America), *Shiwu bao* 32 (10 July 1897); "Taiwushi bao lun buwa" (The Times on Hawaii), *Shiwu bao* 39 (17 September 1897); "Lusong duli lun" (On Luzon Independence), *Dongya bao* 4; "Meirizhan dianhui zhi" (Wire Reports on the American-Spanish War), *Changyan bao* 1 (17 August 1898).

37 "Lun Meifei yingdu zhi zhanshi guanxi yu zhongguo" (On the Relevance for China of the U.S.-Philippine War and the Anglo-Boer War), *Qingyi bao* 32 (13 December 1899).

38 "Lun diguozhuyi zhi fada ji ershi shiji shijie zhi qiantu," *Kaizhi lu* 1 (10 May 1901); rpt. in Zhang and Wang, eds., *Xinhai geming qianshinian jian shilun xuanji* (Selected Editorials from the Decade Preceding the Xinhai Revolution) (Hong Kong: Sanlian shudian, 1962), vol. 1, pt. 1, pp. 53–58. The *Kaizhi lu* was published in Yokohama by Feng Ziyou and Zheng Guanyi from 1899 or 1900 to 1901. At the time, Zheng was working for Liang Qichao's *Qingyi bao* (Journal of Pure Critique) and the *Kaizhi lu* was distributed through the former paper's network. The *Kaizhi lu*, however, was severely critical of Liang's organization, the *Baohuang hui*, and was forced to cease publication when Liang's *Qingyi bao* withdrew its funding and distribution support.

39 "Lun diguozhuyi zhi fada ji ershi shiji zhi qiantu": 55.

40 Ai Mengluzhe, "Menglu zhuyi," *Zhejiang chao* 2–3 (April–May 1903).

41 For the formulation of the above phrases, I am indebted to Kristin Ross, *The*

Emergence of Social Space: Rimbaud and the Paris Commune (Minneapolis: University of Minnesota Press, 1988): 41.

42 Since the epidemic started in Chinatown, Chinese in particular were prevented from traveling to the United States from the islands. See Ma, *Revolutionaries, Monarchists, and Chinatowns*: 31–32), for how the outbreak was handled in Hawaii; see below for how the epidemic was figured in China slightly later.

43 Over U.S. $30,000 was collected in the first month (Glick, *Sojourners and Settlers*: 277).

44 The *Xin Zhongguo bao* was the first journal for Chinese in Hawaii and was intended for distribution in high schools and middle-class Hawaiian Chinese circles. See Fang Hanji, *Zhongguo jindai baokan shi* (History of Modern Chinese Periodicals) (Taiyüan: Shanxi renmin chubanshe, 1981), 1:199; C. E. Glick, *Sojourners and Settlers*: 277; *Revolutionaries, Monarchists, and Chinatowns*: 61.

45 "Hanman lu" (Record of the Wide Ocean) was originally published as an appendix to *Xin dalu youji jielu* (Selected Memoir of Travels in the New World); it was renamed "Xiaweiyi youji" (Travel Diary of Hawaii) and is hereafter cited as such. In Liang Qichao, YBSZJ 7:149–60; cite on 149.

46 Liang Qichao, "Xiaweiyi youji": 149.

47 During 1898–99, among many other things, Liang had helped organize the reform movement and implement its various provisions; he had seen the reforms crushed and his beloved emperor Guangxu placed under house arrest by the Empress Dowager's coup d'état; he had fled Beijing for his life, knowing that his comrades, Tan Sitong and Kang Guangren, were to be executed (Liang called Tan the "first Chinese martyr"); he had settled in Yokohama in exile and had begun publishing a new journal—the *Qingyi bao*—while also reading widely in the available political-philosophical literature in Japan and writing a truly astounding number of essays and articles.

48 Liang, "Xiaweiyi Youji": 151.

49 Joseph Levenson has characterized this whole portion of the diary as "thoroughly conventional . . . : heavy seas—mal de mer—heavier seas—waves like thunder—like snow-capped mountains." Levenson, *Liang Ch'i-ch'ao and the Mind of Modern China* (Berkeley: University of California Press, 1959): 64.

50 "Taipingyang yu yu," originally published in *Qingyi bao* 54 (15 August 1900).

51 Liang Qichao, "Ershi shiji Taipingyang ge" (Song of the Twentieth-century Pacific). Written in January 1900, the poem was published in February 1902 in the first issue of Liang's *Xinmin congbao* (New People's Miscellany). Reprinted in YBSWJ 45:17–19; cite on 19.

52 Rengong was Liang Qichao's courtesy name. "Ershi shiji Taipingyang ge": 17

53 "Ershi shiji Taipingyang ge": 18.

54 The similarity of Liang's locution to the American claim that the Pacific was "America's lake" is unmistakable; it indicates that the latter claims were by no

means accepted by Liang, even though, as with the American locution, Hawaii and the Hawaiians are effectively erased.

55 With the final burning of Chinatown on 20 January 1900, Liang condemned the Qing government's inability to assist the Hawaiian Chinese. See Glick, *Sojourners and Settlers*: 276.

56 "Xiaweiyi Youji": 156.

57 Ibid.: 156–60. He is referring to the number of white cabinet ministers in both King Kalakaua's and Queen Liliuokalani's governments.

58 Queen Liliuokalani had attempted to surrender to the United States directly, rather than to Samuel Dole, leader of the white settlers, later president of the short-lived Hawaiian Republic. However, the United States under Grover Cleveland was not interested in annexing the islands at the time.

59 "Xiaweiyi youji": 160.

60 Liang was not aware of the deliberate effort by missionaries to force English on the Hawaiian native population; Hawaiian language schools had been closed down and English declared the "national language" in 1896. Haunani Kay Trask, *From a Native Daughter*: 21.

61 "Xiaweiyi youji": 160.

62 In particular, see his 1901 essay "Mieguo xinfa lun" (On the New Rules for Destroying Countries), in which he brings all of these issues into play to spin a startlingly prescient rendition of modern world history. Originally published in *Qingyi bao* (16 July–24 August 1901); rpt. in YBSWJ 6:32–47.

63 "Lun jinshi guomin jingzheng zhi dashi ji zhongguo qiantu" (On Recent Trends in the Competition between Peoples and China's Future), originally published in *Qingyi bao* 30 (15 October 1899); rpt. in YBSWJ 4:56–61; cites 56, 57. Also see Chen Jian'an, "Ershi shiji chunian de xin wenhua yundong" (The New Culture Movement at the Beginning of the Twentieth Century), in Hu Weixi, ed., *Xinhai geming yu zhongguo sixiang wenhua* (Shanghai: Huadong shida chubanshe, 1991): 153–68, for a discussion of the centrality in the late Qing of the rearticulation of *guo* and *min* into a different conception of the whole.

64 "Ershi shiji Taipingyang ge": 19.

65 "Xiaweiyi youji": 156.

66 Ibid.: 156.

67 For how the French Revolution was seen prior to 1911 in China, see Zhang Kaiyuan, "Faguo dageming yu xiahai geming" (The French Revolution and the Xinhai Revolution), in Liu Zongzhu, ed., *Faguo dageming erbai zhounian jinian lunwenji* (Essays in Commemoration of the 200th Anniversary of the Great French Revolution) (Beijing: Sanlian shudian, 1990): 64–80.

68 I follow Marshall Sahlins's strategy of reading here. According to Sahlins, an event is "a *relation* between a happening and a structure"; that is, an event is only an event when it is endowed with historical significance, which occurs

when the happening to which the event points is "appropriated in and through the cultural scheme" to "acquire historical *significance*." *Islands of History* (Chicago: University of Chicago Press, 1985): xiv.

69 While it may be important to note that Liang was later to turn his back on the French Revolution *as an event*—Xiaobing Tang has noted that after 1903, Liang increasingly chose to emphasize the violence and chaos of the *event*, rather than the abstraction of its ideals (*Global Space and the Nationalist Discourse of Modernity: The Historical Thinking of Liang Qichao* [Stanford: Stanford University Press, 1996]: chaps. 3 and 4)—it is also important to note that Liang did not turn his back on its significance as *history*.

70 "Mieguo xinfa lun": 32–33.

71 Liang Qichao, "Lun jinshi guomin jingzheng zhi dashi ji Zhongguo zhi qiantu" (On the General Trend of Competition between the Peoples of Nations and China's Future), YBSWJ 2:56–67. (Originally published in *Qingyi bao* 30 [25 October 1899].)

72 "Mieguo xinfa lun": 46.

73 Rey Chow, *Woman and Chinese Modernity* (Minneapolis: University of Minnesota, 1991): chap. 3.

74 "Xiaweiyi youji": 160.

75 K. Scott Wong, "Liang Qichao and the Chinese of America: A Re-evaluation of His *Selected Memoirs of Travels in the New World*," *Journal of American Ethnic History* 11.4 (summer 1992): 279.

76 Lin Xie (1874? 76?–1926)—also known as Lin Baishui or Lin Shaoquan—wrote under a number of pseudonyms: prior to 1903 as Xuanfanzi, and after 1903 as Baihuadao ren. Originally from Fujian Province, in 1898, Lin became involved in journalism and education in his hometown. After the 1898 coup, he went to Japan to study, returning to China in 1901 to write for the *Hangzhou Vernacular*. In 1902, Lin helped Cai Yuanpei, Jiang Zhiyou, Zhang Binglin, and Wu Zhihui found the Chinese Educational Association (*Zhongguo jiaoyu hui*) and the Patriotic Girl's School (*Aiguo nüxuexiao*); in 1903 he founded and wrote for the *Zhongguo baihua bao* (China Vernacular Journal). Later that year, he returned to Japan to participate in the anti-Russian volunteer army movement (*Ju E yiyong jun*); in 1905 he joined the Revolutionary Alliance (*Tongmeng hui*), and in 1909 he joined the literary group *Nanshe* (Southern Society). Elected a member of Congress after the 1911 revolution, he was executed in 1926 for his excessive criticism of the warlord Zhang Zongchang. See Fang Hanji, *Zhongguo jindai baokan shi*, 1:267–68; Li Hsiao-t'i, *Ch'ing-mo te hsia-ch'eng she-hui ch'i-meng yun-tung, 1901–1911* (Lower-class Enlightenment in the Late Ch'ing Period, 1901–1911) (Taipei: Institute of Modern History, Academia Sinica, 1992): 19; Tao Yinhui, *Cai Yuanppei Nianpu* (Ts'ai Yuan-p'ei: A Chronological Biography) (Taipei: Institute of Modern Chinese History, Academia Sinica, 1976), 1:90–91.

77 The *Hangzhou Vernacular Journal* was founded in 1901 and ran for almost ten years. It printed 700 to 800 copies per issue, of which more than twenty were given as gifts to the Qiushi Shuyuan of Hangzhou (a "new style" academy). Copies of the journal were also distributed free to the Hangzhou Qingchun Menwai teahouse, where it was read aloud for those who could not read. In 1903, the journal became a leading organ of the Zhejiang branch of the *Guangfu hui* (Restoration Society). In 1906, editorial changes led to a moderation of the journal's politics, although a special issue on Qiu Jin was published upon her capture and execution in 1907. For the journal (and a dispute about its dates), see Fang Hanji, *Zhongguo jindai baokan shi*, 1:263–65; Li Hsiao-t'i, *Ch'ing-mo*, chap. 3; and *Xinhai geming shiqi qikan jieshao* (Introduction to Journals from the Xinhai Revolution Period) [hereafter QKJS] (Beijing: Renmin chubanshe, 1982), 2:63–80.

78 Lin Xie, "Preface," *Zhongguo baihua bao* 1 (19 December 1903).

79 Printed in *Hangzhou baihua bao* 20–23 (25 December 1901–24 January 1902). [Hereafter cited as HZBHB, with the issue number.]

80 See subsequent chapters for more essays by Lin on these topics.

81 An outline of events: toward the end of December 1899, a white doctor in Hawaii reported to health authorities a case of the plague, from which two people (Chinese) had died. Authorities converged on Chinatown and began a quarantine and fumigation operation. Fires were at first used to destroy the houses and personal effects of people who had died; then, fires were set to destroy adjacent properties. A month later, on 20 January 1900, fire was set to the thirty-eight-acre area identified as the breeding ground of the pestilence; the flames spread and eventually destroyed Honolulu's Chinatown. The health authorities contended that the fire got out of control due to a sudden shift in the wind. Some 4,500 people (mostly Chinese) were displaced; of the 61 dead, 35 were Chinese, 15 Hawaiians, 13 Japanese, 7 whites, and one unidentified.

82 "Tanxiangshan huaren shounie ji," HZBHB 21: n.p.

83 In the general tradition of oral storytelling, the essay is both conscious of the audience and self-conscious at the same time, an effect achieved not only through the use of colloquial language but also through the essay's very structure (broken into sections designed to be read aloud in installments).

84 The idea of "brotherhood" was intelligible from within a popular secret society idea of communities of action against the status quo, as well as from popular local dramas.

85 HZBHB 21.

86 HZBHB 22.

87 By 1904 in China there was a wide recognition of the "yellow peril" discourse deployed in the United States and Europe, as the numerous essays on the issue published in Chinese journals attest. See, e.g., "Huanghuo bian" (Distinguish-

ing the Yellow Peril), *Jingzhong ribao* (14–19 March 1904); a reprise of the issue in the same journal, now cast into a scientific light, "Lun Huanghuo zhi shuo bu heyu xueli," *Jingzhong ribao* (23–24 July 1904); "Lun Huanghuo" (On the Yellow Peril), *Dongfang zazhi* 2 (10 April 1904); "Lun Huanghuo" (On the Yellow Peril), *Beijing zashi* 1 (14 May 1904); among many others.

88 HZBHB 22.

89 HZBHB 22.

90 As historian Chen Jian'an notes, the vast majority of both reformers and revolutionists at the time were intensely suspicious of unleashing "the people's" energies, particularly after what was widely viewed as the disaster brought upon China by the Boxer Rebellion. Chen Jian'an, "Ershi shiji chunian de xin wenhua yundong": 167–68.

91 It might well be claimed that for the Qing state, the overseas Chinese constituted a much more dependable and desirable *active* source of support—financial and political—than the rebellious and unruly "people" and the wayward local entrepreneurs who resided within the boundaries of the Qing empire itself. For the efforts of the Qing state through the late nineteenth and into the twentieth century to weld the overseas Chinese more fully to state-directed economic projects, see Yen Ching-hwang, "The Overseas Chinese and Late Ch'ing Economic Modernization," *Modern Asian Studies* 16.2 (1982). This is also clear in Sun Zhongshan's praxis as well as in his later writings. See Jiang Yihua, "Sun Zhongshan de minzu zhuyi yu Zhongguo jindai minzu xingcheng de jincheng" (Sun Zhongshan's Nationalism and the Constitutive Process of the Chinese People), in *"Sun Zhongshan yu Yazhou" guoji xueshu taolunhui lunwenji* (Guangdong: Zhongshan daxue chubanshe, 1994): 406–23.

92 The model Chinese citizen as entrepreneur has been taken up with a vengeance in Chinese scholarship recently, where successful overseas Chinese entrepreneurs are now lauded as the citizen par excellence. This, however, is a different topic, which cannot be pursued here.

93 The focus in most studies of this process is generally on the *nanyang* (Southern Seas) Chinese. See Wang Gungwu, *China and the Overseas Chinese* (Singapore: Times Academic Press, 1991). In one of the earliest histories of overseas Chinese as a corporate body (in *Minbao* 25–26 [1909–1910]), overseas Chinese (*huaqiao*) are identified as those residing in the *Nanyang*.

94 For the incorporation of Chinese into the global labor market in Hawaii, see Edna Bonacich and Lucie Cheng, eds., *Labor Immigration under Capitalism: Asian Immigrant Workers in the United States before World War II* (Berkeley: University of California Press, 1984).

95 For example, see "Lun Taipingyang shang lieguo zhengjing dashi" (On the Power Competition in the Pacific), *Waijiao bao* 43 (May 1903); "Shijie zhengci"

(Weltpolitik), *Hubei xuesheng jie* 1 (12 February 1903); "Dongya shinian waijiao shi" (A History of East Asian Foreign Affairs of the Last Decade), *Jiangsu* 9/10 (17 March 1904); among many others.

Chapter 4. Recognizing Colonialism

1 Cited by Xue Fucheng in *The European Diary of Hsieh [Xue] Fucheng: Envoy Extraordinary of Imperial China*, trans. Helen Hsieh Chien (New York: St. Martin's Press, 1993): 19.

2 Benjamin Schwartz's characterization. See his *In Search of Wealth and Power: Yen Fu and the West* (Cambridge: Harvard University Press, 1964): 43.

3 James Pusey, *China and Charles Darwin* (Cambridge: Harvard University Press, 1983). As Pusey points out, in Yan Fu's interpretation, Darwinism was never simply "a theory for describing" the world, but a "program for changing the world" (5).

4 In English in the text, with a parenthetical notation that it can be translated as *ziyou* or *duli*.

5 "Lun diguo zhuyi zhi fada ji ershishiji zhi qiantu" (On the Development of Imperialism and the Future of the Twentieth Century World), *Kaizhi lu* 1 (10 May 1901); rpt. in Zhang Dan and Wang Renzhi, eds., *Xinhai geming qianshinian jian shilun xuanji* [hereafter SLXJ] (Hong Kong: Sanlian shudian, 1962), vol. 1, pt. 1, pp. 53–58; cite on 57–58.

6 Late-Qing interest in the Philippines has generally been discussed through a focus on Sun Zhongshan's assistance to the Filipinos in obtaining arms in Japan for their struggle. In these accounts, the Philippines emerges in cameo appearance on China's (or Sun's own) already constituted revolutionary stage, where Chinese interest in the Philippines is kept outside the unfolding of Chinese history rather than integrally incorporated into the unfolding of that history and related to how Chinese intellectuals came to imagine their own modern history and revolutionary moment. See, e.g., Marius Jansen, *The Japanese and Sun Yat-sen* (Stanford: Stanford University, 1954); Harold Schiffrin, *Sun Yat-sen and the Origins of the Chinese Revolution* (Berkeley: University of California Press, 1968); Li Yun-han, "Dr. Sun Yat-sen and the Independence Movement of the Philippines (1898–1900)," *China Forum (Zhongguo xuebao)* 1.2 (July 1974): 201–4; Duan Yuanzhang, "Sun Zhongshan he tongshiqi yazhou qita minzhu geming xianfeng de bijiao" (A Comparison of Sun Zhongshan and Asian Democratic Revolutionary Pioneers of the Same Era), *Jindaishi yanjiu* 42.6 (November 1987): 70–84; Qi Zhifen, "Sun Zhongshan he Feilubin duli zhanzheng—zhongfei youyishi shang de yiye" (Sun Zhongshan and the Philippine War of Independence—a Page in the History of Sino-Filipino Friendship), *Jindaishi yanjiu* 14.4 (October 1982): 240–45; Zhou Nanjing, "Feilubin duli zhanshi yu zhong-

guo renmin" (The Philippine War of Independence and the Chinese People), *Huaqiao xuehui tongxun* 2 (1985): 1–8; Feng Ziyou, "Gemingdang yu feilubin zhishi zhi guanxi" (The Relationship between the Revolutionary Party and Filipino Activists), *Zhonghui mingguo kaiguoqian gemingshi* (Shanghai: Shangwu Press, 1944), 2:116–25; and Feng, "Zhongguo ribao yu Feilubin Qing lingshi shesong ji" (The China Daily Reports on the dealings between the Filipinos and the Qing consul), *Geming yishi*, 2d ed. (Taiwan: Shangwu Press, 1952), 1:190–91.

7 For a discussion of how Liang Qichao saw this problem in relation to his studies on the French Revolution, see Xiaobing Tang, *Global Space and the Nationalist Discourse of Modernity: The Historical Thinking of Liang Qichao* (Stanford: Stanford University Press, 1996).

8 "Synthesis" is Liang Qichao's characterization of his teacher's endeavor. See Liang's *Intellectual Trends of the Ch'ing Period (Qingdai xueshu gailun)*, trans. Immanual C. Y. Hsu (Cambridge: Harvard University Press, 1959): 91.

9 For more on Kang, see Hsiao Kung-ch'uan, *A Modern China and a New World: K'ang Yu-wei, Reformer and Utopian* (Seattle: University of Washington Press, 1975); Tang Zhijun, *Kang Youwei yu wuxu bianfa* (Kang Youwei and the Wuxu Reforms) (Beijing: Xinhua shuju, 1984); Li Zehou, "Kang Youwei sixiang yanjiu" (Study of Kang Youwei's Thought), in *Zhongguo jindai sixiang shilun* (Historical Essays on Modern Chinese Thought) (Beijing: Renmin chubanshe, 1979): 92–181; and Hao Chang, *Chinese Intellectuals in Crisis* (Berkeley: University of California Press, 1987), chap. 2.

10 Arif Dirlik, *Anarchism in the Chinese Revolution* (Berkeley: University of California Press, 1991): 63.

11 *Xin Guangdong* (New Guangdong), rpt. in SLXJ 1:269–311; cite on 276.

12 This was because of their long history of interaction with the non-Chinese world, the diffusion of their people across the globe, and their well-defined separate linguistic traditions. In addition, Ou maintained that because the current leadership of Chinese reformism (Kang, Liang, himself, and others) was overwhelmingly Guangdongese, the province was peculiarly well suited for "independence."

13 Mary Rankin, *Early Chinese Revolutionaries* (Cambridge: Harvard University Press, 1971): 80. For more on Zou Rong, see "Introduction" by John Lust, in Tsou Jung, *The Revolutionary Army: A Chinese Nationalist Tract of 1903* (The Hague: Mouton, 1968): 18–24; for the *Subao* case, see Rankin, chap. 4; John Lust, "The *Su-bao* Case," *Bulletin of the School of Oriental and African Studies* (University of London, 1964): 27; and Fang Hanji, *Zhongguo jindai baokanshi* (History of Modern Chinese Periodicals) (Taiyuan: Shanxi renmin chubanshe, 1981), 1:230–49.

14 Zou died in prison in early 1905. Zhang was released in 1905 and, his revolutionary reputation secured, went to Tokyo to take up the editorship of Min-

bao (People's Journal), the newly established mouthpiece of Sun Zhongshan's Revolutionary Alliance.

15 See the exchanges in 1906–7 between Liang Qichao and Hu Hanmin in the *Xinmin congbao* and the *Minbao*, respectively. For accounts of these exchanges, see Arif Dirlik, "Socialism and Capitalism in Chinese Socialist Thinking: The Origins," *Studies in Comparative Communism* 21.2 (summer 1987): 131–52; and Tang, *Global Space*: chap. 4.

16 In the Cuban revolution, such diverse observers as Tang Caichang, an oppositional intellectual executed by the Qing state in 1900 for antidynastic activity, saw an exemplary instance of how transnational alliances could be mobilized for national purposes, while Zhang Zhidong, a leading Qing official, saw a positive example of a people's desire for independence. See Zhang Zhidong, "Quan xuepian" (Exhortation for Learning) (March–April 1898); and Tang Caichang, who also in 1898 wrote of the example of Cuba as one that Chinese should follow in their quest for sovereignty, in his "Lun xingya yihui" (On the Awake Asian Society), *Xiang bao* 65 (20 May 1898); rpt. *Tang Caichang Ji* (Works of Tang Caichang) (1980): 177–79. For details, see Rebecca E. Karl, "Secret Sharers: China and the Non-West at the Turn of the Twentieth Century" (Ph.D. diss., Duke University, 1995): chap. 4.

17 For documents relating to the historical relationship between Luzon and China, see Zhongshan daxue, ed., *Zhongguo gujizhong youguan feilubin zhiliao huibian* (Compendium of Materials from Ancient Chinese Sources on the Philippines) (Guangzhou: Zhongshan daxue chubanshe, 1980). Luzon was the name used in the Chinese historical records; many of the late Qing essays parenthetically explain that Luzon is the Philippines.

18 See, for instance, *Qingyi bao* 13 (30 April 1899).

19 *Qingyi bao* 9 (22 March 1899).

20 The changes can be tracked particularly well through the *Qingyi bao* reportage from May through August 1899.

21 *Qingyi bao* 33 (23 December 1899).

22 *Qingyi bao* 24. Aguinaldo is translated saying: "Insignificant Philippines! Strong Philippines! . . . You have separated yourself from the constraints of Spain, raising your head in the world and issuing a declaration for freedom and independence! Since then, a year has passed." The extract concludes with a commentator remarking that, since the American army is clearly in trouble, "the complete independence of the Philippines is surely not far off."

23 "Lun jinshi guomin jingzheng zhi dashi ji zhongguo qiantu" (On the Recent Trends in People's Competition and China's Future), *Qingyi bao* 30 (15 October 1899); in YBSWJ 4: 56–61.

24 "Lun Feilubin dao zhi duli," *Qingyi bao* 25 (26 August 1899).

25 Ou (1869–1912) worked closely with Liang and Kang in the post-1898 period;

his thought presents a mixture of their reformist ideas. However, although he was never allied with Sun Zhongshan, Ou's writings consistently carried a strong revolutionary tone. These orientations are evident in Ou's *Xin Guangdong* (New Guangdong).

26 Ou, "Lun Feilubin dao zhi duli."

27 Ibid. Ou is referring here to the waves of Chinese who emigrated to Luzon beginning in the Ming dynasty.

28 This type of "stateless colonization" was also generally associated with the British East India Company's takeover of India.

29 Ou, "Lun feilubin dao zhi duli."

30 For example, *Zhengyi tongbao* (Journal of Political Technique), which was devoted to exploring the "national essence" (*guocui*) of politics, published an editorial in 1903 that stated, "The Philippines is smaller than China; Philippine independence is more difficult (to achieve) than China's. Yet there are quite a few elites working hard, sacrificing blood in pursuit of [their country's] future freedom . . . China can learn from this." Untitled editorial comment preceding the reprint of Mayamoto Tahira, "Preface," to the Japanese translation of Mariano Ponce, *History of the War for Philippine Independence* (see note 58 below for full cite and discussion).

31 Johannes Fabian, *Time and the Other: How Anthropology Makes Its Object* (New York: Columbia University Press, 1983): 31. The denial of coevalness is an epistemological condition and is the precondition for a Western anthropological praxis which represses the conditions of possibility and the historical effects of its own production of knowledge. The historical Chinese hierarchy was selectively more flexible than was the nineteenth-century Euro-America colonial/anthropological version, and its historical effects were also very different from the Euro-American version.

32 Ou, "Lun feilubindao zhi duli."

33 See Marilyn B. Young, *The Rhetoric of Empire: American China Policy, 1895–1901* (Cambridge: Harvard University Press, 1968): chap. 6.

34 Ou, "Lun Feilubindao zhi duli."

35 "Feilubin mindang qiyi ji," HZBHB 15–19 (5 November–15 Dec. 1901).

36 Reprinted in SLXJ, vol. 1, pt. 1, pp. 58–63.

37 The valorization of "righteous uprising" in the context of the rebellion by the Boxers—who loudly proclaimed their "righteousness" and incorporated the character for "righteous" (*yi*) into their name (*Yihe tuan*)—can only be thought a challenging act on Lin's part.

38 Lin, "Feilubin mindang qiyi ji," HZBHB 15.

39 *Sun Yatsen and the Origins of the Chinese Revolution* (Berkeley: University of California Press, 1968): 99–100.

40 On the Boxers, see Joseph Esherick, *The Origins of the Boxer Uprising* (Berkeley:

University of California Press, 1987), and Paul Cohen, *History in Three Keys: The Boxers as Event, Experience, and Myth* (New York: Columbia University Press, 1997).

41 Lin, "Feilubin mindang qiyi ji," HZBHB 16.

42 *The Wretched of the Earth* (New York: Grove Press 1965). Fanon marks out a three-stage theory of "native intellectuals": unqualified assimilation of colonial culture along with the adoption of the same prejudices as the colonial masters against "natives"; a return to the people and the rediscovery of the "authentic self" in the native country; a phase of violence to overthrow colonialism followed by the installation of the native elites into positions of state power which marks national liberation.

43 Lin seemed untroubled by the question of the constitution of individual consciousness and individual self-actualization in the process of mobilizing against injustice; in this respect, he was wedded to a sense of subjectivity not dependent upon an originating encounter with "difference" and did not bother about the historicity of the construction of a national subject as an individual subjectivity.

44 On this point in a different historical context, see Abdallah Laroui, *The Crisis of the Arab Intellectual: Traditionalism or Historicism?* (Berkeley: University of California Press, 1976).

45 Historians Hu Fengyang and Zhang Wenjian suggest that the renewed interest in *qun* can be correlated to the sociological works coming in from the West. While this correlation is surely important, it cannot be drawn so axiomatically. There were a variety of pressures on Chinese intellectuals to rethink *qun*, and while a sociological sensibility and vocabulary borrowed from the West and Japan were among those pressures, the underlying social dimensions demanding such a rethinking cannot be effaced. See Hu and Zhang, *Zhongguo jindai shixue sichao yu liupai* (Trends and Schools in Modern Chinese Historiography) (Shanghai: Huadong shida chubanshe, 1991): 188–200.

46 Benjamin Elman, *Classicism, Politics and Kinship: The Ch'ang-chou School of New Text Confucianism in Late Imperial China* (Berkeley: University of California Press, 1990): 301–2.

47 This is particularly apparent in Kang's *Datong shu* (Book of Great Unity).

48 Pusey, *China and Charles Darwin*: 60–68. As Pusey points out (64), Yan Fu never mentions that Darwin's major point was that "struggle within the species" was "the ultimate cause of the transformation of the species."

49 The preface to this essay was first published in *Zhixin bao* 18 (17 May 1897); the complete essay is in YBSWJ 2:3–7.

50 Hao Chang, *Liang Ch'i-chao and Intellectual Transition in China, 1890–1907* (Cambridge: Harvard University Press, 1971): 99–100.

51 Lin, "Feilubin mindang qiyi ji," HZBHB 17.

52 For a similar reading of Rizal in the Philippines, see Vincent Raphael, "Nationalism, Imagery, and the Filipino Intelligentsia in the Nineteenth Century," *Critical Inquiry* 16 (spring 1990): 591–611.

53 Rizal was popular among exile intellectuals in Japan. Ma Junwu wrote a biography of him, based upon accounts narrated by Filipino revolutionaries he met in Tokyo. See Ma, "Feilubin zhi ziguozhe" (A Filipino Patriot), *Xinmin congbao* 27 (12 March 1903). Ma also published a translation of Rizal's final poem, "Mi Ultima Adiós," written on the eve of his execution. Also see Tang Tiaoding [Erhe], "Feilubin haojie zhuan," *Xinshijie xuebao* 10 (February 1903); and "Feilubin wangguo canzhuan lue," *Hubei xuesheng jie* (1903).

54 For more on the writer-patriot as hero, see Tang, *Global Space*: chap. 2.

55 Lin, "Feilubin mindang qiyi ji," HZBHB 19.

56 For detailed documentation of these news reports see Karl, *Secret Sharers*: 259–64.

57 The scope of circulation of Ponce's *History of the War for Philippine Independence* is difficult to ascertain, but it appears that it was widely known among those who read the newest books to emerge from the centers of progressive politics and thinking. Diaries of the period—such as those by Gu Yuanguang, Sun Baoxuan, and Song Shu, all major figures on the late Qing literati scene—indicate that Ponce's *History* was readily available. Gu Yuanguang, *Yishu jingyanlu* (Translated Books I Have Read) (n.p.), 1:23, notes, after a brief summary of the contents, that "one can really get a feel for the tragedy of losing one's country." Also see Sun Baoxuan, *Wangshanlu riji* (Diary of the Master of Wangshan Studio), 2 vols. (Shanghai: Shanghai guji chubanshe, 1983); and *Song Shu ji* (Song Shu's Diary), 2 vols. (Beijing: Zhonghua shuju, 1993). According to Ponce's own retrospective account, "the book had a good sale of several thousand copies" among Chinese. See Ponce, *Sun Yat-sen: The Founder of the Republic of China* (Manila: Filipino-Chinese Cultural Foundation, 1965 [orig., 1912 in Spanish and 1913 in Chinese]): 10.

58 The Chinese title was *Feilubin duli zhanshi*; it was translated by "Zhongguo tongshi shangxin ren" (Similarly Heartbroken Chinese), originally published by Shanghai's Shangwu Press in 1902, and reissued in 1913. The translation carries a preface by Miyamoto Tahira written in 1901. Also published in 1902, and sometimes found appended to Ponce's *History*, were biographical sketches of the leaders of the revolution. For a detailed account of the publication history of the book, see Karl, "Secret Sharers": 250–53.

59 For changing historiography on the revolution in the Philippines, see Ruby Paredes, "Introduction" to Santiago V. Alvarez, *The Katipunan and the Revolution: Memoirs of a General*, trans. Paula Carolina S. Malay (Manila: Ateneo de Manila University Press, 1992). Also see Teodoro Kalaw, *The Philippine Revolu-*

tion (Manila: Jorge B. Vargas Filipiniana Foundation, Reprint Series 1, 1969); Teodoro Agoncillo, *The Revolt of the Masses: The Story of Bonifacio and the Katipunan* (Manila: University of the Philippines, 1956).

60 Ponce was a veteran of the late-nineteenth-century *illustrado* movement, which was led by mestizo and Chinese-native members of the small Filipino bourgeoisie, many of whom had been educated in Spain. A liberal reformist movement, it strove for a more favorable status for the Philippines within the Spanish colonial structure. After the Spanish crackdown on the *illustrado*, the *Katipunan*, a secret society with revolutionary goals, was formed in 1892 with Andres Bonifacio at its head. A split emerged within the *Katipunan* between Aguinaldo and Bonifacio during a showdown over leadership in 1896. Ponce followed Aguinaldo. For Ponce's biographical information, see M. M. Norton, *Builders of a Nation* (Manila: E. C. McCullough and Co., 1914); Han Lih-wu, "Introduction" to 1965 reprint of Ponce, *Sun Yat-sen: El Fundador de la República de China;* Bernadita R. Churchill, "Sun Zhongshan shidai de feilubin minzu zhuyi" (Philippine Nationalism in Sun Zhongshan's Era), trans. Wang Ning, in *Sun Zhongshan he tade shidai* (Sun Zhongshan and His times) (Zhonghua shuju, 1987): 328–41; Maria Liuset Camagay, "Liangge minzhuzhuyizhe jian de youyi: Sun Zhongshan yu Maliannuo Ponsi" (The Friendship between Two Nationalists: Sun Zhongshan and Mariano Ponce), trans. Qu Ayin, in *Sun Zhongshan he tade shidai:* 342–51.

61 Authority (*zhengtong lun*) was of key importance to Chinese intellectuals. In his 1902 *Xin Shixue* (New Historiography), Liang Qichao leveled an attack on the preoccupation in Chinese historiography with the question of "authority," which, he asserted, stemmed from crude political need rather than from methodological considerations. For a general discussion, see Wendy Larson, *Literary Authority and the Modern Chinese Writer: Ambivalence and Autobiography* (Durham, N.C.: Duke University Press, 1991).

62 "Feilubin duli zhanshi xu" (Preface to the History of the Philippine War for Independence): 1b.

63 For Ponce in Japan, see Enrique J. Corpus, "Japan and the Philippine Revolution," *Philippines Social Science Review* 6.4 (October 1934): 249–98.

64 "Feilubin duli zhanshi xu": 1a–1b.

65 Ponce's book concentrates on the anti-Spain part of the revolution. As a translator of the book explains in his preface, this is because Ponce did not want to jeopardize whatever chance there might be of reaching a settlement with the United States: "As for the Americans, these portions are omitted; I guess that the gentleman writing the book was reluctantly forced to do this, out of fear. Nevertheless, there is a subtle message in the nuances and those in the know will surely forgive him." Tang Tiaoding, "Felubin zhanshi duduan" (Fragments from the History of the War in the Philippines), *Xinshijie xuebao* 14 (1903): 6.

66 "Feilubin duli zhanshi xu": 18b–19a.

67 Speech reprinted in *Qingyi bao* 24 (16 August 1899).

68 Tang Tiaoding [Erhe] (1871–1940) was a Muslim from Hangzhou. A student of Chen Fuchen [Jieshi] in both Hangzhou and Shanghai until 1901, and a co-editor of the *Xinshijie xuebao*, Tang received a government scholarship to go to Japan in 1902, where he studied at the Saika Gakko, a military prep school. In 1903, Tang joined the anti-Russian volunteer corps in Tokyo and was sent by the corps to China to negotiate with Yuan Shikai on opposing the Russians. Failing in this mission, he returned to Shanghai, where he joined Zhang Binglin and others in activities intended to force the Qing to oppose Russia's aggression. He returned to Japan in 1904 to study medicine and married a Japanese woman in 1905. After 1911, he established a medical school in Hangzhou, and upon Cai Yuanpei's recommendation, became the chancellor of Peking Medical College. He wrote many books on medicine, was the translator from Japanese of many Southern Manchurian Railway surveys, and became an official in the Japanese-sponsored Beijing government in 1937. See Howard Boorman, *Biographical Dictionary of Republican China* (New York: Columbia University Press, 1970), 3:228–30; Ma Shulun, *Wo zai liushi sui yiqian* (Autobiography at Sixty) (Shanghai: Shenghuo shudian, 1947): 10–20.

69 Tang Tiaoding, "Feilubin zhanshi duduan" (Fragments on the History of the War in the Philippines), *Xinshijie xuebao* 14 (12 April 1903); this essay was subsequently reprinted in June 1904 in the first issue of the *Cuixin bao* (New Essence Journal), a short-lived journal published in Zhejiang with Ma Shulun as one of the major supporters.

70 Tang, "Feilubin zhanshi duduan": 2–4.

71 Robert Young, *White Mythologies: Writing History and the West* (New York: Routledge, 1990): 140.

72 Both terms derive from Homi K. Bhabha: "mimicry" pointing to the "not quite/not white" reflection of colonial discourse by its ostensible objects ("Of Mimicry and Man," *October* 28 [1984]: 125–33); and "hybridity" pointing to the actual moment at which colonial and native knowledges are articulated into active forms of resistance ("Signs Taken for Wonders," *Critical Inquiry* 12.1 [1985]: 144–65).

73 This is true, even taking into account the problematic historical category of "colonial experience" as a way of designating a homogeneous global space called "the third world" or "the non-West." For a clear articulation of this problem, see Aijaz Ahmad, "Jameson's Rhetoric of Otherness and 'National Allegory,'" *Social Text*, no. 16 (winter 1987); revised in Aijaz Ahmad, *In Theory: Classes, Nations, Literatures* (London: Verso, 1992).

74 My emphasis on the particularity of the historical moment comes from a recognition that, as Harry Harootunian puts it, citing Tony Bennett, "there are no forms that are forever 'oppositional' or 'dominant'; rather their functioning

and effects depend politically on the place they occupy within the changing set of relationships that define their position." Harootunian, *Things Seen and Unseen: Discourse and Ideology in Tokugawa Nativism* (Chicago: University of Chicago Press, 1988): 15.

75 This, of course, is one of the central arguments of Edward Said, *Orientalism* (New York: Pantheon, 1979).

76 Tang, "Feilubin zhanshi duduan": 3.

77 Ibid.: 7–8.

78 Ibid.: 4.

79 Ibid.: 8.

80 In other essays of the same time, Tang was to utopianize failure as the measure and marker of the contemporary global era for non-Euro-American peoples, for, as he argued, in this era what counted most was the claim on history that activity—successful or not—made. See his "Feilubin haojie zhuan" (Biographies of Filipino Heroes), *Xinshijie xuebao* 10 (12 February 1903): 10–16.

81 For these, see Hu Fengyang and Zhang Wenjian, *Zhongguo jindai shixue sichao yu liupai*: chap. 4; Yu Danchu, "Zhongguo jindai aiguo zhuyi de '*wangguo* shijian' chukao" (Preliminary Investigation into Modern Chinese Patriotic "Mirrors on the History of Lost Countries"), *Shijie lishi* (World History) 1 (1984): 22–32; Duan Ruli, comp., *Wangguo jian* (Mirror of *wangguo*) (Shanghai: n.p., 1917). For individual discussions of various late Qing *wangguo* histories see Rebecca E. Karl, "Secret Sharers."

82 Taken from a line of José Rizal's poem, as translated by Ma Junwu.

83 "Feilubin wangguo canzhuang jilue" (1): 1.

84 Liang Qichao, "Lun meifei yingdu zhi zhanshi guanxi yu zhongguo" (On the Relevance for China of the American-Philippine War and the Anglo-Transvaal War) *Qingyi bao* 32 (13 December 1899); in YBSWJ 11:1–3.

85 Lydia N. Yu-Jose notes a trend in Japan at the turn of the century to claim that Filipinos were racially related to Japanese; this emerged from historical research demonstrating that on certain Philippine islands to which Japanese had emigrated, there had been widespread intermarriage, leading to racial mixing, thus making Filipinos partially "Japanese." See Yu-Jose, *Japan Views the Philippines, 1900–1944* (Manila: Ateneo de Manila, 1992), chaps. 1–2.

86 "Feilubin wangguo canzhuang jilue" (2): 10.

87 "Feilubin wangguo canzhuang jilue" (1): 2, 3.

88 Ibid.: 3.

89 Anonymous, untitled essay in *Zhejiang chao* 2.

90 For Japanese representational practices, see Stefan Tanaka, *Japan's Orient: Rendering Pasts into History* (Berkeley: University of California Press, 1993).

91 The newness of an awareness of "visualism" is clear when the student reaction to the Osaka incident is compared to an earlier Chinese account of an exhibi-

tion, contained in a travelogue by the Jiangsu merchant Li Gui, who went to the United States as part of an official Chinese delegation to the centennial celebrations (1876). Li wrote glowingly of the Philadelphia Expo and of the range of items on display, noting the ingenuity of manufactures and the colorfulness of handicrafts. He wrote proudly of China's exhibit; approvingly of Egypt's and Turkey's booths ("the style of their things was indeed a wonder"); competitively of India's ("The volume of things from India was half of that from China. India's tea production increases every year, but the taste of their tea is not so good."). The only booths of which he wrote dismissively were Peru's and Chile's, which exhibited a "preserved pigmy and numerous painted masks, bows, and many things made of animal bones." Li evinces no recognition of the representational aspects of the exhibition, or of the structures of meaning in its organizational form. Li Gui, *Huanyou dichou xinlu* (New Account of a Trip around the World), published 1879 with preface by Li Hongzhang; reprinted in Zhong Shuhe, ed., *Zouxiang shijie congshu* (From East to West: Chinese Travelers before 1911), (Changsha: Yuelu chubanshe, 1985), 6: 209, 214, 221. For a partial translation of Li's notes on the women's pavilion, see Arkush and Lee, eds., *Land without Ghosts: Chinese Impressions of America from the Mid-Nineteenth Century to the Present* (Berkeley: University of California Press, 1989): 41–48.

92 The racism argument is made by Frank Dikötter, *The Discourse of Race in Modern China* (Stanford: Stanford University Press, 1992): 113–14; the culturalist argument is made by most historians who have written on the issue.

93 "Feilubin wangguo canzhuang jilue" (1): 6.

94 Ibid.: 4.

95 Ibid.: 5–6.

96 Ibid.: 12.

97 The phrase is Arif Dirlik's, *Anarchism*: 63.

98 Ou Jujia, "Zhongguo lidai geming shuo" (Brief Historical Outline of Chinese Revolutions), *Qingyi bao* 31 (25 October 1899).

99 Unsigned Chinese "Preface" to Fukomoto Nichinan, *Telansifa'er* (The Transvaal), trans. Hangzhou hezong yishu ju (1902): n.p.

100 "Nanfei gongheguo da tonglin Gulujia jianzhuan" (A Brief Biography of Determination of President Kruger of the South African Republic), *Jingzhong ribao* (18 July 1904).

101 On vocabulary/language change, see the inspiring passage in Joseph Levenson, *Confucian China and Its Modern Fate*, 3:156–63.

102 Most recently, during the People's Power uprising in 1986 that overthrew Ferdinand Marcos.

103 On this point for the May Fourth period, see Rey Chow, *Woman and Chinese Modernity: The Politics of Reading between East and West* (Minneapolis: University of Minnesota Press, 1991): "In their patriotic attempts to rejuvenate China

through language and literature by appealing to the 'Chinese people,' Chinese intellectuals of the early twentieth century became at the same time a 'class' in formation" (92).

104 It is worth noting that at any time in the past century when intellectuals have engaged in such displacements, "the people" have been excluded from political participation on the basis of their purported "backwardness" and insufficient preparation for inclusion. For contemporary China, see Xudong Zhang, "Nationalism, Mass Culture, and Intellectual Strategies," *Social Text*, no. 55 (summer 1998): 109–40.

Chapter 5. Promoting the Ethnos

1 Unsigned Chinese "Preface" to Fukumoto Nichinan, *Telansifa'er* (The Transvaal), trans. Hangzhou hezong yishu ju (Hangzhou: Hangzhou hezong yishu ju, 1902): n.p.

2 I draw here from insights provided by Naoki Sakai in his discussion of Meiji and Taishō "Japan." As Sakai notes, "Discursive formation of a much higher complexity than a geographic proper name is required in order that the unity of a group thus named be a social reality." See *Translation and Subjectivity: On "Japan" and Cultural Nationalism* (Minneapolis: University of Minnesota Press, 1997): 43.

3 The particular specification of what made Chinese "Chinese"—that is, the ideological specification of nationhood—was not so much the issue as was the prior conceptual problem. For more on "ideologies of peoplehood" as a theoretical problem, see Richard G. Fox, introduction to his *National Ideologies and the Production of National Cultures* (Washington, D.C.: American Anthropological Association, 1990): 3. For the emergence of the term *minzu*, traced to Japanese borrowing, see Han Qichun and Li Yifu, "Hanwei 'minzu' yizi de chuxian ji qi shiyong qingkuang" (The Appearance in Chinese of the Term Minzu and Its Usages), *Minzu Yanjiu* (Minzu Research) 2 (1984): 36–43. For post 1911 issues of *minzu* usage, particularly in contrast to *renmin* (the masses), see Joseph Levenson's discussion in *Revolution and Cosmopolitanism* (Berkeley: University of California Press, 1971): 1–18.

4 See Hao Chang, *Liang Ch'i-chao and Intellectual Transition in China, 1890–1907* (Cambridge: Harvard University Press, 1971): 257.

5 Yan Fu, "On Our Salvation" (1895), cited in Benjamin I. Schwartz, *In Search of Wealth and Power: Yen Fu and the West* (Cambridge: Harvard University Press, 1964): 88.

6 See Hou Yijie, *Ershi shijichu zhongguo zhengzhi gaige fengchao* (Trends in Political Reform in Early-Twentieth-Century China) (Beijing: Renmin chubanshe, 1993).

7 For *shunmin* and *nuli*, see Wu Yingnan et al., eds., *Qingmo shehui sichao* (Late Qing Trends in Social Thought) (Fuzhou: Fujian Renmin chubanshe, 1990): 38–39.

8 Cited in Zhang Kaiyuan, "Characteristics of the Trend of Patriotism in the 1911 Revolution," *Papers Presented at the International Colloquium on the 1911 Revolution and the Founding of the Chinese Republic* (Washington, D.C.: Center for Chinese Research Materials, n.d.): 7.

9 Chen Tianhua, *Jingshi zhong*; rpt. in Chai Degeng, ed., *Xinhai geming* (The Xinhai Revolution) (Shanghai, 1957), 1: 529.

10 "Feizhou duliguo you chuxian yi" (Another Independent Country Emerges in Africa), *Jingzhong ribao* (4 November 1904).

11 Needless to note, "Africa" was not named as such, nor understood as a continent among others by Chinese chroniclers until the mid-nineteenth century. Indeed, "the image of 'darkest Africa,' as an expression of geographical ignorance or as one of cultural arrogance was a nineteenth-century invention" in Europe (Philip Curtin, *The Image of Africa: British Ideas and Action, 1780–1850* [Madison: University of Wisconsin Press, 1964]: 9) and missionaries were this invention's biggest promoters (Patrick Brantlinger, "Victorians and Africans: The Genealogy of the Myth of the Dark Continent," in Henry Louis Gates, ed., *"Race," Writing, and Difference* [Chicago: University of Chicago Press, 1985]: 197).

12 Wei Yüan, *Haiguo tuzhi* [Treatise on Maritime States] (Taipei, 1967), juan 20: 1301.

13 Articles about the mistreatment of Chinese in South Africa began to appear regularly in 1903–4 in the *Waijiao bao* (Foreign Affairs Journal), *Jiangsu*, *Dongfang zazhi* (Eastern Miscellany), and Liang Qichao's *Xinmin congbao* (New People's Miscellany), among others. The latter published, with commentary, letters written by Chinese laborers that were forwarded to the journal by the Johannesburg Chinese Guild in June 1904. Most of the reports note that, in the post–Boer War recovery of gold mining, the Chinese were being used to replace "black slaves" who refused to work, and that the Chinese were treated even worse than the "black slaves." A compendium of the letters from South Africa was published in Tianjin in 1906.

In 1895, a small branch of the *Xingzhong hui* (Arise China Society) was founded in Johannesburg by Yang Quyun, who arrived there after having fled China in the wake of Sun Zhongshan's first failed uprising that year. See J. Y. Wong, *The Origins of an Heroic Image: Sun Yat-sen in London, 1896–1897* (London: Oxford University Press, 1986): 123.

14 Blacks were known in China as slaves imported by the Portuguese to their colony at Macao and later as slaves to others. Nevertheless, as Wei Yüan indicates, until the nineteenth century there was no recognition that "black" and "white" denoted separate peoples; they were merely two variations on an unChinese theme. See excerpts from early documents in Ai Zhouchang, ed., *Zhongfei guanxishi wenxuan, 1500–1918* (Selected Writings from the History of Sino-African Relations, 1500–1918) (Shanghai: Huadong shifan daxue chuban-

she, 1989); Ai Zhouchang, "Jindai shiqi de zhongguo yu feizhou" (China and Africa in the Modern Era), *Xiya feizhou* 1 (1984).

15 A "planetary system" encompasses the world into a systemic totality, and then attempts to manage that totality from a center proclaimed as the self. See Enrique Dussel, *The Invention of the Americas: Eclipse of "the Other" and the Myth of Modernity* (New York: Continuum, 1995). For an account of Africa in Chinese history, see Philip Snow, *Star Raft* (Ithaca: Cornell University Press, 1988), and J. J. L. Duyvendak, *China's Discovery of Africa: Lectures Given at the University of London on January 22 and 23, 1947* (London: Arthur Probsthain, 1949).

16 Liang Qichao, "Mieguo xinfa lun" (On the New Rules for Destroying Countries), YBSWJ 6:32.

17 For how the trope of "slavery" was conjoined to the trope of "women as slaves" (*nüzi wei nuli*) in the late Qing, see my "'Slavery,' Gender, and Citizenship in China's Turn of the Century Global Context," in Rebecca Karl and Peter Zarrow, eds., *Rethinking the 1898 Reforms: Political and Cultural Change in Modern China* (Cambridge: Harvard University Council on East Asian Publications, 2002).

18 In commentaries on Spencer, Yan Fu concentrated on what he considered to be the primary arena of struggle: that between whites and yellows. In 1902, Liang wrote in *Xinshi xue* (New Historiography) that humankind could be divided into two large categories, the "historical races" and the "unhistorical races," with whites and yellows pertaining to the former and reds and blacks to the latter.

19 Minor disruptions to this include Lin Shu's translation of Harriet Beecher Stowe's *Uncle Tom's Cabin* under the title *Heinu xu tianxia* (A Black Slave's Cry to Heaven) in 1905, recommended for classroom use in 1906 by the Ministry of Education (*Xuebu*) as an appropriate way to "touch people's human emotions while promoting their love of country" (*Sichuan xuebao* 9 [September 1906]). For a translation of Lin's preface, see David Arkush and Leo Ou-fan Lee, *Land without Ghosts* (Berkeley: University of California Press, 1988): 77–80. Another disruption to the image was the victory of Abyssinia over Italy in 1896, which was occasionally alluded to but never amplified.

20 "Xingmeng ge" (Song to Awaken from a Dream), *Anhui suhua bao* 8 (27 July 1904): 33–34, 36–37.

21 These came via wire services, through Japan, usually from British-generated war news. See *Wuzhou shishi huibao* (Compendium on World Events); the *Yadong shibao* (East Asian Times); and *Qingyi bao*. For details, see Karl, "Secret Sharers: China and the Non-West at the Turn of the Twentieth Century" (Ph.D. diss., Duke University, 1995): 351–57.

22 *Yadong shibao* 17 (20 November 1899). Published in Shanghai under nominal Japanese ownership, this journal was founded in June 1898. With its sixth issue, Tang Caichang became editor-in-chief; when Tang, who led the abortive uprising in the Yangzi Valley associated with the *Baohuang hui*, was executed in mid

1900, the paper was closed down. Also associated with the journal was Wang Kangnian.

23 *Yadong shibao* 17.

24 "Telansifa'er da tongling zhuanlue" (Brief Biography of the President of the Transvaal), *Wuzhou shishi huibao* 2 (20 September 1899): n.p.

25 Du Shizhen (Jiefeng), from Shanghou District in Zhejiang Province, attended the Yangzheng School in Hangzhou in 1900; he was a classmate of Ma Shulun and Tang Tiaoding (Erhe), all of whom were students of Chen Fuchen (Jieshi). In 1902, they moved to Shanghai and founded the *Xinshijie xuebao*. According to Ma Shulun, Du was, along with himself and Tang, a special favorite of Chen's, and during their school years they were nicknamed the "san jie" (three stars [or heroes]). In 1902, as they were preparing to graduate, the school nominated all three for government scholarships in Japan, but Du was unable to take his up due to an altercation with officials. Tang and Ma went to Japan in early 1903; it is unclear if Du ever did. See Ma Shulun, *Wo zai liushi sui yiqian* (My Life before Sixty) (Shanghai: Shenghuo shudian, 1947): 10–20.

26 Du Shizhen, "Duguo datongling Gulujia liezhuan" (Brief Biography of the Transvaal President, Kruger), *Xinshijie xuebao* 6–8 (14 November–14 December 1902), n.p.

27 Paul Kruger was said to claim that the Boers were God's chosen people for the task of bringing the British to their knees. See J. S. Marais, *The Fall of Kruger's Republic* (London: Clarendon Press, 1961).

28 As Gandhi—who arrived in South Africa in 1910—summarized:

> Napoleon is said to have described the English as a nation of shop-keepers . . . They hold whatever dominions they have for the sake of their commerce. Their army and their navy are intended to protect it. When the Transvaal offered no such attractions, the late Mr. Gladstone discovered [in the 1870s] that it was not right for the English to hold it. When it became a paying proposition [in the 1880s], resistance led to war. Mr. Chamberlain soon discovered [in the 1890s] that England enjoyed a suzerainty over the Transvaal. It is related that someone asked the late President Kruger whether there was gold on the moon. He replied that it was highly unlikely because, if there were, the English would have annexed it.

Mahatma Gandhi, *Hind Swaraj* (1910); cited in Partha Chatterjee, *Nationalist Thought and the Colonial World: A Derivative Discourse?* (Minneapolis: University of Minnesota Press, 1986): 87–88.

29 J. A. Hobson, *Imperialism: A Study* (Ann Arbor: University of Michigan Press 1965 [1902]). The war was for him a "paradigm for explaining the international consequences of capitalist underconsumption and oversavings," through which he—and many after him, until Lenin rearticulated the issue—defined imperial-

ism as an essentially economic endeavor, albeit one whose benefits redounded not to the nation or to the state but to a few "financiers," who used the state to advance their own interests. Philip Seigelman, "Introduction" to *Imperialism*: xiii. The crucial difference between Hobson and Lenin is between imperialism as a policy pursued for the gain of a small minority (Hobson) and imperialism as a necessary stage of capitalism (Lenin).

30 Cited in Stephen Koss, *The Pro-Boers* (Chicago: University of Chicago Press, 1973): 55–56.

31 Elisaveta Kandyba-Foxcroft, *Russia and the Anglo-Boer War, 1899–1902* (Pretoria: CUM Books, 1981): 51.

32 Kandyba-Foxcroft notes that Russian essays depicted the Boers as "the last representatives of a heroic age of simple patriarchal living and a prophetlike loftiness of soul" (ibid.: 39).

33 Theodore Shanin, *The Roots of Otherness: Russia's Turn of the Century* (New Haven: Yale University Press, 1986).

34 The *Waijiao bao*, an influential paper in the first decade of the twentieth century, was founded in Shanghai in January 1902 and edited by Zhang Yüanji, also the editor-in-chief of Shanghai's Shangwu (Commercial) Press. It was one of the first journals to focus on foreign and diplomatic affairs and is generally considered "reformist" for its advocacy of monarchical constitutionalism and its tepid support for expelling foreigners (*paiwai*). For details, see Manying Ip, *The Life and Times of Zhang Yuanji* (Beijing: Shangwu Press, 1985).

35 "Lun Yingte zhanji," *Waijiao bao* 11 (22 May 1902).

36 Ibid.

37 Du Shizhen, "Duguo datongling Gulujia liezhuan" (6): n.p.

38 Ibid. (7): n.p.

39 Ibid.

40 Ibid. (8): n.p.

41 Anarchists were the only ones at the time to completely reject the state. There is no evidence that Du was an anarchist, although he was broadly familiar with early-century socialism; indeed, he was the translator for the *Xinshijie xuebao* of several essays on socialism, which he copiously annotated. These were mostly excerpts from Hisamatsu Yoshinori's *Kinsei shakai shugi hyoron* (A Commentary on Modern Socialism), *Xinshijie xuebao* 11–15 (27 February–27 March 1903).

42 The tensions inherent in the accommodation of the Boers to "civilization" are clear in the heroic biographies of Paul Kruger, published in 1902–3. In these, Kruger became the defender of the essence of the Boer *minzu* by being singularly identified with the Boer project. By redefining his exemplary defense of *minzu* in relation to "the modern," Kruger, the Boers, and the Transvaal's imperfect fit into "civilization" were accommodated. See, e.g., Du Shizhen, "Duguo datongling Gulujia liezhuan"; "Nanfei gongheguo da tongling Gulujia jianzhuan" (A

Biography of Determination of President Kruger of the South African Republic), *Jingzhong ribao* (18 July 1904); "NanA Zhanji" (A Record of the South African War), *Yunnan* 1 (15 October 1906); "Nan A duli yingxiong gulujia lüe zhuan" (Brief Biography of Kruger, Hero of South African Independence), *Youxue yibian* 6–7 (12 April, 11 May 1903).

43 Henry Louis Gates Jr., "Writing 'Race' and the Difference It Makes," in Gates, ed., *"Race," Writing, and Difference*: 11.

44 A further difference was that there were no personal relations between Chinese and Boers; the Chinese thus viewed the war from afar and their perspectives and information were thoroughly mediated by Japanese reports (from which they received most of their information).

45 See, "Zhanchang xingshi" (Contours of the Battlefield), *Huibao* 129 (19 November 1899).

46 For landscape as a theoretical issue, see Brett de Bary, "Karatani Kojin's Origins," in Masao Miyoshi and Harootunian, eds., *Postmodernism and Japan* (Durham, N.C.: Duke University Press, 1989): 235–58.

47 A report in *Qingyi bao* 38 (11 March 1900) notes that a Japanese observer was sent to investigate why the Transvaal wouldn't submit to "England's obvious superiority in weapons and numbers of troops." The observer, Captain Hichiro Hiraoka, wrote a report for internal use under the title *Eito-sense ni ekeru gunji-jo no kansatsu* (Military Studies in the Anglo-Boer War); in 1902, the Ministry of Defense printed a public volume based on Hichiro's reports, *Boa-senjutsu no kenkyū* (Study of War Tactics during the Boer War).

48 "Ji yingte zhanzheng jinshi," *Yadong shibao* 19.

49 The latter problem recalled to the Japanese the "mistakes" made by their own army during the pacification of Taiwan a few years earlier (1895). "Yingguo zhi lujun" (The British Army), *Qingyi bao* 36 (20 February 1900).

50 "Duguo zhi bingzhi zhanshu" (Battle Strategy and Military System in the Transvaal), *Qingyi bao* 32 (13 December 1899). Howard Bailes notes: "Boer styles of warfare exercised a peculiar fascination over British military commentators. Many . . . wrote rhapsodically of their enemy's prowess" ("Military Aspects of the War," in Peter Warwick, ed., *The South African War: The Anglo-Boer War, 1899–1902* [London: Longman, 1980]: 69.)

51 Fukumoto (1857–1921) was a "prolific writer and journalist who traveled widely in Asia before settling down as publisher of the *Kyūshū Nippō* (Kyushu Daily)" (Miyazaki Tōten, *My Thirty-three Years' Dream*, trans. Eto Shinkichi and Marius Jansen (Princeton: Princeton University Press, 1982): 196n). He was a member of the Lower House of the Diet; joined the *Seikyōsha* (Society for Political Education); and was an editor of *Nihonjin* (The Japanese), a journal advocating the formation of a "Japanese identity"—a *kokusui* (Ch: *guocui*; national essence) compatible with Japan's projected new standing in the world. He had deep links

to Sun Zhongshan and Miyazaki Tōten, Sun's closest Japanese associate, as well as to Inukai Ki and Uchida Ryohei, government supporters of Sun's plots against the Qing. Fukumoto was intimately involved in Sun's planning for the Huizhou (Waichow) uprising in October 1900 (a failed endeavor supported by the Guangdong Triad Society), having been introduced to Sun earlier by Suenaga Setsu. See Miyazaki, My Thirty-three Years' Dream: 196–97; *Gendai jinmei jiten* (Dictionary of People of the Modern Era); Kenneth Pyle, *The New Generation in Meiji Japan* (Stanford: Stanford University Press, 1970); Marius Jansen, *The Japanese and Sun Yat-sen* (Cambridge: Harvard University Press, 1954); Martin Bernal, "Liu Shih-p'ei and National Essence," in Charlotte Furth, ed., *The Limits of Change* (Cambridge: Harvard University Press, 1976): 90–112.

52 Fukumoto Nichinan, "Nan A gailun" (Situation in South Africa), *Qingyi bao* 35 (10 February 1900). The Boers' low cultural level and their excellent physiques remained two oft-noted characteristics; yet, as some commentators later surmised, without "culture," the Boers might be able to achieve battle victory over the British, but they would not be able to defend the victory enduringly in the global arena. See "Lun Yingte zhanji," *Waijiao bao* 11 (22 May 1902).

53 Sun was apparently quite interested in the Boer War, according to George Lynch, a British journalist who interviewed Sun in mid 1900 and commented on the number of articles and books on South Africa piled up in Sun's Yokohama study. George Lynch, *The War of Civilizations* (London, 1901): 283. Also see Harold Schiffrin, *Sun Yat-sen*: 302, 307; Marius Jansen, *The Japanese and Sun Yat-sen*: 115. It is likely that Sun's interest was facilitated by Fukumoto.

54 Schiffrin, *Sun Yat-sen*: 277.

55 "Zhina baoquan fenhai lun" (Arguments for the Preservation or Dismemberment of China), *Jiangsu* 3; rpt. *Sun Zhongshan quanji* (Collected Works of Sun Zhongshan) (Beijing: Zhonghua shuju, 1981), 1:218–24.

56 James T. Liu, *The Chinese Knight-Errant* (Chicago: University of Chicago Press, 1967). Also see C. T. Hsia's description of the chivalrous man or woman (*xia*) of the traditional Chinese novel (*The Classic Chinese Novel: An Introduction* [New York: Columbia University Press, 1968]: 30).

57 Liang Qichao, "Ji dongxia" (On Eastern [Japanese] Knights), *Shiwu bao* 39 (17 September 1897); rpt. YBSWJ 2:29; also see Liang, "San xiansheng zhuan" (Biography of Three Gentlemen), *Zhixin bao* 34 (16 October 1897); rpt. YBSWJ 1:115.

58 Mai Menghua, "Zong xiapian" (Respect the Knight-errant), *Shiwu bao* 32 (10 July 1897).

59 "Lun Zhongguo zhi minqi keyong" (On the Utility to China of the People's Spirit), *Qingyi bao* 57 (14 September 1900). While Mai extols the utility of "people's spirit," he specifically distances himself from the Boxers, whom he labels "bandits."

60 For *shishi* in Japan, see Thomas H. Huber, "Men of High Purpose and the Politics of Direct Action, 1862–1864," in Tetsuo Najita and Victor Koschmann, eds., *Conflict in Modern Japanese History: The Neglected Tradition* (Princeton: Princeton University Press, 1982): 107–27. For a discussion of *shishi* in pre-1911 China, see Zhao Junyi, *Xinhai geming yu dalu langren* (The Xinhai Revolution and the "Mainland Ronin") (Beijing: Zhongguo dabaikeshe chubanshe, 1991).

61 Also see Zhuang You, "Guomin xin linghun" (The New Spirit of a National People), *Jiangsu* 5 (May 1903); Zhuang lists five types of "spirit" needed to build a national people; among them is "youxia," or a roaming knight-errant spirit, which he describes as a wandering spirit that is not content with the status quo but that acts to change things (through revolution, assassination, bloodshed, or republicanism). Essay reprinted in Zhang Dan and Wang Renzhi, eds., *Xinhai geming qianshinian jian shilun xuanji* (Selected Editorials from the Decade Preceding the Xinhai Revolution) (Hong Kong: Sanlian shudian, 1962), vol. 1, pt. 2, pp. 571–76.

62 Liang Qichao, "Zhongguo zhi wushi dao," YBSZJ 6:1–15 (1904). Also see "Junguomin sixiang puji lun" (On the Popularization of Military Citizens Thinking) *Hubei Xuesheng Jie* 3 (1903). For more, see Qu Lihou, *Qingmo minchu minzuzhuyi jiaoyu sichao* (Trends in Nationalist Education in Late Qing and Early Republican China) (Taipei: Chung-hua wen-hua fu-hsing yun-tung t'ui-hsing wei yuan hui, 1984): chap. 2.

63 The abundance of military heroic types in popular dramas, fiction, opera, etc., had made the type well respected among nonelites already.

64 Sang Bing, *Qingmo xin zhishijie de shetuan yu huodong* (Societies and Activities in Late Qing New Intellectual Circles) (Beijing: Sanlian-Harvard Yenching, 1995): chap. 7.

65 Sang Bing, *Qingmo xinzhishijie*: 262.

66 This view substantially adopted the Boers' own self-representations. See Ken Smith, *The Changing Past: Trends in South African Historical Writing* (Cincinnati: Ohio University Press, 1988): 57–69.

67 "Yingguo duguo zhuquan wenti" (The Problem of Sovereignty between England and the Transvaal), *Qingyi bao* 33 (23 December 1899), which explains the legal status of the Transvaal. In brief, the problem emerged from ambiguities in the 1881 and 1884 Pretoria and London treaties, where England's suzerainty over the South African Republica was first affirmed (1881) and then apparently dropped (1884). The Transvaal argued, in 1898, that since the 1884 treaty did not mention "suzerainty," there was no British suzerainty; the British argued that the 1881 treaty was the operative master-treaty, with the 1884 treaty representing a revision of selected articles. See T. R. H. Davenport, *South Africa: A Modern History*, 4th ed. (Toronto: University of Toronto Press, 1991): 180–83.

68 *Nan A xinjianguo shi* (History of a Newly Established Country in South Africa),

trans. Chen Zhixiang (Shanghai: Wenming shuju, 1902); and Fukumoto, *Telansifa'er* (Transvaal). There was also *Yingte zhanji* (A Record of the Anglo-Transvaal War), trans. Dongya shanlin xueguan (East Asian Good Neighbor Society), ed. Xia Qingyi (Shanghai: Kaiming shudian, 1904), written by a Japanese, although not Fukumoto.

69 "Nan A gailun" (Situation in South Africa), *Qingyi bao* 35 (10 February 1900).

70 By mid-Meiji, Fukuoka was dominated by mining concerns; the *Genyōsha* (Dark Ocean Society) emerged in the 1880s in part as a reaction to these developments. See E. H. Norman, "The Genyosha: A Study in the Origins of Japanese Imperialism," *Pacific Affairs* 17.3 (September 1944): 261–84.

71 Carol Gluck, *Japan's Modern Myths* (Princeton: Princeton University Press, 1985): 178–89; Tessa Morris-Suzuki, *Re-inventing Japan: Time, Space, Nation* (New York: M. E. Sharpe, 1998).

72 Fukumoto elaborated this by condemning British actions in South Africa as "sins" against a transhistorical value of justice. "Lun yingren shidazui" (On the Ten Great Sins of the English), *Yadong shibao* 21 (28 April 1900). Through this essay he critiqued the assumption that modernity's content was exhausted by capitalist "modernization." For him, the agrarianism of the Boers did not signify the binary obverse of "modernity"; it was not, in Harry Harootunian's words, a "traditionalism" that figured a lack requiring completion. H. D. Harootunian, "The Benjamin Effect: Modernism, Repetition, and the Path to Different Cultural Imaginaries," in Michael P. Steinberg, ed., *Walter Benjamin and the Demands of History* (Ithaca: Cornell University Press, 1996): 62–87. By the same token, Fukumoto's recuperation of the Boers as a paradigmatic symbol intended to explode the historicist march of capitalism conceals the political implications of such a perspective in late Meiji Japan, where concern with the "natural community" of the *minzoku* almost inevitably went hand in hand with support for Japanese imperialism in Asia. Fukumoto's organizational affiliations bear out this relationship. See Gluck, *Japan's Modern Myths*, chap. 6; Naoki Sakai, *Translation and Subjectivity*, chaps. 3–4.

73 For the antimodernist tendencies of Tokyo-based anarchists, see Arif Dirlik, *Anarchism in the Chinese Revolution* (Berkeley: University of California Press, 1991): chap. 3.

74 See Arif Dirlik, "Socialism and Capitalism in Chinese Socialist Thinking: The Origins," *Studies in Comparative Communism* 21.2 (summer 1988): 131–52; Martin Bernal, *Chinese Socialism to 1907* (Ithaca: Cornell University Press, 1976): 129–97.

75 Fukumoto, *Nan A xinjianguo shi* xu: 1–2.

76 Ibid.: 3.

77 The *Youxue yibian* was begun by the Hunan Translation Society, founded in Japan in 1902 by eight Hunanese students. Among them were Yang Desheng (Shouren), author of *Xin Hunan*, and Yang Du. The journal published annotated trans-

lations of Japanese or Western-language materials, as well as exchanges of letters from Hunanese students. A monthly magazine, it endured for an entire year and published twelve issues in all.

78 According to Hao Chang, based upon the musings in the fragmented *Ziyou shu* (Book of Freedom), Liang synthesized his interpretation of liberalism in his famous March 1902 essay entitled "Lun zhengfu yu renmin zhi quanxian" (On the Boundaries between the Government and the People), wherein Liang "accepted the classically liberal concept of government as a night watchman" while upholding the "collectivistic notion that over and above government and the people there exists the state, which must be regarded as having an independent personality of its own and as the locus of the highest sovereignty of the country." *Liang Ch'i-ch'ao*: 191–93.

79 "NanA duli yingxiong Gulujia luezhuan" (Brief Biography of Kruger, Hero of South African Independence), *Youxue yibian* 6–7 (12 April, 11 May 1903); cite 6: n.p. Translated from the Japanese paper *Keiyo ho*.

80 "NanA duli yingxiong Gulujia luezhuan," *Youxue yibian* 6: n.p.

81 Ibid. 7: n.p.

82 On the latter, see Kathy Le Mons Walker, *Chinese Modernity and the Peasant Path* (Stanford: Stanford University Press, 1999); Roxann Prazniak, *Of Camel Kings and Other Things: Rural Rebels against Modernity in Late Imperial China* (Totowa, N.J.: Rowman and Littlefield, 1999).

83 Liang Qichao used "puppet" to describe the situation up until 1903, after which he dropped this critique. The anti-Manchuists used "slave." For Liang's initial description of "puppetry" see "Kueilei shuo" (On Puppets), YBSZJ 2:42 (originally published in *Qingyi bao* 9 [22 March 1899]).

84 Gonghe fuhansheng (Restore the Han Republican Student), "Lun Minzu zhuyi" (On Ethno-nationalism), *Jingzhong ribao* (8–10 December 1904).

85 Speech delivered in Tokyo marking the first anniversary of *Minbao*, mouthpiece of the Revolutionary Alliance, printed in *Minbao* 10 (2 December 1906): 10.

86 Liang Qichao, "Mieguo xinfa lun," YBSWJ 6:36–38.

87 Liang elsewhere called this "invisible dismemberment" (*wuxing de guafen*). ("Lun jinshi guomin jingzheng zhi dashi ji Zhongguo zhi qiantu" (On the General Trend of Competition between Peoples and China's Future), YBSWJ 2:56–67; *Qingyi bao* 30 (25 October 1899).

88 Liang, "Mieguo xinfa lun": 38.

89 Ibid.: 46, 45.

90 For more on this particular issue as a theoretical proposition, see Etienne Balibar, "The Nation Form: History and Ideology," in Balibar and Wallerstein, *Race, Nation, Class: Ambiguous Identities* (New York: Verso 1991): 86–106.

91 Hao Chang, *Liang Ch'i-ch'ao*: 166.

92 Xiaobing Tang, *Global Space*: chaps. 3–4.

93 Hao Chang, *Liang Ch'i-ch'ao*: 166.

94 See in particular Liang Qichao, "Guojia sixiang bianqian yitong lun" (On Transformations and Differences in Thinking on the State), *Qingyi bao* 94–95 (October 1901); rpt. YBSWJ 6:12.

95 "Nan A Zhanji" (A Record of the South African War), *Yunnan* 1 (1906): n.p. *Yunnan*, published in Tokyo by Yunnanese students, was affiliated with the Revolutionary Alliance.

96 The formulation is adapted from Etienne Balibar, who writes: "Under certain conditions, *only* imaginary communities are real" ("The Nation Form: History and Ideology": 93).

97 For a discussion of the deep structures of Zhang's and Liu's radical thought, see Hao Chang, *Chinese Intellectuals in Crisis* (Berkeley: University of California Press, 1987): chaps. 4 and 5. As Chang demonstrates, Zhang Binglin's political radicalism was heavily informed by his understandings of Yogacara Buddhism, particularly after 1903; Liu's intellectual orientation, meanwhile, can be traced to the radicalism of the Yangzhou school of Han Learning.

98 The anti-Manchu revolution thus did not represent a historical choice against anti-imperialism by Chinese intellectuals, as Chinese historians have claimed, because it was intellectually conceived and justified completely within the paradigm of anticolonial/anti-imperialist revolution. Indeed, Chinese historians still find it difficult to explain why anti-Manchuism took priority over anti-Western imperialism, and most explanations have rested upon a staged labeling of late Qing intellectuals as "immature" or "petty bourgeois," or on explications of post-Ming Chinese scholarly sources for anti-Manchu sentiment. Western scholarship has often taken the latter route while dismissing the former. For recent Chinese articulations, see Tao Xu, *Wanqing minzu zhuyi sichao* (Late Qing Nationalism) (Beijing: Renmin chubanshe, 1995): 203–22; Geng Yunzhi, "Lun Qingmo de fanman geming sichao" (On Late Qing Anti-Manchu Revolutionism), in Zhongnan diqu xinhai gemingshi yanjiuhui et al., eds., *Xinhai fengyun yu jindai zhongguo* (Modern China and the Xinhai Revolution) (Guiyang: Guizhou renmin chubanshe, 1991): 38–75.

99 For scholarly bases of anti-Manchuism, as articulated by *guocui* (national essence) scholars, see Charlotte Furth, "The Sage as Rebel: The Inner World of Chang Ping-lin," in Furth, ed., *The Limits of Change*: 113–50; Martin Bernal, "Liu Shih-p'ei and National Essence," in *The Limits of Change*: 90–112; Laurence A. Schneider, "National Essence and the New Intelligentsia," in *The Limits of Change*: 57–89; Shimada Kenji, *Pioneer of the Chinese Revolution: Zhang Binglin and Confucianism*, trans. Joshua Fogel (Stanford: Stanford University Press, 1990); Kauko Laitinen, *Chinese Nationalism in the Late Qing Dynasty: Zhang Binglin as an Anti-Manchu Propagandist* (London: Curzon Press, 1990).

100 This political understanding stands in contrast to the New Culture–May Fourth period (1915–1925) when, as Arif Dirlik has shown, global capitalism became the basis for a local recognition of capitalist incursion in China, which helped make relevant to China a radical Marxist or Marxian politics that specifically situated itself against capitalism as an organizing schema. *Origins of Chinese Communism*: 71.

Chapter 6. *Performing on the World Stage in Asia*

1 Cited in Wong Young-tsu, *Search for Modern Nationalism: Zhang Binglin and Revolutionary China, 1869–1936* (New York: Oxford University Press, 1989): 64.

2 Liang Qichao, "Zhongguoshi xulun" (Introductory Essay to a History of China), *Yinbingshi wenji* (Collected Essays from the Ice-Drinkers Studio) [hereafter YBSWJ, with citations by *juan* number] (Taipei: Zhonghua shuju, 1984), 6:1–12.

3 Liang, "Zhongguoshi xulun": 11–12.

4 For a discussion linking this essay to developments in Liang's historical consciousness, see Xiaobing Tang, *Nationalist Discourse and the Global Space of Modernity: The Historical Consciousness of Liang Qichao* (Stanford: Stanford University Press, 1996): chap. 2.

5 *Wenming* is one of the terms whose "meaning" was in transition throughout the late Qing. D. R. Howland makes the case that up until the mid-1890s, *wenming* can be tied firmly to a "Chinese civilizational worldview" that was dependent upon the centrality of language and texts to its definition (*Borders of Chinese Civilization* [Durham, N.C.: Duke University Press, 1996]: intro. and chap. 1). As documented throughout this book, *wenming* was quickly being diffused in meaning—to cover unlettered peoples such as the Boers and unliterary pursuits such as revolution; it was thus taking on the meaning of "modern" or "modernity."

6 The general essay was entitled "Dili yu wenming zhi guanxi" (The Relationship between Geography and Modern Civilization), published in February 1902; the next three are: "Yazhou dili dashi lun" (Discourse on General Geographical Trends in Asia) (March 1902); "Zhongguo dili dashi lun" (Discourse on General Geographical Trends in China) (April 1902); and "Ouzhou dili dashi lun" (Discourse on General Geographical Trends in Europe) (June 1902). All were originally published in Liang's journal *Xinmin congbao* and are reprinted in YBSWJ 4—respectively, 106–16; 69–77; 77–101; and 101–6.

7 Also see Liang's "Dongji yuedan" (A Critique of Japanese Booklists) *Xinmin congbao* 9, 11 (June–July 1902); rpt., YBSWJ 4:82–102, in which he notes: "So-called world history . . . for the Japanese is actually the history of the West" (91); and "what the Japanese call Eastern, as opposed to Western, indicates

only Asia, and the main protagonist in Asia is actually China . . . Even though these books are called 'Histories of the East,' they are really nothing but histories of China . . . This is insufficient to merit the designation 'History of the East'" (98).

8 Liang, "Yazhou dili dashi lun": 69–70.

9 For the European invention, see Edward Said, *Orientalism* (New York: Pantheon, 1979); for the Japanese *toyo*, see Stephan Tanaka, *Japan's Orient: Rendering Pasts into History* (Berkeley: University of California Press, 1993).

10 Liang, "Yazhou dili dashi lun": 73.

11 Ibid.: 70.

12 The numbers of Chinese students in Japan skyrocketed at this point: from just over several hundred in the beginning of the century, the number reached over eight thousand in 1905, even while only a small minority of this eight thousand was actually active in politics. See Wang Qisheng, *Zhongguo liuxuesheng de lishi quzi* (In the Historical Footsteps of Chinese Students Abroad) (Hankou: Hubei jiaoyu chubanshe 1992): 95.

13 John W. Witek, "Understanding the Chinese: A Comparison of Matteo Ricci and the French Jesuit Mathematicians Sent by Louis XIV," in Charles E. Ronan and Bonnie B. C. Oh, eds., *East Meets West: The Jesuits in China, 1582–1773* (Chicago: University of Chicago Press, 1988): 71.

14 Wei Yüan, *Haiguo tuzhi* (Illustrated Gazeteer on Maritime States); originally published in 1844 and reprinted in 1847. Citations are to the 1847 edition, 7 vols., reprinted in Taipei, 1967.

15 Ibid., 2:679.

16 Xu Jiyu, *Yinghuan zhilue* (A Short Account of Maritime Circuits) (1848; rpt. Taipei, 1967), 1:24 (for the decision on transcriptions) and 59 (for the cited text).

17 Ibid., 1:60.

18 As we have seen, the turn of the century also saw the emergence of: *dongfang* (the East), previously used to refer only to Japan, but now denoting "the East" or "the Orient" in relation to the West; *yuandong* (the Far East), which also adopted the "West's" perspectival lens; *dongya* (East Asia); and *taipingyang* (the Pacific).

19 Zhao Junyi, *Xinhai geming yu dalu langren* (The Xinhai Revolution and "Mainland Ronins") (Beijing: Zhongguo dabaikeshu chubanshe, 1991): 16–17. This could be contrasted to what Stefan Tanaka describes as the late Meiji construct of Asia: "The totality described through this historical perspective incorporated the separation of politics or history from a culture that was frozen in the past." *Japan's Orient*: 200.

20 Howland, *Borders*: intro. Stefan Tanaka analyzes this in his discussion of Meiji Japanese constructions of *toyo* (the Orient), which, he notes, often served to legitimize the Meiji state's will to hegemony over Asia, and were thus intended

to discursively *distance* Japan from China and its neighbors in order to tie Japan firmly to Europe. Stefan Tanaka, *Japan's Orient*. Also see Yumiko Iida, "Fleeing the West, Making Asia Home: Transpositions of Otherness in Japanese Pan-Asianism, 1905–1930," *Alternatives* 22 (1997): 409–32.

Even prior to these distancings, as Harry Harootunian has demonstrated, the dehistoricization of China in the late Tokugawa period (early 1800s) had already helped Tokugawa thinkers produce a concept of a homogeneous "Japan." Thus, when the actual historicity of mid-nineteenth-century China, in all its decline and despair, was incorporated into Meiji Japanese thought, such luminaries as Fukuzawa Yukichi began to advocate a "dissociation from Asia" (that is, from China). See H. D. Harootunian, "The Function of China in Tokugawa Thought," in Akira Iriye, ed., *The Chinese and Japanese: Essays in Political and Cultural Interactions* (Princeton: Princeton University Press, 1980): 9–36; and his extended working out of this issue in *Things Seen and Unseen: Discourse and Ideology in Tokugawa Nativism* (Chicago: Chicago University Press, 1988).

21 He used *tongzhong* specifically to encourage Chinese students to go to Japan to study modern scientific and technological subjects. Howland notes that Zhang Zhidong often used *tongwen tongzhong* and that in this official usage *tongzhong* was explicitly linked to *tongwen* and remained narrow in its conceptualization. *Borders*: 261–62n22.

22 Zhang Binglin, "Lun Yazhou yize wei chunchi" (It is Best for Asia to Stand together Firmly), *Shiwu bao* 18 (February 1897).

23 For China's official relationship to Japan in this period, see Douglas R. Reynolds, *China, 1898–1912: The Xinzheng Revolution and Japan* (Cambridge: Harvard University Press, 1993).

24 For an analysis of early pan-Asianism that focuses on Sun Zhongshan, see Prasenjit Duara, "Transnationalism and the Predicament of Sovereignty: China, 1900–1945," *American Historical Review* 102 (October 1997): 1030–51; for a comprehensive anthology of the field of Sun Zhongshan pan-Asia studies see *"Sun Zhongshan yu yazhou" guoji xueshu taolunhui lunwen ji* (Collection of Essays from the "International Conference on Sun Zhongshan and Asia"), ed. Guangdong-sheng Sun Zhongshan yanjiuhui (Guangzhou: Zhongshan daxue chubanshe, 1994).

25 For Wang Jingwei's pan-Asianism in relation to his wartime stance, see Hwang Dongyoun, "Some Reflections on Wang Jingwei's Collaboration," *Working Papers in Asian-Pacific Studies* (Duke University, 1998). Hwang demonstrates that Wang's pan-Asianism emerges quite logically from Sun Zhongshan's earlier version.

26 "Wei wairen zhi nuli yu wei Manzhou zhengfu zhi nuli wubie" (There Is No Difference between Being a Slave of Foreigners and Being a Slave of the Manchus), *Tongzi shijie* 24 (2 May 1903); rpt. Zhang Dan and Wang Renzhi, eds., *Xinhai geming qianshinianjian shilun xuanji* (Selected Editorials from the Decade Preceding

the Xinhai Revolution) (Hong Kong: Sanlian shudian, 1962), vol. 1, pt. 2, pp. 526–27.

27 Liang Qichao, "Mieguo xinfa lun," YBSWJ 6:35 (*Qingyi bao* 32 [July–August, 1901]).

28 Ibid.: 36.

29 Ibid.

30 For example: *Yindu chanshi zhanshi* (The Wars of Nibbling away at India), trans. Wang Younian, *Lixue yibian* (Journal of Translations to Encourage Learning) 1–12 (3 April 1901–22 February 1902); *Indu shi* (History of India), trans. Wang Benxiang (Shanghai: Chiwenshe 1903); *Indu miewang shi* (The History of the Destruction and Loss of India), ed. and trans. Xia Qingfu (Shanghai: Kaiming shudian, 1902); "Yindu miewang zhi yuanyin" (The Reasons for India's Destruction and Perishing), *Zhejiang chao* 1.5 (17 February, 15 June 1903).

31 "Fengehou zhi wumin" (My People after Partition), *Jiangsu* 8–10 (January–March 1904): n.p. The Boxers had also worn red turbans to distinguish themselves; however, there is no evidence that "red turbans" denote anything but Indians, although Boxers were often called "slaves" of the Qing.

32 Ibid.

33 Allen's essay, "Indu li yinguo shi'er yi shuo," appeared in *Wanguo gongbao* 94 (October–November 1896); among the twelve "advantages" to British colonization of India, Allen lists the institution of the rule of law, education, building railroads, and so on. Timothy Richards used the same forum to promote similar views. For a discussion, see Yuan Weishi, *Wanqing dabianjuzhong de sichao yu renwu* (Intellectual Trends and Figures in the Late Qing Transformations) (Shenzhen: Haitian chubanshe, 1992): chap. 7; and Hu Fengyang and Zhang Wenjian, *Zhongguo jindai shixue sichao yu liupai* (Trends and Schools of Modern Chinese Historiography) (Shanghai: Huadong shida chubanshe, 1991): 149–73.

34 Founded in 1887 in Shanghai by American and British missionaries—Alexander Williamson, Young J. Allen, Joseph Edkins, Timothy Richards, William A. P. Martin, and others—the SDK's purpose was to make accounts of Western history, science, and religion available in China. Among its books were several on the English experience of colonizing India, such as *Daying zhili yindu xinzheng kao* (Investigation into the New Policies of the British Empire's Rule in India). For the SDK's publishing activities, see Hu Fengyang and Zhang Wenjian, *Zhongguo jindai shixue sichao yu liupai*: 149–73. Xie Honglai (1873–1916) went on to become the director of the YMCA publications department.

35 J. P. Drège, *La Commercial Press de Shanghai, 1897–1949* (Paris: Collège de France, Institute des Hautes Études Chinoises, 1978): 9. This endeavor was not successful, in part due to the untransferability of the India readers to China, and in part because a new wave of textbook writing more relevant to the Chinese context

got under way in 1900, sponsored by a new wing of the Commercial Press and others involved in the new-style schools.

36 Ding Muqin, "Qinquan tongbao saochu mixin" (A Warning to Our Compatriots to Sweep away Superstitions), *Beijing nübao* 1091 (10 September 1908).

37 Xuan Pushi, *Zuijin zhina geming yundong xu* (Preface to *The Recent Chinese Revolutionary Movement*), by Tano Katsuji (Shanghai: Xinzhi she, 1903): 5.

38 As with Chinese forgings of relationships with Ponce of the Philippines, there is a significant class dimension to these recognitions of commonality: one condition of possibility for the mutual recognition of "sameness"—however universally articulated—was the shared elite social status of the Chinese and other Asians in Japan with whom they were in contact. "Difference" could thus be transposed into "sameness" when cultural standards and social status were similar.

39 It is only after 1905 that one sees essays on Vietnam in the periodical press. For example, see Nanguo henren (an alias), "Yuenan wangguo shimo tan" (A Complete Account of the Loss of Vietnam), *Guofeng bao* 1–2 (1910–1911); in addition to the numerous 1908–1911 *wangguo shi* compilations, which include Vietnam among the other more usual suspects.

40 David Marr, *Vietnamese Anticolonialism* (Berkeley: University of California Press, 1971): chaps. 4–5.

41 Howland, *Borders*: 43–53. Excerpts from Liang's and Phan's *bitan* were published as the seventh installment of Liang's *Ziyou shu* (Book of Freedom), under the title "Ji yuenan wangren zhi yan" (A Record of the Words of a Lost Person from Vietnam), *Xinmin congbao* 67 (19 April 1905).

42 Hue-Tam Ho Tai, *Radicalism and the Origins of the Vietnamese Revolution* (Cambridge: Harvard University Press, 1992): 21.

43 David Marr calls this book "Vietnam's first revolutionary history book" (*Vietnamese Anticolonialism*: 144). The Chinese version was one of a book series, "Mirror on Popular Current Events," edited by Liang and published by the Guangzhi shuju. (Other books in the series include one on China's national debt; the Russo-Japanese War and the Division of Manchuria; the history of railroads in China; an explanation of "spheres of influence"; and one on Korea and Tibet.)

44 One version can be found in *Anhui baihua bao* (Anhui Colloquial Journal) 1 (5 October 1908); others can be found in several Yunnan publications of 1906–9. I have found no evidence that this drama was ever performed.

45 "*Yuenan wangguo shi* qianlu" (Preface to *History of the Loss of Vietnam*) (Shanghai: Guangzhi shuju, 1905): 6.

46 Hue-Tam Ho Tai, *Radicalism and the Origins of the Vietnamese Revolution*: 58.

47 Huang Guo'an, Su Deji, and Yang Libing, eds., *Jindai zhongyue guanxishi zhiliao xuanbian* (Selected Documents on the History of Modern Chinese and Vietnamese Relations) (Guangxi renmin chubanshe, 1990), 3:763–68.

48 In 1912, Phan began using Guangzhou as a base for his "Vietnam Restoration Society," through which he advocated a republican revolution. Several former Revolutionary Alliance members were active in this society, and under the dual sponsorship of Phan's society and the Revolutionary Alliance the "Arise China Awaken Asia Society" (*Zenhua xingya hui*) was formed to assist the Vietnamese resistance. Phan was the vice-chairman of this organization, and Zeng Jingya, an Alliance member, was chairman. Yuan Shikai suppressed the organization upon the request of the French in 1913. See Zeng Jingya, "Zhongyue geming zhishi zuzhi 'Zenhua xingya hui' jinxing kangfa douzheng huiyi" (Reminiscences on the Chinese-Vietnamese Revolutionaries' Organization "Arise China Awaken Asia Society" and the Promotion of the anti-French Struggle), in *Guangdong wenshi zhiliao* (Guangzhou: Guangdong renmin chubanshe, 1978), 22:205–35.

49 Phan's memoirs note that he participated in and jointly managed, with Zhang Ji and others, the *Tōa Dōmeikai* (Ch: *Dongya tongmeng hui*; East Asia League). Kawamoto Kuniye states that this league is one and the same as the Asian Solidarity Society. "The Viet-nam Quang Phuc Hoi and the 1911 Revolution," trans. Okui Yaeko, in Eto Shinkichi and Harold Z. Schiffrin, eds., *The 1911 Revolution in China: Interpretive Essays* (Tokyo: University of Tokyo Press, 1984), 115–27; 125. Also see Tang Zhijun, "Guanyu yazhou heqin hui" (On the Asian Solidarity Society), in Wuchang Xinhai geming yanjin zhongxin, eds., *Xinhai geming yu jindai zhongguo: 1980–1989 nian lunwen xuan* (The Xinhai Revolution and Modern China: A Selection of Essays Written from 1980 to 1989) (Wuhan: Hubei renmin chubanshe, 1991): 223; Hue-Tam Ho Tai, *Radicalism and the Origins of the Vietnamese Revolution*: 59.

50 It had long been one goal of Zhang Binglin's "national essence" (*guocui*) studies to decenter Confucius in Chinese learning through the recovery of the writings of the *zhuzi*, or the "Hundred Schools and Nine Streams." For Zhang, the Manchu promotion of imperial Confucianism had served to quash the genuine diversity of Chinese learning. See Shimada, *Pioneer*: 90–95.

51 *Guomin bao* 4 (10 August 1901).

52 This point is derived from a related discussion in Shimada, *Pioneer*: 56–7. Zhang's own interest in Mahayana Buddhism also led him to claim that China and India were the only genuinely "historical" Asian countries, and that both needed to recover their pasts from the hands of foreigners.

53 As Lydia Liu has noted, distinctions between anthropological notions of culture and historical notions of civilization (both expressed in Chinese by *wenming* or *wenhua*) were just being worked out at this time. Liu Shipei and Zhang Binglin were two of the foremost scholars involved in this endeavor. See Liu, *Translingual Practice: Literature, National Culture, and Translated Modernity* (Stanford: Stanford University Press, 1995): chap. 9.

54 Indeed, secondary discussions of the Asian Solidarity Society present the organization and its content as an expected and flawed climax of the pre-1911 intellectual trajectory and unique cultural attitudes of Zhang Taiyan. This reading is essentially limited. See Tang Zhijun, "Guanyu yazhou heqin hui"; Wang Youwei, "Shixi Zhang Taiyan 'Yazhou heqin hui yuezhang'" (A Preliminary Analysis of Zhang Taiyan's "Constitution for the Asian Solidarity Society"), *Xueshu yuekan* 6 (1976): 68–70; Tao Zhigong, "Bayu" (Afterword) to the society's constitution, as reprinted in *Xinhai geming congkan* 1.

55 Liu Shipei, "Zhongguo minzu zhi" (Sketch of the Chinese Ethnos), *Liu Shenshu xiansheng yishu* (Posthumous Works of Liu Shenshu [Shipei]) (no publisher, 1937), vol. 17, chap. 18: 53b–54a.

56 Liu Yazi and Liu Wuji, *Su Manshu (Su Xuanying) Nianpu ji qita* (A Chronological Biography of Su Manshu and Other Matters) (Shanghai: Beixin shuju, 1928). Su's participation in the society is not mentioned here, but contemporary participants and chroniclers place him firmly in the membership. See below for more details.

57 *Zhang Puquan [Ji] xiansheng nianpu* (A Chronological Biography of Mr. Zhang Puquan [Ji]), no publisher, no date, no author: 455.

58 It is difficult to ascertain how many Indian students were there. According to "Wangguo zhi xuesheng" (Students of a Lost Country), *Jingzhong ribao* (12 May 1904), there were twenty; the report notes that due to financial difficulties and the unwillingness of Indian merchants in Yokohama to assist them because of pressure from British and Japanese authorities, the students' original activities had ceased. By 1907, a group had apparently reorganized.

59 "Ji yindu xipoqi wang jinianhui shi" (A Report on the Commemorative Meeting for the Indian, King Shivaji), *Minbao* 13 (5 May 1907): 93–97. For an annotated translation, see Shimada Kenji, *Pioneer*: 78–82. In the report Zhang likened Shivaji to Zhu Yuanzhang, the Han Chinese military hero who had led the overthrow of the Mongol Yuan dynasty to establish the Ming dynasty (mid-fourteenth century). For a discussion of Shivaji, see James W. Laine, "Shivaji as Epic Hero," in Gunther D. Sontheimer, ed., *Maharashtra: Culture and Society, Folk Culture, Folk Religion, and Oral Tradition* (New Delhi: Oxford University Press, 1995): 1–24.

60 Takeuchi Zensaku, a Japanese socialist involved in the organization, dates the founding to the summer of 1907. "Meiji makki ni okeru chūnichi kakumei undō no kōryū" (Late-Meiji Exchanges between Chinese and Japanese Revolutionary Movements), *Chūgoku kenkyū* 5 (September 1948): 74–95. Chinese historian Tang Zhijun dates it to April 1907. "Guanyu yazhou heqin hui": 221–28. Those involved in the Shivaji memorial only met on 20 April; thus the organization must have formed after that.

61 "Yazhou heqin hui yuezhang" (The Constitution of the Asian Solidarity So-

ciety), in *Zhang Taiyan xuan ji* (*Selected Works of Zhang Taiyan* [hereafter ZTYXJ]), ed. Zhu Weijing and Qi Yihua (Shanghai: Renmin chubanshe, 1981): 429.

62 Tao Zhigong lists the following Chinese participants in addition to the ones named above: Su Manshu, Tao himself, Chen Duxiu, Lü Fu, and Luo Xiangtao. Tao, "Bayu" (Afterword to the society's constitution), in *Xinhai gemingshi congkan* (Journal of Xinhai Revolution History) 1 (1940). Takeuchi lists Sakai Toshihiko, Yamakawa Hitoshi, Morita Ariaki, Morichika Umpei, Ōsugi Sakae, and himself as the Japanese participants. He notes that the anarchist Kōtoku Shūsui was in sympathy, although it is unclear if Kōtoku ever attended the society's meetings.

63 Both Tao and Takeuchi mention a Mr. D (or Dai) as the leader of the Indians, while Zhang Binglin (Taiyan) records a Mr. Boluohan and a Mr. Baoshen as his contacts among the Indians. For Zhang's account, see "Song Yindu Boluohan Baoshen erjun xu" (Preface Sent to Two Indian Gentlemen, Boluohan and Baoshen), *Minbao* 13 (5 May 1907): 97–100. (I have been no more successful than Joshua Fogel in tracking down the identity of these two men; for Fogel's efforts, see Shimada, *Pioneer*: 158n101.) As for the "Mr. D," this may very well refer to the Bengali Taraknath Das (1884–1958), who fled India in 1905 for Japan; he moved to San Francisco in 1906 and established the journal *Free Hindustan*, becoming a major publicist for the Indian cause in the United States. See *The Dictionary of National Biography* (Calcutta, 1971–74), 1:363–64; also see Janice R. and Stephen R. MacKinnon, *Agnes Smedley: The Life and Times of an American Radical* (Berkeley: University of California Press, 1988): 357 n10.

64 Shyamaji established a bi-weekly journal, "Indian Sociologist," in London in 1905; the paper was subtitled: "an organ of freedom and political, social, and religious reform." Within two years, he had initiated anticolonial centers in Paris, San Francisco, Tokyo, and Berlin. On his connection to Indian students in Tokyo, see T. R. Sareen, *Indian Revolutionaries, Japan, and British Imperialism* (New Delhi: Sterling, 1993): 12; A. C. Bose, *Indian Revolutionaries Abroad, 1905–1922: In the Background of International Developments* (Patna: Bharati Bhawan, 1971): chaps. 1–3; and Naito Masao, "Meiji Intellectuals and India," in Okhata Kohei, ed., *Nihon to Indo* (Japan and India) (Tokyo: University of Tokyo Press, 1978): 33–36. Also see indications of this network in Liu Shipei, "Yazhou xianshi lun" (On Recent Trends in Asia), *Tianyi bao* 2.3 (1907).

65 It is assumed by Chinese historians that Zhang Taiyan was the author of the Chinese text and its inclusion in his selected works makes this assumption a "fact." However, Takeuchi suggests that Zhang Taiyan's name was used by Zhang Ji and Liu Shipei—the real authors—because Taiyan was more famous. The English text was either written by the Indian participants or was translated from the Chinese by Su Manshu. Takeuchi suggests Indian authorship; Chinese historians suggest Su Manshu's translation. (Despite efforts, I have been unable to locate a copy of the English version.)

66 Takeuchi records that the pamphlet was printed on 100-jin weight paper (good-quality paper), relatively large in size (54cm x 21cm). With the English text on the back and Chinese on the front, the pamphlet was folded seven times; the Chinese text was thus on the inside and the English text on the outside. He comments: "Judging from the way it was folded, the Chinese might be considered the more important text, but in fact, it was the English text that was more clearly visible. The English text was four pages long and the Chinese text was five." "Meiji makki": 78.

67 Vietnamese, Korean, and Japanese intellectuals trained in the traditional fashion would have been able to read the classical Chinese text.

68 The India House was inaugurated in late 1906 by Surendramohan Bose (perhaps the Mr. Baoshen of Zhang Taiyan's acquaintance?) and the aforementioned Mr. D, a student at Tokyo's Imperial University; it was located at 17 Gondawara-chō in Aoyama. Bose wrote to Shyamaji Krishan Verma, then in London, informing him of the formation of this collective. Sareen, *Indian Revolutionaries*: 12; Bose, *Indian Revolutionaries Abroad*: 66–70.

69 The Socialist Lecture Group (C: *Shehui zhuyi jiangxi hui*; J: *Shakaishugi kōshūkai*) was also called the Friday Lecture Group (C: *Jinyao hui*; J: *Kinyō kai*) in order to circumvent Japan's Public Security laws prohibiting socialists from organizing. For more on these groups and on Chinese anarchists in Tokyo, see Arif Dirlik, *Anarchism in the Chinese Revolution* (Berkeley: University of California Press, 1991): chap. 2.

70 One of the Vietnamese involved was Phan Boi Chau. It is almost certain that Mariano Ponce was involved, although no direct evidence places him at the society's meetings.

71 Marius Jansen notes that the society was forcefully disbanded by the Japanese authorities in 1908 because it "did not constitute the kind of Greater Asian movement that the Tokyo government favored" (*The Japanese and Sun Yat-sen*: 124).

72 For reports on the society's activities, see essays written by Zhang Taiyan and Tang Zengbi, *Minbao* 16–22 (1907–1908). For Tang Zengbi's involvement in the society, see Zhou Nianchang, "Tongmeng huiyuan Tang Zenbi xiansheng ersanshi" (A Few Things about Tang Zengbi, Member of the Revolutionary Alliance), *Jiangxi shehui kexue* (1981): 81–87.

73 There is a conspicuous absence of Islam here. Zhang Binglin, the ostensible author of the constitution, generally placed Islam into the same category as Christianity: "harmful" and "obstructive" of people's thinking. See Shimada Kenji, *Pioneer*: 30, 120.

74 ZTYXJ: 428.

75 Aijaz Ahmad, *In Theory: Classes, Nations, Literatures* (London: Verso, 1992), 102.

Ahmad is responding to Fredric Jameson, "Third World Literature in the Era of Multinational Capitalism," *Social Text*, no. 15 (fall 1986): 65–88.

76 As discussed in chapter 3 above, clearly the Manchu takeover had been figured as *wangguo* in the traditional sense; here *wangguo* is being made into the equivalent of modern colonization.

77 "Yazhou xianshi lun," *Tianyi bao* 2/3 (30 November 1907); reprinted in *Wuzhengfu zhuyi sixiang zhiliao xuan* (Selection of Materials on Anarchist Thought), ed. Ge Maochun et al. (Beijing: Beijing daxue chubanshe, 1984), 1:120–33. Citations are from the reprinted text.

78 Liu, "Yazhou xianshi lun": 120.

79 Ibid.: 123, 124.

80 Ibid.: 123–4. The phrase *ruozhong* (weak peoples) started to appear more frequently than the phrase *tongzhong* (same race/kind) at this point. By the 1920s, *ruozhong* coexisted with the phrase *bei yapo renmin* (oppressed peoples).

81 Needless to say, these are exaggerated claims for the centrality of Chinese linguistic culture. Yet the point of these claims is not to reinscribe Sinocentricity, but precisely the opposite.

82 Liu, "Yazhou xianshi lun": 125.

83 Dirlik, *Anarchism*: 52.

84 For the distinction between "space" and "place"—where "space" dynamizes "place," or, "space is a practiced place"—see Michel de Certeau, "Spatial Stories," in *The Practice of Everyday Life* (Berkeley: University of California Press, 1988): 117.

85 For more on this epistemological dilemma, see Partha Chatterjee, *Nationalist Thought and the Colonial World: A Derivative Discourse?* (New Jersey: Zed Books, 1986): chaps. 1–2.

86 Dirlik, "Critical Reflections on 'Chinese Capitalism' as Paradigm," *Identities* 3.3 (1997): 303–30.

Chapter 7. Re-creating China's World

1 Min Yi, "Bosi Geming" (Persian Revolution), *Minbao* 25 (1 January 1910): 7. "Min Yi" was the sobriquet for essays discussed collectively among the *Minbao* editors, and then written by Hu Hanmin or Wang Jingwei, or both. It was the composite voice of *Minbao*. See Fang Hanji, *Zhongguo jindai baokan shi* (History of Modern Chinese Journals) (Taiyuan: Shanxi renmin chubanshe: 1981), 2:367. The "success" of the Persian revolution gave way almost immediately to big-power rivalry over the territory, and thus in the end hardly constituted a successful bid for independence.

2 For commentary on the Portuguese revolution, see Yuan Yü, "Putaoya geming ji" (Record of the Portuguese Revolution), *Guofeng bao* 25 (13 October 1910): 1–5.

The essay begins with the following comment: "Last year in April was the Turkish revolution, where the Sultan ceded his position to his brother; in July was the Persian revolution, in which the Persian king gave his position to his son; this year on October 3 the Portuguese also had a revolution, where the Portuguese king was forced to abdicate completely and was replaced by a republican government. In two years, there have been three revolutions; of them, only the Portuguese one can be said to be truly a change for the better" (p. 1).

3 Entitled *Aiji jinshi shi* (Modern History of Egypt), the text was serialized in *Qingyi bao* 47–74 (7 June 1900–30 March 1901) with the Japanese author's preface in issue 45. It was subsequently reprinted in various single-volume editions: first in 1902 by the Commercial Press of Shanghai, as the second volume in the press's new Imperialism Series (*diguo congshu*), translated by the overseas students translation and compilation bureau (Chuyang xuesheng bianji suo), with no preface or editorializing in the text. Zi Ye, later editor at the Commercial Press, asserts in his memoir that it was actually translated by Liang Qichao, and that the press's Imperialism Series was "China's first modern history series." Zi Ye, "Liang Qichao he Shangwu yinshu guan" (Liang Qichao and the Commercial Press), in *Shangwu yinshuguan jiushi nian* (Shanghai's Commercial Press at Ninety) (Shanghai: Shangwu, 1988): 497. In 1903, the book was republished as the ninth volume in the Commercial Press's first popular History Series, the *Lishi congshu*; this version notes the translator as Zhang Chiwei, and carries a preface by Zhang Yüanji.

4 Shiba Shiro (Tokai Sanshi [1852–1922]), was the famed author of the political novel *Strange Encounters with Elegant Women* (Ch: *Jiaren qiyu*; J: *Kajin no kigū*), translated by Liang Qichao for the *Qingyi bao* in 1899–1900. Written from 1885 through 1897, the novel was serialized, and then published in eight volumes in Japan. It concerns the travels and travails of a Japanese political refugee who wanders the world, encountering political refugees from other countries. For Tokai Sanshi and this novel in Japan, see Chris Hill, "History and Circulation: Narratives of the Nation-State in Late-Nineteenth-Century Japan" (Ph.D. diss., Columbia University, 1999).

5 In addition to Zhang Yüanji's commentary (presented below), there were: Chen Huai, "Du *Aiji jinshi shi* bawei" (Epilogue upon Reading *The Modern History of Egypt*), *Xinshijie xuebao* 12 (13 March 1903); "Aiji bainian xingshuai ji" (Egypt's Rise and Fall in the Past Century), *Jingji congbian* 1–7 (March 1903); "Aiji wangguo canzhuang ji" (A Record of the Tragic Perishing of Egypt), *Youxue yibian* 8, 11 (10 June and 5 October 1903); and "Aiji bianzheng kao" (Investigation into Egyptian Reforms), *Zhengyi tongbao* (1907). Aside from the last piece—which is a summary of Lord Milner's work *England in Egypt*—the others are in the same general vein; Lord Milner's book was edited by the Shanghai-based missionary Timothy Richards and published in Chinese in three volumes under

the name *Aiji bianzheng kao* (Investigation into Egyptian Reforms), trans. Yin Pao Lo (Ren Baoluo) (Shanghai: Christian Literature Society, 1907); the excerpt from this book is the only place where Egypt is identified as "African" and not "Asian."

6 Liang Qichao, "Mieguo xinfa lun" (On the New Rules for Destroying Countries), *Qingyi bao* (16 July–24 August 1901); rpt. in YBSWJ 3:32–47.

7 Kitamura was a founding member of the *Tohokyokai* (C: *Dongfang xiehui*; East Asian Association) (1891), which had the stated objective of providing Japan with information on Asian countries and peoples. Zhao Bizhen (1873–1956) was one of the most prolific late Qing translators from Japanese, particularly of early socialist texts such as Fukui Junzo's *Kinsei shakaighugi* (*C: Jinshi shehui zhuyi*; Modern Socialism) (1899); and Kōtoku Shūsui's *Nijuseiki no kaibutsu teikokushugi* (C: *Ershi shiji zhi guaiwu: diguo zhuyi*; Imperialism: The Specter of the Twentieth Century) (1902). On Zhao, see Tian Youlong and Tang Daiwang, "Makesi xueshuo de zaoqi yijiezhe Zhao Bizhen" (An Early Translator and Introducer of Marxism, Zhao Bizhen), *Chousuo* 1 (1983): 118–20.

The Kitamura/Zhao book on Egypt was published as the eighth volume in a series launched by Liang Qichao through the Guangzhi publishing company in Shanghai. The series has ten volumes, seven of which were written by Kitamura and translated by Zhao; the latter are all on "Asia," understood as what in Europe was called the Orient. The historical point of all of these volumes was to explain the reasons for civilizational decline. Zhao, in his annotations to all of the volumes, objects to this characterization. For fuller discussion, see Rebecca E. Karl, "Secret Sharers: China and the Non-West and the Turn of the Twentieth Century" (Ph.D. diss., Duke University, 1995): chap. 9.

8 *Aiji shi* (History of Egypt): 18a–18b. The editorial comments are set off from the text with the words "*yizhe yue*" (the translator says).

9 Kitamura devotes two chapters to Arabi Pasha; see *Aiji shi*: 19b, 20a; and for full citations to Arabi Pasha's proclamations and patriotic statements, see *Aiji shi*: 24a–27b.

10 *Aiji shi*: 32a.

11 Zhang Yüanji, "*Aiji jinshi shi* xu" (Preface to *History of Modern Egypt*), *Waijiao bao* 12: n.p. In her otherwise comprehensive biography of Zhang, Manying Ip does not mention this preface. Manying Ip, *The Life and Times of Zhang Yuanji, 1867–1959* (Beijing: Commercial Press, 1985). Zhang's chronological biography (*nianpu*) notes that the preface was written in March 1903, and that on 15 May 1903 the preface, along with an afterword by Zhang, were published. I have compared the two preface texts—the one attached to the volume and the one in the *Waijiao bao*—and they are identical. See *Zhang Yüanji nianpu* (Shanghai: Shangwu, 1991): 45.

12 Zhang Yüanji, "Aiji jinshi shi xu": n.p.

13 Ibid.

14 Hong Fei (a.k.a. Zhang Zhongduan), "Tuerji lixian shuo" (On the Turkish Constitution), *Henan* 7 (5 August 1908): 19–27. Zhang (1881–1911), a native of Henan province, was a member of the Revolutionary Alliance and one of the founding editors of *Henan*.

15 Ibid.: 23.

16 Ibid.: 25.

17 Indeed, in the passage that follows the above citation, Zhang registered his doubts about the current configuration of the Turkish national project by adding a warning about the historic expansionism of Islam, which had struck fear into the "blond-haired and blue-eyed" Europeans in the past, thus echoing Zhang Taiyan's suspicions about Islam.

18 Hong Fei, "Tuerji lixian shuo": 26–27.

19 Ibid.: 27.

20 For an analysis of constitutionalism and the groups involved, see Chang Yü-fa, *Qingji de lixian tuanti* (Constitutionalists of the Ch'ing Period) (Taipei: Institute of Modern History, Academia Sinica, 1971).

21 For the general argument, see Wang Jingwei, "Minzu de guomin" (An Ethno-National People), *Minbao* 1–2, where Wang strives to separate the Revolutionary Alliance's notion of "constitutionalism" from that advocated by their opponents (specifically Liang Qichao). Hu Hanmin was also quite prolific in his refutations of Liang's arguments for a monarchical constitution built around the dynasty. For the comparison to Turkey, see (Wang) Jingwei, "Lun Geming zhi chushi" (On Revolutionary Trends), *Minbao* 25 (1 January 1910): 1–19. On pp. 16–17 and then on p. 19, Wang Jingwei explicitly states this point. In his conclusion he states that just as in the 1876 Turkish case, the only purpose the Qing constitution could have is to consolidate the power of the monarchy, while interfering with and circumscribing the freedoms of the people.

22 "Shuxuejie yifenzijun lai han hou" (Results of a Letter from an Educated Person), *Xin shiji* 65 (11 September 1908): 2–3.

23 "Tuerqi tiedao de bagong" (The Turkish Railroad Strike), *Xin shiji* 72 (14 November 1908): 5–7.

24 "Xiaonian tuerqi zhi zuzhi" (The Organization of the Young Turks), *Nanfeng bao* 6–7 (July–August 1911).

25 It is nowhere recognized in this essay—or others—that the only thing that held the exiled activists together was a consensus about the need for the sultanate to go. See M. Şükrü Hanioğlu, *The Young Turks in Opposition* (New York: Oxford University Press, 1995).

26 Of these varieties, the most developed are the essays I will discuss here: (1) Min Yi, "Tuerqi geming" (The Turkish Revolution), *Minbao* 25 (1 January 1910): 1–7; and (2) Hu Hanmin, "Jiu Tuerqi geming gao woguo junren" (On What the

Turkish Revolution Can Tell Our Military), *Minbao* 25 (January 1910): 1–25. Hu Hanmin was one of the Revolutionary Alliance's most prolific analysts.

27 Min Yi, "Tuerqi geming": 1.

28 Ibid.: 2.

29 Ibid.: 4.

30 Ibid.: 5.

31 Ibid.: 5–6. This is quite a different account of Greek independence than that provided in *Xila dulishi* (History of Greek Independence) (Shanghai: Guangzhi shuju, 1903), which places the whole movement in a civilizational decline framework.

32 Hu Hanmin, "Jiu Tuerqi geming gao woguo junren": 1–25; cite on 2–3. The Banner armies were the preserve of the Manchu's ruling house, whereas there were, by the early twentieth century, plenty of Han-Chinese-led armies that had grown out of the efforts to suppress the major mid-nineteenth-century peasant rebellions that threatened the dynasty's survival.

33 Hu Hanmin, "Jiu Tuerqi geming gao woguo junren": 5, 6.

34 Ibid.: 6, 7.

35 Ibid.: 10.

36 Ibid.: 14.

37 Ibid.: 16, 24, 25.

38 Marshall Berman, *All That Is Solid Melts into Air* (New York: Simon and Schuster, 1983): 15.

Conclusion

1 Chen Duxiu, "Shuo Guojia" (On the Nation), *Anhui suhua bao* 5 (14 June 1904); rpt. *Chen Duxiu zhuozuo xuan* (Selected Works of Chen Duxiu) (Shanghai: Shanghai renmin chubanshe, 1991): 1:55–57; cite on 56.

2 The term is Hao Chang's, in *Chinese Intellectuals in Crisis* (Berkeley: University of California Press, 1987): intro.

3 *Waiguo* is generally rendered in English as *foreign* and its literal meaning is "outer states." In common usage both in the late Qing and in contemporary times, however, *waiguo* refers more specifically to the Euro-American world, and usually not to all non-Chinese foreigners.

4 As Derek Gregory has pointed out, "Discourse is not an unproblematic reflection of the world, but instead an intervention in the world." *Geographical Imaginations* (London: Blackwell, 1994): 8.

5 A good example here is Prasenjit Duara's *Rescuing History from the Nation: Questioning Narratives of Modern China* (Chicago: University of Chicago Press, 1995). Duara includes a chapter or two on India because it provides a "comparative" perspective on China, even though he argues throughout the book that "na-

tion" is a faulty historical category. Yet his only basis of comparison is "national."

6 For example, L. S. Stavrianos's *Global Rift: The Third World Comes of Age* (New York: William Morrow, 1981) and others in the classical world systems idiom, which explicitly attempt to connect the world together in dialectical fashion. Despite the unquestioned value of these works, their reliance upon strictly economic and socioeconomic histories structure them as narratives of center (West)/periphery (non-West) interaction, where the direction is established by the nature and structure of the questions asked, for it is precisely the multiple destructions of regional trade structures that are tracked in world systems theories, which yield the seeming impossibility of systems that circumvent the structuring economic structures of Euro-American-led global capitalism.

7 David Harvey, *The Condition of Postmodernity: An Enquiry into the Origins of Cultural Change* (London: Blackwell, 1989): 264.

8 Frederick Buell, *National Culture and the New Global System* (Baltimore, Md.: Johns Hopkins University Press, 1994): 338.

9 G. W. F. Hegel, *Elements of the Philosophy of Right*, ed. Allen Wood, trans. H. B. Nisbet (Cambridge: Cambridge University Press, 1991), sec. 278: 315–16.

Appendix

1 The opera has a number of short scenes; preceding each scene is a list of characters on stage and a description of props, if any, which give a clue to where the action takes place (Beijing Opera does not use elaborate sets). I have placed these indications, along with stage directions, in parentheses.

2 Following Confucius's saying, *sanshi erli* (at thirty, I stood on my feet), the thirtieth birthday is particularly important: many prominent literati and others wrote their autobiographies upon reaching thirty to evaluate their achievements and to establish future goals.

3 There are four major role types in Beijing opera: *sheng, jing, chou, dan. Dan* is a female character—military or otherwise—of which there are none in this opera. The other three are also divided into civilian (*wen*) and military (*wu*) classifications. *Sheng*, a principal male character, is subdivided into *laosheng, xiaosheng*, and *wusheng. Laosheng* is normally an older man, a court official or general, and sings with a rich baritone voice (Wang was a *laosheng* actor); *xiaosheng* is generally a younger man, a scholar or a lover, with a higher-pitched voice; *wusheng*, a military type, must be highly skilled in acrobatics. *Jing*, also called "painted face" (*hualian*) for the heavy makeup that is part of his costume, is a male role that is either evil or good, often a warrior, bandit, crafty minister, upright judge, or loyal statesman. *Chou*, a clown, is often a stupid or ribald

character. Colin Mackerras, *The Chinese Theatre in Modern Times: From 1840 to the Present* (Amherst: University of Massachusetts, 1975): 23–25. We are introduced to four *sheng*, two *jing*, and two *chou*, all ministers of the Polish court. The Polish emperor is a *xiaosheng*, indicating his youth.

4 There are three modes of line delivery in Beijing opera: *chang* (singing); *bai* (declaiming); and *shi* (versifying). I have indicated the mode of delivery if it is not *bai*, the most frequently used mode.

5 Dynastic symbols of longevity and historical vitality.

6 The king of Poland was elected by the nobility beginning in 1572, at the end of the Jagiellon dynasty (1386–1572), generally seen as having presided over Poland's golden years.

7 Augustus (Sigismund II, r. 1548–1572) was the last king of the Jagiellon dynasty, itself the last native Polish dynasty.

8 When a foreign emissary arrived at the Qing court, his banner or flag was raised at his temporary residence. *Xiaqi*, or "taking the flag down," thus indicates a departure.

9 The first two characters used for this minister's name (*kesi*) indicate he is meant to represent a thoughtful person. Given the depiction, however, the name is sarcastic. It could also be a reference to Thaddeus Kosciuszko, leader of a national uprising in 1794 after the second partition of Poland.

10 From the characters in his name, he is identified as a "Polish slave" (*bonu*): a person with few independent thoughts and little likelihood of acting boldly.

11 A martial type, as indicated by the characters in his name (*wu*).

12 One with an "inferiority complex" (*suo*), as indicated by the characters in his name.

13 The controversy over war and appeasement is a reference to debates within the Qing court over the prosecution of the Sino-Japanese War in 1894–95 and, in the context of 1904, of debates in the Qing court and general society over whether China should fight Russian expansion in Manchuria/Korea.

14 It is no coincidence that the person charged with saving Poland is "Liske." Each of the accounts of Poland circulating in China at the time tells a version of the legend of Poland's origins, which involves three brothers—Luke (Rus), Chake (Czeck), and Liske (Lek)—who one day find themselves on the banks of a river: "Suddenly a mythic bird called to Liske to go the place of Poland and to stop there. Liske began reclaiming the land in the location of Poland. This is the beginning of the history of the country of Poland." Cited from "Bolanguo de gushi" (The Story of the Country of Poland), *Hangzhou baihua bao* 1–3 (1901): 1b–2a.

15 Reference to historical Ottoman and Islamic incursions in Europe.

16 The Chinese had deemed the Japanese an "uncivilized tribe" prior to the Japanese victory in the Sino-Japanese War of 1894–5; Russians also referred to the

Japanese as inferiors, a characterization they revised after the Japanese victory in the Russo-Japanese War of 1905.

17 Refers to a river eddy, a dramatic change in the current that obstructs passage. It could also be a play on the word "*hui*," "return" or "turn back," or on the word for Islam (as in *huijiao*).

18 Refers to a large obstacle in the middle of a river that blocks passage up or downstream. It also refers to the word "lan" (as in *Bolan*, or Poland).

19 This name is significant. The surname, Wang, uses the most common "king" character; however, the given name, "guonu," means "slave." The full name is hence a homonym for "*wangguo nu*" ("slave of a lost [perished] country"). See chapter 2 for discussion.

20 Poland, when it was a unified state, was landlocked. The natural-barrier thesis, seasickness, and naval incompetence are thinly veiled references to the repeated defeats of the Chinese navy in battle. During the Opium War–era defense of Guangzhou, Lin Zexu unsuccessfully relied on natural barriers preventing entrance to the Bogue; in the Sino-French War of 1885, the navy was defeated before even setting sail; and in the Sino-Japanese War of 1894–95, the Chinese navy was again destroyed before it left port. The unseaworthiness of the Chinese naval men in all these battles was well known.

21 Refers to the common practice in the late Qing for army commanders to claim a large number of soldiers under their command, when the actual number was sometimes less than a third of that claimed. Here, merely halving the number claimed is deemed relatively honest.

22 A play on words: foreign guns (*yangqiang*) vs. smoking pipes (*yanqiang*); reference to the opium/foreign invasion linkage that was established in the 1839–1842 Opium War.

23 Refers to the method of showing promotion up the bureaucratic ranks in dynastic China.

24 A principle of Sunzi's *Art of War*: if troops have no room for escape, they will fight for their lives out of desperation and will thus win the battle. Wang seems to be parodying the habit of citing textual authority for proposed actions.

25 The two ministers sent as negotiators are those identified as the "slave" and the one with an "inferiority complex"; the assignment thus bodes ill from the outset.

26 For a total indemnity of 200 million taels, precisely the amount required of China by Japan in the Treaty of Shimoneseki (1895) signed to conclude the Sino-Japanese War.

27 Reference to the ceding of Taiwan to Japan in the Treaty of Shimoneseki.

28 This may be a misprint; it should probably read "3,000" not "30,000." See next note.

29 The 3,000 here seems more likely than the 30,000 cited above; 3000 corre-

sponds to the number of troops per country allowed to be stationed on Chinese territory as stipulated in the Boxer Protocol of 1901.

30 Referring to the most-favored nation clause of the Treaty of Shimoneseki, which opened the doors to the scramble among the foreign powers in China for spheres of influence and territorial concessions.

31 Reference to the Han acceptance of Manchus as rulers of China.

32 The three factions commonly identified in the Chinese court after the summer 1898 coup.

33 The Darwinian phrase that had gained broad usage by the early 1900s in China: "*yousheng, liebai*," "the fit win, the unfit lose."

34 Reference to the endemic usage of opium in the late Qing military.

BIBLIOGRAPHY

A Ying. *Wanqing wenxue congchao: xiaoshuo xiqu yanjiu juan* (Compendium of Late Qing Literature, Volume on the study of Novels and Dramas). 2 vols. Beijing: Zhonghua shuju, 1960.

Agoncillo, Teodoro. *The Revolt of the Masses: The Story of Bonifacio and the Katipunan.* Philippines: University of the Philippines, 1956.

Ahmad, Aijaz. *In Theory: Classes, Nations, Literatures.* London: Verso, 1992.

———. "Jameson's Rhetoric of Otherness and 'National Allegory." *Social Text*, no. 16 (winter 1987): 3–25.

"Ai Jiangnan" (Alas, Jiangnan). *Jiangsu* 1 (27 April 1903).

Ai Mengluzhe. "Menglu zhuyi" (The Monroe Doctrine). *Zhejiang chao* 2–3 (April–May 1903).

Ai Zhouchang, ed. *Zhongfei guanxishi wenxuan (1500–1918)* (Selected Writings from the History of Sino-African Relations [1500–1918]). Shanghai: Huadong shifan daxue chubanshe, 1989.

———. "Jindai shiqi de zhongguo yu feizhou" (China and Africa in the Modern Era). *Xiya feizhou* 1 (1984).

"Aiji bainian xingshuai ji" (Egypt's Rise and Fall in the Past Century). *Jingji congbian* 1 (24 March 1903).

Aiji bianzheng kao (Investigation into Egyptian Reforms). Trans. Yin Pao Lo (Ren Baoluo). Shanghai: Christian Literature Society, 1907.

"Aiji bianzheng kao" (Investigation into Egyptian Reforms). *Zhengyi tongbao* 2 (11 March 1902).

"Aiji wangguo canzhuang ji" (A Record of the Tragic Perishing of Egypt). *Youxue yibian* 8 (10 June 1903).

Allen, Young J. "Indu li yingguo shi'er yi shuo" (Twelve Advantages of Britain in India). *Wanguo gongbao* 94 (October–November 1896).

Anderson, Benedict. *Imagined Communities: Reflections on the Origin and Spread of Nationalism.* 2d ed. London: Verso, 1991.

Anderson, Mark. "The Foreign Relations of the Family State: The Empire of Ethics, Aesthetics, and Evolution in Meiji Japan." Ph.D. diss., Cornell University, 2000.

Anhui baihua bao (Anhui Colloquial Journal).

Arkush, R. David, and Leo O. Lee, eds. *Land without Ghosts: Chinese Impressions of America from the Mid-Nineteenth Century to the Present*. Berkeley: University of California Press, 1989.

Armstrong, William N. *Around the World with a King: The Story of the Circumnavigation of His Majesty King David Kalakaua*. 1904. Rutland, Vt.: Tuttle Publishers, 1977.

Bailes, Howard. "Military Aspects of the War." In Peter Warwick, ed., *The South African War: The Anglo-Boer War 1899–1902*. Essex, England: Longman, 1980.

Balibar, Etienne. "The Nation Form: History and Ideology." In Balibar and Immanuel Wallerstein, eds. *Race, Nation, Class*. London: Verso, 1991.

Balibar, Etienne, and Immanuel Wallerstein, eds. *Race, Nation, Class*. London: Verso, 1991.

Barnett, Suzanne Wilson. "Wei Yuan and Westerners: Notes on the Sources of the *Hai-kuo T'u-chih*." *Ch'ing-shih wen't'i* 2.4 (November 1970): 1–20.

Beijing nübao (Beijing Women's Daily).

Beijing zazhi (Beijing Journal).

Benjamin, Walter. "Theses on the Philosophy of History." *Illuminations*. New York: Schocken Books, 1978.

Berman, Marshall. *All That Is Solid Melts into Air*. New York: Simon and Schuster, 1983.

Bernal, Martin. "Liu Shih-p'ei and National Essence." In Charlotte Furth, ed., *The Limits of Change*. Cambridge: Harvard University Press, 1976.

Bhabha, Homi K. "Difference, Discrimination, and the Discourse of Colonialism." In Francis Barker, ed., *The Politics of Theory*. Essex, England: University of Essex, 1983.

———. "Of Mimicry and Man: The Ambivalence of Colonial Discourse." *October* 28 (1984): 125–33.

———. "The Other Question." *Screen* 24.6 (1983): 18–35.

———. "Signs Taken for Wonders." *Critical Inquiry* 12.1 (1985): 144–65.

"Bolanguo zhi gushi" (The Story of the Country of Poland). *Hangzhou baihua bao* 1–3, 1901.

Bonacich, Edna, and Lucie Cheng, eds. *Labor Immigration under Capitalism: Asian Immigrant Workers in the United States before World War II*. Berkeley: University of California Press, 1984.

Boorman, Howard, *Biographical Dictionary of Republican China*. Vol. 3. New York: Columbia University Press, 1970.

Bose, A. C. *Indian Revolutionaries Abroad, 1905–1922: In the Background of International Developments*. Patna: Bharati Bhawan, 1971.

Bourdieu, Pierre. *Outline of a Theory of Practice*. Cambridge: Cambridge University Press, 1977.

Brantlinger, Patrick. "Victorians and Africans: The Genealogy of the Myth of the

Dark Continent." In Henry Louis Gates, ed., *"Race," Writing, and Difference*. Chicago: University of Chicago Press, 1985.

Brewer, Anthony. *Marxist Theories of Imperialism: A Critical Survey*. 2d ed. New York: Routledge, 1990.

Britton, R. S. *The Chinese Periodical Press, 1800–1912*. Taipei: Cheng-wen, 1966.

Buell, Frederick. *National Culture and the New Global System*. Baltimore: Johns Hopkins University Press, 1994.

Camagay, Maria Liuset. "Liangge minzhuzhuyizhe jian de youyi: Sun Zhongshan yu Maliannuo Ponsi" (The Friendship between Two Nationalists: Sun Zhongshan and Mariano Ponce). Trans. Qu Ayin. In Wang Ning, ed., *Sun Zhongshan he tade shidai* (*Sun Zhongshan and His Times*). Beijing: Zhonghua shuju, 1987.

Caplan, Caren, "The Politics of Location as Transnational Feminist Critical Practice." In Inderpal Grewal and Caren Kaplan, eds., *Scattered Hegemonies: Postmodernity and Transnational Feminist Practices*. Minneapolis: University of Minnesota Press, 1994.

Certeau, Michel de. *The Practice of Everyday Life*. Berkeley: University of California Press, 1986.

Chang, Hao. *Chinese Intellectuals in Crisis: Search for Order and Meaning*. Berkeley: University of California Press, 1987.

———. *Liang Ch'i-chao and Intellectual Transition in China, 1890–1907*. Cambridge: Harvard University Press, 1971.

Chang P'eng-yüan. *Liang Ch'i-ch'ao yü Ch'ing-chi ke-ming* (Liang Ch'i-ch'ao and the Late Ch'ing Revolution). Taipei: Institute of Modern Chinese History, Academica Sinica, 1982.

Chang Yü-fa. *Qingji de lixian tuanti* (Constitutionalists of the Ch'ing Period). Taipei: Modern History Institute, Academia Sinica, 1971.

Changyan bao (The Verax).

Chatterjee, Partha. *The Nation and Its Fragments: Colonial and Postcolonial Histories*. Princeton: Princeton University Press, 1993.

———. *Nationalist Thought and the Colonial World: A Derivative Discourse?* Minneapolis: University of Minnesota Press, 1993.

———. "Whose Imagined Community." In Gopal Balakrishnan, ed. *Mapping the Nation*. London: Verso, 1996.

Chen Duxiu. *Chen Duxiu zhuozuo xuan* (Selected Works of Chen Duxiu). Shanghai: Shanghai renmin chubanshe, 1991.

———. "Lun Xiqu" (On Drama). In *Chen Duxiu zhuozuo xuan* (Selected Works of Chen Duxiu), 1:86–90. Shanghai: Shanghai renmin chubanshe, 1991.

———. "Shuo Guojia" (On the Nation). In *Chen Duxiu zhuozuo xuan* (Selected Works of Chen Duxiu), 1:55–57. Shanghai: Shanghai renmin chubanshe, 1991.

Chen Huai. "Du Aiji Jinshi Shi Bawei" (Epilogue upon Reading *The Modern History of Egypt*). *Xinshijie xuebao* 12 (13 March 1903).

Chen Jian'an. "Ershi shiji chunian de xin wenhua yundong" (The New Culture Movement at the Beginning of the Twentieth Century). In Hu Weixi, ed., *Xinhai geming yu zhongguo sixiang wenhua* (The Xinhai Revolution and China's Intellectual Culture). Shanghai: Huadong shida chubanshe, 1991.

Chen Jieshi (Fuchen). *Dushi* (Independent History). *Xinshijie Xuebao* 2 (1902).

Chen Qubing. "*Guazhong lanyin* xinju bianyan" (Preface to the New Opera *Guazhong lanyin*). *Jingzhong Ribao* (1 October 1904).

———. "Lun xiju zhi youyi" (On the advantages of Drama). *Jingzhong Ribao* (21 August 1904).

Chen Tianhua. *Jingshi zhong* (A Bell to Warn the World). 1904. In Chai Degeng, ed., *Xinhai geming* (The Xinhai Revolution). 8 vols. Shanghai, 1957.

Chen Zhixiang. *Nan A xinjianguo shi xu* (Preface to *History of a Newly Established Country in South Africa*). Shanghai: Wenming shuju, 1902.

Chilcote, Ronald. *Theories of Development and Underdevelopment*. Boulder, Colo.: Westview, 1984.

Chow, Rey. *Woman and Chinese Modernity: The Politics of Reading between West and East*. Minneapolis: University of Minnesota Press, 1991.

Chu, Samuel, and Kwang-Ch'ing Liu, eds. *Li Hung-Chang and China's Early Modernization*. New York: M. E. Sharpe, 1994.

Churchill, Bernadita R. "Sun Zhongshan shidai de feilubin minzu zhuyi" (Philippine Nationalism in Sun Zhongshan's Era). Trans. Wang Ning. In Wang Ning, ed., *Sun Zhongshan he tade shidai* (Sun Zhongshan and His Times). Beijing: Zhonghua shuju, 1987.

Cohen, Paul. *Discovering History in China: American Historical Writing on the Recent Chinese Past*. New York: Columbia University Press, 1984.

———. *History in Three Keys: The Boxers as Event, Experience, and Myth*. New York: Columbia University Press, 1997.

Cooper, Fredrick. "Conflict and Connection: Rethinking Colonial African History." *American Historical Review* 99 (1994). 1516–45.

Corpus, Enrique J. "Japan and the Philippine Revolution." *Philippines Social Science Review* 6.4 (October 1934): 249–98.

Cuba Commission Report: A Hidden History of the Chinese in Cuba. 1877. Baltimore: Johns Hopkins University Press, 1993.

Curtin, Philip. *The Image of Africa: British Ideas and Action, 1780–1850*. Madison: University of Wisconsin Press, 1964.

Da Jindao. "Shuo Guojia" (On the Nation). *Xinbaihua bao* 1–2 (spring 1904).

Da Yunwan. "Wang Xiaonong de mingming" (Wang Xiaonong's Fate and Reputation). *Jiangsu xiju* 12 (1980): 38.

Dalu (The Continent).

Davenport, T. R. H. *South Africa: A Modern History*. 4th ed. Toronto: University of Toronto Press, 1991.

De Bary, Brett. "Karatani Kojin's Origins." In Masao Miyoshi and H. D. Harootunian, eds., *Postmodernism and Japan*. Durham, N.C.: Duke University Press, 1989.

Deleuze, Gilles, and Félix Guattari. *A Thousand Plateaus: Capitalism and Schizophrenia*. Trans. Brian Massumi. Minneapolis: University of Minnesota Press, 1986.

Derrida, Jacques. *Limited, Inc*. Evanston, Ill.: Northwestern University Press, 1988.

Dianhua bao (Yunannese Journal).

"Diansheng gailiang xiqu jishi" (A Record of Opera and Drama Reform in Yunnan Province). *Dianhua bao* 2 (May 1908).

Dictionary of National Biography. Calcutta, 1971–74.

Dikötter, Frank. *The Discourse of Race in Modern China*. Stanford: Stanford University Press, 1992.

Ding Muqin. "Qinquan tongbao saochu mixin" (A Warning to Our Compatriots to Sweep Away Superstitions). *Beijing nübao* 1091 (10 September 1908).

Ding Wenjiang. *Liang Rengong xiansheng nianpu changpian chugao* (Chronological Biography of Liang Rengong [Qichao], First Draft). Taibei: Shijie shuju, 1958.

Ding Zeliang. "Zhang Binglin yu Yindu minzu jiefang douzheng" (Zhang Binglin and the Indian People's Liberation Struggle). *Lishi yanjiu* 1 (1957): 26–40.

Dirks, Nicholas B. ed. *Colonialism and Culture*. Ann Arbor: University of Michigan Press, 1992.

Dirlik, Arif. *After the Revolution: Waking to Global Capitalism*. Middletown, Conn.: Wesleyan University Press, 1994.

———. *Anarchism in the Chinese Revolution*. Berkeley: University of California Press, 1991.

———. "Chinese History and the Question of Orientalism." *History and Theory: Studies in the Philosophy of History*, Theme Issue 35: Chinese Historiography in Comparative Perspective (1996).

———. "Critical Reflections on 'Chinese Capitalism' as Paradigm." *Identities* 3.3 (1997): 303–30.

———. *Origins of Chinese Communism*. NY: Oxford University Press, 1989.

———. "Reversals, Ironies, Hegemonies: Notes on the Contemporary Historiography of Modern China." *Modern China* 22.3 (July 1996): 243–84.

———. "Socialism and Capitalism in Chinese Socialist Thinking: The Origins." *Studies in Comparative Communism* 21.2 (summer 1987): 131–52.

Ditmer, Lowell, and Samuel S. Kim, eds. *China's Quest for National Identity*. Ithaca: Cornell University Press, 1993.

Dolby, William. *A History of Chinese Drama*. New York: Harper and Row, 1976.

Dongfang zazhi (Eastern Miscellany).

"Dongya shinian waijiao shi" (A History of East Asian Foreign Affairs of the Last Decade). *Jiangsu* 9–10 (17 March 1904).

Drake, Fred. *China Charts the World: Hsu Chi-yu and His Geography of 1848*. Cambridge: Harvard University Press, 1975.

Drège, J. P. *La Commercial Press de Shanghai, 1897–1949*. Paris: Collège de France, Institute des Hautes Études Chinoises, 1978.

Drinnon, Richard. *Facing West*. New York: Schocken Books, 1990.

Du Shizhen. "Duguo datongling Gulujia liezhuan" (Brief Biography of the Transvaal President, Kruger). *Xinshijie xuebao* 6–8 (14 November–14 December 1902).

Duan Ruli. *Wangguo jian* (Mirror on *wangguo*). Shanghai: Taidong tushuju, 1917.

Duan Yuanzhang. "Sun Zhongshan he tongshiqi yazhou qita minzhu geming xianfeng de bijiao" (A Comparison of Sun Zhongshan and Asian Democratic Revolutionary Pioneers of the Same Era). *Jindaishi yanjiu* 42.6 (November 1987): 70–84.

Duara, Prasenjit. "De-constructing the Chinese Nation." *Australian Journal of Chinese Affairs* 30 (July 1993): 1–26.

———. "Nationalists among Transnationals: Overseas Chinese and the Idea of China, 1900–1911." In Aihwa Ong and Donald Nonini, eds., *Underground Empires*. New York: Routledge, 1997.

———. *Rescuing History from the Nation: Questioning Narratives of Modern China*. Chicago: University of Chicago Press, 1996.

———, "Transnationalism and the Predicament of Sovereignty: China, 1900–1945." *American Historical Review* 102.4 (October 1997): 1030–51.

"Duguo zhi bingzhi zhanshu" (Battle Strategy and Military System in the Transvaal). *Qingyi bao* 32 (13 December 1899).

Dussel, Enrique. *The Invention of the Americas: Eclipse of "the Other" and the Myth of Modernity*. New York: Continuum, 1995.

Duyvendak, J. J. L. *China's Discovery of Africa: Lectures Given at the University of London on January 22 and 23, 1947*. London: Arthur Probsthain, 1949.

Eber, Irene. "Poland and Polish Authors in Modern Chinese Literature and Translation." *Monumenta Serica* 31 (1974): 403–45.

Elman, Benjamin. *Classicism, Politics, and Kinship: The Ch'ang-chou School of New Text Confucianism in Late Imperial China*. Berkeley: University of California Press, 1990.

"Ershi shiji zhi taipingyang," *Zhejiang Chao* 2 (18 March 1903).

"Ershi shiji zhi zhongguo" (Twentieth-Century China). *Guomin bao* 1 (10 May 1901). Rpt. in Zhang Dan and Wang Renzhi, eds., *Xinhai geming qianshinian jian shilun xuanji* (Selected Editorials from the Decade Preceding the Xinhai Revolution), vol. 1. Hong Kong: Sanlian shudian, 1962.

Esherick, Joseph. *The Origins of the Boxer Uprising*. Berkeley: University of California Press, 1987.

Fabian, Johannes. *Time and the Other: How Anthropology Makes Its Object*. New York: Columbia University Press, 1983.

Fang Hanji. *Zhongguo jindai baokan shi* (History of Modern Chinese Periodicals). 2 vols. Taiyüan: Shanxi renmin chubanshe, 1981.

———. "Zaoqi de xinwen dianxun" (Early News Wire Services). In Fang Hanji, ed., *Baoshi yu baoren* (Journal History and Journalists). Beijing: Xinhua chubanshe, 1991.

Fanon, Franz. *The Wretched of the Earth*. New York: Grove Press, 1965.

"Feizhou duliguo you chuxian yi" (Another Independent Country Emerges in Africa). *Jingzhong ribao* (4 November 1904).

Feng Ziyou. "Gemingdang yu feilubin zhishi zhi guanxi" (The Relationship between the Revolutionary Party and Filipino Activists). In *Zhonghua minguo kaiguoqian gemingshi* (History of the Revolution before the Founding of the Republic of China), vol. 2. Shanghai: Shangwu Press, 1944.

———. "Zhongguo ribao yu Feilubin Qing lingshi shesong ji" (The China Daily Reports on the dealings between the Filipinos and the Qing consul). In *Geming yishi* (Reminiscences of the Revolution), 2d ed. Vol. 1. Taipei: Shangwu Press, 1952.

"Fengehou zhi wumin" (My People after Partition). *Jiangsu* 8–10 (January–March 1904).

Fitzgerald, John. *Awakening China: Politics, Culture, and Class in the Nationalist Revolution*. Stanford: Stanford University Press, 1996.

Fox, Richard G. *National Ideologies and the Production of National Cultures*. Washington, D.C.: American Anthropological Association, 1990.

Friedman, Edward. "Reconstructing China's National Identity: A Southern Alternative to Mao-Era Anti-Imperialist Nationalism." *Journal of Asian Studies* 53.1 (February 1994).

Fukumoto Nichinan. "Lun yingren shidazui" (On the Ten Great Sins of the English). *Yadong shibao* 21 (28 April 1900).

———. "Nan A gailun" (Situation in South Africa). *Qingyi bao* 35 (10 February 1900).

———. *Telansifa'er* (The Transvaal). Trans. Hangzhou hezong yishu ju. Hangzhou: Hangzhou hezong yishu ju, 1902.

———. *Nan A xinjianguo shi* (History of a Newly Established Country in South Africa). Trans. Chen Zhixiang. Shanghai: Wenming shuju, 1902.

Furth, Charlotte, ed. *The Limits of Change*. Cambridge: Harvard University Press, 1976.

Gan Yang. "A Critique of Chinese Conservatism in the 1990s." *Social Text*, no. 55 (summer 1998): 45–66.

Gates, Henry Louis Jr. "Writing 'Race' and the Difference It Makes." In Gates, ed., *"Race," Writing, and Difference*. Chicago: University of Chicago Press, 1985.

Ge Maochun et al., eds. *Wuzhengfu zhuyi sixiang zhiliao xuan* (Selection of Materials on Anarchist Thought). 2 vols. Beijing: Beijing daxue chubanshe, 1984.

Gellner, Ernest. *Nations and Nationalism*. Ithaca: Cornell University Press, 1983.

———. *Thought and Change.* London: Weidenfeld and Nicholson, 1964.

Geng Yunzhi. "Lun Qingmo de fanman geming sichao" (On Late-Qing Anti-Manchu Revolutionism). In Zhongnan diqu xinhai gemingshi yanjiuhui, eds., *Xinhai fengyun yu jindai zhongguo* (Modern China and the Xinhai Revolution). Guizhou: Renmin chubanshe, 1991.

Glick, C. E. *Sojourners and Settlers: Chinese Migrants in Hawaii.* Honolulu: University of Hawaii Press, 1980.

Gluck, Carol. *Japan's Modern Myths: Ideology in the Late Meiji Period.* Princeton: Princeton University Press, 1980.

Gonghe Fuhansheng. "Lun Minzu zhuyi" (On Ethno-nationalism). *Jingzhong ribao* (8–10 December 1904).

Greenberg, Michael. *British Trade and the Opening of China 1800–42.* New York: Monthly Review Press, 1951.

Greer, Richard A. "The Royal Tourist Kalakaua's Letters Home from Tokyo to London." *Hawaiian Journal of History* 5 (1971): 75–109.

Gregory, Derek. *Geographical Imaginations.* Cambridge, Mass.: Blackwell, 1994.

Grewal, Inderpal, and Caren Kaplan, eds. *Scattered Hegemonies.* Minneapolis: University of Minnesota Press, 1994.

Gu Yuanguang. *Yishu jingyanlu* (Translated Books I Have Read). Shanghai: n.p., n.d.

Guangdongsheng Sun Zhongshan yanjiuhui, ed. *"Sun Zhongshan yu yazhou" guoji xueshu taolunhui lunwen ji* (Collection of Essays from the "International Conference on Sun Zhongshan and Asia"). Guangzhou: Zhongshan daxue chubanshe, 1994.

"Guazhong lanyin." *Dalu* 2.5 (3 July 1904).

Guofeng bao (Journal of National Trends).

Halliday, Jon. *A Political History of Japanese Capitalism.* New York: Pantheon, 1975.

Han Lih-wu. "Introduction." In Marianno Ponce, *Sun Yat-sen: Founder of the Republic of China*, trans. Nick Joaquin. Manila: Filipino-Chinese Cultural Foundation, 1965.

Han Qichun and Li Yifu. "Hanwei 'minzu' yizi de chuxian ji qi shiyong qingkuang" (The Appearance in Chinese of the Term *Minzu* and Its Usages). *Minzu Yanjiu* 2 (1984): 36–43.

Hangzhou baihua bao (Hangzhou Vernacular Journal).

Hansheng. "Feilubin wangguo canzhuang jilue" (Brief Outline of the Tragic Loss of the Philippines). *Hubei xuesheng jie* 5, 7 (27 May, 21 September 1903).

Harootunian, H. D. "The Benjamin Effect: Modernism, Repetition, and the Path to Different Cultural Imaginaries." In Michael P. Steinberg, ed., *Walter Benjamin and the Demands of History.* Ithaca: Cornell University Press, 1996.

———. "The Function of China in Tokugawa Thought." In Akira Iriye, ed., *The Chinese and Japanese: Essays in Political and Cultural Interactions.* Princeton: Princeton University Press, 1980.

———. *Things Seen and Unseen: Discourse and Ideology in Tokugawa Nativism*. Chicago: University of Chicago Press, 1988.

Harvey, David. *The Condition of Postmodernity*. New York: Blackwell, 1989.

Hawaii's Queen Liliuokalani. *Hawaii's Story*. Boston: Lothrop, Lee, and Shepard, 1895.

Hegel, G. W. F. *Elements of the Philosophy of Right*. Ed. Allen Wood, trans. H. B. Nisbet. Cambridge: Cambridge University Press, 1991.

Hevia, James L. *Cherishing Men from Afar: Qing Guest Ritual and the Macartney Embassy of 1793*. Durham, N.C.: Duke University Press, 1995.

Hichiro Hiraoka. *Eito-sense ni ekeru gunji-jo no kansatsu* (Military Studies in the Anglo-Boer War). In Ministry of Defense, *Boa-senjutsu no kenkyū* (Study of War Tactics during the Boer War). N.p., 1902–3.

Hill, Christopher. "History and Circulation: Narratives of the Nation-State in Late Nineteenth Century Japan." Ph.D. diss., Columbia University, 1999.

Hobson, J. A. *Imperialism: A Study*. Ann Arbor: University of Michigan Press, 1965.

Hong Fei [Zhang Zhongduan]. "Tuerji lixian shuo" (On the Turkish Constitution). *Henan* 7 (5 August 1908).

Hou Yijie. *Ershi shijichu zhongguo zhengzhi gaige fengchao* (Trends in Early-Twentieth-Century Chinese Political Reform). Beijing: Renmin chubanshe, 1993.

Howland, D. R. *Borders of Chinese Civilization: Geography and History at Empire's End*. Durham, N.C.: Duke University Press, 1996.

Hsia, C. T. *The Classic Chinese Novel: An Introduction*. New York: Columbia University Press, 1968.

Hsiao Kung-ch'uan. *A Modern China and a New World: K'ang You-Wei, Reformer and Utopian*. Seattle: University of Washington Press, 1975.

Hubei xuesheng jie (Hubei Students World).

Hu Fengyang and Zhang Wenjian. *Zhongguo jindai shixue sichao yu liupai* (Trends and Schools in Modern Chinese Historiography). Shanghai: Huadong shida chubanshe, 1991.

Hu Hanmin. "Jiu Tuerqi geming gao woguo junren" (On What the Turkish Revolution Can Tell Our Military). *Minbao* 25 (1 January 1910).

Huang, Philip. *Liang Ch'i-ch'ao and Modern Chinese Liberalism*. Seattle: University of Washington Press, 1972.

Huang Guo'an, Su Deji, and Yang Libing, eds. *Jindai zhongyue guanxishi zhiliao xuanbian* (Selected Documents on the History of Modern Chinese and Vietnamese Relations). Nanning: Guangxi renmin chubanshe, 1990.

"Huanghuo bian" (Distinguishing the Yellow Peril). *Jingzhong ribao* (14–19 March 1904).

Huber, Thomas H. "Men of High Purpose and the Politics of Direct Action, 1862–1864." In Tetsuo Najita and Victor Koschmann, eds., *Conflict in Modern Japanese History: The Neglected Tradition*. Princeton: Princeton University Press, 1982.

Hunt, Michael. *The Making of a Special Relationship: The United States and China to 1914.* New York: Columbia University Press, 1983.

Hwang Dongyoun. "Some Reflections on Wang Jingwei's Collaboration." Working Papers in Asian-Pacific Studies, Duke University Asia-Pacific Studies Institute, 1998.

Iida Yumiko. "Fleeing the West, Making Asia Home: Transpositions of Otherness in Japanese Pan-Asianism, 1905–1930." *Alternatives* 22 (1997): 409–32.

Indu miewang shi (The History of the Destruction and Loss of India). Ed. and trans. Xia Qingfu. Shanghai: Kaiming shudian, 1902.

Indu shi (History of India). Trans. Wang Benxiang. Shanghai: Chiwen she, 1903.

Ip, Manying. *The Life and Times of Zhang Yuanji, 1867–1959.* Beijing: Shangwu Press, 1985.

Jameson, Fredric. "Cognitive Mapping." In Cary Nelson and Laurence Grossberg, eds., *Marxism and the Interpretation of Culture.* Urbana: University of Illinois Press, 1988.

———. "Foreword." In Liu Kang and Xiaobing Tang, eds., *Politics, Ideology, and Literary Discourse in Modern China.* Durham, N.C.: Duke University Press, 1993.

———. *The Political Unconscious: Narrative as a Socially Symbolic Act.* Ithaca: Cornell University Press, 1981.

———. "Third World Literature in the Era of Multinational Capitalism." *Social Text,* no. 15 (fall 1986): 65–88.

Jansen, Marius B. *The Japanese and Sun Yatsen.* Stanford: Stanford University Press, 1954.

"Ji yindu xipoqi wang jinianhui shi" (A Report on the Commemorative Meeting for the Indian King Shivaji). *Minbao* 13 (5 May 1907).

"Ji yingte zhanzheng jinshi" (Record of Recent Developments in the Anglo-Transvaal War). *Yadong shibao* 19 (28 February 1900).

Jian Bocan et al., comp. *Zhongguo jindai shi zhiliao congkan* (Anthology of Materials on Modern Chinese History). Shanghai: n.p., 1953.

Jiangsu (Jiangsu Journal).

Johnson, David, and Evelyn Rawski, eds. *Popular Culture in Late Imperial China.* Berkeley: University of California Press, 1985.

"Junguomin sixiang puji lun" (On the Popularization of Military Citizens Thinking). *Hubei xuesheng jie* 3 (1903).

Kaizhi lu (Journal of New Learning).

Kalaw, Teodoro. *The Philippine Revolution.* Manila: Jorge B. Vargas Filipiniana Foundation, Reprint Series 1, 1969.

Kandyba-Foxcroft, Elisaveta. *Russia and the Anglo-Boer War, 1899–1902.* Pretoria: CUM Books, 1981.

Karl, Rebecca. "Creating Asia: China in the World at the Beginning of the Twentieth Century." *American Historical Review* 103.4 (October 1998): 1096–1118.

———. "Race, Ethnos, History in China at the Turn of the Twentieth Century." In Peter Osborne and Stella Sandford, eds., *Philosophies of Race and Ethnicity*. London: Athlone Press, 2002.

———. "Secret Sharers: Chinese Nationalism and the Non-Western World at the Turn of the Twentieth Century." Ph.D. diss., Duke University, 1995.

———. " 'Slavery,' Gender, and Citizenship in China's Turn of the Century Global Context." In Rebecca Karl and Peter Zarrow, eds., *Rethinking the 1898 Reforms: Cultural and Political Change in Modern China*. Cambridge: Harvard University Council on East Asian Publications, 2002.

———. "Staging the World in Late-Qing China: Globe, Nation, and Race in a 1904 Beijing Opera." *Identities* 6.4 (winter 2000): 551–606.

Kawamoto Kuniye. "The Viet-nam Quang Phuc Hoi and the 1911 Revolution." Trans. Okui Yaeko. In Eto Shinkichi and Harold Z. Schiffrin, eds., *The 1911 Revolution in China: Interpretive Essays*. Tokyo: University of Tokyo Press, 1984.

Kim Key-Hiuk. "The Aims of Li Hung-chang's Policies towards Japan and Korea, 1870–1882." In Samuel Chu and Kwang-Ch'ing Liu, eds., *Li Hung-Chang and China's Early Modernization*. New York: M. E. Sharpe, 1994.

Kitamura Saburo. *Aiji shi* (History of Egypt). Trans. Zhao Bizhen. Shanghai: Guangzhi shuju, 1903.

Koschmann, Victor. "Asianism's Ambivalent Legacy." In P. Katzenstein and Takashi Shiraishi, eds., *Network Power: Japan and Asia*. Ithaca: Cornell University Press, 1997.

Koss, Stephen. *The Pro-Boers*. Chicago: University of Chicago Press, 1973.

Kuhn, Thomas. *The Structure of Scientific Revolutions*. Chicago: University of Chicago Press, 1970.

Laine, James W. "Shivaji as Epic Hero." In Gunther D. Sontheimer, ed., *Maharashtra: Culture and Society, Folk Culture, Folk Religion, and Oral Tradition*. New Delhi: Oxford, 1995.

Laroui, Abdallah. *The Crisis of the Arab Intellectual: Traditionalism or Historicism?* Berkeley: University of California Press, 1976.

Larson, Wendy. *Literary Authority and the Modern Chinese Writer: Ambivalence and Autobiography*. Durham, N.C.: Duke University Press, 1991.

Lazarus, Neil. *Nationalism and Cultural Practice in the Postcolonial World*. Cambridge: Cambridge University Press, 1999.

Lee, Gregory B. *Troubadours, Trumpeters, Troubled Makers: Lyricism, Nationalism, and Hybridity in China and Its Others*. Durham, N.C.: Duke University Press, 1995.

Lee, Leo Oufan and Andrew Nathan. "The Beginnings of Mass Culture: Journalism and Fiction in the Late Ch'ing and Beyond." In Johnson and Rawski, eds., *Popular Culture in Late Imperial China*. Berkeley: University of California Press, 1985.

Lenin, V. I. *Imperialism: The Highest Stage of Capitalism*. New York: International Publishers, 1939.

Leonard, Jane. *Wei Yuan and China's Rediscovery of the Maritime World*. Cambridge: Harvard University Press, 1984.

Leung, Edwin Pak-wah. "Li Hung-chang and the Liu-ch'iu (Ryuku) Controversy, 1871–1881." In Samuel Chu and Kwang-Ch'ing Liu, eds., *Li Hung-Chang and China's Early Modernization*. New York: M. E. Sharpe, 1994.

Levenson, Joseph. *Confucian China and Its Modern Fate: A Trilogy*. Berkeley: University of California Press, 1965.

———. *Liang Ch'i-ch'ao and the Mind of Modern China*. Berkeley: University of California Press, 1959.

———. *Revolution and Cosmopolitanism: The Western Stage and the Chinese Stages*. Berkeley: University of California Press, 1971.

Li Gui. *Huanyou dichou xinlu* (New Account of a Trip around the World). 1879. In Zhong Shuhe, ed., *Zouxiang shijie congshu* (From East to West: Chinese Travelers before 1911), vol. 6. Changsha: Yuelu chubanshe, 1985.

Li Hsiao-t'i. *Ch'ing-mo te hsia-ch'eng she-hui ch'i-meng yun-tung, 1901–1911* (Lower-Class Enlightenment in the Late Ch'ing Period, 1901–1911). Taipei: Institute of Modern History, Academia Sinica, 1992.

Li Yun-han, "Dr. Sun Yat-sen and the Independence Movement of the Philippines (1898–1900)." *China Forum (Zhongguo xuebao)* 1.2 (July 1974): 201–04.

Lixue yibian (Journal of Translations to Encourage Learning).

Li Zehou. *Zhongguo jindai sixiangshi lun* (Essays on Modern Chinese Intellectual History). Beijing: Renmin chubanshe, 1986.

———. "Kang Youwei sixiang yanjiu" (Study of Kang Youwei's Thought). In *Zhongguo jindai sixiang shilun* (Historical Essays on Modern Chinese Thought). Beijing: Renmin chubanshe, 1979: 92–181.

Liang Qichao. "Aiguo Lun" (On Patriotism). YBSWJ 3:65–77.

———. "Bolan miewang ji" (Record of the Destruction of Poland). *Shiwu bao* 1 (29 August 1896).

———. "Dili yu wenming zhi guanxi" (The Relationship between Geography and Modern Civilization). YBSWJ 10:106–10.

———. "Dongji yuedan" ("A Critique of Japanese Booklists"). YBSWJ 4:82–102.

———. "E tu zhanji xu" (Preface to *Russo-Turkish War*). YBSWJ 3:33–34.

———. "Ershi shiji Taipingyang ge" (Song of the Twentieth-Century Pacific). YBSWJ 45:17–19.

———. "Guafen weiyuan" (A Note of Warning on Dismemberment). YBSWJ 4:19.

———. "Guojia sixiang bianqian yitong lun" (On Transformations and Difference in Thinking on the State). YBSWJ 6. 12–23.

———. *Intellectual Trends of the Ch'ing Period* (Qingdai xueshu gailun). Trans. Immanual C. Y. Hsu. Cambridge: Harvard University Press, 1959.

———. "Ji dongxia" (On Eastern [Japanese] Knights). YBSWJ 2:29.

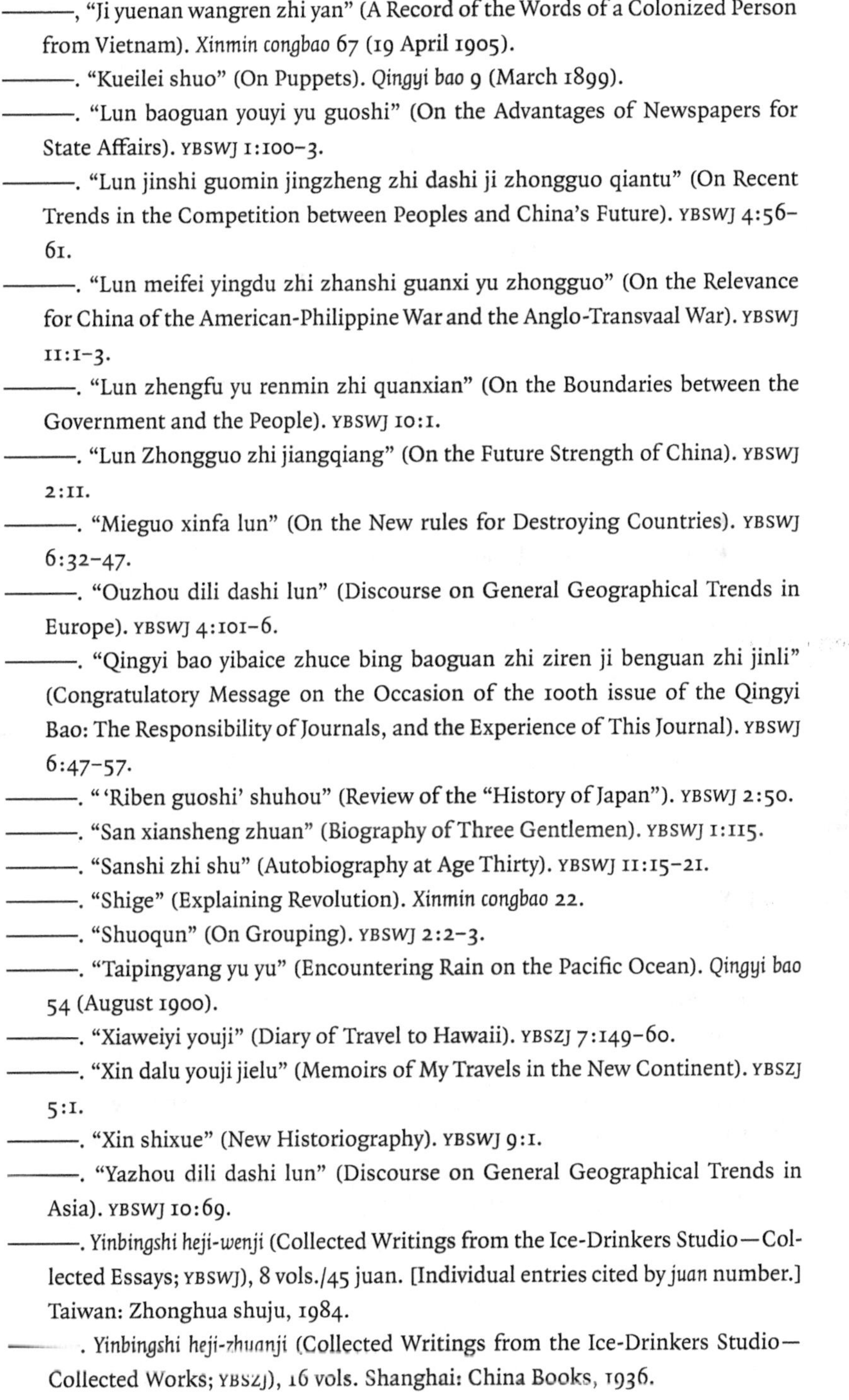

———, "Ji yuenan wangren zhi yan" (A Record of the Words of a Colonized Person from Vietnam). *Xinmin congbao* 67 (19 April 1905).

———. "Kueilei shuo" (On Puppets). *Qingyi bao* 9 (March 1899).

———. "Lun baoguan youyi yu guoshi" (On the Advantages of Newspapers for State Affairs). YBSWJ 1:100–3.

———. "Lun jinshi guomin jingzheng zhi dashi ji zhongguo qiantu" (On Recent Trends in the Competition between Peoples and China's Future). YBSWJ 4:56–61.

———. "Lun meifei yingdu zhi zhanshi guanxi yu zhongguo" (On the Relevance for China of the American-Philippine War and the Anglo-Transvaal War). YBSWJ 11:1–3.

———. "Lun zhengfu yu renmin zhi quanxian" (On the Boundaries between the Government and the People). YBSWJ 10:1.

———. "Lun Zhongguo zhi jiangqiang" (On the Future Strength of China). YBSWJ 2:11.

———. "Mieguo xinfa lun" (On the New rules for Destroying Countries). YBSWJ 6:32–47.

———. "Ouzhou dili dashi lun" (Discourse on General Geographical Trends in Europe). YBSWJ 4:101–6.

———. "Qingyi bao yibaice zhuce bing baoguan zhi ziren ji benguan zhi jinli" (Congratulatory Message on the Occasion of the 100th issue of the Qingyi Bao: The Responsibility of Journals, and the Experience of This Journal). YBSWJ 6:47–57.

———. "'Riben guoshi' shuhou" (Review of the "History of Japan"). YBSWJ 2:50.

———. "San xiansheng zhuan" (Biography of Three Gentlemen). YBSWJ 1:115.

———. "Sanshi zhi shu" (Autobiography at Age Thirty). YBSWJ 11:15–21.

———. "Shige" (Explaining Revolution). *Xinmin congbao* 22.

———. "Shuoqun" (On Grouping). YBSWJ 2:2–3.

———. "Taipingyang yu yu" (Encountering Rain on the Pacific Ocean). *Qingyi bao* 54 (August 1900).

———. "Xiaweiyi youji" (Diary of Travel to Hawaii). YBSZJ 7:149–60.

———. "Xin dalu youji jielu" (Memoirs of My Travels in the New Continent). YBSZJ 5:1.

———. "Xin shixue" (New Historiography). YBSWJ 9:1.

———. "Yazhou dili dashi lun" (Discourse on General Geographical Trends in Asia). YBSWJ 10:69.

———. *Yinbingshi heji-wenji* (Collected Writings from the Ice-Drinkers Studio—Collected Essays; YBSWJ), 8 vols./45 juan. [Individual entries cited by *juan* number.] Taiwan: Zhonghua shuju, 1984.

———. *Yinbingshi heji-zhuanji* (Collected Writings from the Ice-Drinkers Studio—Collected Works; YBSZJ), 16 vols. Shanghai: China Books, 1936.

———. "Yuenan wangguo shi qianlu" (Preface to *History of the Loss of Vietnam*). Shanghai: Guangzhi shuju, 1905.

———. "Zhongguo dili dashi lun" (Discourse on Geographical Trends in China). YBSWJ 10:77.

———. "Zhongguoshi xulun" (Introductory Essay to a History of China), YBSWJ 6:11–12.

———. "Zhongguo zhi wushi dao" (Chinese Bushido). YBSZJ 24:1–57.

———. Ziyou shu (Book of Freedom). YBSZJ 2:1–97.

Lin Xie. "Preface." *Zhongguo baihua bao* 1 (19 December 1903).

———. "Tanxiangshan huaren shounie ji" (Account of the Suffering of Chinese in Hawaii). *Hangzhou baihua bao* 20–23 (December 1901–January 1902).

———. "Feilubin mindang qiyi ji." *Hangzhou baihua bao* 15–19 (5 November–15 December 1901).

Liu Danian. "Zhongguo jindaihua de daolu yu shijie de guanxi" (China's Path to Modernization and Its Relationship to the World). In Chinese Academy of Social Sciences, ed., *Zouxiang jindai shijie de Zhongguo* (China on the Path toward the Modern World). Chengdu: Renmin chubanshe, 1992.

Liu, James T. *The Chinese Knight-Errant*. Chicago: University of Chicago Press, 1967.

Liu, Lydia. *Translingual Practice: Literature, National Culture, and Translated Modernity—China, 1900–1937*. Stanford: Stanford University Press, 1995.

Liu Shipei. "Yazhou xianshi lun" (On Recent Trends in Asia). In Ge Maochun et al., eds., *Wuzhengfu zhuyi sixiang zhiliao xuan* (Selection of Materials on Anarchist Thought), vol. 1. Beijing: Beijing daxue chubanshe, 1984.

———. "Zhongguo minzu zhi" (Sketch of the Chinese Ethnos). *Liu Shenshu xiansheng yishu* (Posthumous Works of Liu Shenshu [Shipei]). N.p., 1937.

Liu Yazi and Liu Wuji. *Su Manshu (Su Xuanying) nianpu ji qita* (A Chronological Biography of Su Manshu (Su Xuanying) and Other Matters). Shanghai: Beixin shuju, 1928.

Lo Jung-pang, ed. *Kang You-wei: A Biography and Symposium*. Tucson: University of Arizona Press, 1967.

"Lun diguo zhuyi zhi fada ji ershi shiji zhi qiantu" (On the Development of Imperialism and the Future of the Twentieth Century World). In Zhang Dan and Wang Renzhi, eds., *Xinhai geming qianshinian jian shilun xuanji* (Selected Editorials from the Decade Preceding the Xinhai Revolution). Hong Kong: Sanlian shudian, 1962.

"Lun Huanghuo" (On the Yellow Peril). *Beijing zazhi* 1 (14 May 1904).

"Lun Huanghuo" (On the Yellow Peril). *Dongfang zazhi* 2 (10 April 1904).

"Lun Meibu hebing zhi gu" (On the Annexation of Hawaii by America). *Shiwu bao* 32 (10 July 1897).

"Lun Taipingyang shang lieguo zhengjing dashi" (On the Power Competition in the Pacific). *Waijiao bao* 43 (May 1903).

"Lun Yingte zhanji" (On the Anglo-Transvaal War). *Waijiao bao* 11 (22 May 1902).

"Lusong duli lun" (On Luzon Independence). *Dongya bao* 4.

Lust, John. "Introduction." In Tsou Jung, *The Revolutionary Army: A Chinese Nationalist Tract of 1903*. The Hague: Mouton, 1968.

———. "The Su-bao Case." In *Bulletin of the School of Oriental and African Studies*. London: University of London, 1964.

Lynch, George. *The War of Civilizations*. London: N.p., 1901.

Ma, L. Eve Armatrout. *Revolutionaries, Monarchists, and Chinatowns: Chinese Politics in the Americas and the 1911 Revolution*. Honolulu: University of Honolulu Press, 1990.

Ma Shulun. *Wo zai liushi sui yiqian* (Autobiography at Sixty). Shanghai: Shenghuo shudian, 1947.

Mackerras, Colin. *Chinese Theater: From Its Origins to the Present Day*. Honolulu: University of Hawaii Press, 1985.

———. *The Chinese Theatre in Modern Times: From 1840 to the Present*. Amherst: University of Massachusetts Press, 1975.

———. *The Rise of the Peking Opera, 1770–1870*. London: Oxford University Press, 1972.

MacKinnon, Janice R., and Stephen R. *Agnes Smedley: The Life and Times of an American Radical*. Berkeley: University of California Press, 1988.

Mahan, Alfred T. "Hawaii and Our Future Sea Power." *Forum* 15 (1893).

Mai Menghua. "Lun Zhongguo zhi minqi keyong" (On the Utility to China of the People's Spirit). *Qingyi bao* 57 (14 September 1900).

———. "Zong xiapian" (Respect the Knight-errant). *Shiwu bao* 32 (10 July 1897).

Mallon, Florencia. "Cycles of Reverberation? Dialogues among the Fragments: Restrospect and Prospect." In Steve Stern et al., eds., *Confronting Historical Paradigms: Peasant, Labor, and the Capitalist World System in Africa and Latin America*. Madison: University of Wisconsin Press, 1993.

Mao Zedong, "The Chinese Revolution and the Chinese Communist Party." [December 1939]. *Selected Works of Mao Tse-tung*, vol. 2. Peking: Foreign Language Press, 1967.

Marais, J. S. *The Fall of Kruger's Republic*. London: Clarendon Press, 1961.

Marr, David. *Vietnamese Anticolonialism*. Berkeley: University of California Press, 1971.

Marumoto, Maraji. "Vignette of Early Hawaii-Japanese Relations: Highlights of King Kalakaua's Sojourn in Japan on His Trip around the World as Recorded in His Personal Diary." *Hawaiian Journal of History* 10 (1976): 53–62.

Mayamoto Tahira. "Feilubin duli zhanshi xu" (Preface to the History of the Philippine War for Independence). *Zhengyi tongbao* 21, 22 (December 1902).

"Meirizhan dianhui zhi" (Wire Reports on the American-Spanish War). *Changyan bao* 1 (17 August 1898).

Min bao (People's Voice).

Min Yi. "Bosi Geming" (Persian Revolution). *Minbao* 25 (1 January 1910).

Miyazaki, Tōten. *My Thirty-three Years' Dream*. Trans. Eto Shinkichi and Marius Jansen. Princeton: Princeton University Press, 1982.

Mohanty, Chandra. "Under Western Eyes: Feminist Scholarship and Colonial Discourse." In Chandra Mohanty, Russo, and Lourdes, eds., *Third World Women and the Politics of Feminism*. Bloomington: Indiana University Press, 1991.

Morris-Suzuki, Tessa. *Re-Inventing Japan: Time, Space, Nation*. New York: M. E. Sharpe, 1998.

Mudimbe, V. Y. *The Invention of Africa: Gnosis, Philosophy, and the Order of Knowledge*. Bloomington: Indiana University Press, 1988.

Naito Masao. "Meiji Intellectuals and India." In Okhata Kohei, ed., *Nihon to Indo* (Japan and India). Tokyo: University of Tokyo Press, 1978.

Najita, Tetsuo. "Introduction: A Synchronic Approach to the Study of Conflict in Modern Japanese History." In Tetsuo Najita, and Victor Koschmann, eds., *Conflict in Japanese History: The Neglected Tradition*. Princeton: Princeton University Press, 1982.

Nanfeng bao (Southern Journal).

Nanguo henren. "Yuenan wangguo shimo tan" (A Complete Account of the Loss of Vietnam). *Guofeng bao* 1–2 (1910–1911).

Naoki Sakai. *Translation and Subjectivity: On "Japan" and Cultural Nationalism*. Minneapolis: University of Minnesota Press, 1997.

Negri, Antonio, and Michael Hardt. *Labor of Dionysus: A Critique of the State-Form*. Minneapolis: University of Minnesota Press, 1991.

———. *Empire*. Cambridge: Harvard University Press, 2000.

Nelson, Cary, and Laurence Grossberg, eds. *Marxism and the Interpretation of Culture*. Urbana: University of Illinois Press, 1988.

Nordyke, Eleanor C., and Richard C. K. Lee. "The Chinese in Hawaii: A Historical and Demographic Perspective." *Hawaiian Journal of History* 23 (1989): 196–216.

Norman, E. H. "The Genyosha: A Study in the Origins of Japanese Imperialism." *Pacific Affairs* 17.3 (September 1944): 261–84.

Norton, M. M. *Builders of a Nation*. Manila: E. C. McCullough and Co., 1914.

Osborne, Peter. *The Politics of Time: Modernity and Avant-Garde*. London: Verso, 1995.

Ou Jujia. "Lun Feilubin dao zhi duli" (On the Independence of the Philippine Islands). *Qingyi bao* 25 (26 August 1899).

———. *Xin Guangdong* (New Guangdong). In Zhang Dan and Wang Renzhi, eds., *Xinhai geming qianshinian jian shilun xuanji* (Selected Editorials from the Decade Preceding the Xinhai Revolution). Vol. 1. Hong Kong: Sanlian shudian, 1962.

———. "Zhongguo lidai geming shuolue" (Brief Historical Outline of Chinese Revolutions). *Qingyi bao* 31 (25 October 1899).

Ouyang Yuqing. "Huiyi chun liu" (Recollections of the Spring Willow [Society]). *Ouyang Yuqing quanji* (Collected Works of Ouyang Yuqing). Shanghai: Shanghai wenyi chubanshe, 1990.

Paredes, Ruby. "Introduction." In Santiago V. Alvarez, *The Katipunan and the Revolution: Memoirs of a General*. Trans. Paula Carolina S. Malay. Manila: Ateneo de Manila University Press, 1992.

Peng Shuzhi. "Minbao yu Indu duli yundong" (Minbao and the Indian Independence Movement). *Nanya yanjiu* 1 (1982): 1–10.

Ponce, Mariano. *Sun Yat-sen: The Founder of the Republic of China*. Trans. Nick Joaquin. Manila: Filipino-Chinese Cultural Foundation reprint, 1965.

Prakash, Gyan. "Writing Post-Orientalist Histories of the Third World: Perspectives from Indian Historiography." *Society for the Comparative Study of Society and History* 32.2 (April 1990): 383–408.

Prazniak, Roxann. *Of Camel Kings and Other Things: Rural Rebels against Modernity in Late Imperial China*. Totowa, N.J.: Rowman and Littlefield, 1999.

Price, Don. *Russia and the Roots of the Chinese Revolution, 1896–1911*. Cambridge: Harvard University Press, 1974.

Pusey, James. *China and Charles Darwin*. Cambridge: Harvard University Press, 1983.

Pyle, Kenneth. *The New Generation in Meiji Japan*. Stanford: Stanford University Press, 1970.

Qi Zhifen. "Sun Zhongshan he Feilubin duli zhanzheng—zhongfei youyishi shang de yiye" (Sun Zhongshan and the Philippine War of Independence—A Page in the History of Sino-Filipino Friendship). *Jindaishi yanjiu* 14.4 (October 1982): 240–45.

Qingyi bao (Journal of Pure Critique).

Qu Lihou. *Qingmo minchu minzuzhuyi jiaoyu sichao* (Trends in Nationalist Education in Late Qing and Early Republican China). Taipei: Chung-hua wen-hua fu-hsing yun-tung t'ui-hsing wei yuan hui, 1984.

Rancière, Jacques. *Disagreement: Politics and Philosophy*. Trans. Julie Rose. Minneapolis: University of Minnesota Press, 1999.

———. *The Names of History: On the Poetics of Knowledge*. Trans. Hassan Melehy. Minneapolis: University of Minnesota Press, 1994.

Rankin, Mary. *Early Chinese Revolutionaries*. Cambridge: Harvard University Press, 1971.

Ren Jianshu. *Chen Duxiu Zhuan* (Biography of Chen Duxiu). 2 vols. Shanghai: Shanghai renmin chubanshe, 1989.

Reynolds, Douglas R. *China, 1898–1912: The Xinzheng Revolution and Japan*. Cambridge: Harvard University Press, 1993.

Ricoeur, Paul. *Lectures on Ideology and Utopia*. Ed. G. H. Taylor. New York: Columbia University Press, 1986.

Ross, Kristin. *The Emergence of Social Space: Rimbaud and the Paris Commune*. Minneapolis: University of Minnesota Press, 1988.

Sahlins, Marshall. *Islands of History*. Chicago: University of Chicago Press, 1985.

Said, Edward. *Orientalism*. New York: Pantheon, 1979.

Sang Bin. *Qingmo xin zhishijie de shetuan yu huodong* (Societies and Activities in Late Qing New Intellectual Circles). Beijing: Sanlian-Harvard Yenching, 1995.

Sareen, T. R. *Indian Revolutionaries, Japan, and British Imperialism*. New Delhi: Sterling, 1993.

Schiffrin, Harold. *Sun Yat-sen and the Origins of the Chinese Revolution*. Berkeley: University of California Press, 1968.

Schwarcz, Vera. *The Chinese Enlightenment: Intellectuals and the Legacy of the May Fourth Movement of 1919*. Berkeley: University of California Press, 1986.

Schwartz, Benjamin. *In Search of Wealth and Power: Yen Fu and the West*. Cambridge: Harvard University Press, 1964.

Seigel, James T. *Fetish, Recognition, Revolution*. Princeton: Princeton University Press, 1997.

Shanin, Theodore. *The Roots of Otherness: Russia's Turn of the Century*. New Haven: Yale University Press, 1986.

Shiba Shiro [Tokai Sanshi]. *Aiji jinshi shi* (Modern History of Egypt). *Qingyi bao* 47–74 (7 June 1900–30 March 1901).

Shibue Tamotsu. *Bolan shuaiwang shi* (The History of the Decline and Loss of Poland). Trans. Xue Gongxia [Zhilong]. Shanghai: n.p., 1904.

"Shijie zhengci" (Weltpolitik). *Hubei xuesheng jie* 1 (12 February 1903).

"Shijie zhi xinshi" (A New History of the World). *Jingshi wenchao* 3 (1902).

Shimada Kenji. *Pioneer of the Chinese Revolution: Zhang Binglin and Confucianism*. Trans. Joshua Fogel. Stanford: Stanford University Press, 1990.

"Shuxuejie yifenzijun lai han hou" (Results of a Letter from an Educated Person). *Xin shiji* 65 (11 September 1908): 2–3.

Sichuan xuebao (Sichuan Journal of Education).

Smith, Ken. *The Changing Past: Trends in South African Historical Writing*. Cincinnati: University of Ohio Press, 1988.

Smith, Neil. *Uneven Development: Nature, Capital, and the Production of Space*. New York: Blackwell, 1984.

Snow, Philip. *Star Raft*. Ithaca, N.Y.: Cornell University Press, 1988.

Soja, Edward. *Postmodern Geographies: The Reassertion of Space in Critical Social Theory*. London: Verso, 1988.

Song Shu. *Song Shu Ji* (Song Shu's Diary). 2 vols. Beijing: Zhonghua Shuju, 1993.

M. Şükrü Hanioğlu. *The Young Turks in Opposition*. New York: Oxford University Press, 1995.

Stavrianos, S. *Global Rift: The Third World Comes of Age*. New York: William Morrow, 1981.

Stern, Steve. "Introduction: Africa, Latin America, and the Splintering of Historical Knowledge: From Fragmentation to Reverberation." In Stern et al., eds., *Confronting Historical Paradigms: Peasant, Labor, and the Capitalist World System in Africa and Latin America*. Madison: University of Wisconsin Press, 1993.

Su Yi. *Jingju erbainian gaiguan* (An Overview of Peking Opera's 200 Years). 3d ed. Beijing: Yanshan chubanshe, 1989.

Suleri, Sara. *The Rhetoric of English India*. Chicago: University of Chicago Press, 1992.

Sun Baoxuan. *Wangshanlu riji* (Diary of the Master of Wangshan Studio). 2 vols. Shanghai: Shanghai guji chubanshe, 1983.

Sun Zhongshan. "Zhina baoquan fenhai lun" (Arguments for the Preservation or Dismemberment of China). *Sun Zhongshan quanji* (Collected Works of Sun Zhongshan), vol. 1. Beijing: Zhonghua shuju, 1981.

Tai, Hue-Tam Ho. *Radicalism and the Origins of the Vietnamese Revolution*. Cambridge: Harvard University Press, 1992.

"Taiwushi bao lun buwa" (The Times on Hawaii). *Shiwu bao* 39 (17 September 1897).

Takeuchi, Zensaku. "Meiji makki ni okeru chūnichi kakumei undō no kōryū" (Late-Meiji Exchanges between Chinese and Japanese Revolutionary Movements), *Chūgoku kenkyū* 5 (September 1948): 74–95.

Tanaka Issei. "The Social and Historical Context of Ming-Ch'ing Local Drama." In Johnson and Rawski, eds., *Popular Culture in Late Imperial China*. Berkeley: University of California Press, 1985.

Tanaka, Stefan. *Japan's Orient: Rendering Pasts into History*. Berkeley: University of California Press, 1993.

Tang Caichang. "Lun xingya yihui" (On the Awake Asian Society). *Xiang bao* 65 (20 May 1898).

Tang Tiaoding. "Felubin zhanshi duduan" (Fragments from the History of the War in the Philippines). *Xinshijie xuebao* 10–14 (1902).

Tang Wenquan. *Dongfang de juexing: jindai zhongyin minzu yundong dingwei guanzhao* (The Awakening of the East: A Reflection on the Position of National Movements in Modern China and India). Changsha: Hunan renmin chubanshe, 1991.

Tang, Xiaobing. *Global Space and the Nationalist Discourse of Modernity: The Historical Thinking of Liang Qichao*. Stanford: Stanford University Press, 1996.

Tang Zhijun. "Guanyu yazhou heqin hui" (On the Asian Solidarity Society). In Wuchang Xinhai geming yanjiu zhongxin, eds., *Xinhai geming yu jindai zhongguo: 1980–1989 nian lunwen xuan* (The Xinhai Revolution and Modern China: A Selection of Essays Written from 1980 to 1989). Wuhan: Hubei renmin chubanshe, 1991.

———. *Kang Youwei yu wuxu bianfa* (Kang Youwei and the Wuxu Reforms). Beijing: Xinhua shuju, 1984.

———. *Kang Youwei Zhenglun ji* (Collected Political Essays of Kang Youwei). 2 vols. Beijing: Zhonghua shuju, 1981.

———. "Shixi Zhang Taiyan 'Yazhou heqin hui yuezhang'" (A Preliminary Analysis of Zhang Taiyan's "Constitution for the Asian Solidarity Society"). *Xueshu yuekan* 6 (1976): 68–70.

Tao Xu. *Wanqing minzu zhuyi sichao* (Late Qing Ethno-Nationalism). Beijing: Renmin chubanshe, 1995.

Tao Yinhui. *Cai Yuanppei Nianpu* (Ts'ai Yuan-p'ei: A Chronological Biography). Taipei: Institute of Modern Chinese History, Academia Sinica, 1976.

Tao Zhigong. "Bayu" (Afterword to the Society's Constitution). In *Xinhai gemingshi congkan* 1 (1940).

"Telansifa'er da tongling zhuanlue" (Brief Biography of the President of the Transvaal). *Wuzhou shishi huibao* 2 (20 September 1899).

Thongchai Winnichakul. *Siam Mapped: A History of the Geo-Body of a Nation*. Honolulu: University of Hawaii Press, 1994.

Tian Youlong and Tang Daiwang. "Makesi xueshuo de zaoqi yijiezhe Zhao Bizhen" (An Early Translator and Introducer of Marxism, Zhao Bizhen). *Chousuo* 1 (1983): 118–20.

Tongzi shijie (Children's World).

Trask, Haunani Kay. *From a Native Daughter: Colonialism and Sovereignty in Hawai'i*. Monroe, Maine: Common Courage Press, 1993.

"Tuerqi tiedao de bagong" (The Turkish Railroad Strike). *Xin shiji* 72 (14 November 1908): 5–7.

Vogeley, Nancy. "Turks and Indians: Orientalist Discourse in Postcolonial Mexico." *Diacritics* 25.1 (1995): 3–20.

Waijiao bao (Foreign Affairs Journal).

Waley, Arthur. *The Opium Wars through Chinese Eyes*. Stanford: Stanford University Press, 1958.

Waley-Cohen, Joanna. *The Sextants of Beijing: Global Currents in Chinese History*. New York: W. W. Norton, 1999.

Walker, Kathy Le Mons. *Chinese Modernity and the Peasant Path*. Stanford: Stanford University Press, 1999.

Wang Gungwu. *China and the Overseas Chinese*. Singapore: Times Academic Press, 1991.

Wang Hui, "Contemporary Chinese Thought and the Question of Modernity." Trans. Rebecca E. Karl. *Social Text* 55 (summer 1998): 9–44.

Wang Jiaqian. *Wei Yuan nianpu* (A Chronological Biography of Wei Yuan). Taipei: Academia Sinica, Institute of Modern History, 1964.

Wang Jingwei. "Lun Geming zhi chushi" (On Revolutionary Trends). *Minbao* 25 (1 January 1910).

———. "Minzu de guomin" (An Ethno-National People). *Minbao* 1–2 (1905).

Wang Qisheng. *Zhongguo liuxuesheng de lishi quzi* (In the Historical Footsteps of Chinese Students Abroad). Hankou: Hubei jiaoyu chubanshe, 1992.

Wang Shaochou. *Jindai zhongri wenhua jiaoliu shi* (History of Modern Sino-Japanese Cultural Exchange). Beijing: Zhonghua shuju, 1992.

Wang, Te-wei. *Fin-de-siècle Splendor: Repressed Modernities of Late Qing Fiction, 1849–1911.* Stanford: Stanford University Press, 1997.

Wang Youwei. "Shixi Zhang Taiyan 'Yazhou heqing hui yuezhang'" (A Preliminary Analysis of Zhang Taiyan's "Constitution for the Asia Solidarity Society"). *Xueshu yuekan* 6 (1976): 68–70.

"Wangguo zhi xuesheng" (Students of a Lost Country). *Jingzhong ribao* (12 May 1904).

Warwick, Peter. *The South African War: The Anglo-Boer War, 1899–1902.* Essex: Longman, 1980.

"Wei wairen zhi nuli yu wei Manzhou zhengfu zhi nuli wubie" (There Is No Difference between Being a Slave of Foreigners and Being a Slave of the Manchus). *Tongzi shijie* 24 (2 May 1903). In Zhang Dan and Wang Renzhi, eds., *Xinhai geming qianshinianjian shilun xuanji* (Selected Editorials from the Decade Preceding the Xinhai Revolution), vol. 1, pt. 2. Hong Kong: Sanlian shudian, 1962.

Wei Yüan. *Haiguo tuzhi* (Treatise of Maritime States). 60 juan. 1843. Taibei: Shangwu, 1967.

Wen Gongjen, ed. *Manshu dashi wenji* (Mr. [Su] Manshu's Writings). 2 vols. Hong Kong: Xuelin Shudian, 1953.

White, Hayden. *Metahistory.* Baltimore: Johns Hopkins University Press, 1973.

Wigen, Kären Wigen, and Martin Lewis. *The Myth of Continents: A Critique of Metageography.* Berkeley: University of California Press, 1998.

Wilson, Andrew. "Zhang Zhidong and the Manila Consulate-General: A Study in Methods and Motives." *Papers on Chinese History,* Harvard University, 3 (spring 1994): 116–34.

Wilson, Rob. "Blue Hawaii: *Bamboo Ridge* as 'Critical Regionalism.'" In Arif Dirlik, ed., *What Is in a Rim? Critical Perspectives on the Pacific Region Idea.* Boulder, Colo.: Westview Press, 1993.

Witek, John W. "Understanding the Chinese: A Comparison of Matteo Ricci and the French Jesuit Mathematicians Sent by Louis XIV." In Charles E. Ronan and Bonnie B. C. Oh, eds., *East Meets West: The Jesuits in China, 1582–1773.* Chicago: University of Chicago Press, 1988.

Wong, J. Y. *The Origins of an Heroic Image: Sun Yat-sen in London, 1896–1897.* Oxford: Oxford University Press, 1986.

Wong, K. Scott. "Encountering the Other: Chinese Immigration and Its Impact on Chinese and American Worldviews, 1875–1905." Ph.D. diss., University of Michigan, 1992.

———. "Liang Qichao and the Chinese of America: A Re-evaluation of His *Selected Memoirs of Travels in the New World.*" *Journal of American Ethnic History* 11.4 (summer 1992): 3–24.

Wong Young-tsu. *Search for Modern Nationalism: Zhang Binglin and Revolutionary China, 1869–1936.* London: Oxford University Press, 1989.

Worsely, Peter. *The Three Worlds*. Chicago: University of Chicago Press, 1984.

Wu Qianjie, ed. *Ershi shiji Zhongguo xiju wutai* (The Twentieth-Century Drama and Stage). Shandong: Qingdao chubanshe, 1992.

Wu Tingjia. *Wuxu sichao zongheng lun* (A Complete Discussion of Trends in Thought of the *Wuxu* Period). Beijing: Renmin chubanshe, 1988.

Wu Yingnan et al., eds. *Qingmo shehui sichao* (Late Qing Trends in Social Thought). Fuzhou: Fujian Renmin chubanshe, 1990.

Wuzhou shishi huibao (Compendium on World Events).

Xia Qingyi, ed. *Yingte zhanji* (A Record of the Anglo-Transvaal War). Trans. Dongya shanlin xueguan. Shanghai: Kaiming shudian, 1904.

Xia Shaohong. *Jueshi yü chuanshi: Liang Qichao de wenxue daolu* (Enlightenment and Eternity: Liang Qichao's Literary Path). Shanghai: Renmin chubanshe, 1991.

Xiang bao (Hunan Journal).

"Xiaonian tuerqi zhi zuzhi" (The Organization of the Young Turks). *Nanfeng bao* 6–7 (July–August 1911).

Xila dulishi (History of Greek Independence). Shanghai: Guangzhi shuju, 1903.

Xinhai geming shiqi qikan jieshao (Introduction to Journals of the Xinhai Revolutionary Period). 5 vols. Comp. Chinese Academy of Social Sciences. Beijing: Renmin chubanshe, 1982.

"Xingmeng ge" (Song to Awaken from a Dream). *Anhui suhua bao* 8 (27 July 1904).

Xinmin congbao (New People's Miscellany).

Xin Shiji (New Era).

Xin Zhongguo bao (New China Journal).

Xu Banmei. *Huaju quangshiqi huiyi lu* (Recollections on the Initial Period of Spoken Drama). Beijing: Zhongguo xiju chubanshe, 1957.

Xu Jiyu. *Yinghuan zhilüe* (A Short Account of Maritime Circuits). 10 vols. 1848. Taipei, 1967.

Xuan Pushi. *Zuijin zhina geming yundong xu* (Preface to *The Recent Chinese Revolutionary Movement* [by Tano Katsuji]). Shanghai: Xinzhi she, 1903.

Xue Fucheng. *The European Diary of Hsieh [Xue] Fucheng: Envoy Extraordinary of Imperial China*. Trans. Helen Hsieh Chien; with introduction and annotation by Douglas Howland. New York: St. Martin's Press, 1993.

Yadong shibao (East Asian Times).

Yang Ming, ed. *Dianju shi* (History of Yunnan Drama). Beijing: Zhongguo xiju chubanshe, 1986.

Yang Tianshi. "Xinhai geming shiqi de Chen Qubing" (Chen Qubing during the Xinhai Revolution Period). *Jindaishi yanjiu* 3 (1984): 255–80.

Yen Ching-hwang. "The Overseas Chinese and Late Ch'ing Economic Modernization." *Modern Asian Studies* 16.2 (1982): 217–32.

"Yindu chanshi zhanshi" (The Wars of Nibbling Away at India). Trans. Wang Younian. *Lixue yibian* 1–12 (3 April 1901–22 February 1902).

"Yindu miewang zhi yuanyin" (The Reasons for India's Destruction and Perishing). *Zhejiang chao* 1, 5 (17 February, 15 June 1903).

"Yingguo duguo zhuquan wenti" (The Problem of Sovereignty between England and the Transvaal). *Qingyi bao* 33 (23 December 1899).

"Yingguo zhi lujun" (The British Army). *Qingyi bao* 36 (20 February 1900).

Young, Marilyn B. *The Rhetoric of Empire: American China Policy, 1895–1901*. Cambridge: Harvard University Press, 1968.

Young, Robert. *White Mythologies: Writing History and the West*. New York: Routledge, 1990.

Youxue yibian (Journal of Translations by Overseas Students).

Yu Danchu. "Zhongguo jindai aiguo zhuyi de '*wangguo* shijian' chukao" (Preliminary Investigation into Modern Chinese Patriotic "Mirrors on the History of Lost Countries"). *Shijie lishi* 1 (1984): 23–32.

Yu-Jose, Lydia. *Japan Views the Philippines, 1900–1944*. Manila: Ateneo de Manila, 1992.

Yuan Weishi. *Wanqing dabianjuzhong de sichao yu renwu* (Intellectual Trends and Figures in the Late Qing Transformations). Shenzhen: Haitian chubanshe, 1992.

Yuan Yü. "Putaoya geming ji" (Record of the Portuguese Revolution). *Guofeng bao* 25 (13 October 1910).

Zeng Hailin. *Huang Zunxian yu jindai zhongguo* (Huang Zunxian and Modern China). Beijing: Sanlian shudian, 1988.

Zeng Jingya. "Zhongyue geming zhishi zuzhi 'Zenhua xingya hui' jinxing kangfa douzheng huiyi" (Reminiscences on the Chinese-Vietnamese Revolutionaries' Organization "Arise China Awaken Asia Society" and the Promotion of the Anti-French Struggle). *Guangdong wenshi zhiliao*, vol. 22. Guangzhou: Guangdong renmin chubanshe, 1978.

Zhang Binglin [Taiyan]. "Lun Yazhou yize wei chunchi" (It Is Best for Asia to Stand together Firmly). *Shiwu bao* 18 (February 1897).

———. "Song Yindu Boluohan Baoshen erjun xu" (Preface Sent to Two Indian Gentlemen, Boluohan and Baoshen). *Minbao* 13 (5 May 1907).

———. "Yazhou heqin hui yuezhang" (The Constitution of the Asian Solidarity Society). In Zhu Weijing and Qi Yihua, eds., *Zhang Taiyan xuan ji* (Selected Works of Zhang Taiyan). Shanghai: Renmin chubanshe, 1981.

———. "Zheng Chou Man lun" (On the Correct Hatred of the Manchus). *Guomin bao* 4 (10 August 1901).

Zhang Dan and Wang Renzhi, eds. *Xinhai geming qianshinian jian shilun xuanji* (Selected Editorials from the Decade Preceding the Xinhai Revolution). Hong Kong: Sanlian shudian, 1962.

Zhang Guotu. *Zhongguo fengjian zhengfu de huaqido zhengce* (The Policies of China's Feudal Government toward Overseas Chinese). Xiamen: Xiamen Daxue Chubanshe, 1989.

Zhang Guyu. "Shanghai Jingju Yiwang" (Reminiscences of Shanghai's Beijing

Opera). In *Shanghai wenshi zhiliao xuanji* 61.1. Shanghai: Renmin chubanshe, 1989.

Zhang Kaiyuan. "Characteristics of the Trend of Patriotism in the 1911 Revolution." In *Papers Presented at the International Colloquium on the 1911 Revolution and the Founding of the Chinese Republic*. Washington, D.C.: Center for Chinese Research Materials, n.d.

———. "Faguo dageming yu xinhai geming" (The French Revolution and the Xinhai Revolution). In Liu Zongzhu, ed., *Faguo dageming erbai zhounian jinian lunwenji* (Essays in Commemoration of the 200th Anniversary of the Great French Revolution). Beijing: Sanlian shudian, 1990.

Zhang Mingjiu. "'Yinghuan zhilue' yu 'Haiguo tuzhi' bijiao yanjiu" (A Comparative Analysis of the *Yinghuan zhilue* and the *Haiguo tuzhi*). *Jindaishi yanjiu* 6 (1992): 68–81.

Zhang Puquan [Zhang Ji]. *Zhang Puquan xiansheng quanji* (Complete Works of Zhang Puquan). Taipei: Zhongyang wenwu gongying she, 1951.

Zhang, Xudong. "Nationalism, Mass Culture, and Intellectual Strategies." *Social Text*, no. 55 (summer 1998): 109–40.

Zhang Yuanji. "Aiji jinshi shi xu" (Preface to History of Modern Egypt). *Waijiao bao* 12 (15 May 1903).

Zhang Yuanji nianpu. (A Chronological Biography of Zhang Yuanji). Shanghai: Shangwu, 1991.

Zhang Zengqun. "Jindai zhongguo yu shijie: jige youguan wenti de kaocha" (Modern China and the World: Investigations on Several Relevant Questions). In Chinese Academy of Social Sciences, ed., *Zouxiang jindai shijie de Zhongguo* (China on the Road to the Modern World). Chengdu: Renmin chubanshe, 1991.

Zhang Zhongduan. "Tuerji lixian shuo" (On the Turkish Constitution). *Henan* 7 (5 August 1908): 19–27.

"Zhanchang xingshi" (Contours of the Battlefield). *Huibao* 129 (19 November 1899).

Zhao Junyi. *Xinhai geming yu dalu langren* (The Xinhai Revolution and the "Mainland Ronin"). Beijing: Zhongguo dabaikeshu chubanshe, 1991.

Zhejiang chao (Tides of Zhejiang).

Zhengyi tongbao (Journal of Political Technique).

Zhong Shuhe, ed. *Zouxiang shijie congshu* (From East to West: Chinese Travelers before 1911). Changsha: Yuelu chubanshe, 1985.

Zhongguo baihua bao (China Vernacular Journal).

Zhongguo chuqi huaju shiliao (Historical Documents on the Beginning Period of Chinese Spoken Drama). Beijing: n.p., 1980.

Zhongguo tongshi shangxin ren. *Feilubin duli zhanshi* (History of the Philippine War of Independence). Shanghai: Shangwu yinshu guan, 1902.

Zhongshan daxue, ed. *Zhongguo gujizhong youguan feilubin zhiliao huibian* (Compendium of Materials from Ancient Chinese Sources on the Philippines). Guangzhou: Zhongshan daxue chubanshe, 1980.

Zhou Nanjing. "Feilubin duli zhanshi yu zhongguo renmin" (The Philippine War of Independence and the Chinese people). *Huaqiao xuehui tongxun* 2 (1985): 1–8.

Zhou Nianchang. "Tongmeng huiyuan Tang Zenbi xiansheng ersanshi" (A Few Things about Tang Zengbi, Member of the Revolutionary Alliance). *Jiangxi shehui kexue* (1981): 81–87.

Zhou Xinfang, ed. *Wang Xiaonong xiqu ji* (Wang Xiaonong's Collected Dramas). Beijing: Zhonggua xiju chubanshe, 1957.

Zhu Weijing and Qi Yihua, eds. *Zhang Taiyan xuan ji (Selected Works of Zhang Taiyan).* Shanghai: Renmin chubanshe, 1981.

Zhuang You. "Guomin xin linghun" (The New Spirit of a National People). *Jiangsu* 5 (May 1903).

Zi Ye. "Liang Qichao he Shangwu yinshu guan" (Liang Qichao and the Commercial Press). In *Shangwu yinshuguan jiushi nian* (Shanghai's Commercial Press at Ninety). Shanghai: Shangwu yinshu guan, 1988.

Zito, Angela. *Of Body and Brush: Grand Sacrifices as Text/Performance in Eighteenth-Century China.* Chicago: University of Chicago Press, 1997.

Zongli Yamen archives, Box 01–21/20–6. Academia Sinica, Taipei, Taiwan.

INDEX

Rebecca E. Karl is Assistant Professor of History and East Asian Studies at New York University.

Library of Congress Cataloging-in-Publication Data
Karl, Rebecca E.
Staging the world : Chinese nationalism at the turn of the twentieth century / Rebecca E. Karl
p. cm. — (Asia-Pacific)
Includes bibliographical references and index.
ISBN 0-8223-2852-6 (cloth : alk. paper) —
ISBN 0-8223-2867-4 (pbk. : alk. paper)
1. Nationalism—China. I. Title. II. Series.
JC311 .K32 2002
320.54'0951'09034—dc21 2001054468

www.ingramcontent.com/pod-product-compliance
Lightning Source LLC
LaVergne TN
LVHW020506100826
845148LV00003B/703
9780822328674